Canada and the Crown

Essays on Constitutional Monarchy

Edited by
D. Michael Jackson and Philippe Lagassé

Institute of Intergovernmental Relations
Queen's Policy Studies Series
School of Policy Studies, Queen's University
McGill-Queen's University Press
Montreal & Kingston • London • Ithaca

The Institute of Intergovernmental Relations

The Institute is the only academic organization in Canada whose mandate is solely to promote research and communication on the challenges facing the federal system.

Current research interests include fiscal federalism, health policy, the reform of federal political institutions and the machinery of federal-provincial relations, Canadian federalism and the global economy, and comparative federalism.

The Institute pursues these objectives through research conducted by its own associates and other scholars, through its publication program, and through seminars and conferences.

The Institute links academics and practitioners of federalism in federal and provincial governments and the private sector.

The Institute of Intergovernmental Relations receives ongoing financial support from the J. A. Corry Memorial Endowment Fund, the Royal Bank of Canada Endowment Fund, the Government of Canada, and the governments of Manitoba and Ontario. We are grateful for this support, which enables the Institute to sustain its program of research, publication, and related activities.

L'Institut des relations intergouvernementales

L'Institut est le seul organisme universitaire canadien à se consacrer exclusivement à la recherche et aux échanges sur les enjeux du fédéralisme.

Les priorités de recherche de l'Institut portent présentement sur le fédéralisme fiscal, la santé, la modification des institutions politiques fédérales, les mécanismes des relations fédérales-provinciales, le fédéralisme canadien dans l'économie mondiale et le fédéralisme comparatif.

L'Institut réalise ses objectifs par le biais de recherches effectuées par ses chercheurs et par des chercheurs de l'Université Queen's et d'ailleurs, de même que par des congrès et des colloques.

L'Institut sert de lien entre les universitaires, les fonctionnaires fédéraux et provinciaux et le secteur privé.

L'Institut des relations intergouvernementales reçoit l'appui financier du J. A. Corry Memorial Endowment Fund, de la Fondation de la Banque Royale du Canada, du gouvernement du Canada et des gouvernements du Manitoba et de l'Ontario. Nous les remercions de cet appui qui permet à l'Institut de poursuivre son programme de recherche et de publication ainsi que ses activités connexes.

Library and Archives Canada Cataloguing in Publication

Canada and the Crown : essays on constitutional monarchy / edited by D. Michael Jackson and Philippe Lagassé.

(Queen's policy studies series)
Includes revised papers from the conference, The Crown in Canada, a Diamond Jubilee Assessment held in Regina, October 26-28, 2012.
Includes bibliographical references.
Issued in print and electronic formats.
Includes chapter abstracts in French.
ISBN 978-1-55339-204-0 (pbk.).—ISBN 978-1-55339-205-7 (epub).
978-1-55339-206-4 (pdf)

1. Constitutional history—Canada. 2. Monarchy—Canada. 3. Federal government—Canada. I. Jackson, D. Michael, editor of compilation II. Lagassé, Philippe, editor of compilation III. Queen's University (Kingston, Ont.). Institute of Intergovernmental Relations IV. Series: Queen's policy studies series

JL15.C35 2013 320.471 C2013-905548-7
C2013-906526-1

Cover photo: The Queen's personal Canadian flag is flown on Parliament Hill on Accession Day, February 6, 2012, marking the Diamond Jubilee of Queen Elizabeth II. The Canadian Press / Sean Kilpatrick

Contents

Part 4. First Nations and the Crown

Acknowledgements

Diamond Jubilee Conference on the Crown, Regina, October 2012

Organizing Partners

Province of Saskatchewan
Office of the Lieutenant Governor
Executive Council
Provincial Capital Commission

JOHNSON SHOYAMA GRADUATE SCHOOL OF
PUBLIC POLICY

Johnson-Shoyama Graduate School of Public Policy
University of Saskatchewan and University of Regina

In cooperation with

MASSEY

COLLEGE

Massey College in the University of Toronto

IIGR

Institute of Intergovernmental Relations, Queen's University

Sponsors

The Mosaic Company (principal funding partner)

Whitecap-Dakota First Nation (donor)

University of Regina

Office of the President, University of Regina

Conference Officers

Honorary Chair	Her Honour the Honourable Vaughn Solomon Schofield, SOM, SVM, Lieutenant Governor of Saskatchewan
Patron	The Honourable A. Raynell Andreychuk, Senator
Co-chairs	John Fraser, CM, Master of Massey College
	Rick Mantey, Cabinet Secretary & Clerk of the Executive Council, Government of Saskatchewan
Secretary	Dr. D. Michael Jackson, CVO, SOM, CD
Coordinator	Kendra Gellner, Johnson-Shoyama Graduate School of Public Policy
Advisory Committee	The Honourable Serge Joyal, PC, OC, OQ, Senator
	Dr. Christopher McCreery, MVO, Private Secretary to the Lieutenant Governor of Nova Scotia
	Dr. Ken Rasmussen, Associate Director, Johnson-Shoyama Graduate School of Public Policy
	Dr. David E. Smith, OC, FRSC, Professor Emeritus of Political Studies, University of Saskatchewan
Remarks	Chief Perry Bellegarde, Federation of Saskatchewan Indian Nations
	Brad Delorey, Director of Public Affairs, The Mosaic Company
	The Honourable Wayne Elhard, Provincial Secretary of Saskatchewan
	André Juneau, Director, Institute of Intergovernmental Relations, Queen's University
	George Lafond, Treaty Commissioner for Saskatchewan (discussant)
	The Honourable Bill McKnight, PC, former Treaty Commissioner (discussant)
	The Honourable Andrew Scheer, Speaker of the House of Commons
	Nathan Tidridge, author of *Canada's Constitutional Monarchy* (discussant)

Publication of *Canada and the Crown: Essays on Constitutional Monarchy*

Editorial Committee

Editors Dr. D. Michael Jackson, CVO, SOM, CD

Dr. Philippe Lagassé

Members John Fraser, CM

Senator Serge Joyal, PC, OC, OQ

Rick Mantey

Dr. Christopher McCreery, MVO

Dr. Ken Rasmussen

Dr. David E. Smith, OC, FRSC

Publishers

IIGR

André Juneau, Institute of Intergovernmental Relations

Mary Kennedy, Institute of Intergovernmental Relations

Mark Howes, School of Policy Studies, Queen's University

Valerie Jarus, School of Policy Studies, Queen's University

Ellie Barton, Copy Editor

McGill-Queen's University Press

Principal Funding Partner

The Mosaic Company

Foreword

By His Excellency the Right Honourable David Johnston, Governor General of Canada

As Governor General of Canada, I continually emphasize the importance of our national symbols and institutions, including the Canadian Crown—a fundamental part of our remarkably successful federation. Given its long history and considerable complexity, it is perhaps unsurprising that the role of the Crown in Canada is not widely understood. For this reason, I welcome the present volume of essays, which makes a significant contribution to our understanding of this vital institution.

Our unique system of government derives from a centuries-old tradition of constitutional monarchy with origins in England and France. This system has continued to evolve within Canada to meet our country's particular needs and circumstances. It is very much a shared Crown, comprising a Parliament that consists of the Sovereign, the House of Commons, the Senate, and the thirteen provincial and territorial legislatures. The Crown also enjoys close ties with First Nations dating back more than two centuries. Within this constitutional monarchy operates our system of responsible government, defined by the late Eugene Forsey as "government by a Cabinet answerable to, and removable by, a majority of the assembly." This balanced Crown, which I find quintessentially Canadian, both performs a symbolic, unifying role and fulfils a very real purpose in safeguarding our democratic rights and freedoms.

In practice, Canada's constitutional monarchy functions through both written rules and unwritten conventions. Many of its features find expression in the key documents of our nation, including the Royal Proclamation of 1763 and the Constitution Acts, 1867 to 1982, the latter of which includes the Canadian Charter of Rights and Freedoms. As a symbol, however, the Crown is more than the sum of our written documents: it embodies and provides space for our values and beliefs as Canadians. As Her Majesty The Queen once said, "The Crown represents the basic political ideals which all Canadians share. It stands for the idea that individual people matter more than theories; that we are all subject to the rule of law. These ideals are guaranteed by a common loyalty, through the Sovereign, to community and country."

Just as Canada itself is an experiment in peace, tolerance, and diversity, the Crown can be viewed as an idea put into practice that we continually seek to improve. Evolving peacefully, our constitutional monarchy allows us to blend tradition with modern circumstances in an effort to ensure justice, fairness, and equality of opportunity. The result is a system of government that, while far from perfect, is admired around the world for its ability to forge consensus and stability.

I commend the authors and editors of these essays for shedding light and new perspectives on the Canadian Crown. This collection is a most worthy and remarkable achievement. May it inspire many more.

His Excellency the Right Honourable David Johnston, C.C., C.M.M., C.O.M., C.D., Governor General and Commander-in-Chief of Canada
Photo by: Sgt Serge Gouin, Rideau Hall.

Avant-propos

Par Son Excellence le très honorable David Johnston, Gouverneur général du Canada

En tant que Gouverneur général du Canada, je mets sans cesse l'accent sur l'importance de nos institutions et symboles nationaux, y compris la Couronne canadienne — élément fondamental du remarquable succès de notre fédération. On ne se surprend guère que le rôle de la Couronne au Canada soit si peu connu, vu sa longue histoire et sa complexité considérable. C'est pourquoi je salue la publication de ce recueil, qui enrichira sensiblement nos connaissances à l'égard de cette institution essentielle.

Notre système de gouvernement s'inspire de traditions de la monarchie constitutionnelle française et anglaise qui remontent à plusieurs siècles. Ce système unique a évolué de manière à répondre aux besoins et aux circonstances propres au Canada. Les pouvoirs sont partagés, la Couronne étant formée d'un Parlement comprenant le Souverain, la Chambre des communes, le Sénat et les treize législatures provinciales et territoriales. En outre, la Couronne entretient des rapports étroits avec les Premières Nations depuis plus de deux cents ans. C'est dans le contexte de cette monarchie constitutionnelle qu'opère notre régime de gouvernement responsable, que feu Eugene Forsey a décrit comme un gouvernement « qui doit répondre à l'assemblée et qui est révocable par la majorité de celle-ci ». Cette répartition fondamentalement canadienne des pouvoirs de la Couronne joue un rôle symbolique et unificateur, tout en protégeant effectivement nos droits et libertés démocratiques.

Dans la pratique, la monarchie constitutionnelle du Canada répond à des règles écrites autant qu'à des conventions non écrites. Plusieurs de ses caractéristiques trouvent leur expression dans les documents clés de notre nation, y compris la Proclamation royale de 1763 et les *Lois constitutionnelles* de 1867 et de 1982, la plus récente comportant la Charte canadienne des droits et libertés. Sur le plan symbolique, par contre, la Couronne est plus que la somme de nos documents; elle incarne les valeurs et les croyances des Canadiens et donne libre cours à leur expression. Comme Sa Majesté la Reine l'a déjà dit, « la Couronne représente les idéaux politiques fondamentaux que partagent tous les Canadiens. Elle symbolise l'idée que les personnes sont plus importantes que les théories et que nous sommes tous sous l'autorité de la loi. Par l'intermédiaire du Souverain, ces idéaux sont garantis par une loyauté commune envers la collectivité et le pays. »

À l'image du Canada, qui constitue en soi une expérience en matière de paix, de tolérance et de diversité, on peut considérer la Couronne comme une idée devenue réalité que nous nous efforçons sans cesse d'améliorer. Suivant pacifiquement son cours, notre monarchie constitutionnelle permet de marier la tradition à la modernité, dans l'intérêt de la justice, de l'équité et de l'égalité des chances. Il en résulte un système de gouvernement qui, malgré ses failles, suscite l'admiration du monde entier par sa capacité de forger le consensus et la stabilité.

Je félicite les auteurs et les réviseurs de ces essais, qui ont su faire la lumière sur la Couronne canadienne et engendrer de nouvelles perspectives. Le présent recueil est une réalisation méritoire et remarquable. Puisse-t-il en inspirer beaucoup d'autres.

Preface

André Juneau

In the twenty-first century, attention to the constitutional monarchy in Canada has increased markedly among academics and those involved in public policy, government, and the law. Given its mandate to study the dynamics of the Canadian federation, the Institute of Intergovernmental Relations at Queen's University was pleased to be the organizing partner of a conference, "The Crown in Canada: Present Realities and Future Options," held in Ottawa in 2010. We were also pleased to publish through McGill-Queen's University Press the resulting book, *The Evolving Canadian Crown*, edited by Jennifer Smith and D. Michael Jackson, which appeared early in 2012, the year of the Diamond Jubilee of Queen Elizabeth II.

The institution of the Crown understandably took on an even higher profile among the Canadian public in Diamond Jubilee Year. It was therefore timely indeed that a second conference on the Crown took place in October 2012, this time at Government House in Regina. Called "The Crown in Canada: A Diamond Jubilee Assessment," the conference was co-sponsored by the Government of Saskatchewan and the Johnson-Shoyama Graduate School of Public Policy at the Universities of Regina and Saskatchewan, with generous support from The Mosaic Company and the Whitecap Dakota First Nation. The Institute of Intergovernmental Relations was glad to be involved in this conference, which brought together leading academics and practitioners from across Canada to examine and debate issues of the Canadian Crown, including notably its roles in Quebec and among the First Nations.

The Institute now has the privilege of publishing *Canada and the Crown: Essays on Constitutional Monarchy*, an outcome of the Jubilee conference. The editors, D. Michael Jackson and Philippe Lagassé, decided, appropriately, that the two chapters on the Crown in Quebec should appear in the original French rather than in translation. They also made the welcome decision to enlarge the scope of the book beyond the topics discussed at the conference. The nineteen contributors to this volume, both established and emerging scholars, offer intriguing and challenging perspectives on the Crown in Canada. The result is a stimulating appraisal of the monarchical institution that remains at the heart of Canada's governance. I am therefore delighted that His Excellency the Right Honourable David Johnston, Governor General of Canada, consented to honour this book with a foreword.

André Juneau
Director
Institute of Intergovernmental Relations
Queen's University, Kingston

Contributors

Richard Berthelsen

Richard Berthelsen served as private secretary to the lieutenant governor of Ontario from 1997 to 2003. From 1990 to 1997 he was policy and program officer in the Office of the Secretary to the Governor General. He is a frequent media commentator for CTV and the *Globe and Mail* and a consultant on protocol, machinery of government, and honours issues.

Alexander Bolt, CD

Alexander Bolt is a lieutenant-colonel in the Canadian Forces, serving in the Office of the Judge Advocate General. He holds the position of director of the Directorate of International and Operational Law. He has twice deployed on international operations: in 2002–2003 as legal advisor to the battle group serving with the NATO Stabilization Force in Bosnia and in 2008 as legal advisor to a Canadian Forces task force in Afghanistan.

James W. J. Bowden

James W. J. Bowden is a graduate student at the University of Ottawa and is writing his master's thesis on the powers of the Crown under responsible government. He is co-author of "No Discretion: On Prorogation and the Governor General" and "Writing the Unwritten: The Officialization of Constitutional Conventions in Canada, the United Kingdom, New Zealand, and Australia."

Linda Cardinal

Linda Cardinal is full professor at the School of Political Studies at the University of Ottawa. She is also research chair in francophone studies and public policy and principal investigator of the Community-University Research Alliance on knowledge-based community governance in the area of language planning. From 2006 to 2007 she held the chair in Canadian Studies at the Université Sorbonne-Nouvelle Paris 3 (France).

Phillip Crawley, CBE

Phillip Crawley is publisher and CEO of the *Globe and Mail*. He oversees the strategy and operations of the newspaper, websites including globeandmail.com, reportonbusiness.com, and globeinvestor.com, and magazines including *Report on Business*. Mr. Crawley has held a variety of senior executive positions with media companies in Europe, Asia, and New Zealand. He was made a Commander of the Order of the British Empire by the Queen in 2012 for his charitable work.

Stephanie Danyluk

Stephanie Danyluk has a master's degree in history from the University of Saskatchewan. She is a research analyst in the Department of Self-Government at Whitecap Dakota First Nation. She has conducted community-based research on Indigenous knowledge, history, and culture with a number of First Nations and Métis communities in Canada.

John Fraser, CM

John Fraser has been master of Massey College at the University of Toronto since 1995. Prior to this, he was editor of *Saturday Night*. He continues a freelance career with feature articles for *Maclean's*, the *Globe and Mail*, and numerous magazines and journals. He is the author of ten books, including the internationally-acclaimed *The Chinese: Portrait of a People* (1980) and *The Secret of the Crown: Canada's Affair with Royalty* (2012). He was appointed a Member of the Order of Canada in 1992.

Carolyn Harris

Carolyn Harris is lecturer at the University of Toronto, School of Continuing Studies. She completed her PhD in history at Queen's University in 2012. An expert in the history of the monarchy, she has been interviewed by a wide variety of media outlets. Her writing concerning the historical context for current royal events has appeared in publications including the *Globe and Mail* and the *Ottawa Citizen*.

Robert E. Hawkins, DCL

Robert E. Hawkins is professor of law in the Johnson-Shoyama Graduate School of Public Policy at the University of Regina. He served as president of the University of Regina. Prior to that, he was vice-president at Nipissing University, dean of arts at St. Francis Xavier University, and associate dean of law at the University of Western Ontario. He was a Queen's National Scholar at the Faculty of Law, Queen's University.

Ian Holloway, QC, CD

Ian Holloway is dean of law at the University of Calgary. Prior to this appointment, he served two terms as dean of law at the University of Western Ontario and a term as associate dean at the Australian National University. He is a member of the Bars of Nova Scotia and Ontario and was appointed Queen's Counsel in 2003. He also served as law clerk to the chief justice of the Federal Court of Canada.

D. Michael Jackson, CVO, SOM, CD

Chief of Protocol of Saskatchewan from 1980 to 2005, Michael Jackson coordinated ten visits by members of the Royal Family, wrote educational booklets on the Crown, and established the province's honours program. He was a research fellow at the University of Regina from 2006 to 2011 and co-editor of *The Evolving Canadian Crown* (2012). The Queen named him a Lieutenant of the Royal Victorian Order in 1987 and Commander in 2005. He is a Member of the Saskatchewan Order of Merit (2007).

The Honourable Serge Joyal, PC, OC, OQ

Serge Joyal was a Liberal member of the House of Commons for Montreal from 1974 to 1984 and was summoned to the Senate in 1997. He served as co-chair of the joint Senate–House of Commons committee on the patriation of the Constitution, 1980–81, and as secretary of state of Canada, 1982–84. He was made Chevalier de l'Ordre national de la Légion d'honneur of France in 1995 and Officier in 2008, Officer of the Order of Canada in 1996, and Officier de l'Ordre national du Québec in 2004.

Philippe Lagassé

Philippe Lagassé is associate professor with the Graduate School of Public and International Affairs at the University of Ottawa. His areas of academic specialization include machinery of government related to foreign policy and national security affairs, the nature and scope of executive power in the Westminster tradition, and Canadian civil-military relations and defence policy. His research focuses on prerogative power and the respective roles of Parliament, Cabinet, and the Crown in national defence.

Nicholas A. MacDonald

Nicholas MacDonald is a doctoral candidate with the Faculty of Law at the University of Ottawa. He holds a master's degree in political management from Carleton University. He is co-author of "No Discretion: On Prorogation and the Governor General" and "Writing the Unwritten:

The Officialization of Constitutional Conventions in Canada, the United Kingdom, New Zealand, and Australia."

Christopher McCreery, MVO

Christopher McCreery has been private secretary to the lieutenant governor of Nova Scotia since 2009. He is one of the Commonwealth's foremost experts on orders, decorations, and medals. Prior to his appointment as private secretary, Dr. McCreery worked for the Privy Council Office, the Leader of the Government in the Senate, the Speaker of the Senate, and Senator Michael Kirby. In 2010 the Queen appointed him a Member of the Royal Victorian Order.

J. R. (Jim) Miller, SOM, FRSC

Jim Miller is the Canada Research Chair in Native-Newcomer Relations and professor of history at the University of Saskatchewan. He served as president of the Canadian Historical Association in 1996–97, was appointed to the governing board of the Social Sciences and Humanities Research Council of Canada (SSHRC) in 1998, and was elected a Fellow of the Royal Society of Canada in 1998. In 2010, SSHRC awarded him its Gold Medal for Achievement in Research. He was appointed a Member of the Saskatchewan Order of Merit in 2013.

Peter H. Russell, OC, FRSC

Peter Russell is professor emeritus of political science and principal of Senior College at the University of Toronto, where he has taught political science since 1958. His scholarly work has focused on constitutional, judicial, and Aboriginal politics in Canada as well as in a comparative context, especially with other Westminster parliamentary democracies. Peter Russell is an Officer of the Order of Canada and a Fellow of the Royal Society of Canada.

David E. Smith, OC, FRSC, D.Litt

David E. Smith is distinguished visiting professor at Ryerson University, emeritus professor of political studies at the University of Saskatchewan, and former senior policy fellow at the Johnson-Shoyama Graduate School of Public Policy. He is author of numerous books on Canadian politics, including *The Invisible Crown: The First Principle of Canadian Government* (1995), *The Republican Option in Canada, Past and Present* (1999), and *The People's House of Commons* (2007). Dr. Smith was elected a Fellow of the Royal Society of Canada in 1981. He was appointed an Officer of the Order of Canada in 2013.

John D. Whyte, LL.D

John Whyte was recently Senior Policy Fellow at the Johnson-Shoyama Graduate School of Public Policy at the University of Regina. He served as director of constitutional law in the Saskatchewan Department of the Attorney General from 1979 to 1982, advising Saskatchewan on the 1982 constitutional amendments. He was dean of law at Queen's University from 1987 to 1992. From 1997 to 2002 he served as Saskatchewan's deputy minister of justice and deputy attorney-general. He received an honorary doctorate from York University, Toronto, in 2013.

Introduction: The Enduring Canadian Crown

D. Michael Jackson

Cet ouvrage et celui qui l'a précédé, The Evolving Canadian Crown, *sont tous deux le fruit de conférences sur le thème de la Couronne tenues à Ottawa en 2010 puis à Regina en 2012, qui ont mis en lumière le regain d'intérêt du public et des chercheurs pour l'institution de la monarchie constitutionnelle au Canada, intérêt encore accentué en 2012 par le Jubilé de la reine Elizabeth II. De fait, la dynamique suscitée par la Couronne canadienne a sensiblement évolué sous l'effet de la nomination de gouverneurs généraux apolitiques à partir de 1999, du ferme soutien que le gouvernement conservateur de Stephen Harper apporte à la Couronne depuis 2006 et de l'attitude favorable adoptée par Rideau Hall sous le mandat de l'actuel gouverneur général, David Johnston.*

La première section, « Canadian Encounters with the Crown », traite des questions suivantes : l'influence du gouverneur général lord Lorne et de sa femme, la princesse Louise ; le débat historique suscité par la Couronne au Québec ; les rapports entre les médias et la Couronne ; et la difficulté d'éduquer les Canadiens sur l'institution monarchique. Dans la section « Crown and Constitution » sont ensuite examinés les aspects d'« efficacité» et de « dignité » de la Couronne, la loi sur la succession au trône et les arguments en faveur de l'idée républicaine au Canada. La section « The Crown in Practice » aborde ces différents thèmes : l'évolution de la Couronne provinciale et du poste de lieutenant-gouverneur ; le discours du Trône ; recours aux manuels de Cabinet pour clarifier les conventions constitutionnelles ; le rôle des secrétaires de gouverneur ; et l'usage des prérogatives de la Couronne pour autoriser le déploiement des Forces canadiennes à l'étranger. Dans la dernière section, « First Nations and the Crown », on fait remonter l'enjeu de la gouvernance autochtone au Canada à la guerre de 1812 et même avant. En conclusion, on décrit les trois conceptions héréditaire, collective et constitutionnelle de la Couronne, avant de proposer des moyens d'enrichir l'ensemble du débat sur la Couronne canadienne.

Complex and sometimes controversial, nuanced and even perplexing, the Crown nonetheless endures at the core of Canada's governance. It is far more than a colourful symbol, although of course that is one of its most prominent—and attractive—features. As Jennifer Smith so aptly wrote in this book's predecessor volume, *The Evolving Canadian Crown,*

> The Canadian Crown is steeped in symbolism, to be sure, and in many respects it is this symbolic face that the public sees and knows. More than that, however, the institution is tightly woven into the fabric of the Canadian constitution and parliamentary system of government, itself loosely patterned on the British model. The symbolic light of the Crown illuminates many of the formal processes of parliamentary government. It also engages the conduct of government and politics.[1]

The above-mentioned book resulted from a conference held in the Parliament Buildings in Ottawa in June 2010, "The Crown in Canada: Present Realities and Future Options." The conference was both evidence and a result of the blossoming of academic and public interest in the Canadian version of the monarchy after several decades of relative indifference. The landmark 1995 study *The Invisible Crown* by David E. Smith,[2] dean of Canadian scholars of the Crown (and a welcome contributor both to the present book and to its predecessor), began the momentum by drawing long-overdue attention to the monarchical institution's importance for Canadian government and federalism. The Golden Jubilee of Queen Elizabeth II in 2002 gave renewed visibility to the public and ceremonial face of the Crown, even if some of its detractors took advantage of the opportunity to call for its abolition. Then two high-profile governors general, Adrienne Clarkson (1999–2005) and Michaëlle Jean (2005–2010), changed the dynamics of the national vice-regal office, which had languished for twenty years under a series of former politicians. True, these two incumbents veered toward an interpretation of the Crown that appeared to undermine its rationale in substituting a presidential-style governor general for the Sovereign, yet this very approach stimulated meaningful debate on the monarchy in Canada.

The dynamics of the Crown changed still further with the election of Stephen Harper's Conservative government in 2006. Whether in a minority situation (2006–2011) or a majority (from 2011), this administration clearly demarcated itself with respect to the Crown from its Liberal and Progressive Conservative predecessors of the past four decades. Gone were the attempts to gloss over or quietly bury the monarchical nature of the Canadian polity so well documented by David E. Smith. In quick succession came the Queen's presence in France at the ninetieth anniversary of the Battle of Vimy Ridge in 2007; publication in 2008 of a long-suppressed educational booklet, *A Crown of Maples,*[3] followed in 2009 by a new citizenship study guide, *Discover Canada,* which gave a prominent place to the monarchy;[4] a much-delayed tour by the Prince of Wales and Duchess of Cornwall in 2009 and a major tour by the Queen and the Duke of Edinburgh in 2010, featuring Canada Day in Ottawa and the centennial of the Canadian navy in Halifax; then, in 2011, a brilliantly successful tour, including Quebec, of the newlywed Duke and Duchess of Cambridge (Prince William and Catherine), followed in short order by the restoration of the historic names Royal Canadian Navy, Royal Canadian Air Force and Canadian Army, which had been jettisoned in 1968.

These monarchical manifestations could be dismissed as mere window-dressing, or at best as a revival of the "dignified" face of the Crown, to reprise Walter Bagehot's well-known phrase. Yet symbolic gestures reflect inner realities and policy options. Sure enough, during the same period the "efficient" face of the Crown, to again quote Bagehot, rose to prominence in the dissolution and prorogation controversies of 2008 and 2009. Arguments pro and con—well summarized in *The Evolving Canadian Crown*[5]—drew more attention to the "reserve powers" of the governor general than had been the case since the "King-Byng affair" of 1926. The Ontario Liberal government's prorogation controversy in 2012 simply directed media and public attention to the same issue with another political party in another jurisdiction. The constitutional role of the Crown had emerged from its obscurity.

The Queen's Diamond Jubilee Year in 2012 accentuated public interest in the Crown. By then, Governor General David Johnston, nominated by Prime Minister Harper in 2010, was well established in office. Once again, the vice-regal dynamics had changed—but this time, in contradistinction to the previous regimes, the Crown and the Sovereign were front and centre at Rideau Hall. A Diamond Jubilee program, featuring a widely distributed commemorative medal as well as postage stamps, a website, displays, and community grants, publicized the historic sixtieth anniversary of the reigning monarch. A Canadian delegation led by the governor general and prime minister travelled to London for the spectacular Jubilee celebration, during which the Queen unveiled a new Canadian portrait of herself for display at Rideau Hall, replacing the one banished during Michaëlle Jean's tenure. Parliamentarians of all stripes, except, of course, the Bloc Québécois, vied with themselves to praise Queen Elizabeth and the monarchy when adopting a Diamond Jubilee resolution in the House of Commons. The Prince of Wales and Duchess of Cornwall made a brief but well-received tour to three provinces. Opinion polls, transitory and fluctuating as they always are, appeared to register a rebound in the popularity of the monarchy, or at least its "dignified" side.

At the same time, the age-old issue of Quebec's attitude to the Crown reared its head during the province's 2012 election, when Parti Québécois leader Pauline Marois, soon to be premier, railed against the office of lieutenant governor and the monarchy as instruments of Ottawa and anglophone domination. In 2013, the debate over the Succession to the Throne Act revealed fault lines in Canada's approach to the monarchy. The debate was not about ending male primogeniture or removing the bar to the monarch's marrying a Roman Catholic—both measures were widely applauded—but the legitimacy of doing so by assenting to a British law without a constitutional amendment, and one involving provincial consent at that. In June 2013, two law professors in Quebec filed a court challenge on just those grounds. (Questions about a possible split in the line of succession became moot when the first child born to the Duke and Duchess of Cambridge on July 22, 2013, was a boy, but the constitutional debate remains.) Then, a month later, another court challenge was mounted in Ontario against the citizenship oath of allegiance to the Queen, a matter thought to have been resolved by the Federal Court of Canada in the 1994 *Roach* case which was also rejected by the Ontario Superior Court in 2009 on another motion filed in 2005. The same Ontario court dismissed the new motion in September 2013.

Fault lines exist, too, in varying reactions to the government's use of the "efficient" side of the Crown to achieve its political goals. In 2012, a newly formed organization called Your Canada – Your Constitution challenged executive dominance through royal prerogative powers and, by clear implication, the monarchy that conferred them.[6] Is the use of prerogative powers indeed too far-reaching? Is responsible government, over which the Crown presides and which it is supposed to protect, at risk?

Evidently there is ample reason and fertile ground for continued discussion and study of the Crown in Canada, and the Diamond Jubilee Year provided a timely opportunity to do so. Accordingly, the Government of Saskatchewan and the Johnson-Shoyama Graduate School of Public Policy at the University of Regina and the University of Saskatchewan convened a second conference on the Crown at Government House in Regina in October 2012. In this, they were ably supported by The Mosaic Company, the Whitecap-Dakota First Nation, Friends of the Canadian Crown, Massey College at the University of Toronto, and the Institute of Intergovernmental Relations at Queen's University, which had been the organizing partner of the 2010 conference. Entitled "The Crown in Canada: A Diamond Jubilee Assessment," the 2012 conference brought together an eclectic group of Canadian scholars, public servants, elected representatives, educators, vice-regal staff members, and even a lieutenant governor designate. Their discussions ranged from the monarchy's position in Quebec and its relations with First Nations, through the media, education on the Crown, and a republican option for Canada, to the succession to the throne, the effectiveness of the provincial Crown, and the conundrum for parliamentary democracy of an institution that must be at the same time "dignified" and "efficient."

Revised versions of the conference papers—and of commentaries on two of these papers—are included as chapters in this book. However, as editors we sought to broaden the scope of the present volume even beyond the already varied topics addressed at the 2012 conference. In particular, we invited some emerging scholars, as well as established writers, to submit their ideas. One of the gratifying aspects of contemporary scholarship on the Crown is the interest, indeed enthusiasm, it has elicited among a new generation of students and academics; this was apparent at the Regina conference and is evident in social media such as blogs and Twitter as well as in more traditional vehicles.

The resulting book may surprise readers by its diversity. After all, it deals at one and the same time with historical topics such as the War of 1812 (marking its bicentennial) and the nineteenth-century vice-regal court of Lord Lorne and Princess Louise, and the very contemporary issues of cabinet manuals and international deployments of the Canadian Forces. What do all these topics have to do with the Crown? Everything, we submit. Precisely because the Crown is so multifaceted, it touches on multiple layers of Canada's governance and political culture. The "dignified" is a cover for an "efficient" that is complex and momentous. That is why we believe studies of the Crown in Canada are so fascinating and rewarding. We hope readers of this volume will share our view.

****

The volume is organized into four parts. In Part 1, "Canadian Encounters with the Crown," the contributing authors look at both individual and collective experiences of the monarchical institution.

Historian Carolyn Harris, one of a new generation of scholars, affirms that the period 1878–1883, when the Marquis of Lorne was governor general, not only prefigured but ushered in a uniquely Canadian version of the monarchy. Lord Lorne was married to Princess Louise, a talented daughter of Queen Victoria, and Dr. Harris makes the case in her chapter "Lord Lorne, Princess Louise, and the Emergence of the Canadian Crown" that the royal couple helped assert Canada's sovereignty vis-à-vis the United States; identified the Crown with the regions, francophone Canadians, and First Nations; and adapted the monarchy to the more informal, egalitarian nature of Canadian society. "The Marquis of Lorne and Princess Louise," concludes Dr. Harris, "set crucial precedents that defined a distinct role for the Crown in Canada from the nineteenth century to the present reign."

Writing, too, from a historical perspective, Serge Joyal examines the vexing issue of the Crown in Quebec. In a provocative essay entitled "La Couronne au Québec: de credo rassurant à bouc émissaire commode," Senator Joyal challenges the mantra of nationalistes and souverainistes, reiterated by Pauline Marois in 2012, that the Crown has been a symbol of federal and anglophone domination of the people of Quebec. Jacques Parizeau once said that "les Québécois n'ont pas la fibre monarchique." Not so, counters the senator: for two centuries before the Treaty of Paris in 1763, Canadiens were subjects of the kings of France; for two centuries afterwards, although with some dissent, they viewed their British successors, from George III to Elizabeth II, at least as benign sovereigns and even as guardians of their language, religion, and culture. They defended the monarchy against American republican invaders in 1776 and 1812: "les

Canadiens ... étaient monarchistes, affectueusement monarchistes : ils aimaient leur roi," affirms Senator Joyal. And, from Papineau to Cartier, Laurier to Duplessis, French Canadians saw constitutional monarchy as the locus of their liberty. Members of the Royal Family were enthusiastically received in Quebec. This changed abruptly in the 1960s with the rise of the sovereigntist movement. Now, argues Senator Joyal, Québécois, still imbued with a victim mentality despite their undoubted success as a modern society, treat the Crown as a "convenient scapegoat" for a lack of confidence in their past and in their dynamic future. "Peut-être aussi, inconsciemment, craint-on ce qu'on pourrait y découvrir et qui pourrait heurter notre prétendue modernité." This historical revisionism contradicts Quebec's motto, *Je me souviens*.

Point counterpoint. In her commentary, Linda Cardinal applauds Senator Joyal's initiative in drawing attention to the neglected phenomenon of the Crown in Quebec. However, for her there is another "convenient scapegoat": a Quebec seen as conservative, retrograde, and even reactionary before the Quiet Revolution of the 1960s. Was this society really monarchical? Recent Quebec historiography, says Dr. Cardinal, differs from the senator's interpretation in the way it looks at the British Empire, the roots of democratic, even republican, opinion in Quebec, and the pertinence of the monarchy. The role of the Crown in Quebec will continue to be debated, but Senator Joyal and Dr. Cardinal show that it is far more complex than popular perception would suggest.

Whether in Quebec or in the rest of Canada and beyond, the media inevitably shape public opinion on the Crown. At the 2012 conference, Phillip Crawley, publisher of the *Globe and Mail*, and author John Fraser engaged in an unscripted dialogue about the Crown and the media. They agreed that "the media and the Crown were hopelessly intertwined" and needed each other. The low point for the Royal Family was the "hacking scandal" in the United Kingdom. In Canada, more positive media coverage and editorial treatment of the Crown and its Canadian representatives reflect a renewed interest in, and more balanced coverage of, the institution, along with inevitable questioning of it.

But are Canadians aware of what the Crown really means to their governance? Peter H. Russell, in "Educating Canadians on the Crown – A Diamond Jubilee Challenge," identifies a "knowledge gap" about the Crown's vital role in our parliamentary democracy. According to him, we fail to see the fundamental differences between our Westminster system and the American presidential system, to grasp the "duality at the top" in ours, and to understand the role of the vice-regal reserve powers in constraining the elected government. Dr. Russell defends this duality at the top, as he does unwritten conventions and vice-regal interventions. However, he says, it may be advantageous, if not to codify these conventions, at least to summarize them in a cabinet manual—another debatable issue. Above all—and this is scarcely debatable—Dr. Russell deplores the abysmal state of civics education in our schools, well documented by Ontario teacher Nathan Tidridge.[7] The Diamond Jubilee challenges us to do something about the widespread ignorance of the way we are governed.

Part 2, "Crown and Constitution," deals specifically with the way we are governed. The heart of the matter, of course, is the Constitution, monarchical since before Confederation, but enshrined in the British North America Act of 1867 and entrenched in the Constitution Act, 1982.

"The Crown in Canada Today: How Dignified? How Efficient?" by David E. Smith examines in the Canadian context the classic formulation by Walter Bagehot of the passive and active roles of the monarchy: symbol and government.[8] The author acknowledges the rejuvenation of the visual image of the Crown by the Conservative government of Prime Minister Harper. But in Canada, he says, there cannot be the same personal bond between Sovereign and people as in the United Kingdom. Given the unique constitutional and political circumstances of this country, Dr. Smith argues that the efficiency of the Crown has been much more in evidence here in Canada. Whereas "the Crown as an emblem of monarchy seemed to be evaporating, the Crown as instrument of government assumed new form and prominence." The prorogation debate in 2008 did not call into question the utility of the Crown; on the contrary, it portrayed the governor general as an impartial umpire. With the executive engaging increasingly in extra-parliamentary, populist politics, the governor general may become an "efficient" vehicle for transforming Canada from a parliamentary democracy into an electoral democracy—for example, through Senate reform. Paradoxically, the new visibility of the governor general makes the office more exposed and more vulnerable. For the Canadian Crown, concludes Dr. Smith, the Queen is now viewed as the "principal" and the governor general as the "agent." Does this suggest that the former is to be lauded as the "dignified" and the latter treated warily as the "efficient"?

In offering a commentary on Dr. Smith's chapter, Robert E. Hawkins actually provides a sequel: "'Inefficient Efficiency': The Use of Vice-Regal Reserve Powers." Professor Hawkins agrees with David Smith that the most prominent characteristic of the Canadian Crown is its efficiency, but he is more sanguine about the end result. Indeed, describing yet another paradox, he contends that "what makes our Crown efficient is not its efficiency, but its very inefficiency." The vice-regal representatives safeguard their neutrality by "not acting"—unless there is a genuine constitutional emergency where, as neutral players, they may intervene to safeguard the constitutional order. Professor Hawkins suggests five such scenarios where an impartial vice-regal arbiter could make "the democratic voice of the people heard." Assuredly, paradox abounds in the institution of the Crown!

Another paradoxical feature in this democratic yet monarchical form of government is the hereditary succession to the throne. Ian Holloway, in "The Law of Succession and the Canadian Crown," evokes, like David Smith and Robert Hawkins, the Bagehotian distinction between the dignified and efficient dimensions of the Crown. But unlike them, he focuses on the dignified, and even extends it to a third dimension, the "mystical." Dean Holloway sees this dimension as essential to a system of government grounded "in the mists of history," and he deplores a Canadian "anti-historicism" that assesses everything in terms of the present. The succession is in itself counterintuitive, regulated as it is by eighteenth-century laws requiring the monarch to be of a certain family and religion in the United Kingdom. The irony is that the succession is firmly entrenched in Canadian constitutional law: the Canadian monarch must be the same as the monarch of the United Kingdom; the office of the Sovereign can be changed only with the consent of both houses of Parliament and all ten provincial legislatures. (Presumably Dean Holloway disagrees with the process used in the 2013 Succession to the Throne Act.) He dismisses the "canard" that Canada could simply not proclaim the Prince of Wales as Sovereign on the death of the Queen: under common law, the succession is automatic.

The dignified, indeed mystical, side of the Crown is duly noted by our next author, John D. Whyte, but in "A Case for the Republican Option" he applies rigorous logical analysis to an institution that by definition is scarcely logical. Having a constitutional monarch for Canada, despite its undoubted historical and moral resonances, he says, is irrelevant and even misleading. Is there any good reason why Canada should remain a monarchy and not become a parliamentary republic? Responding in the negative, Professor Whyte makes five claims: there is no longer a "fit" between monarchy and Canada's constitutional culture; republican ideas provide a more coherent basis for our political organization; civic republican theory captures better than monarchy the concepts of the Canadian state; Aboriginal claims for political recognition would be better advanced and defended through civic republican theory; and civic republicanism matches the chief moral imperatives governing the Canadian political community. Professor Whyte, who has described himself as a "reluctant republican," draws these conclusions from a profound reflection on constitutional theory. Other authors in this book may take issue with his emphasis on the hereditary nature of monarchy rather than its constitutional side, and may challenge his apparent equating of liberal democracy with republicanism. Yet John Whyte raises probing questions that deserve our attention.

After these examinations of constitutional theory, the next five chapters in Part 3, "The Crown in Practice," draw our attention to specific and contemporary issues of the Canadian Crown "at work."

Christopher McCreery reviews the evolution of the Crown in the provinces, signalling its intimate link with Canadian federalism. (This timely topic is of course intrinsic to Serge Joyal's chapter, "La Couronne au Québec.") Dr. McCreery reminds us of the short shrift given to the office of lieutenant governor and the institution of the provincial Crown during much of Canada's first century, despite the landmark ruling of the Judicial Committee of the Privy Council in the 1892 *Maritime Bank* case that the national and provincial Crowns were coordinate in status. Since at least the 1970s, however, there has been a major rehabilitation of the Crown in the provinces and the position of vice-regal representatives. The lieutenant governors may still be federal appointees, but they are certainly no longer viewed either by the courts or by politicians and the public as federal agents. Their "efficient" constitutional role continues in tandem with that of the governor general. However, Dr. McCreery makes the intriguing observation that their "dignified" role has expanded significantly. In yet another paradox, these erstwhile agents of Ottawa now represent to the public both the federal and the provincial Crowns, in what the author calls "cross-pollination" or "seepage" between the two jurisdictions. This occurs domestically with, for example, the conferring of honours and attention to the First Nations, but even internationally, with some provinces recruiting their lieutenant governors for missions abroad. Above all, the lieutenant governors vigorously promoted the monarchy at a time when official Ottawa, including Rideau Hall, was trying to hide it.

Turning to an issue that affects all jurisdictions, Richard Berthelsen critiques a prominent royal function in "The Speech from the Throne and the Dignity of the Crown." Referring once again to Walter Bagehot, he points out that the dignified and efficient sides of the Crown intersect uniquely in the speech from the throne, where the governor gives voice in highly ceremonial form to the government's plans. Mr. Berthelsen sees an "inherent contradiction" in requiring the vice-regal person to step into the political or policy realm by speaking for the partisan government of the day. Lest the author seem iconoclastic, he observes that in 1989 federal cabinet minister Mitchell Sharp alleged that the throne speech had "been converted from its original purpose into a vehicle of government propaganda." To buttress Sharp's claim, Mr. Berthelsen quotes chapter and verse from verbose, partisan throne speeches in jurisdictions as varied as Canada and its provinces and territories, Australia and its states, and Commonwealth realms in the Caribbean and the South Pacific. By contrast, the throne speeches at the Parliament at Westminster—and l'Assemblée nationale du Québec—are paragons of brevity and non-partisanship. The irony of the latter will strike Senator Joyal and Dr. Cardinal, but Mr. Berthelsen sees it as a worthy model to emulate.

In "Cabinet Manuals and the Crown," James W. J. Bowden and Nicholas A. MacDonald deal with a topic that has generated much discussion and some controversy. Like veteran academics Peter Russell and Robert Hawkins, these two emerging scholars eschew codification of convention. Again like Dr. Russell, but this time not Professor Hawkins, they advocate cabinet manuals as a way to "officialize" the norms of constitutional conventions and in so doing to clarify the role of the Crown. "When some conventions are misunderstood or misinterpreted or even ignored or flaunted," they say, "a cabinet manual may serve a useful purpose in reminding political actors of how constitutional conventions are meant to work." Mr. Bowden and Mr. MacDonald cite the 1968 *Manual of Official Procedure of the Government of Canada* as a good example of "officialization." The authors believe that at the time of the 2008 prorogation controversy, reference to this manual would have shown that the prime minister was in fact acting in accordance with constitutional convention. So, too, it clarifies the "caretaker role" of the government during an election period, and even the prerogatives of mercy and state funerals. While not all will be convinced, the authors make a compelling case for reinforcing the Crown through officialization of convention.

Christopher McCreery returns to the forum with "Confidant and Chief of Staff: The Governor's Secretary." The private secretary to the Queen, the secretary to the governor general, and the secretaries to the lieutenant governors all serve in differing degrees as chiefs of staff, administrative heads, official conduits, and advisers to their principals. Dr. McCreery traces the history of the governor's secretary to pre-Confederation days, indeed as far back as New France, and recounts conflicting views on the tenure and power of the incumbents. The practice that eventually prevailed for the governor general's office is to have the term of the secretary match more or less that of the vice-regal incumbent, a notable exception being the legendary Esmond Butler. With deputy minister status, the secretary to the governor general enjoys considerable autonomy, although not as much as the equivalent position in Australia. The secretaries to the provincial lieutenant governors are in a different league. Dr. McCreery relates the chequered history of these offices, which have never attained the prestige of their counterparts in the Australian states. However, he demonstrates that their scope has considerably developed in the past four decades, just like that of the lieutenant governors which he described in his earlier chapter. Although none of the Canadian vice-regal secretaries, national or provincial, can compare with the influence and autonomy of the private secretary to the Queen, for Dr. McCreery they still play a crucial role in "ensuring vice-regal autonomy from the potential machinations of the political executive."

One cannot think of a better example of the efficient side of the Crown than that of military deployment. Alexander Bolt analyzes this in "Crown Prerogative Decisions to Deploy the Canadian Forces Internationally: A Fitting Mechanism for a Liberal Democracy." The title says it all: the political executive deploys the Forces, and such use of the royal prerogative is entirely appropriate. The author admits that this may appear archaic, illiberal, and to some, even unlawful. Should Parliament not make such decisions or at least be involved in them? Lieutenant-Colonel Bolt responds with a resounding "no." Examining the nature and history of the royal prerogative, he concludes that it provides legitimate and long-standing domestic legal authority for deployment of the Canadian Forces; there is no requirement for parliamentary approval. Then, if Parliament does not *have* to be involved in military deployment decisions, *should* it be? The author believes that this would actually be harmful to both Parliament and the Forces: partisan considerations would inevitably come into play, and government accountability would be diluted. Moreover, military deployment requires a rapid response and confidential liaison with allies. In a ringing defence of the system of responsible government, Lieutenant-Colonel Bolt asserts that for military deployment, Canada is best served by cabinet responsibility and by the parliamentary roles of holding the executive accountable and approving appropriations. Contrary to current attacks against it, the royal prerogative is neither "pre-democratic" nor anti-democratic. Instead, it is a "fitting mechanism for a liberal democracy."

We begin this book in a historical mode. Appropriately, we do the same in the last part, "First Nations and the Crown," which draws our attention to one of the most historic and arguably most meaningful relationships for the monarchy in Canada, and certainly one where both its dignified and its efficient roles have been manifest.

Another emerging scholar, Stephanie Danyluk, hearkens back two hundred years in "'Recollecting Sovereignty': First Nations–Crown Alliance and the Legacy of the War of 1812." The First Nations were crucial allies to the British Crown in that conflict. Ms. Danyluk makes the point that, while serving under a common command, they did not view themselves as subordinate, nor did they surrender their sovereignty to the Crown. She demonstrates through written records and oral histories that the First Nations were self-governing nations, involved in a treaty relationship with the Crown, which the Crown promised to uphold. But in the case of the "Western Indian Nations" the promises were not fulfilled; instead, these First Nations were abandoned to the expansionist Americans. In the 1860s and 1870s, some Dakota peoples, moving across the border from the United States, appealed—with little success—for the Crown to honour its promises. Ms. Danyluk asserts that the War of 1812 established a precedent for shared sovereignty today between the two parties and for a "third order of government" for the First Nations under the Crown. While John Whyte considers this option unfeasible, or at least undesirable, it is very much part of current scholarly thinking.

In "The Aboriginal Peoples and the Crown," J. R. (Jim) Miller evokes the same notion of First Nations–Crown alliance as Ms. Danyluk and recalls the same initiatives of the Dakota peoples in Western Canada. But he expresses the relationship in terms of "kinship" and traces it back even further than the War of 1812, to Champlain and New France, the Hudson's Bay Company, trade in the seventeenth and eighteenth centuries, and the landmark Royal Proclamation of 1763, which served as "foundation of the territorial treaty system" and symbol of the protective role of the Crown. This kinship was (and is) taken very seriously by the First Nations and was at the centre of their protocols, especially for treaty negotiations. It was for good reason, says Dr. Miller, that the Aboriginal peoples called Queen Victoria "mother" and her son the Prince of Wales "brother." They "enlarged the circle of kinship" to include the Queen and Canadians; they viewed the relationship as one of family—certainly not one of subordination. The failure on the Canadian side to respect the spirit of the treaties, and above all the passing of the Indian Act in 1872, turned the First Nations peoples into legal dependants rather than "kin-like partners." For Dr. Miller, reflecting on protests like the Idle No More movement, it is essential to restore the lapsed kinship and treaty relationship between Canada and the First Nations embodied in the Crown.

My co-editor, Philippe Lagassé, entitles his Conclusion to this volume "The Contentious Canadian Crown." He could equally have called it the "controversial" or "challenging" Crown. The very complexity of this Crown causes confusion and even division when it is examined. Commentators talk at cross-purposes, says the author, because they are assessing in isolation different facets of a multifaceted institution. In reviewing not only the chapters in the present book but the entire spectrum of current debate on Canada's monarchical polity, Dr. Lagassé has undertaken an ambitious initiative. In this, he has succeeded admirably. He clarifies the issues by grouping them under three headings: the hereditary Crown—its familial and British aspects; the communal Crown—building a sense of political community and Canadian nationhood; and the constitutional Crown—the source of sovereign authority. In the latter, he encapsulates and demystifies the monarchical constitution. Dr. Lagassé carefully summarizes and evaluates the pros and cons of the Crown in its multiple dimensions. "Debates and discussions about Canada's constitutional monarchy," concludes Dr. Lagassé, "are better served when the Crown's complexity is acknowledged and embraced." I leave it to the reader to appreciate his lucid explanation of this complex institution.

****

The multiple adjectives used to describe the Canadian Crown testify to the complexity whereof Philippe Lagassé speaks. Twenty years after writing *The Invisible Crown: The First Principle of Canadian Government* in 1995, David E. Smith would undoubtedly retain "the first principle of Canadian government" in the title. But would he drop the "invisible" if he published a new edition (following the welcome 2013 reprint)? If so, it would be due in large part to his own scholarly achievements, as well as to the events and policy evolution that have taken place in the past two decades. Certainly, Dr. Smith continues to point to the centrality of constitutional monarchy in our political order, even if it is not properly understood or its principles always realized. For example, in his latest work, on parliamentary opposition, he queries whether we still accept that there is no constituent power outside the Crown-in-Parliament.[9]

That Crown could variously be described as puzzling, intriguing, elusive, even amorphous. French adjectives like *insaissisable* and *fuyant* come to mind. It has also been termed "inconvenient."[10] Perhaps one of the best descriptors is that of Australian scholar Anne Twomey: the "chameleon Crown."[11] As in Australia, so too in Canada the Crown has proved resilient, constantly evolving, and adaptive to ever-changing circumstances. David E. Smith speaks in his chapter in this book of "regal persistence" in Canada. Serge Joyal, quoting a popular song in Quebec, says that "comme dans la chanson *La Maladie d'amour* ... 'elle dure, elle dure la ...' monarchie." Contested, contentious, complicated, or confusing, the enduring, even endearing, Canadian Crown is inseparable from the unique story of this country of ours.

Notes

1. Jennifer Smith, "Introduction," in *The Evolving Canadian Crown*, ed. Jennifer Smith and D. Michael Jackson (Montreal and Kingston: McGill-Queen's University Press, 2012), 1.
2. David E. Smith, *The Invisible Crown: The First Principle of Canadian Government* (Toronto: University of Toronto Press, 1995). Reprinted with a new preface by the author (University of Toronto Press, 2013).
3. Kevin S. MacLeod, *A Crown of Maples: Constitutional Monarchy in Canada / La Couronne canadienne: La monarchie constitutionnelle au Canada* (Ottawa: Department of Canadian Heritage, 2008; new edition, 2012).
4. *Discover Canada: The Rights and Responsibilities of Citizenship / Découvrir le Canada: Les droits et responsabilités liés à la citoyenneté* (Ottawa: Minister of Citizenship and Immigration, 2009; new edition, 2011).
5. See the following chapters in *The Evolving Canadian Crown*: Patrick J. Monahan, "The Constitutional Role of the Governor General;" Andrew Heard, "The Reserve Powers of the Crown: The 2008 Prorogation in Hindsight;" and Robert E. Hawkins, "Written Reasons and Codified Conventions in Matters of Prorogation and Dissolution."
6. See the website of Your Canada, Your Constitution, www.ycyc-vcvc.ca.
7. Nathan Tidridge, "Ontario Civics Textbooks and Their Errors concerning the Canadian Crown," presented at the conference "The Crown in Canada: A Diamond Jubilee Assessment," Regina, October 2012. See also Carolyn Alphonso, "Incorrect Textbooks Being Used to Teach Civics," *Globe and Mail*, April 15, 2013.
8. In 1867, Walter Bagehot wrote *The English Constitution* (London: Oxford University Press, 1961), in which he made a classic distinction between the "dignified" aspect of government (the monarchy) and the "efficient" side (the cabinet and House of Commons).

9. David E. Smith, *Across the Aisle: Opposition in Canadian Politics* (Toronto: University of Toronto Press, 2013), 167-68.
10. Mark Lovewell, "The Inconvenient Crown," *Literary Review of Canada* 20, no. 5 (2012).
11. Anne Twomey, *The Chameleon Crown: The Queen and Her Australian Governors* (Sydney: Federation Press, 2006).

Part 1

Canadian Encounters with the Crown

1

Royalty at Rideau Hall: Lord Lorne, Princess Louise, and the Emergence of the Canadian Crown

Carolyn Harris

En 1878, le gendre de la reine Victoria, John Campbell (lord Lorne), devient le quatrième gouverneur général du Canada depuis la Confédération. Pour nombre d'historiens, cette nomination et celle d'autres gouverneurs généraux natifs de Grande-Bretagne au XIXe *siècle et au début du XX*[e] *témoignent du maintien de l'identité britannique du Canada au-delà de la Confédération. Mais l'arrivée en 1878 de lord Lorne et de sa femme, la princesse Louise, est l'occasion pour les Canadiens d'affirmer leur identité nationale naissante en exprimant leurs attentes à l'égard du nouveau couple vice-royal, devenu en quelque sorte canadien. Cette année-là, trois aspects clés de cette identité naissante sont ainsi mis en lumière dans les journaux, la correspondance et les imprimés grand public qui rendent compte de la nomination de lord Lorne et de l'arrivée du couple.*

Ces aspects sont la fidélité du Canada à la Couronne (contrairement aux États-Unis), le caractère démocratique de sa société sans distinction de classes (contrairement à la Grande-Bretagne) et le rapport proprement canadien à la nature et aux sports d'hiver. L'accueil enthousiaste fait au couple en déplacement de Halifax à Ottawa, ainsi que l'inquiétude de la population que le couple veuille être traité avec la même déférence que les autres membres de la famille royale, traduisait en ce XIXe *siècle l'émergence d'une culture nationale unique. C'est en répondant à ces attentes que lord Lorne et la princesse Louise ont acquis une grande popularité dès leurs premiers mois au pays. Leur arrivée en 1878 aura favorisé l'élaboration d'une identité canadienne distincte à la fois de celles de la Grande-Bretagne et des États-Unis.*

"I am longing to hear an account of your reception in Canada and how everything goes off. I hear they have gone to a great deal of trouble and expense to do you honour—you know what a Canadian I am in feeling so you can imagine the interest I take in all that will be going on there now."

—Letter from Prince Arthur, Duke of Connaught, to his sister, Princess Louise, Marchioness of Lorne, November 23, 1878.[1]

The Canadian Crown

On July 24, 1878, British prime minister Benjamin Disraeli asked Queen Victoria's son-in-law, John Campbell, Marquis of Lorne, to become the fourth governor general of Canada since Confederation.[2] Loyalty to the Crown united the diverse provinces, and the Dominion's place in the British Empire appeared to protect Canada's territorial integrity from American expansion. Lorne's appointment also reflected the long-standing personal relationship between Queen Victoria's family and the newly self-governing Dominion. The Queen's endorsement of the union of Canada (East and West), New Brunswick, and Nova Scotia in 1867 had been crucial to overcoming Maritime opposition to Confederation.[3] The Queen had also selected Ottawa as the new Dominion's capital.[4] Queen Victoria's eldest son, the future Edward VII, had completed a successful tour of British North America in 1860; her second son, Prince Alfred, Duke of Edinburgh, had toured the Maritimes in 1861; and her third son, Prince Arthur, Duke of Connaught, who would ultimately serve as governor general from 1910 to 1916, had completed part of his military training in Montreal in 1869/70.

Lord Lorne and his wife, Princess Louise Caroline Alberta, however, would be the first royal couple to travel together to Canada and reside in Rideau Hall in an official capacity. The presence of the royal couple in Canada served as tangible proof of the connection with the Crown, a connection that had contributed to Confederation and continued to affirm the Dominion's independence from the United States. Louise's and Lorne's activities in Canada set important precedents for the structure of royal visits, the significance of a royal presence to the Dominion's place in the British Empire and to its subsequent sovereignty as an independent state, and popular perceptions of how royalty should behave in an egalitarian Canadian society.

The importance of Lorne and Louise to the development of Canada's nationhood was well known during their lifetimes, but their significance has faded into relative obscurity. In his 1884 study of Canada under the administration of Lord Lorne, J. E. Collins credited the royal couple with professionalizing the visual arts in Canada by founding the Royal Canadian Academy of Arts and the National Gallery of Canada.[5] Lorne's own prodigious published writings in the late nineteenth and early twentieth centuries encompassed the scope of his activities in Canada, including poetry commemorating the naming of the province of Alberta after his wife.[6] H. V. Ross singled out Louise as a nation-builder among Canada's vice-regal consorts in a 1907 article, writing, "If the Princess entertained less munificently than her predecessor [Lady Dufferin], she was, if anything, more active in those solid works that make for the lasting betterment of a country."[7] When Louise died in 1939, having been widowed for twenty-five years and away from Canada for more than half a century, Prime Minister William Lyon Mackenzie King paid tribute to her lifelong interest in Canadian affairs, stating, "In the death of Princess Louise, Canada has lost a true friend who never failed to retain a very special interest in the country which was so much a part of her earlier life."[8] After Louise's death and the appointment of Canadian-born governors general following the Second World War, the contributions of Lorne and Louise to Canadian nationhood received little attention, with the exception of W. Stewart MacNutt's 1955 study.[9] Biographies of the royal couple focused on the impact of Canada on the lives of Louise and Lorne rather than their influence on how Canadians viewed themselves.[10] The most recent scholarship concerning Lorne and Louise in Canada places their extensive travels in Canada within the context of popular responses to the broader British Empire rather than the development of the Dominion.[11]

The official arrival of Lorne and Louise in Halifax on November 25, 1878, and their subsequent journey to Ottawa was widely scrutinized by Canadians as the most significant royal visit since Confederation. As a prince who already had extensive experience living in Canada and viewed himself as "Canadian," the Duke of Connaught correctly predicted the intense interest that his sister and brother-in-law would receive from the moment of their arrival. The range of popular responses to Lorne's appointment as governor general and his arrival in Canada with Louise, however, reflected the unique Canadian political and social climate during the decades immediately following Confederation. Although loyalty to the monarch remained a quality that united inhabitants from the various provinces, the advent of Confederation prompted a national debate about what the role of the Crown and the Royal Family should be in the self-governing Dominion. Amid the enthusiastic coverage of the arrival of Lorne and Louise in the Canadian press was a growing consensus that the monarchy played a different role in Canada than it did in Great Britain.[12]

Contemporary analyses of the unique place of the monarchy in Canada during Lorne's term in Ottawa covered three broad themes that have had a profound impact on the Canadian Crown to the present day. The first was the view that the physical presence of members of the Royal Family in Canada helped guarantee Canadian territorial sovereignty, reflecting Great Britain's commitment to defend Canada against an American invasion. Lorne's years as governor general coincided with annexationist sentiment in America. The presence of Queen Victoria's daughter in

Canada was widely believed to affirm the Dominion's territorial integrity. The second theme, closely related to the issue of territorial sovereignty, was that all regions of the Dominion of Canada should receive regular royal visits to affirm the personal relationship between each province and the Crown. Although the British government had assumed in 1867 that Confederation would inevitably lead to centralization, Lorne and Louise discovered a strong tradition of regional autonomy in Canada and responded by making personal visits to the various provinces.[13] A third theme was the importance of maintaining an egalitarian, informal society in Canada rather than recreating the rigid social hierarchy of the British court. Canadians expected members of the Royal Family to engage with people from diverse backgrounds and participate in Canadian pastimes such as winter sports. From the beginning of their time in Canada, Louise and Lorne attempted to respond to both the political and the social expectations of the monarchy in the newly self-governing Dominion. Their acceptance of a uniquely Canadian role for royalty influenced the subsequent history of royal visits to Canada and created the social conditions for a distinct Canadian Crown that would continue to evolve with Canada's emergence as a modern sovereign state.

The Governor General and the Princess

Of all the members of Queen Victoria's family in the 1870s, Louise and Lorne were best suited to adapt the British conception of royalty to the unique political and cultural expectations of the Canadian people. Louise was born in 1848, the sixth of the Queen's nine children. From a young age, she was skeptical of formal court ceremonies, writing to her friend Louisa Bowater in 1866, "I shall be so pleased to see you at Court, and will try and behave very well when you pass [to curtsey to the Queen] because I have always had an inclination to laugh when I see anyone I know."[14] In contrast to her sisters Helena and Beatrice, who accepted the Queen's seclusion after the death of the Prince Consort in 1861, Louise attempted to persuade her mother to appear in public. Louise had read newspaper articles criticizing the Queen's absence from London,[15] and she demonstrated a sensitivity to popular opinion that was not shared by all members of her family. Louise also became the first British princess to attend a public educational institution, taking sculpture classes at the National Art Training School in Kensington.[16] The Princess's most innovative decision was her choice of Lorne, the heir to the Duke of Argyll, as a husband. All four of Louise's sisters married German princes, and there had not been a marriage between a princess and a British subject since 1515. The 1871 marriage was popular among all social classes in Great Britain, as it appeared to demonstrate Louise's love for her homeland and absence of pretention.[17]

Lorne's appointment as governor general at the comparatively young age of thirty-three was greeted with some skepticism in the British press. The London correspondent for the *New York Times* argued that Lorne's "greatest achievement in life is his marriage to a Princess" and that Disraeli may have decided to send the royal couple to Canada because of Louise's "cleverness and feminine discretion."[18] In contrast, Canadian newspapers identified positive attributes that Lorne would bring to Canadian political and social life. The Toronto *Mail* observed,

> The young Lord, who as Head of our Canadian Government, represents the Queen, has had great advantages. He is the son of the distinguished statesman, the Duke of Argyll, he has himself been for many years in parliament; he is a scholar and author of some distinction. He is a personal friend of the Governor General, and he will have the benefit of Lord Dufferin's experienced advice.[19]

In addition to the qualities described by the *Mail*, Lorne shared Louise's love of foreign travel, interest in the arts, and critical attitude toward traditional institutions. After completing his education at Eton and Cambridge, Lorne published an article entitled "The Handicaps of a University Education," arguing that universities should spend less time teaching the classics and more time providing practical training for future colonial officials.[20] Lorne gained first-hand experience by travelling extensively to countries in the British Empire, including Canada, prior to his marriage. For Lorne, the invitation to become governor general was an opportunity to return to a region that he had already visited and to apply his political and cultural experience within the nascent Dominion.

Canada and the United States

While the earliest press coverage of Lorne's appointment as governor general focused on the qualities that suited the royal couple to an extended residence in Canada, the three themes that defined the emergence of a distinctly Canadian Crown after Confederation quickly became the focus of commentary. The perception that the physical presence of royalty in Canada protected the Dominion's integrity from encroachments of the United States was part of the 1878 souvenir book, *Royalty in Canada*. The author, Charles R. Tuttle, who had published *The Comprehensive History of the Dominion of Canada* the previous year,[21] argued that Louise's arrival was a key moment in the history of Canada: "The presence of the Princess in Canada will have more than social significance; it will have great political influence. It will carry us through that transition state where our destinies seem to be balancing between Imperialism and Republicanism. It will arrest our drifting into the republic of the United States."[22] This prediction appeared within the context of a detailed comparison between Canada's growing economic links with the United States in the nineteenth century on the one hand, and its cultural values of loyalty to the Crown and pride in being part of the British Empire on the other. Tuttle assumed that the presence of the royal couple would reinforce the Dominion's political and cultural links to the monarchy and thereby protect it from American imperialism.

Tuttle noted approvingly that even the American press recognized the significance of the arrival of the royal couple and their extended residence in Canada.[23] The political magazine *Harper's Weekly*, which typically dismissed Canada's allegiance to the monarchy, observed, "If Canada's loyalty to the mother country needed strengthening . . . nothing could have been better devised than the appointment of the Marquis and the Princess."[24] In the Canadian press, the presence of royalty was considered so important that the *Montreal Gazette* expressed regrets that the Duke of Connaught had not been chosen as governor general over Lorne.[25]

Lorne and Louise would have been aware of their perceived importance to Canada's continued presence in the British Empire. Lorne had consulted extensively with his predecessor, Lord Dufferin, before coming to Canada,[26] and Louise had learned of the political situation through correspondence with her brothers. The Duke of Connaught had written from Montreal in February 1870, following a visit to the United States, "I earnestly pray that this Dominion may never be given over to the States as it will be the ruination of it; for I feel certain that British rule is the only really free one; for in the states mob tyranny is something fearful, and bribery and corruption are practised to any amount."[27] The time Louise and Lorne devoted to travelling across British North America and bestowing regal names on new settlements and provinces demonstrated that they took the threat of annexation seriously and sought to unify what is now Canada as a single dominion.

The royal couple's arrival journey from Halifax to Ottawa in 1878 encompassed the four original provinces that joined Confederation in 1867, and their subsequent travels to British Columbia and what was then the Northwest Territories displayed their commitment to a unified British North America. The couple visited British Columbia in 1882 to reinforce the connection between this distant province and the federal government at a time of political tension between Victoria and Ottawa regarding the terminus for the Canadian Pacific Railway.[28] Louise chose Regina as the name of the future capital of Saskatchewan in honour of the Queen.[29] In 1880, Lorne explained his vision for Canada in a letter to Queen Victoria: "Next year, I hope to get a new province in our 'North West' named after [Louise], which will have a population equal to that of Greece and Denmark together, for we have room for four or five such Provinces there. . ."[30] Louise and Lorne not only symbolized Canada's loyalty to the Empire but acted to ensure that the Northwest Territories would become a series of Canadian provinces instead of American states.

The precedent set by the royal couple endured after Canada became independent of the British Empire and developed its own sovereignty. The physical presence of members of the Royal Family in Canada continues to be a marker of Canadian authority over disputed regions. During the Cold War, the Canadian Arctic became strategically significant due to its proximity to Russia and the United States. In 1969, the American oil tanker the *SS Manhattan* became the first ship to travel through the Northwest Passage, prompting the introduction of the Arctic Waters Pollution Prevention Act in the House of Commons, which would create a 100 nautical-mile pollution-prevention zone under Canadian control.[31] Prime Minister Pierre Trudeau was not a monarchist, but he enjoyed a warm relationship with Queen Elizabeth II[32] and recognized that the best way to attract international attention to the issue of Canadian Arctic sovereignty was a royal tour.[33] In 1970, to commemorate the hundredth anniversary of the Northwest Territories joining the Dominion of Canada, the Queen, Prince Philip, Prince Charles, and Princess Anne visited remote communities on the Arctic Circle. As the Northwest Passage becomes increasingly accessible to sea traffic due to global warming, royal visits continue to symbolize Canadian sovereignty over its Arctic waters. The 2012 working visit of the Earl and Countess of Wessex to Iqaluit reaffirmed the Crown's historic ties to the region.

The Crown and the Provinces

The practice of royal visits encompassing the full range of Canadian geography was another precedent set in the nineteenth century that continues to shape the structure of royal tours of Canada. In Great Britain, the royal presence was concentrated in London and the regions that surrounded royal estates. The long-standing tradition of royal progresses came to an end during the reign of King Charles I,[34] limiting opportunities for the public outside the capital to see the monarch. Queen Victoria lived in relative seclusion after the death of Prince Albert and performed comparatively few public engagements during the second half of her reign. In contrast, the inhabitants of British North America expected a royal tour to encompass as many regions and major population centres as possible. When the future King Edward VII visited North America in 1860, he toured the major centres of Newfoundland, Prince Edward Island, Nova Scotia, New Brunswick, and Canada East and West.[35] After Confederation, Canada's provinces maintained unique regional identities dating from their time as distinct colonies and expected to maintain individual relationships with the Crown within the British Empire.[36]

Lorne and Louise ensured that an inclusive approach to royal visits continued after Confederation. As the royal couple visited the towns along the Intercolonial Railway during their arrival tour of Canada, Lorne's speeches referenced the places they intended to visit on subsequent tours.

For example, when the royal train stopped in Moncton, Lorne responded to the official welcome by saying, "It would have been a satisfaction to us had we been able to make a more extended tour of New Brunswick, and we look forward to the day when we can visit the capital and chief centres of the population."[37] The following year, Louise and Lorne completed a full tour of the province, including a visit to Fredericton, demonstrating their commitment to the individual provinces and recognizing the long history of regional autonomy in Canada.[38] During the 1879 visit to New Brunswick, Lorne and Louise met with descendants of American loyalists and Acadians, affirming the Crown's gratitude for their loyalty and protection of their interests.[39]

The royal couple's policy of connecting with all regions of Canada has become standard practice throughout the Commonwealth during the reign of Elizabeth II. Some of the most successful Canadian royal tours consisted of long-distance train journeys that crossed the entire country, such as those of King George VI and Queen Elizabeth in 1939 and Queen Elizabeth II and the Duke of Edinburgh in 1959. This format allowed visiting royalty to engage with a broad cross-section of the Canadian population and to reinforce their personal relationships with the individual provinces, developing the modern-day "compound monarchy" (the term introduced by David E. Smith in *The Invisible Crown* to describe Canada's adaptation of monarchy to federalism).[40] Once multiweek whistle-stop tours fell out of fashion in the 1960s, shorter royal visits took place that covered different regions of Canada. Most recently, the Duke and Duchess of Cambridge's 2011 tour covered Ottawa, Montreal, Quebec City, Charlottetown, Yellowknife, and Calgary, while the 2012 Diamond Jubilee visit by the Prince of Wales and Duchess of Cornwall encompassed Saint John, Toronto, and Regina. Although the precedents set by the travels of Louise and Lorne after Confederation reflected the Canadian federal structure, the current Queen has applied this approach to all her Commonwealth tours. Elizabeth II established a pattern early in her reign, ensuring that major cities and counties in the United Kingdom received a visit from the monarch every three or four years and that more remote regions were part of a tour every eight to ten years.[41] The Queen visited all regions of the United Kingdom for her Diamond Jubilee, while members of the Royal Family toured the Commonwealth realms. The ambitious travel program undertaken by Louise and Lorne between 1878 and 1883 has become an integral aspect of the Crown's personal relationship with all Commonwealth realms.

An Egalitarian Court

In addition to setting a post-Confederation precedent for the geographical scope of royal tours, Louise and Lorne accepted Canadian cultural expectations that they would engage with a more diverse social circle. The royal couple's social life became the third theme that dominated Canadian press coverage of their time in the Dominion. Just as loyalty to the Crown differentiated Canadians from Americans, rejection of a strict social hierarchy governed by ancestry made Canada distinct from Great Britain. Precedents had already been set by the first two post-Confederation vice-regal consorts, Lady Monck and Lady Lisgar, who publicized their "At Homes" in the Ottawa newspapers.[42] The Dufferins introduced fancy dress balls to Rideau Hall but, according to Ross, "nothing won [Canadians] over more completely than the sweetness and urbanity of [Lady Dufferin], whose cordial manner broke down all barriers between herself and those who were privileged to meet her."[43] Lady Dufferin was a shrewd observer of Canadian social customs and adapted her manner accordingly. Upon hearing of Lord Lorne's appointment as her husband's successor, she expressed her thoughts to Queen Victoria's private secretary, Sir Henry Ponsonby, who recorded the conversation as follows: "The real difficulty was how Louise would treat people in Canada—if as royalty, there would be trouble, but if in the same way Lady Dufferin did they would be flattered."[44] Canadians took pride in Louise's presence in Canada because of their loyalty to the Crown, but they expected her to socialize differently in Ottawa than she did in London.

Even the most enthusiastic Canadian observers of Lorne's appointment as governor general stated that British royal ceremonial etiquette and pageantry would be out of place in the more egalitarian Canadian society. The Toronto *Globe* stated, "The Canadian people are by no means wealthy and there will be cause for regret if the presence of the Marquis and his wife is the signal for extravagance in equipage or dress."[45] The writer hoped that they would set an example of a prudently managed household to the Canadian people. Another Canadian newspaper expressed concern that the society ladies of Ottawa were practising "the backward walk" and that their husbands might have to wear knee breeches.[46] Only the Quebec City newspapers expressed any enthusiasm for a Canadian "court" that would be similar to the one in London.[47] While Queen Victoria was critiqued for simplifying court and public ceremonies during her widowhood,[48] Louise and Lorne were expected to interact with Canadians from a variety of social backgrounds without the kind of ostentation associated with the royal court in London.

The royal couple made clear from their arrival that they intended to conform to Canadian social expectations. On her first day in Halifax, Louise slipped ashore incognito to attend church in thanksgiving for the end of the difficult transatlantic voyage.[49] At Lorne's swearing-in on the following day, Louise wore a simple black dress with jet jewellery, as she was still in mourning for her mother-in-law, the Duchess of Argyll.[50] Both Lorne and Louise made an excellent first impression on the assembled dignitaries gathered to greet them and on the crowds that had poured into Halifax for the royal couple's arrival.[51] Although Prime Minister John A. Macdonald's absence from the welcoming party due to excessive drinking on the train from Ottawa fuelled rumours from the Liberal Opposition that he disapproved of Lorne's appointment,[52] the first real test of protocol did not occur until the royal party reached Montreal. After a public welcome so enthusiastic that Lorne's speech was drowned out by cheering crowds,[53] Louise made the royal couple even more popular by her response to the protocol concerns of a vice-regal aide. The aide attempted to insist that ladies received by the Princess must don full court dress, including the low-cut ball gowns abhorred by the Quebec Roman Catholic clergy.[54] Louise reputedly replied, "I should not have cared if they had come in blanket coats."[55] The royal couple maintained this perspective throughout their time in Canada. In 1881, journalist Annie Howells Frechette observed in *Harper's Magazine*, "So unaffected is the life at Rideau Hall that it shows almost a republican sensibility compared with the ceremony and parade kept up in many of the great houses in England. No court etiquette is observed and only the rules of good manners are adhered to."[56] By conforming to Canadian social customs, Lorne and Louise demonstrated that royalty in Canada played a different role than in Great Britain, establishing the cultural conditions for the emergence of a distinct Canadian Crown.

During their first winter in Canada, Louise and Lorne discovered that a key element of Canadian culture and social life was participation in winter sports such as curling, skating, and tobogganing. These were not simply activities for passing long winters but part of a culture of engagement with the wilderness that united Canadians from diverse backgrounds, in the same manner as loyalty to the Crown. As Collins observed in 1883, "In nothing is Canada distinctly national, save in her games and sports."[57] Sporting activities were a key aspect of previous royal visits to Canada. The Prince of Wales had attended a lacrosse game in 1860, and the Duke of Connaught had thrown himself into hunting and winter sports during his military training in Canada.[58] When Lorne and Louise arrived in Montreal, the welcoming crowds included delegations from the local sport clubs. The *St. Joseph Gazette* reported, "At the intersection of Dorchester with Beaver Hill streets, the Montreal Lacrosse club had improvised an arch. A large number of the members of the Lacrosse and Snow Shoe Clubs, dressed in their peculiar costumes, were clustered on top of the arc . . ."[59] The royal couple gained immense popularity during their first year in Canada through their enthusiastic participation in winter sports. Louise took skating lessons and hosted tobogganing parties at the Rideau Hall toboggan slide, which had been installed by the Dufferins.[60] Lorne became president of the vice-regal curling club and received praise for "playing a fine lead."[61] Participation in winter sports demonstrated that the royal couple were "Canadians" during their time in Canada, assimilating into the nascent national culture.

Having expressed their enthusiasm for the comparative informality of Canadian society, Lorne and Louise proceeded to broaden the range of people in Canada who enjoyed personal contact with royalty. As Louise's elder brother, the Prince of Wales, was a bachelor at the time of his tour of British North America, most of the delegations he received consisted of men alone.[62] The presence of the Princess in Canada allowed Canadian women's organizations to request royal patronage. For example, the Ladies' Educational Association of Montreal requested that the Princess become their patroness.[63] Louise, who was visiting Montreal, responded to the delegation with a speech accepting the request and expressing her own opinions on the subject of women's education.[64] The Princess's personal engagement granted a Canadian women's organization unprecedented access to royal patronage and further demonstrated Louise's enthusiasm for comparatively informal Canadian social etiquette. In Great Britain, Lorne often gave addresses on Louise's behalf, as it was not customary for ladies make speeches.[65]

In addition to receiving delegations from women's organizations, the royal couple made lasting connections with French Canadians and members of the First Nations. Lorne and Louise were both fluently bilingual and engaged with French-Canadian society to a greater degree than any vice-regal couple since Confederation. When the Prince of Wales had visited Montreal, he had been surrounded by English Canadians at all times.[66] By contrast, in St. Thomas, Quebec, Louise addressed the crowds in French: "Au nom de la reine, je vous remercie des délicates allusions que contient votre adresse, et je vous remercie en mon nom des bonnes choses que vous m'avez dites."[67] In Ottawa, the royal couple engaged with the French-Canadian political elite, who had largely socialized separately from English Canadians during the terms of the previous three governors general.[68] Louise in particular enjoyed French-Canadian society, as she found that many politicians from Quebec and their wives were well educated, had made the grand tour of Europe, and shared her artistic interests.[69] The warm relations established between the royal couple and First Nations leaders were not unprecedented, as the Prince of Wales had received First Nations leaders and recognized their communities in 1860.[70] Nevertheless, Louise and Lorne received particular praise from native leaders for shaking hands with them as equals during the couple's visit to Victoria, British Columbia, in 1881.[71] Lorne also met with native leaders throughout his solo tour of the Northwest Territories in 1881,[72] reinforcing the personal relationship between the First Nations and the Crown. The royal couple's relative informality and personal engagement with the leaders of French Canada and the First Nations set important precedents for future royal visits and popular perceptions of the Canadian Crown.

Royal visits to Canada during the reign of Queen Elizabeth II continue to follow the pattern set by Louise and Lorne. Some of the most iconic images of the Queen and her family in Canada show them behaving informally and/or engaging in local sporting activities. These images include Hilton Hassel's painting of Princess Elizabeth and the Duke of Edinburgh square dancing at Rideau Hall in 1951, which became a Canadian Christmas card design in 1958, and the Queen dropping the first puck at a Vancouver Canucks game during her Golden Jubilee tour of Canada in 2002. At the time of the Queen's Diamond Jubilee in 2012, *Ottawa Citizen* columnist Dan Gardner rebuked a republican who commented that Elizabeth II could not be Queen of Canada because "she wouldn't know a hockey puck from a piece of tar." Gardner noted the Queen's attendance at Canadian games over the decades and argued that "in another very practical sense, and one that too many republicans refuse to acknowledge, she has such a deep connection with this country that to call her a foreigner seems quite false."[73] The Queen's children and grandchildren also engage with Canadian pastimes. The Duke and Duchess of Cambridge received extensive praise for conversing at length with ordinary Canadians during their 2011 tour. Both Prince William in 2011 and Prince Charles in 2012 played street hockey with Canadian children.

Louise's and Lorne's public engagement with women, French Canadians, and First Nations demonstrated the Crown's ability to unify Canadians from diverse backgrounds after Confederation. The popular view of the monarchy as a protector of French-Canadian linguistic and cultural rights lasted until the Quiet Revolution of the 1960s. Back in 1939, while touring Canada with King George VI, Queen Elizabeth wrote, "The French people in Quebec & Ottawa were wonderfully loyal; & [in] Montreal there must have been 200,000 people, all very enthusiastic & glad to have an excuse to show their feelings."[74] The cheering crowds in Quebec City and Montreal during the Duke and Duchess of Cambridge's 2011 tour suggest that French-Canadian attitudes toward the monarchy may be becoming favourable once more, after decades of hostility following the Quiet Revolution.

The perception of a personal relationship between the Crown and the First Nations has continued to the present day. In 2012, Prince Charles and the Duchess of Cornwall visited the First Nations University in Regina, meeting with youth entrepreneurs. Most recently, Chief Theresa Spence of the Attawapiskat First Nation wrote to the Queen in January 2013 to request Governor General David Johnston's presence at meetings between First Nations leaders and Prime Minister Stephen Harper to address the issues facing native communities in Canada.

The Lasting Impact

Louise and Lorne did not maintain the near-universal popularity of their first year in Canada during their entire period of residence. Louise was injured in a sleighing accident in 1880 and spent much of the final years of Lorne's term as governor general recovering her health in the United Kingdom and Europe.[75] The royal couple also experienced marital difficulties during the early 1880s, and Louise in particular appears to have insisted that they spend long periods of time apart.[76] Unfortunately, Louise's long absences from Canada during the final years of Lorne's term fuelled rumours that the Princess disliked Canadians or that the royal couple did not get along with Sir John and Lady Macdonald.[77] By the time Lorne declined to extend his term as governor general by an additional year in 1883, the couple had a mixed reputation in Canada. They were still praised for their political and social successes, but Louise's frequent absences from Canada prevented them from enjoying the same lasting acclaim as their immediate predecessors in Rideau Hall.

Despite the problems the royal couple experienced during the final years of Lorne's term as governor general, their ability to embrace Canadian political and social expectations of royalty at the time of their arrival in Canada did set lasting precedents for the Canadian Crown. The popular perception that the presence of members of the Royal Family in Canada helped to guarantee territorial sovereignty continues to the present reign with royal visits to the Arctic symbolizing Canadian authority over the Northwest Passage. The unprecedented scope of the royal couple's travels during their time in Canada reinforced the notion of a compound monarchy, with each individual province as well as the federal government enjoying a personal relationship with the Crown. Canadian social etiquette also had a profound effect on the manner in which Louise and Lorne interacted with diverse groups of ordinary Canadians. In Canada, the royal couple behaved much more informally than they did in Great Britain, disregarding court protocol, participating in winter sports, and meeting a more varied social circle than they would have previously encountered. Their engagement with women, French Canadians, and First Nations set the tone for subsequent royal visits, demonstrating the ability of the Crown to unify Canadians from diverse backgrounds. The Marquis of Lorne and Princess Louise set crucial precedents that defined a distinct role for the Crown in Canada from the nineteenth century to the present reign.

Notes

1. Elizabeth Longford, ed., *Darling Loosy: Letters to Princess Louise 1856-1939* (London: Wiedenfeld and Nicolson, 1991), 216.
2. Robert M. Stamp, *Royal Rebels: Princess Louise and the Marquis of Lorne* (Toronto and Oxford: Dundurn Press, 1988), 114.
3. Richard Gwyn, *John A., The Man Who Made Us: The Life and Times of John A. Macdonald,* vol. 1, *1815–1867* (Toronto: Vintage Canada, 2007), 370-89.
4. Sandra Gwyn, *The Private Capital: Ambition and Love in the Age of Macdonald and Laurier* (Toronto: McClelland & Stewart, 1984), 36-37.

5. J. E. Collins, *Canada under the Administration of Lord Lorne* (Toronto: Rose Publishing Company, 1884), 401-2.
6. John Campbell, Marquis of Lorne, *Memories of Canada and Scotland* (London: Sampson Low, Marston, Searle & Rivington, 1883), 63.
7. H. V. Ross, "Vicereines of Canada: Being Sketches of the Nine Ladies Who Have Led Canadian Social Life at Ottawa since Confederation," *Canadian Magazine of Politics, Arts, Science and Literature* 29 (May–October 1907): 228.
8. D. Blake McDougall, *Princess Louise Caroline Alberta* (Edmonton, AB: Legislature Library, 1988), http://www.assembly.ab.ca/lao/library/louise/index.htm.
9. W. Stewart MacNutt, *Days of Lorne: Impressions of a Governor General* (Fredericton, NB: Brunswick Press, 1955).
10. See David Duff, *The Life Story of H.R.H. Princess Louise Caroline Alberta, Duchess of Argyll* (Bath: Cedric Chevers, 1971); Jehanne Wake, *Princess Louise: Queen Victoria's Unconventional Daughter* (London: Collins, 1988); and Stamp, *Royal Rebels.*
11. See R. W. Sandwell, "Dreaming the Princess: Love, Subversion, and the Rituals of Empire in British Columbia," in *Majesty in Canada: Essays on the Role of Royalty,* ed. C. M. Coates (Toronto: Dundurn, 2006).
12. Christopher Moore, *1867: How the Fathers Made a Deal* (Toronto: McClelland & Stewart, 1997), 231-52.
13. See Paul Romney, *Getting It Wrong: How Canadians Forgot Their Past and Imperilled Confederation* (Toronto: University of Toronto Press, 1999), 150-53; and Robert C. Vipond, *Liberty and Community: Canadian Federalism and the Failure of the Constitution* (Albany: State University of New York Press, 1991), 52.
14. Longford, *Darling Loosy*, 8.
15. Wake, *Princess Louise*, 80-81.
16. Jerrold M. Packard, *Victoria's Daughters* (New York: St. Martin's Press, 1998), 127.
17. Longford, *Darling Loosy*, 142-43.
18. *New York Times*, September 9 and 11, 1878, quoted in Stamp, *Royal Rebels*, 118.
19. "Canada's New Governor: Enthusiasm in the Dominion. The Marquis of Lorne's Appointment Hailed with Delight by the Canadian Press," The *Mail*, reprinted in the *New York Times*, July 31, 1878.
20. MacNutt, *Days of Lorne*, 3-4.
21. Charles R. Tuttle, *The Comprehensive History of the Dominion of Canada* (Montreal: H.B. Bigney, 1877).
22. Charles R. Tuttle, *Royalty in Canada: Embracing Sketches of the House of Argyll* (Montreal: Tuttle and Simpson, 1878), 24-25.
23. Tuttle, *Royalty in Canada*, 112-13.
24. *Harper's Weekly*, article by George William Curtis, quoted in Tuttle, *Royalty in Canada*, 112.
25. *Montreal Gazette*, editorial by Thomas White Esquire, quoted in Tuttle, *Royalty in Canada*, 116.
26. Stamp, *Royal Rebels*, 119.
27. Longford, *Darling Loosy*, 119.
28. Sandwell, "Dreaming the Princess," 45.
29. Wake, *Princess Louise*, 245.
30. Longford, *Darling Loosy*, 219.

31. N. D. Bankes, "Forty Years of Canadian Sovereignty Assertion in the Arctic: 1947-1987," *Arctic* 4, no. 4 (December 1987): 288.
32. John English, *Just Watch Me: The Life of Pierre Trudeau 1968–2000* (Toronto: Alfred Knopf, 2009), 229.
33. Arthur Bousfield and Garry Toffoli, *Fifty Years the Queen: A Tribute to Queen Elizabeth II on Her Golden Jubilee* (Toronto: Dundurn Press, 2002), 141.
34. Michelle Anne White, *Henrietta Maria and the English Civil Wars* (Aldershot: Ashgate Publishing, 2006), 22.
35. Ian Radforth, *Royal Spectacle: The 1860 Visit of the Prince of Wales to Canada and the United States* (Toronto: University of Toronto Press, 2004), xii.
36. Vipond, *Liberty and Community*, 85.
37. Collins, *Canada under the Administration of Lord Lorne*, 38.
38. D. Michael Jackson and Lynda M. Haverstock, "The Crown in the Provinces: Canada's Compound Monarchy," in *The Evolving Canadian Crown*, ed. Jennifer Smith and D. Michael Jackson (Montreal and Kingston: McGill-Queen's University Press, 2012), 11-30.
39. *The International Portrait Gallery* (London: Cassell and Co., 1878), 159.
40. David E. Smith, *The Invisible Crown: The First Principle of Canadian Government* (Toronto: University of Toronto Press, 1995; reprinted with a new preface by the author, 2013).
41. Robert Hardman, *Our Queen* (London: Hutchinson, 2011), 247.
42. S. Gwyn, *Private Capital*, 145.
43. Ross, "Vicereines of Canada," 228.
44. S. Gwyn, *Private Capital*, 185.
45. The *Globe*, quoted in Tuttle, *Royalty in Canada*, 115.
46. Longford, *Darling Loosy*, 45.
47. Collins, *Canada under the Administration of Lord Lorne*, 202.
48. Stanley Weintraub, *Victoria: An Intimate Biography* (New York: Truman Talley Books, 1987), 355-56.
49. McDougall, *Princess Louise Caroline Alberta*.
50. Wake, *Princess Louise*, 218-19.
51. "Lord Lorne and Princess Louise: State Entry into Canada," Reuter's telegram, *The Glasgow Herald*, November 26, 1878.
52. Bousfield and Toffoli, *Fifty Years the Queen*, 58; Packard, *Victoria's Daughters*, 200.
53. "Lorne and Louise: An Enthusiastic Reception of the Lornes in Montreal," *St. Joseph Daily Gazette*, November 30, 1878.
54. S. Gwyn, *Private Capital*, 185; MacNutt, *Days of Lorne*, 202-3.
55. S. Gwyn, *Private Capital*, 185.
56. Annie Howells Frechette, "Life at Rideau Hall," in *Improved by Cultivation: English-Canadian Prose to 1914*, ed. R. G. Moyells (Peterborough, ON: Broadview Press, 1994), 123-24.
57. Collins, *Canada under the Administration of Lord Lorne*, 393.
58. Gillian Pouter, *Becoming Native in a Foreign Land: Sport, Visual Culture and Identity in Montreal, 1840–85* (Vancouver: UBC Press, 1999), 181.
59. "Lorne and Louise: An Enthusiastic Reception of the Lornes in Montreal," *St. Joseph Daily Gazette*, November 30, 1878.
60. Frechette, "Life at Rideau Hall," 126; Wake, *Princess Louise*, 224-25.

61. John Kerr, *The History of Curling and Fifty Years of the Royal Caledonian Curling Club* (Edinburgh: David Douglas, 1890), 328.
62. For example, the welcoming party in St. John's, Newfoundland, was all male. See Radforth, *Royal Spectacle*, 88.
63. Collins, *Canada under the Administration of Lord Lorne*, 46.
64. Ibid., 46-47.
65. Wake, *Princess Louise*, 291.
66. Radforth, *Royal Spectacle*, 264.
67. Collins, *Canada under the Administration of Lord Lorne*, 42.
68. S. Gwyn, *Private Capital*, 186.
69. MacNutt, *Days of Lorne*, 205-6.
70. Radforth, *Royal Spectacle*, 208.
71. Wake, *Princess Louise*, 253.
72. Stamp, *Royal Rebels*, 172-77.
73. Dan Gardner, "Truly, The Queen of Canada," *Ottawa Citizen*, August 29, 2012.
74. William Shawcross, ed., *Counting One's Blessings: The Select Letters of Queen Elizabeth the Queen Mother* (New York: Farrar, Straus and Giroux, 2012), 237.
75. Wake, *Princess Louise*, 234-42.
76. Longford, *Darling Loosy*, 55.
77. S. Gwyn, 188-90; Stamp, *Royal Rebels*, 200-1.

2

La Couronne au Québec : de credo rassurant à bouc émissaire commode

Serge Joyal

For over 350 years, Canadians of French origin were ardent and loyal subjects of the kings of France and England. Twice they took up arms so that Canada could remain under the British Crown, in gratitude for the rights and freedoms they had benefited from. And they never missed an opportunity to publicly recall their allegiance to the Crown each time a member of the Royal Family visited Quebec. This loyalty was inseparable from their faithfulness to the Catholic Church, part of an age-old alliance between the Throne and the Altar.

From the beginning of the 1960s, a demanding and aggressive nationalism appeared, determined to get rid of everything that could have caused the economic and religious domination of French Canadians. It attacked the Crown as a symbol of an outdated colonial past. Vengeful in tone and concealing the true nature of constitutional monarchy, these expressions of opposition to the Crown have become a constant feature, inseparable from public debate on the future of Quebec and uniting partisans of all sides. And since the mid-1990s, key figures in English Canada have criticized the relevance of the Crown, widening the grounds for calling the Canadian monarchy into question. Yet the arguments put forward fifty years ago have not really evolved. The debate is mired in ignorance—evidence of a form of political immaturity.

Tout le monde a une opinion sur la monarchie, la Couronne, la Reine ou sur l'un ou l'autre membre de la famille royale, opinion qui tient plus souvent du potin ou des courants de la mode « genre tendance »… Yann Martel, l'écrivain de Saskatoon, déclarait en 2012: « Je ne suis pas monarchiste, ni anti-monarchiste d'ailleurs»[1]. C'était avant de recevoir la médaille du Jubilé de Diamant de la Reine Elizabeth II. À l'autre bout, Jacques Parizeau, dans son testament politique en 2009, disposait à sa façon de la question : « Les Québécois n'ont pas la fibre monarchique ».[2] Le premier ministre Charest, quant à lui, prenait ses distances avec les évènements entourant le Jubilé. « M. Charest s'occupe d'économie, il n'a pas le temps pour s'occuper des médailles »,[3] déclarait son bureau. Plusieurs députés fédéraux n'ont guère fait montre de plus d'enthousiasme face à l'opportunité de distribuer des médailles commémoratives aux plus méritants de leurs électeurs.[4]

En somme, au mieux on aborde le sujet à distance, sans se commettre, conservant une certaine « virginité » de pensée, ou encore, on déclare n'avoir rien à y voir, que la question a trop peu d'importance pour nourrir le début d'une idée. Jour après jour, on occit la monarchie à coup de sondages aux résultats tout aussi convenus et fatals les uns que les autres.[5] Et pourtant, comme dans la chanson *La Maladie d'amour* (1973) de Michel Sardou, « elle dure, elle dure la ... » monarchie.

Toutes ces opinions, en apparence définitives, sont aussi superficielles que profondément ignorantes d'une réalité historique incontournable : le Canada français est le plus ancien territoire en Amérique (du nord et du sud) où règne un monarque, sans interruption, depuis plus de 470 ans. Ce phénomène historique a profondément marqué l'éthos du Canada français, et tenter de comprendre quelles influences cette continuité surprenante et unique a exercées sur la perception que les Canadiens français ont généralement d'eux-mêmes est un exercice qui attire peu d'esprits curieux, tant on prétend être convaincu de sa vétusté. Peut-être aussi, inconsciemment, craint-on ce qu'on pourrait y découvrir et qui pourrait heurter notre prétendue modernité.

Le Canada, dont la possession a été réclamée en 1534 au nom de François Ier, Roi de France, est aujourd'hui, en 2013, gouverné au nom de Elizabeth II, reine du Canada. Pendant près des 230 premières années de son existence (1534-1763), il a été sous la couronne des Rois de France, jusqu'au *Traité de Paris* signé le 10 février 1763. Le « Chemin du Roy » longe toujours le Saint-Laurent de Montréal à Québec sur la rive nord, le buste de Louis XIV occupe fièrement le centre de la Place Royale dans la basse ville de la vieille capitale, et le drapeau du Québec arbore les fleurs de lys, symbole de la monarchie française. Le Mont-Royal à Montréal, ainsi nommé pour honorer le Roi de France, en perpétue le souvenir depuis le premier voyage de Jacques Cartier (1534). Le Roi de France y a incarné l'autorité suprême, le Canada devenant même en 1663 une colonie royale, jusqu'à sa cession cent ans plus tard. Le Souverain était Roi par la grâce de Dieu, il était l'élu de Dieu[6] et détenait sur tous ses sujets un pouvoir bien peu tempéré par la loi. Cet absolutisme, quoique non despotique au pays[7], se fit sentir de tout son poids pendant l'Ancien Régime; il mena, on le sait, aux bouleversements sanglants de la Révolution française.

L'historien réputé Marcel Trudel (1917-2011), un peu plus distant du consensus mou des historiens d'allégeance plutôt nationaliste, a eu l'heur de démontrer dans une analyse incisive que la chute de la Nouvelle-France de Louis XV, et sa transformation en colonie britannique sous George III, ne représentèrent pas pour la population canadienne un choc aussi brutal qu'on a bien voulu y voir des années plus tard quand on s'est mis à rêver que la Nouvelle-France représentait l'âge d'or des Canadiens.[8]

Le fait fondamental que les Canadiens continuaient de demeurer « sujets » d'un roi, cette fois de George III, comme ils l'avaient été de Louis XV, leur garantissait qu'ils pouvaient « se confier en notre protection royale et compter sur nos efforts pour leur assurer les bienfaits des lois de Notre royaume d'Angleterre, »[9] car c'était là le pendant même de la sujétion au Roi. En retour de la soumission, le Roi garantissait à ses sujets sa protection, lui dont l'autorité était de source divine, « by the Grace of God ».

Les Canadiens (s'entend les habitants d'origine française au pays, soulignons-le) étaient monarchistes, affectueusement monarchistes : ils aimaient leur roi. Ils le démontrèrent lors de l'engagement à défendre Québec[10] contre les Américains, le 31 décembre 1775.[11] Sans ce gage de loyauté[12], Québec serait passée aux Américains. Cette première manifestation tangible de fidélité à la Couronne sauva la colonie britannique.

À la Révolution française, lorsque les Canadiens apprirent la décapitation de Louis XVI, le 17 janvier 1793, ils furent bouleversés, stupéfaits. Philippe Aubert de Gaspé (père) écrira, bien des années plus tard en 1866, combien son père avait été atterré en apprenant la nouvelle :

> Mon père venait de recevoir son journal. (Il) bondit tout à coup sur sa chaise, [...] il se prit la tête à deux mains, en s'écriant: Ah! les infâmes, ils ont guillotiné leur Roi!...[13]

On crut même dans les campagnes profondes que l'exécution de Louis XVI était une fausse nouvelle propagée par les Britanniques pour stimuler l'adhésion à la couronne de George III!

Pendant les vingt-deux ans qui ont suivi, jusqu'à la défaite de Napoléon à Waterloo le 18 juin 1815, les Canadiens sont demeurés dans leur immense majorité de fidèles et loyaux sujets du roi George. Ils percevaient alors Napoléon comme le « Corse usurpateur du trône des Bourbons » et n'eurent de cesse d'appuyer l'Angleterre de *John Bull* dans sa campagne incessante contre *Boney*, souscrivant même à l'effort de guerre.[14]

Cette loyauté à la Couronne britannique se manifesta à nouveau douze ans plus tard lors de la seconde invasion américaine. Au cours de la guerre de 1812-14, les Canadiens combattirent spontanément pour repousser les envahisseurs yankees, aussi bien dans la marine sur les Grands Lacs (où ils étaient les seuls à ne pas déserter les navires[15]) qu'à Beaver Dams (Niagara, 24 juin 1813)[16], à Châteauguay, où De Salaberry remporta une victoire décisive contre les Américains (26 octobre 1813)[17], ou encore quelques mois plus tard à Crysler's Farm (Morrisburg, Ontario, 11 novembre 1813), « la victoire qui sauva le Canada », où ils furent les premiers avec des guerriers amérindiens à faire face à la deuxième division du général américain Wilkinson. Il n'y eut aucune hésitation parmi eux à vouloir demeurer sous la Couronne de George III.

L'évêque anglican de Québec, Jacob Mountain, écrivait d'ailleurs dans une lettre le 20 février 1808 :

> Les mépris que les Canadiens catholiques ressentent pour les Bostonnais (c'est ainsi qu'ils appellent les américains) et la crainte qu'ils ont de voir leur pays annexé aux États-Unis, nous assurent de leur fidélité à l'Angleterre.[18]

Mgr Plessis, l'évêque de Québec, était l'un des fervents tenants de l'interprétation que la Conquête de 1760 était un évènement providentiel qui avait épargné aux Canadiens les affres de la Révolution, et le renversement du trône et des autels.

Le témoignage le plus percutant des sentiments prévalant à l'égard de la Couronne, à cette époque, est le discours que prononça Louis-Joseph Papineau, alors président de la Chambre d'assemblée, à l'occasion du décès de George III en 1820 :

> Il est impossible de ne pas exprimer nos sentiments de gratitude pour les bienfaits que nous avons reçus de lui et les sentiments de regret pour sa perte si profondément sentie ici et dans toutes les parties de l'empire.
>
> *Gazette de Québec*, juillet 1820.[19]

L'envolée lyrique de Papineau frappa à ce point l'opinion qu'elle eut des échos jusque dans les journaux à Londres. Dans un manifeste électoral publié en 1827, et endossé par sept députés en vue du Parti patriote, Papineau écrivait :

> Quant au serment de fidélité au roi, il n'y a personne dans la province, quelle que soit sa situation, qui pût, qui osât dire d'aucun membre de cette chambre, qu'il y a manqué. Le peuple de cette province, les électeurs, sont trop bons juges de la loyauté, ils en ont donné des preuves trop convaincantes, pour que l'on suppose qu'ils pourraient choisir pour députés des sujets suspects sur ce point.[20]

Alexis de Tocqueville, qui visita le Bas-Canada à l'été 1831, remarqua les convictions du clergé vis-à-vis la royauté : « ils nous ont paru cependant en général avoir des sentiments de *loyauté* envers le roi d'Angleterre, et soutenir en général le principe de la légitimité ».[21]

Pendant la période tumultueuse de la Rébellion, les Canadiens, en majorité, professèrent une loyauté constante. À cette époque, la jeune Reine Victoria prenait pied dans son siècle, et le rapprochement entre Louis-Philippe et la souveraine, puis entre cette dernière et Napoléon III (scellée pendant la guerre de Crimée, 1853-1856) inaugurèrent une période de détente harmonieuse entre les deux ennemis irréductibles de naguère. Cette nouvelle harmonie favorisa la reprise des relations officielles entre la France et la Province du Canada-Uni, qui se concrétisa en 1855 par la visite de la corvette française *La Capricieuse*, pilotée par le commandant de Belvèze, autorisée par Londres. Le Tricolore et l'Union Jack flottaient côte à côte autant à Québec, Trois-Rivières, Montréal, Chambly, Beauharnois, qu'à Kingston, Toronto, jusqu'aux Chutes du Niagara, et enfin à Ottawa. La bonne entente entre les deux mères patries, sous l'égide de deux souverains impériaux, stimula les éloges enthousiastes et simultanés des deux couronnes.

Lorsque les discussions s'entamèrent en 1864 entre les représentants des différentes colonies britanniques pour former un même Dominion, ceux du Bas-Canada n'hésitèrent pas à proclamer que les colonies devraient être réunies sous la Couronne, incarnation des principes monarchiques qu'ils partageaient profondément. George-Étienne Cartier, un admirateur des institutions parlementaires britanniques, déclara à la Conférence de Halifax de 1864 :

> I am living in a Province in which the inhabitants are monarchical by religion, by habit and by the remembrance of past history. Our great desire and our great object in making efforts to obtain the federation of the Provinces is not to weaken monarchical institutions, but on the contrary to increase their influence. We know very well that, as soon as confederation is obtained, the Confederacy will have to be erected into a Vice-Royalty, and we may expect that a member of the Royal Family will be sent here as the head.[22]

Cartier traduisait fidèlement les convictions prévalant à cette époque : les Canadiens français se voyaient les héritiers d'une longue tradition historique de fidélité au roi, confirmée par leurs principes religieux eux-mêmes définis dans une théologie fondée sur un Dieu protecteur, à l'égal d'un roi. Il y avait ainsi symbiose conceptuelle entre la sujétion à Dieu et la fidélité au roi, entre la protection du roi accordée à ses sujets loyaux et le bonheur éternel promis par Dieu à ses fidèles croyants. Dans cette société à dominante ultramontaine il y avait une cohérence idéologique entre les deux ordres, civil et religieux, qui était lénifiante pour ses habitants.

Le long règne pacifique de la Reine Victoria, marqué par l'apogée de la Révolution industrielle et de l'Empire britannique, eut à la fois des effets bénéfiques, et pervers, bien contre la volonté de la souveraine, précisons-le. Le Canada, qui se développait à une vitesse accélérée grâce à l'ouverture de l'ouest à l'immigration en provenance des îles britanniques (et de l'Europe de l'est), vit émerger une sorte de fièvre impérialiste qui culmina en 1884 avec la fondation de la *Imperial Federation League* à Londres, laquelle eut rapidement trente bureaux au Canada.[23] Cette poussée de loyalisme, qui attira toutes les personnes ayant des liens sentimentaux avec la Grande-Bretagne[24], atteindra son apogée avec le jubilé d'or de la Reine Victoria en 1887. Ce fut l'occasion d'affirmer haut et fort la toute puissance de l'Empire, alors à son zénith, et de se convaincre d'une certaine supériorité des citoyens qui se réclamaient de l'ascendance britannique.

Cette fierté, fortement ressentie, trainait aussi dans son sillage les convictions souvent délétères des loges orangistes qui se réclamaient d'une loyauté indéfectible à la Couronne et au protestantisme, et dont l'ardeur fut portée à son comble suite au procès et à la pendaison de Louis Riel (chef Métis) en 1885, accusé de trahison envers la Couronne. Au cri de « *no more French domination* », les loges s'employèrent à combattre tout ce qui pouvait reconnaître aux Canadiens français l'exercice de leurs droits scolaires traditionnels, l'usage de leur langue et la pratique de leur religion. La croisade des loges orangistes mobilisa la ferveur nationaliste des Canadiens français à lutter contre ce sectarisme qui sapait les principes harmonieux sur lesquels on avait voulu édifier la nouvelle confédération.

Honoré Mercier, premier ministre du Québec (1887-1891), chef du mouvement nationaliste, prit ses distances à l'égard de l'Angleterre. Il déclara en avril 1893 dans un grand discours au parc Sohmer, à Montréal :

> Nous ne devons rien à l'Angleterre; et nous pourrons nous séparer d'elle, quand la majorité, régulièrement consultée, le voudra, sans remords de conscience, sans déchirement de cœur, et même sans verser de larmes…[25]

L'image de l'impartialité de la Couronne à l'égard de tous ses sujets s'en trouva ternie. Chez certains on y voyait une indifférence à l'égard de l'affaiblissement du fait français au Canada.

La réputation de la monarchie en souffrait puisque les loges se réclamaient de William d'Orange, roi d'Angleterre. La Couronne fut toutefois assez sage pour se tenir éloignée de ce fanatisme. Par exemple, en 1860, lorsque le Prince de Galles vint inaugurer à Montréal le *Pont Victoria*[26], une prouesse du génie technique et le pont le plus long de l'Empire britannique, il refusa de rencontrer les représentants des loges de Kingston et le maire de la ville à leur tête, pour éviter « une querelle religieuse et des désordres ».[27] Il ne s'arrêta pas non plus à Belleville.[28]

Au tournant du siècle, le Canada vivra une vague jusque là inconnue de patriotisme et de fierté nationale, stimulée par un concours d'événements qui contribuaient à stimuler une confiance nouvelle en un avenir prometteur. Les Fêtes du Jubilé de diamant à Londres en 1897 avaient vu le Canada reconnu comme le premier Dominion de l'Empire; son premier ministre, Wilfrid Laurier, l'orgueil des Canadiens français, avait été fait Sir à cette occasion, et il avait brillé parmi ses pairs par son intelligence et sa personnalité. Il avait déclaré, à l'Exposition Universelle de Paris qui marquait l'arrivée du nouveau siècle, que le Canada formait maintenant une nation : « Nous sommes de fait une nation, et virtuellement indépendante ».[29] Le XXe siècle serait le siècle du Canada, déclara fièrement Laurier.

Wilfrid Laurier sut le mieux traduire les convictions profondes des Canadiens français à l'égard de la monarchie. C'est à Paris, au cours de sa première visite en 1897, qu'il s'ouvrit sur ses convictions personnelles, lesquelles traduisaient bien le sentiment général ressenti par ses compatriotes. Au cours du banquet donné en son honneur, Laurier rappelle d'abord avec lyrisme à ses hôtes parisiens les liens ancestraux des Canadiens avec la monarchie d'Ancien Régime :

> De nos anciennes luttes, il nous reste à nous, descendants de la France, une relique que nous conservons avec un amour passionné : <u>c'est un drapeau de la France</u>, non pas de la France d'aujourd'hui, mais <u>de l'ancienne monarchie</u>.[30] (Nos soulignés)

Selon Laurier, le lien séculaire avec la couronne française est indissociable de l'identité originelle des Canadiens français. Laurier poursuit en rendant sans hésitation hommage aux institutions britanniques :

> Si, en devenant sujets de la couronne britannique, nous avons su conserver nos anciens droits et même en acquérir de nouveaux, d'un autre côté, nous avons contracté des obligations que, descendants d'une race chevaleresque, nous savons pleinement reconnaître et que nous tenons à honneur à proclamer.
>
> Pour moi, je n'hésite pas à déclarer, parlant ici au nom de mes compatriotes, comme je crois en avoir le droit, que par raison politique et par reconnaissance, je suis profondément attaché aux institutions britanniques.[31]

Il explique ensuite à son auditoire français ce que représente pour lui la Couronne :

> Qu'il me soit permis maintenant de faire une allusion qui m'est toute personnelle. Je me suis laissé dire qu'ici, en France, il est des gens qui s'étonnent de cet attachement que j'éprouve et que je ne cache pas pour la couronne d'Angleterre ; on appelle cela ici du loyalisme. Pour ma part, soit dit en passant, je n'aime pas cette nouvelle expression de *loyalisme*; j'aime mieux m'en tenir à la vieille locution française de *loyauté*.[32]

Il termine alors son intervention par cette déclaration qui eut son effet : « Nous sommes fidèles à la grande nation qui nous a donné la vie[33], nous sommes fidèles à la grande nation qui nous a donné la liberté ».[34]

À cette époque, le patriotisme des Canadiens était soutenu par leur loyauté historique envers les deux mères patries, la France et l'Angleterre, « mais ces deux allégeances nous divisaient et, comme nous prenions ces pays pour modèles, nous négligions d'apprécier nos propres richesses… »[35] et par voie de conséquence de développer une identité mieux enracinée dans le caractère particulier du pays. Les deux guerres mondiales auront pour effet de mettre en évidence cette lacune.[36]

Dès que la Première guerre mondiale fut déclarée, Henri Bourassa, le fougueux député, prit la tête d'un grand nombre de Canadiens français opposés à la guerre, même s'il s'agissait de voler au secours de la France, « la grande nation qui nous a donné la vie ». Bourassa était opposé à la position de principe que toute guerre de l'Empire doive aussi être une guerre canadienne. Il soutenait que le seul devoir des Canadiens français était de prendre les armes quand leur propre pays était attaqué. Dans plusieurs discours qu'il donna[37], Bourassa fut amené à préciser comment lui, chef nationaliste, définissait sa loyauté à l'égard de la Couronne au nom de laquelle les Canadiens français seraient bientôt appelés à servir, « For King and Country ». Il déclare à la Chambre des communes avoir du respect pour l'Angleterre et la Couronne, inspiratrice des libertés :

> Et tant que l'Angleterre sera fidèle à la parole donnée après quatre-vingt ans de luttes pénibles, je veux, et le peuple de ce pays veut, lui rester fidèle.[38]

Bien que viscéralement opposé à l'impérialisme de Joseph Chamberlain, au beau milieu de la guerre il fait droit à l'autorité du souverain :

> En tout ce qui concerne les relations entre l'Angleterre et le Canada […] il ne s'agit nullement, il ne peut s'agir, de conflit entre l'autorité du souverain et les résistances de ses sujets Canadiens…[39]

Bourassa rêvait pour le Canada de « l'indépendance absolue, sous l'autorité nominale du roi d'Angleterre qui serait, en même temps, roi du Canada ».[40] La campagne menée par Bourassa n'empêcha pas les Canadiens français de participer à l'effort de guerre. Environ 14 100[41] soldats canadiens français prirent part à la Première guerre mondiale.[42]

Les convictions monarchistes des Canadiens français allaient trouver une occasion privilégiée de s'exprimer lors des fêtes grandioses du Tricentenaire de Québec en 1908, présidées par le Prince de Galles. La ville de Québec était pavoisée de tricolores et d'Union Jacks reflétant bien la nouvelle *Entente cordiale* (1904) entre l'Angleterre et la France : on célébrait l'harmonie symbolique représentée par les troupes de Montcalm et celles de Wolfe défilant côte à côte sur les Plaines lors d'un « pageant » mémorable. Le futur George V reçut un accueil des plus chaleureux de toute la population emportée par l'esprit de la fête. Adélard Turgeon, ministre des Terres et Forêts, représentant le gouvernement du Québec, souleva alors la question de la conciliation des racines ancestrales des Canadiens français avec la loyauté exprimée à la couronne britannique :

> Mais comment cette affection (pour la France) peut-elle se concilier avec notre loyauté et notre profond attachement pour les Iles britanniques ? [...] Il l'a été par le sens politique de nos hommes d'État, par la largeur de vues de nos compatriotes de langue anglaise, par la clairvoyance et la libéralité de la Métropole et de ses représentants. On a compris que la conservation de l'élément et de la langue française n'était pas une cause de danger, mais un gage de grandeur, de progrès et même de sécurité.[43]

Turgeon exprimait sa confiance dans la raison au delà des préjugés de « race » qui avaient toujours cours dans certains milieux.

Mais la ferveur monarchiste des Canadiens français culminera lorsque le jeune roi George VI débarquera à Québec avec la reine Élisabeth le 17 mai 1939.[44] Une foule exceptionnelle se massa le long du parcours emprunté par le cortège (10,000 personnes)[45] et sur les Plaines d'Abraham, où plus de 100,000 personnes voulurent voir, pour la première fois au pays, un roi et sa jeune épouse au sourire charmeur. L'allégresse populaire était à son comble. Il suffit de recenser les titres à la une des journaux pour s'en convaincre. Les sentiments de loyauté exprimés spontanément aux cris de « Vive le Roi, Vive la Reine » trouvèrent écho dans les Adresses officielles présentées au couple royal, d'abord par le premier ministre Maurice L. Duplessis à l'Assemblée législative, puis par le sénateur Raoul Dandurand au cours du déjeuner offert au Château Frontenac. Il vaut de rapporter l'essentiel des propos tenus par Duplessis, puisqu'ils proviennent d'un politicien qui fera sa réputation avec ses luttes autonomistes contre Ottawa et son refus d'appuyer l'effort de guerre du Canada.

Se tenant devant leurs Majestés assises sur deux trônes placés dans la salle du Conseil législatif, Duplessis déclare alors :

> Notre province a toujours été fidèle à la couronne britannique, elle s'est montrée aussi fidèle aux traditions héritées des ancêtres, au pacte fédératif de 1867 comme à la mission que les hommes d'État anglais de 1791 lui avaient donné : *To remain altogether French.* Ce passé nous tient toujours au cœur et nous ne cesserons de considérer le Trône comme le rempart de nos institutions démocratiques et de nos libertés constitutionnelles.[46]

Duplessis faisait profession de foi en la Couronne comme rempart des institutions démocratiques et des libertés constitutionnelles. Il exprimait en fait l'opinion tenue par les théoriciens de la monarchie constitutionnelle, à savoir que le Souverain est garant, en ultime ressort, de l'ordre constitutionnel :

> The Queen or her representative is the guardian of our democratic Constitution against subversion by a Prime Minister or Cabinet who might be tempted to violate that Constitution and deprive us of our right to self-

government; but it makes sure that we, the people, are not prevented from governing ourselves.[47]

Duplessis avait rappelé qu'il parlait en particulier au nom des Canadiens français.[48]

Au Château Frontenac, Raoul Dandurand, qui était connu pour ses convictions républicaines, ne manqua pourtant pas de rappeler les origines de la devise royale, « Dieu et mon Droit », et de faire acte d'allégeance :

> Sous l'égide de cette devise, ils ont pu clamer, en changeant d'allégeance à l'instar des chevaliers du moyen âge : *le Roi est mort, Vive le Roi!* Aussi, aujourd'hui, répètent-ils à l'adresse de Votre Majesté sans aucune réticence et de plein cœur : *Vive le Roi!*

L'enthousiasme des foules et des édiles pour les jeunes souverains se renouvelèrent le lendemain, lors de leur visite à Montréal. Ils y furent accueilles par le maire Camillien Houde, politicien populiste qui sera lui aussi opposé à la conscription.[49] Les journaux rapportent un emballement populaire comparable.[50] Le maire Houde, reconnu pour son franc parler et pour exprimer les sentiments du petit peuple, présenta à l'Hôtel de ville une Adresse qui ne manquait pas de convictions sincères :

> Ces acclamations enthousiastes dont, particulièrement dans nos murs, une foule innombrable a salué votre passage ont assez dit, croyons-nous, comment une population au cœur franc et loyal peut être fière de ses rois d'aujourd'hui sans avoir pour cela besoin de renier ceux d'autrefois.[51]

Le maire Houde trouva la formule la plus heureuse pour décrire en quelques mots la réalité vécue par les Canadiens français :

> Ici également, vous trouverez une famille qui est la vôtre, famille d'origines, de races et de pensées diverses, qui, en une libre association avec les autres membres du Commonwealth, mais également à sa manière, façonne son destin national.[52]

Selon le maire Houde, le nationalisme des Canadiens français pouvait donc s'exprimer et se développer en toute liberté sous la Couronne.

À son tour la jeune princesse Elizabeth, fille aînée du roi, et son époux, le prince Philip, vinrent à Québec le 9 octobre 1951 et c'est toujours le premier ministre Duplessis qui les accueillit. Il ne manqua pas de rappeler qu'il avait reçu leurs parents en 1939 et renouvela l'expression de sa loyauté à la Couronne, au nom du Québec tout entier :

> Notre province, peuplée en très grande majorité de Canadiens d'origine française, a toujours été fidèle à la Couronne britannique, symbole d'autorité

> et de liberté. Québec est synonyme de loyauté [...] God save Our Gracious King. God save Our Royal Highness.[53]

Cependant, cet engouement populaire pour la monarchie qui s'était exprimé à plusieurs reprises dans le passé commencera à être dénoncé par des ténors nationalistes au milieu des années 1950. Lionel Groulx, l'abbé historien, fut un des premiers à opposer d'une certaine manière le nationalisme de survivance des Canadiens français à la Couronne britannique. Il écrit en 1953 dans un ouvrage intitulé *Pour bâtir* :

> Les hommes de mon âge ne l'ont pas oublié [Lionel Groulx en 1948]: dans nos célébrations patriotiques d'il y a quarante à cinquante ans, quelle est la vertu civique la plus volontiers exaltée par nos orateurs politiques et académiques? L'amour du pays, le culte de la langue et de la culture originelle? Non pas, la loyauté canadienne-française à la couronne britannique.[54] (Notre souligné)

Groulx semblait insinuer que l'un était exclusif de l'autre : on ne pouvait aimer son pays, sa langue et les institutions traditionnelles du Canada français, et faire profession en même temps de loyauté à la Couronne. La Couronne devenait antagoniste, voire antinomique avec le « véritable » nationalisme.

Groulx avait d'ailleurs déjà dénoncé en 1944, dans *Notre maître le passé*[55], l'interprétation antérieure des chefs de l'église (Mgr Hubert, puis Mgr Plessis, et leurs successeurs), à savoir que la conquête du Canada en 1760 avait été « providentielle », en ce qu'elle, selon eux, avait sauvé les Canadiens des affres de la Révolution qui avait renversé le Trône et les autels. Groulx soutenait au contraire que les Britanniques avaient, bien malgré eux, concédé aux Canadiens le droit de pratiquer leur religion. Rien ne leur avait jamais été accordé sans que les Canadiens ne luttent constamment ni ne résistent opiniâtrement. L'intention des Britanniques avait toujours été de les assimiler et de les « protestantiser », le Rapport Durham et l'Acte d'Union à l'appui.

Selon cette interprétation, la cession du Canada par la France, devenue conquête britannique, serait dorénavant vue comme une tragédie collective pour les Canadiens français, qui « ont été en quelque sorte déracinés sur le plan idéologique, les fondements mêmes de leur identité – langue, religion – institutions – ayant été mis en péril ».[56] Cette métaphore de l'arbre déraciné[57] alimentera une conception binaire du pays, à la source des deux irréconciliables solitudes :

> De cette vision essentialiste où les Britanniques sont considérés comme d'éternels conquérants rapaces et les Français comme des victimes plaintives (les autochtones sont exclus) pour mieux maintenir la tension et l'aura tragique de l'opposition binaire condamnant le Canada à ses deux solitudes.[58]

Une nouvelle interprétation historique, toujours teintée de relents théologiques, s'imposait dorénavant chez les bien-pensants du destin national.

Cette conviction manichéenne qui séparait le monde entre les bons Français catholiques et les méchants Anglais protestants, bien dans la tradition d'une certaine orthodoxie judéo-chrétienne qui nourrissait une conception victimaire de l'Histoire, se répandit chez les disciples de Groulx et refit publiquement surface quelques dix années plus tard lorsqu'une nouvelle version de ce nationalisme prendra le virage obligé de la séparation du Québec.

La jeune Reine Elizabeth revint au Québec (à Hull) en 1957, portant pour la première fois le titre de Reine du Canada. En 1959, lors du voyage qui conduisit la souveraine dans toutes les provinces du Canada (où elle inaugura la voie maritime du St-Laurent avec le président américain Dwight D. Eisenhower), la Reine revint également à Québec. La visite de la reine à Montréal provoqua les mêmes accents de loyauté lyrique : le maire Sarto Fournier dansa avec la Reine, au cours d'une soirée mémorable à l'hôtel de ville, dont les annales ont bien relaté les détails savoureux.[59] Personne ne soupçonna que la période de transformation rapide que le Québec allait connaître, perçue comme une Révolution tranquille (aujourd'hui quasi élevée au rang de mythe)[60] allait finir par rejoindre la Couronne et la Souveraine elle-même.

Depuis l'avènement à Québec du gouvernement de Jean Lesage en 1960, la question constitutionnelle avait refait surface. À Ottawa, le gouvernement de Lester B. Pearson s'apprêtait en 1963 à former la Commission Royale d'enquête sur le bilinguisme et biculturalisme dont on espérait que les travaux et les conclusions permettraient de lancer des pourparlers afin de répondre aux revendications du premier ministre Lesage d'un nouveau partage des ressources fiscales et de l'octroi de pouvoirs accrus.

La Reine fut invitée par le premier ministre Pearson à venir à Québec en octobre 1964 marquer le centenaire de la Conférence de Québec, et de Charlottetown, où les Pères de la Confédération avaient convenu d'une entente qui allait donner naissance en 1867 au Canada.

Bien malgré elles, la jeune Souveraine et la monarchie furent entrainées dans un tourbillon de critiques : les mois précédents la visite furent marqués par des appels à la violence de la part du chef du Rassemblement pour l'Indépendance nationale et d'un groupe connu sous le nom de « Armée de Libération du Québec » (ALQ). On intima publiquement à la Souveraine de ne pas mettre les pieds aux Québec, et on évoqua ce qui était survenu à Dallas, l'année précédente, le 22 novembre 1963.[61] C'était la première fois dans l'histoire du pays que des Canadiens français s'en prenaient directement à la Couronne et à la personne même du Souverain. Le gouvernement canadien refusa d'annuler la visite afin d'éviter de créer l'impression de céder au chantage, et le premier ministre Lesage assura que la population réserverait à la Reine une « réception chaude et enthousiaste ».[62]

Pendant toute la journée de la visite de la Reine, le samedi 10 octobre 1964, quelques centaines de manifestants se rassemblèrent autour de l'édifice de l'Assemblée législative, le long du parcours emprunté par le cortège, et là où devait se rendre la Souveraine. Brian Mulroney (âgé de 25 ans), alors chef étudiant à l'Université Laval, était lui-même, à l'occasion de ces manifestations, porte-parole des étudiants opposés à la visite de la Reine.[63]

Les forces de l'ordre, en beaucoup plus grand nombre que les manifestants, chargèrent la foule indistinctement, n'hésitant pas à faire usage de la force et de matraques. Ce jour passa à l'histoire comme « le samedi de la matraque ». À l'intérieur, au Conseil législatif, la Reine, prenant acte des discussions constitutionnelles, rappela en français que toute constitution est perfectible et que c'est à cette tâche que sont conviés les chefs politiques d'aujourd'hui, comme l'avaient été leurs ancêtres lors de la formation du pays :

> Qu'un protocole tracé il y a cent ans ne réponde pas nécessairement à tous les problèmes du jour, cela n'a rien d'étonnant … nous sommes fiers du rôle irremplaçable et de la destinée particulière du Canada français. Pendant quatre cents ans il a conservé sa vigueur, et sa force et, lorsque vous chantez « O Canada », vous vous souvenez que vous êtes nés d'une race fière. C'est à cette fierté, à cette noblesse de cœur, que je m'adresse en rappelant que c'est d'un grand avenir qu'on rêvé les Pères de la Confédération. Leur œuvre vaut d'être poursuivi. Ainsi les cœurs qui ont nourri une telle entreprise n'auront pas battu en vain. En servant les vrais intérêts du Québec, vous servirez ceux du Canada, comme les vrais intérêts du Canada doivent servir ceux du monde entier.[64]

Le premier ministre Jean Lesage se porta, lui, en quelque sorte, à la défense du droit à la dissidence des manifestants :

> Je crois que la pierre de touche consiste dans les garanties qu'un système accorde à ses propres adversaires. Le véritable démocrate luttera pour la liberté de parole de ses contradicteurs et pour que tous les problèmes soient aérés sur la place publique.[65]

Cette journée marqua un tournant dans l'opinion publique; l'événement sera par la suite élevé au rang symbolique d'une présence coloniale étrangère contraire aux intérêts des Canadiens français, en plus d'être cause de troubles et de désordre. Une impression durable avait ainsi été créée. Chaque présence de la Souveraine ou d'un membre de la famille royale fournirait dorénavant l'occasion de manifestations d'opposition publique à la monarchie. La monarchie devenait, pour les indépendantistes de tous crins, un symbole de l'opposition à tout ce que représentait le Canada, et qui devait être honni au Québec.

En 1967, la Reine revint inaugurer l'Exposition Universelle de Montréal et célébrer le Centenaire de la Confédération. Elle reconnut fort à propos la dualité originaire du pays :

> L'expérience qui se poursuit depuis cent ans dans ce pays, avec des défaillances certes, mais aussi avec un espoir grandissant, ne peut laisser indifférente notre époque déchirée [...] C'est en ce sens, me semble-t-il, que le Canada sera grand; non par le pouvoir, mais par le don, le rayonnement et l'exemple.[66]

Ce fut une occasion renouvelée chez les opposants pour crier à « Cent ans d'injustice ». Ce slogan était tamponné à l'encre à l'avers des billets de un dollar, où apparaissait la Reine telle que le photographe Yousuf Karsh l'avait si élégamment représentée.

La Reine sera à nouveau à Montréal à l'été 1976 pour inaugurer les XXIe Jeux Olympiques d'été. L'ambiance était tendue : les travaux entourant la construction des installations avaient soulevé une mer de critiques et le gouvernement de Robert Bourassa à Québec apparaissait à bout de ressources au terme de son mandat. Impopulaire, Bourassa était préoccupé par la réaction publique négative vis-à-vis la présence de la Reine et il craignait avoir à porter le poids politique des critiques. Il demanda même au premier ministre Pierre Elliott Trudeau de décommander la visite : Trudeau refusa.[67] Le chef du Parti Québécois, l'opposition officielle à Québec, s'en mêla, écrivant lui-même à Buckingham Palace pour aviser la Reine de refuser l'invitation du premier ministre fédéral. Bourassa crut s'en sortir en alléguant que le site olympique avait été déclaré territoire international et donc que la Reine n'était pas « en sol québécois! » Finalement, la Reine séjourna au Québec près d'une semaine, assistant à diverses compétitions. Sa présence ne suscita pas l'opposition qu'on avait crainte et on ne rapporta aucun incident fâcheux.[68] Cette visite fut l'occasion pour la Souveraine de préciser sa pensée sur le fait français et l'importance pour le Québec d'en assurer le rayonnement :

> Montréal est au cœur d'une province canadienne qui se veut, et se doit, d'être le centre de rayonnement de la langue et de la culture françaises en Amérique. Au pied du Mont-Royal se côtoient deux peuples d'une égale valeur et d'une égale fierté. [...] La vie quotidienne de ses citoyens témoigne de l'engagement qu'ils ont pris : maintenir ici l'enracinement français et harmoniser des cultures, différentes, sans pour autant compromettre les droits ou les aspirations des deux éléments fondateurs. [...] Pour atteindre cet idéal, il faut une grande générosité, un esprit ouvert et la détermination de vouloir comprendre et apprécier les autres. Ce sont ces qualités [...] dont on fait largement preuve les Canadiens à travers leur histoire. Voilà la grandeur du Canada.[69]

Ce discours marqua les esprits : « Le Québécois qui entendait ces propos ne pouvait se retenir d'admirer la générosité intellectuelle dont témoignaient ces paroles de la souveraine ».[70]

Trois mois plus tard, la controverse entourant la monarchie canadienne réapparaissait en une. Le premier gouvernement indépendantiste conduit par René Lévesque venait d'être élu et ses députés, pour poser un geste d'éclat et établir leur opposition publique à la monarchie, décidèrent d'abord de refuser de prêter le serment d'allégeance prévu à la constitution canadienne.[71] Ils en firent grand cas dans les médias avant de se rendre à l'évidence qu'ils devaient chacun, avant de prendre leur siège, prêter le serment requis, alléguant pour se dédouaner qu'ils prêtaient en fait serment à l' « État du Québec » et qu'ils avaient décidé « de se croiser les doigts ».[72] Le gouvernement Lévesque marqua aussi son opposition de principe à la Couronne en excluant le lieutenant-gouverneur de la cérémonie publique de présentation du nouveau cabinet et en lui retirant la responsabilité traditionnelle de la lecture du Discours du trône, celui-ci en étant réduit à simplement inviter le premier ministre à y procéder – ce que ses successeurs, Jacques Parizeau et Pauline Marois, feront également[73]. On voulait ainsi oblitérer la source du pouvoir législatif toujours détenu par la Couronne du chef de la Province, représentée par le lieutenant-gouverneur.[74] Ce que ce geste ignore, c'est que la souveraineté constitutionnelle des provinces dans leur domaine de juridiction, à l'égal de celle exercée par le fédéral dans ses compétences, derrière laquelle se retranche les gouvernements indépendantistes, a en fait été confirmée par les plus hauts tribunaux du pays (et celui de Londres) par la reconnaissance formelle de l'indépendance du statut de la Couronne provinciale.[75] Encore aujourd'hui, le gouvernement du Québec feint de l'ignorer.[76]

Chaque fois que l'occasion se présentait, on rappelait l'équivalence entre la Couronne et un régime colonial dépassé, insistant qu'il s'agissait d'un système suranné, synonyme d'oppression du caractère des Canadiens français, devenus dorénavant des « Québécois », n'ayant plus aucune appartenance territoriale en commun avec le Canada et les francophones ailleurs au pays, pourtant, en grande majorité, issus de familles d'abord implantées au Québec pendant des générations.

La signature par la Reine de la Proclamation de la loi constitutionnelle de 1982 fournit une nouvelle occasion pour associer cette fois la Souveraine au « coup de force » allégué du gouvernement fédéral contre le Québec, bien que la Reine dans son allocution ait regretté publiquement que le Québec ne fasse pas partie de l'entente formelle :

> Malgré l'absence regrettée du premier ministre du Québec, il n'est que juste d'associer les Québécois et les Québécoises à cette célébration du renouveau. Sans eux le Canada ne serait pas ce qu'il est aujourd'hui. Le Québec fut à la fois l'inspiration et l'agent principal de la transformation profonde qui naquit de cette décision.[77]

Pendant les seize années où Pierre Elliott Trudeau a été premier ministre, le Canada, et la perception qu'en auront les Canadiens, se seront profondément transformés. Cette évolution avait déjà commencé à apparaître de manière visible sous Pearson avec des initiatives qui visaient à renouveler l'identité et les symboles canadiens : l'adoption en 1965 d'un drapeau national, l'Unifolié, puis d'un hymne national, le « O Canada » en 1980, la disparition progressive du terme « Dominion » au profit d'un simple et tout net « Canada », l'élimination du terme « Royal » dans certains services, les Postes, l'aviation, la marine, tout comme l'expression d'une politique étrangère plus indépendante (ainsi que plusieurs autres changements) eurent un impact certain à long terme sur la perception publique de la monarchie et de ses symboles. En 1969, Trudeau autorisa le Gouverneur général Roland Michener à entreprendre pour la première fois, au nom du Canada, un voyage d'État[78] à l'extérieur de l'Amérique du Nord : le Gouverneur général visita de la mi-février à début mars la Jamaïque, la Guyane et les Barbades, pour finir son périple à Trinidad et Tobago. On n'oubliera pas non plus la pirouette du premier ministre Trudeau derrière sa Majesté à Buckingham Palace le 7 mai 1977, qui comportait un certain élément d'irrévérence susceptible d'influencer l'attitude de déférence dont on avait toujours fait preuve à l'égard de la Souveraine.

Pourtant la Reine, qui visita le Canada neuf fois pendant les trois mandats de Trudeau[79], fit preuve d'une grande ouverture lorsqu'elle fut informée de l'intention du gouvernement canadien de procéder au rapatriement de la Constitution canadienne en 1980. Trudeau rapporte dans ses Mémoires qu'il pouvait compter à Londres sur l'intervention de trois femmes d'influence : Margaret Thatcher, premier ministre, Jean Wadds (Haut commissaire du Canada à Londres), et la Reine elle-même, qui était informée régulièrement de la nature des débats qui entouraient l'initiative constitutionnelle. Et pour cause : le projet originaire de résolution contenait la possibilité de tenir un référendum national en cas d'impasse de futures modifications, et l'avenir de la monarchie dans l'ordre constitutionnel canadien pouvait aussi, en principe, faire l'objet de l'une de ses consultations.

Trudeau, pragmatique, savait bien que « although the majority of Canadians are no longer of British descent, there was still, in the 1970s and 1980s, a substantial anglophile and monarchical element in the country ».[80] Trudeau n'entretint jamais le projet d'abolir la monarchie. Lui-même en préserva le caractère; il en respecta la lettre sinon l'esprit.[81] Il n'était certainement pas prêt à risquer du capital politique pour se lancer dans un changement de régime qui aurait amené le Canada à couper ses liens avec la monarchie constitutionnelle[82], bien qu'il fît apporter en 1975 et 1977 des modifications aux *Lettres Patentes* de 1947 définissant le mandat et le rôle du gouverneur-général et qu'il présentât le projet de loi C-60 en 1978, qui restreignaient le rôle de la Reine au bénéfice du Gouverneur général[83], projet de loi qui cependant mourut au feuilleton. Trudeau s'en ouvrira en 1985 après avoir quitté son poste :

> Je disais de la Constitution à peu près ce que je répondais à ceux qui me demandaient de m'attaquer à la monarchie : le système marche à peu près bien, ouvrir le débat à l'heure actuelle diviserait les Canadiens entre eux et créerait d'énormes acrimonies sans résoudre le problème.[84]

Cette opinion à l'effet que le « système » fonctionne efficacement est encore reprise aujourd'hui.[85] Trudeau voyait ainsi la monarchie comme une affaire de raison. Il savait qu'à une époque antérieure elle faisait partie d'un nationalisme exclusif réservé d'abord aux Canadiens d'ascendance britannique qui se l'étaient accaparée comme symbole distinctif. Trudeau percevait les risques associés à une telle exclusion des autres citoyens et en particulier des Canadiens français. Il le reconnut ouvertement en 1998 :

> D'autre part, comme c'était auparavant le cas au Canada, si vous parliez de *nationalisme* canadien dans le sens de la monarchie, de l'Union Jack et de la langue anglaise, vous parliez, réellement du *nationalisme* ethnique. En vérité, le Canada a naguère exercé un nationalisme discriminatoire à l'égard des Canadiens français. Et lorsqu'un nationalisme ethnique est exercé par un groupe ethnique au sein d'un État, il est normal que les groupes minoritaires exercent un *nationalisme* défensif, d'où la naissance du nationalisme canadien français.[86]

Un tel type de nationalisme a tendance à entretenir le « mythe de la conquête » chez les Canadiens français, et le mythe du loyalisme chez les Canadiens d'origine britannique. En d'autres mots, il nourrit le ressentiment des Canadiens français à l'égard du loyalisme dont faisaient preuve leurs compatriotes anglophones à l'égard de la Couronne.[87]

Or il faut bien le reconnaitre : en enchâssant « la charge de la Reine », celle de gouverneur général et de lieutenant-gouverneur dans la Constitution de 1982 (art. 41(a)), sous la formule de l'unanimité, la formule d'amendement la plus exigeante, et ce avec l'accord, à l'origine, des dix provinces y inclus le Québec (alors représenté par son premier ministre René Lévesque), Trudeau savait très bien qu'il assoyait à demeure la monarchie constitutionnelle au Canada, et qu'en fait ce système avait bien servi par le passé les Canadiens et permis l'évolution du pays. Comme il l'avait déjà déclaré en boutade, « Je ne perdrais pas une nuit de sommeil là-dessus ». En cela, il rejoignait l'opinion d'une large majorité de ses compatriotes qui, sans se déclarer monarchiste, reconnaissait que le système canadien fonctionne démocratiquement et qu'il a permis le développement d'une société parmi les plus libres au monde. Le premier ministre du Nouveau-Brunswick, Richard Hatfield, résumait bien cette conviction lorsqu'il déclara au cours d'un banquet offert à la Reine le 15 juillet 1976 :

> Notre attachement à la couronne, Votre Majesté, est une affaire de conviction comme organisation politique souhaitable. C'est une affaire d'engagement à un système qui a été mis à l'épreuve par l'expérience et a duré.[88]

En 1987, après onze ans, la Reine revient à nouveau à Québec. Robert Bourassa, défait à l'automne 1976, avait été réélu le 12 décembre 1985. Suite à d'intenses négociations, il en était arrivé à signer une entente constitutionnelle avec le gouvernement fédéral de Brian Mulroney et les neuf autres provinces pour « ramener le Québec dans le giron constitutionnel canadien ». Bourassa ne craint plus alors d'être photographié en présence de sa Majesté. Le référendum de 1980 est chose du passé; Trudeau a quitté la scène politique au printemps de 1984 et la nouvelle entente [L'Accord du Lac Meech] a été signée « dans l'honneur et l'enthousiasme »[89] le 3 juin avec le premier ministre Mulroney et les neuf autres provinces. Accueillant la souveraine à l'aéroport de Québec, Bourassa commente :

> Je représente la grande majorité des québécois en souhaitant bienvenue à la reine […] le climat est différent [d'alors], c'est évident. Dans la mesure où les québécois acceptent la constitution, la reine est la reine du Canada. C'est normal qu'elle visite l'ensemble du territoire, dont le Québec.[90]

Aucune manifestation publique d'importance ne vint troubler la visite. Au dîner officiel donné en son honneur à l'Assemblée nationale, où assistaient 100 convives triés sur le volet, la Reine déclara :

> Il y a cinq ans, à Ottawa, je disais que la signature de la loi constitutionnelle était une célébration de la diversité du Canada. Je signalais que le Québec était l'inspiration grâce à laquelle s'étaient transformés les rapports entre les multiples collectivités qui ont créé cette culture très riche dont s'enorgueillit le Canada.

Bourassa, avant de proposer « de lever votre verre en l'honneur de Sa Majesté la Reine », conclut : « C'est donc un peuple qui sait se souvenir et qui demeure plus que jamais confiant en son avenir qui vous accueille avec tout le respect dû à vos éminentes fonctions ».[91] On aurait pu conclure qu'une majorité de Québécois s'était réconciliée avec la Couronne et que la Reine était bien révérée comme Reine du Canada, dont le Québec se déclarait fier de faire partie.

La Reine n'est pas venue au Québec depuis 1987, ce qui cependant n'a aucunement contribué à atténuer les débats sur la monarchie toujours présents dans l'opinion publique. Les critiques se manifestèrent en 1996 lorsque Jean-Louis Roux, comédien apprécié, fut nommé lieutenant-gouverneur à Québec. Sous la contrainte de la pression publique, Roux fut amené à démissionner de sa fonction.[92] Le premier ministre du Québec, Lucien Bouchard, saisit l'occasion pour déposer en novembre 1996 à l'Assemblée nationale une motion réclamant l'abolition de la fonction de lieutenant-gouverneur, arguant que le poste était « purement symbolique et une relique du passé colonial », que le processus de nomination prêtait à controverse, nuisait au fonctionnement de l'institution, et qu'à tout le moins ce devait être à l'Assemblée elle-même de choisir démocratiquement le titulaire.[93] Le débat sur la motion du premier ministre ouvrit la porte à tous les arguments et préjugés possibles, et révéla surtout une méconnaissance profonde de l'institution et de son histoire.

Les critiques de cette fonction reprirent lorsque les médias se mirent à publier les allégations impliquant des dépenses personnelles de Lise Thibault, lieutenant-gouverneur du Québec de 1997 à 2007, suite aux accusations criminelles déposées en 2009.[94] Le prestige et la crédibilité rattachés à la fonction en souffrirent inévitablement. En novembre 2012, le nouveau gouvernement de la première ministre Pauline Marois déposa « une motion pour que la fonction de lieutenant-gouverneur au Québec soit abolie ».[95] En janvier 2013, le même gouvernement décida d'abandonner l'initiative de faire choisir par un vote de l'Assemblée nationale le candidat au poste de lieutenant-gouverneur, y voyant une confirmation de la légitimité de la monarchie constitutionnelle.[96] Le Québec, toujours si prompt à défendre ses compétences constitutionnelles, est demeuré coi lors du débat visant à exprimer l'assentiment du Parlement canadien aux modifications apportées par Westminster à la loi concernant la succession au trône, en dépit de l'opinion contraire exprimée par certains constitutionnalistes du crû.[97]

Le premier ministre Jean Chrétien a souvent reconnu lui-même publiquement le respect qu'il entretient à l'égard de la monarchie, au-delà de ses liens personnels avec la Souveraine[98], liens que la Reine a elle-même certainement appréciés pour lui accorder son Ordre du Mérite en 2011. Il est de notoriété que certains des proches conseillers[99] de Chrétien poussaient l'idée de l'abolition de la monarchie comme « projet du millénaire ». L'instinct politique de Chrétien lui suggérait plutôt de ne pas mettre la main dans ce guêpier. Selon ses propres termes : « je n'ai pas voulu imposer cette idée (abolir la monarchie) parce qu'on aurait hurlé au meurtre ».[100]

Mais l'un des faits nouveaux qui a été remarqué dans l'opinion au Québec[101], est l'opposition à la monarchie ou sa remise en question qui se manifeste à l'occasion ailleurs au Canada.[102] L'opinion publique au pays est plus ambivalente sur l'avenir de l'institution[103], et le niveau d'ignorance sur sa véritable nature demeure abyssal.[104]

Des Québécois ne se retrouvent plus les seuls à se questionner sur le rôle et la signification de la monarchie, et son avenir au Canada. C'est maintenant un sujet de réflexion publique, au-delà des barrières linguistiques, qui transcende les atavismes traditionnels des Canadiens français et des Canadiens anglais. Des Canadiens de partout au pays se retrouvent de nos jours dans ce mouvement d'arrachement au passé et à la tradition qui caractérise la modernité.[105] Et la monarchie est incluse dans ces symboles dont on se distance, une institution qui pourtant pendant des siècles avait été vue par une majorité de Canadiens des deux langues comme un point d'appui indéfectible de leur identité.

Au Québec, toute visite de membres de la famille royale ou célébrations reliées à la Couronne suscitent toujours des commentaires partagés. Au cours de la campagne électorale provinciale en 2012, Pauline Marois, chef de l'opposition officielle, déclarait que « la Reine était un symbole que le gouvernement fédéral tentait d'imposer au Québec contre la volonté de ses citoyens ». Elle ajoutait, narquoise, « I'll trade him (Mr. Harper) the royalty for Québec sovereignty ».[106] Le durcissement du ton, destiné à fouetter l'ardeur partisane des militants, frôlait la démagogie facile. D'un futur premier ministre, on se serait attendu à une certaine hauteur de vue par respect pour les institutions qu'il/elle représente. Après tout, la Cour suprême a bien conclu en 1998 que le Québec « ne constitue pas un peuple colonisé ou opprimé ».[107]

Ces attaques faciles plaisent toujours à un certain public qui carbure au « complexe des Plaines d'Abraham »[108]et qui se voit constamment dans un rapport de colonisateur-colonisé.[109] Pour les autres, il est de bon ton de prendre un certain air distant pour éviter le risque de ne pas avoir l'air trop « rétro ». En fait, un grand nombre de Québécois ont beaucoup de difficultés à assumer leur histoire : ils entretiennent « une relation difficile avec leur passé ».[110] Plusieurs ont abandonné tous leurs repères et tentent de s'en créer de nouveaux fondés sur le ressentiment ou la crainte de disparaître. D'une certaine manière, le Québec se retrouve comme « une société d'individus sans ancrage ».[111] Les Québécois ont rompu définitivement avec l'Église catholique; moins de 7% d'entre eux se déclarent pratiquants[112], bien que, « O Contradiction », tous les partis politiques provinciaux refusent de décrocher le crucifix au dessus du fauteuil du Président à l'Assemblée nationale (placé à cet endroit en 1936 par le Premier ministre Duplessis), arguant qu'il représente « notre attachement à notre patrimoine religieux et historique »[113], le seul parlement d'un État démocratique à exhiber de manière ostentatoire un symbole religieux...

En 1977, le gouvernement du Parti Québécois avait d'ailleurs fait disparaître St-Jean Baptiste, le patron des Canadiens français, de la fête du 24 juin, pour en faire bien « laïquement » la « Fête nationale du Québec ».[114] Il est d'autant particulier de rappeler qu'au cours des années 1920, dans un élan de patriotisme centré sur la célébration de héros retrouvés (ou créés), on avait au Québec doublé la fête statutaire de la Reine (dernier lundi avant le 25 mai) avec la « Fête de Dollard », un héros maintenant perdu dans les limbes d'un passé révolu. En 2002, un décret provincial[115] modifia le nom de cette fête, non pas pour rétablir la fête de la Reine, mais plutôt pour ressusciter les Patriotes de 1837/1838 (de nouvelles « saintetés »…), en guise de pied de nez à la monarchie.

En serait-il de même de la réaction des Canadiens d'ascendance britannique ailleurs au pays si on proposait de retirer les symboles qui les rattachent à la monarchie? Ne pourraient-ils pas eux aussi soutenir que ceux-ci représentent leur lien avec un patrimoine ancestral et historique? Si le fonds de l'argument vaut pour l'un, ne vaut-il pas aussi pour l'autre? Le premier ministre Harper se faisait l'écho de cet attachement à l'héritage britannique dans un discours, en 2006, à Londres : « Britain and Canada are eternally bonded by language, culture, economics and values ».[116]

La monarchie est une institution à laquelle les Québécois se sont identifiés pendant près de 350 ans et qui a influencé leur référent psycho-politique. Aujourd'hui, plusieurs la perçoivent comme une domination étrangère alors que le Souverain « représente la nation dans sa continuité historique »[117] et qu'à plusieurs reprises depuis le début de son règne sa Majesté a reconnu l'importance du Québec comme « le centre du rayonnement de la langue et de la culture française en Amérique », la responsabilité du Québec pour « maintenir ici l'enracinement français », et l'influence déterminante du Québec sur la « transformation profonde » du Canada.

Pendant les soixante années de son règne, la Reine Elizabeth II a su refléter les préoccupations des Canadiens français dont elle a été témoin attentif de l'évolution des sentiments et des convictions. Elle a su, dans sa façon d'aborder la réalité canadienne, tenir compte de l'évolution du pays et des perceptions changeantes à l'égard de la Couronne. Par exemple, cette compréhension adaptée au contexte contemporain s'incarne dans la représentation la plus courante de son rôle comme chef de l'État sur le billet de banque canadien où la souveraine apparaît sans insignes royaux, ni autre mention de son titre ou de son identité. Malgré tout, les Québécois semblent toujours figés, avoir une certaine honte de leur passé et faire semblant de l'oublier. Pourtant, « l'avenir ne peut être dans l'amnésie » collective.[118]

Cette rupture des Québécois avec leur passé, réinterprété selon les besoins d'un nationalisme revanchard, les cantonne dans un état de réaction primaire perpétuelle. « Le nationalisme nait de l'opposition : ce qui crée les nations, affirmait Henri Hauser, c'est la lutte, c'est le conflit entre les groupes humains ».[119] On entretient donc ce réflexe défensif commode à l'égard de la monarchie, réflexe qui tient lieu de sécurité artificielle, évitant ainsi aux Québécois d'avoir à assumer la difficile réconciliation des valeurs qu'impose le vouloir vivre commun à des citoyens d'origines et de traditions différentes vivant dans un pays aussi grand qu'un continent.

Ce nationalisme des années 1960 est né d'un sentiment d'humiliation en face de l'élément anglo-saxon, qui avait prise dans l'infériorité économique des Canadiens français. Bien que les Québécois se retrouvent aujourd'hui en position de contrôle dans tous les secteurs qui auparavant leur échappaient[120], ils n'ont pas décroché du mythe qu'ils s'en sont créés. La monarchie incarne pour certains un symbole colonial qui les provoque, « un catalyseur d'autres phénomènes »[121], et ils ont besoin de se rallier contre elle pour se convaincre que leur lutte, leur résistance, sont toujours essentielles à l'affirmation de leur identité. En ce sens, c'est un nationalisme profondément réactionnaire et détourné de la confiance en soi, loin d'une vision originale du pays fondée sur des valeurs humanistes que les Québécois pourraient s'appliquer à construire sur une échelle plus vaste. Ils refusent d'y voir les avantages qu'ils en ont tirés et les opportunités qu'elle représente. En fait, ils cherchent à prendre une revanche définitive sur les Anglais, ne se pardonnant pas d'avoir entretenu une allégeance aussi longue à la Couronne. Est-ce pour se « déculpabiliser », se laver de cette « erreur historique » qu'ils ne peuvent assumer, que des Québécois sont aujourd'hui anti-monarchistes militants?

Certains Québécois ont facilement tendance à se créer des mythes qui deviennent des symboles de l'oppression dont ils se croient victimes. La Couronne, symbole puissant et permanent, est prise en otage dans cet exercice. Elle est une institution qui sera toujours à risque, sous l'œil constant des médias, toujours plus incisifs, qui ne tolèrent aucune faille, si mince soit-elle.[122] Cette affligeante complaisance à dénigrer le passé et les institutions dont nous avons hérité témoigne plus de nos incapacités que de notre confiance intime à façonner l'avenir face à un horizon plus large, susceptible d'améliorer notre prospérité économique commune et une conception plus exigeante des droits et libertés, tout en valorisant la diversité qui a toujours caractérisé ce pays et qui est inscrite au cœur de son existence. Plusieurs Québécois éprouvent toujours beaucoup de difficulté à se définir dans un cadre philosophique qui puisse concilier à la fois leur histoire et une vision humaniste du monde contemporain[123] au-delà des catégories mythiques qui ont servi autrefois à les mobiliser et à les rassurer. Ce carcan complaisant dans lequel ils trouvent leur sécurité immédiate les retient d'imaginer un autre fondement à leur valeur d'être.[124]

Notes

1. Sylvie St-Jacques, « La reine décorera Yann Martel », *La Presse*, 22 août 2012, A30.
2. Jacques Parizeau, *La souveraineté du Québec: Hier, aujourd'hui et demain* (Montréal, Les éditions Michel Brulé, 2009), 152.
3. Guillaume Bourgault-Côté, « Charest n'a pas le temps pour le jubilé », *Le Devoir*, 21 février 2012, disponible enligne : http://www.ledevoir.com/politique/quebec/343248/charest-n-a-pas-le-temps-pour-le-jubile.

4. Guillaume Bourgault-Côté, « Une médaille de la reine? Bof… », *Le Devoir*, 2 février 2012, disponible enligne : http://www.ledevoir.com/politique/canada/341632/une-medaille-de-la-reine-bof.
5. Notes on Polls on the Monarchy, Michael Dewing, Parliamentary Information and Research Service, 2 June 2010, "Recent polls show that more Canadians would prefer replacing the monarchy with an elected head of State than would prefer retaining monarchy. However, one fifth to one quarter of Canadians do not feel it matters one way or the other."
6. Depuis les rois Carolingiens (et Charlemagne) le pouvoir royal est d'origine divine et il s'exerce sous l'égide de la Trinité; par la suite ce sera « Par la grâce de Dieu… ». Archives nationales de France, « Le pouvoir en actes », Hôtel de Soubise, catalogue de l'exposition, 27 mars au 24 juin 2013, Paris, 10.
7. Marc Chevrier, « La République néo-française », *Bulletin d'histoire politique* 17, numéro 3 (2009), 29-57.
8. Marcel Trudel, *Mythes et réalités dans l'histoire du Québec*, Volume I (Éd. Hurtubise HMH, *Cahiers du Québec, coll. Histoire*, 2001), 214, 233.
9. Texte de la Proclamation royale de 1763 : « Dans l'intervalle et jusqu'à ce que ces assemblées puissent être convoquées, tous ceux qui habitent ou qui iront habiter Nos dites colonies peuvent se confier en Notre protection royale et compter Nos efforts pour leur assurer les bienfaits des lois de Notre royaume d'Angleterre ».
10. Justin H. Smith, *Our Struggle for the Fourteenth Colony – Canada and the American Revolution* (G.P. Putnam's Sons, New York & London, The Knickerbocker Press, 1907), 94, 97-98.
11. Gabriel E. Taschereau, « Nouveau rôle de la milice canadienne qui a fait le service pendant le blocus de Québec », 6 mai 1776, publié par la *Literary and Historical Society of Quebec* dans *Historical Documents*, Series 7, 1905, http://www.morrin.org/transactions/docsfromclient/books/40/40_f.html, accédé le 14 septembre 2012.
12. Justin H. Smith, *Our Struggle for the Fourteenth Colony*, 94: "The militia had been assembled and squarely asked whether they would fight. 'Yes,' the Canadians had answered equivocally…"
13. Philippe Aubert de Gaspé, père, *Mémoires*, 1866.
14. Gustave Lanctôt, *Report of the Public Archives for the year 1940*, no XXIII, appendice III, Ottawa, Dominion of Canada, 1941, 23-97.
15. Les Canadiens comptaient pour environ 20% des marins (pour un effectif de 189 hommes, de 1794 à 1801). Contrairement aux Écossais, aux Irlandais et aux Anglais, aucun Canadien ne déserta le service. Bob Garcia, "The Provincial Marine at Amherstburg 1796-1813," Association for Great Lakes Maritime History Annual Conference, Amherstberg, September 16, 2000, disponible enligne: http://www.warof1812.ca/provmarine.htm, accédé le 19 mars 2013.
16. Martin Croteau, « Un rappel de la guerre de 1812 à Montréal – le gouvernement Harper rebaptise l'édifice des douanes en l'honneur d'un combattant », *La Presse*, 11 octobre 2012, A16.
17. Tom Villemaire, "De Salaberry: a Canadian-born hero," *The Kingston Whig-Standard*, 27 August 2012, 2.
18. J. Edmond Roy, « Napoléon au Canada », *Mémoires et comptes rendus de la Société royale du Canada*, Séance de Mai 1911, troisième série, tome V (Londres, Bernard Quartich, 1912), 117.

19. Thomas Chapais, *Cours d'histoire du Canada*, Tome III : 1815-1833 (Québec, Librairie Garneau, 1921), 91-93.
20. Archives nationales du Canada, *Documents relatifs à l'histoire constitutionnelle du Canada 1819-1828* (Ottawa, Imprimeur du Roi, 1935), 413-417. http://www.1837.qc.ca/1837.pl?out=article&pno=document46, accédé le 2 octobre 2012.
21. Alexis de Tocqueville, *Regards sur le Bas-Canada* (Montréal, Typo, 2003), 190.
22. Discours de George-Etienne Cartier donné à l'occasion d'un banquet d'honneur lors de la Conférence des délégués du Canada et des autres provinces à Halifax, les 9 et 10 septembre 1864. Edward Whelan, ed., *The union of the British provinces: a brief account of the several conferences held in the Maritime provinces and in Canada, in September and October, 1864, on the proposed confederation of the provinces, together with a report of the speeches delivered by the delegates from the provinces, on important public occasions* (Charlottetown, G.T. Haszard, 1865), 26-27.
23. Katherine L. Morrison, "The only Canadians: Canada's French and the British Connection," *International Journal of Canadian Studies / Revue intérnationale d'études canadiennes*, No. 37 (2008), 186; John L. Gordon Jr., "Canada and the Imperial Federation Movement," dans *Imperial Canada 1867-1917*, Colin M. Coates, ed. (University of Edinburgh, Centre of Canadian Studies, 1997), 53.
24. John L. Gordon Jr., "Canada and the Imperial Federation Movement," 54.
25. Gilles Gallichan, *Honoré Mercier – la politique et la culture* (Québec, Septentrion, 1994), 70-71.
26. Nommé *Grand Pont Victoria* en 1897 à l'occasion du jubilé de diamant de la Reine, il reprendra son nom de *Pont Victoria* en 1978.
27. P.-J.-O. Chauveau, *Relation du voyage de Son Altesse le prince de Galles en Amérique* (Montréal, E. Senecal, 1860), XVIII à XXV.
28. Ibid.
29. Sir Wilfrid Laurier, *Discours à l'étranger et au Canada* (Montréal, Beauchemin, 1909), 9.
30. Ibid., 34.
31. Ibid., 34.
32. Ibid., 22.
33. Entendre la France monarchique et non républicaine.
34. Sir Wilfrid Laurier, *Discours à l'étranger et au Canada*, 35.
35. Jean Chrétien, *Dans la Fosse aux Lions* (Montréal, Éditions de l'Homme, 1985), 149-150.
36. Les premières manifestations en apparurent lors de la guerre des Boers.
37. Et dans des éditoriaux qu'il signa pour le journal *Le Devoir*, qu'il avait fondé en 1911.
38. Henri Bourassa, Discours du 13 mars 1900 à l'occasion du débat relatif à la guerre sud-africaine, *Débats de la Chambre des communes du Canada*, 5e Session, 8e Parlement, 63-64 Victoria, vol II (Ottawa, S. E. Dawson, 1900), 1823.
39. Henri Bourassa, *Le Problème de l'Empire – Indépendance ou Association impériale* (Montréal, Éditions du *Devoir*, 1916), 38.
40. Ibid., 40.
41. Max Nemni, « Les Canadiens français, la France et les deux guerres mondiales », dans P.-A. Linteau et Serge Joyal [dir.], *France-Canada-Québec : 400*

ans de relations d'exception (Montréal, Les Presses de l'Université de Montréal, 2008), 219 : Nemni s'appuyant sur les travaux d'Elizabeth H. Armstrong.

42. Plus de 161 603 serviront lors de la Deuxième guerre. Voir Max Nemni, « Les Canadiens français, la France et les deux guerres mondiales », 234 : Nemni s'appuyant sur les travaux de Serge Bernier.
43. Jacques Rouillard, compte rendu, « H.V. Nelles, L'Histoire spectacle. Le cas du tricentenaire de Québec » (Montréal, Boréal, 2003), dans *Recherches socio-graphiques, Sciences sociales et littérature* 44, numéro 3, (2003), 573.
44. Renée Gagnon-Guimond, « Leurs Majestés au Québec : la visite royale de 1939 », Cap-aux-Diamants : *la Revue d'histoire du Québec* 5, N° 4 (1990), 23-26. Trois des frères du roi avaient déjà séjourné à Québec, de même que son père et son arrière grand-père. Lui-même s'y était déjà arrêté en 1913, comme officier de marine, alors que son grand oncle, le Duc de Connaught, était gouverneur général du Canada
45. Renée Gagnon-Guimond, « Leurs Majestés au Québec : la visite royale de 1939 », 24 et 25.
46. *Le Devoir*, Montréal, 17 mai 1939, 12.
47. Eugene Forsey, « The Monarchy and the Canadian Constitution » dans *The Silver Jubilee: Royal Visit to Canada* (Ottawa, Deneau & Greenburg, 1977), 54. Malgré ce plaidoyer de loyauté, Duplessis prit plus tard parti contre la participation du Canada à la guerre et il fut défait.
48. *La Presse Canadienne*, « Le Roi remet un message en français à l'adresse de M. Duplessis », *Le Droit*, 17 mai 1939.
49. Il sera emprisonné en 1940 pour avoir défié la loi sur l'enregistrement obligatoire en vue de la conscription votée en dépit des engagements électoraux du Parti Libéral.
50. *Le Devoir* y alla d'un grand titre : « La foule montréalaise acclame et admire les souverains du Canada ». Le journal publia un éditorial où il louangea le roi pour ses propos : « Des paroles que les Canadiens français n'oublieront pas » (*Le Devoir*, 19 mai 1939). Ce journal ne manquera toutefois pas de rester fidèle à sa position anti-impérialiste : « Le roi et la reine nous ont conquis, mais non pas l'impérialisme » (*Le Devoir*, 10 juin 1939). *La Presse* eut ce titre dithyrambique : « Apothéose Royale » (*La Presse*, 19 mai 1939).
51. *Le Devoir*, « L'adresse du maire de Montréal à nos souverains », Volume XXX, N° 114, Montréal, 17 mai 1939.
52. Heather M. Metcalfe, "It's all about war: Canadian opinion and the Canadian approach to international relations, 1935-1939," A Thesis for the Degree of Doctor of Philosophy, Department of History, University of Toronto, 2009, 8.
53. *Le Devoir*, Montréal, 10 octobre 1951, 3.
54. Lionel Groulx, *Pour bâtir* (Montréal, l'Action Nationale, 1953), 15.
55. Lionel Groulx, *Notre maître le passé*, troisième série (Montréal, Granger, 1944).
56. Hélène Quimper et Daniel Drouin, *La Prise de Québec, 1759-1760 / The Taking of Quebec, 1759-1760* (Québec, Commission des champs de bataille nationaux / The National Battlefields Commission et Musée national des beaux-arts du Québec, 2009), 10.
57. Laquelle trouve son origine dans l'œuvre de l'écrivain français nationaliste de droite Maurice Barrès, *Les déracinés* (1897), que Groulx à d'ailleurs lue.
58. Linda Leith, *Introducing Hugh MacLennan's Two Solitudes : A Reader's Guide* (Toronto, ECW Press, 1990), 67, cité par Todd Porterfield, *La peinture d'Histoire*

et l'insoluble question de la souveraineté, dans « Interpellations : trois essais sur Kent Monkman » (Montréal, Université Concordia, 2012), 114.

59. Le maire Fournier toucha de la main l'épaule de la reine, dans un geste familier, ce que le protocole réprouvait assurément… Les journaux anglais en firent largement écho.
60. Alexandre Shields, « Charest est sur le pied de guerre », *Le Devoir*, 1 août 2012, A1. « Cette conception du passé québécois, où l'année 1960 apparaît comme une fracture, relève du domaine du mythe, c'est-à-dire qu'il se fonde à la fois sur le vrai et le faux ».
61. Jacques Lacourcière, *Histoire Populaire du Québec*, Volume V, *1960-1970* (Québec, Septentrion, 2008), 13.
62. Ibid., 132. Le journal *Le Devoir* lança quant à lui une mise en garde : « Si l'on veut que le symbole de la Couronne et la personne de la souveraine restent au dessus des conflits politiques, que nos gouvernements donnent d'abord l'exemple : qu'ils s'abstiennent eux-mêmes de les utiliser à des fins de propagande en les jetant dans la mêlée ». Voir Paul Sauriol, *Le Devoir*, 27 février 1964, cité par Lacourcière, *Histoire Populaire du Québec*, 132.
63. Brian Mulroney, *Mémoires* (Éditions de l'Homme, 2007), 86-87 : il s'en repentira par la suite…
64. Lacourcière, *Histoire Populaire du Québec*, 133.
65. « Allocution de bienvenue […] (du) premier ministre Lesage, à l'endroit d'Elizabeth II, en présence de quelques 240 dignitaires réunis dans la salle du Conseil législatif », *Le Devoir*, Montréal, 12 octobre 1964, 8.
66. « La Reine à l'Expo : Le Canada survivra par le dialogue de ses deux cultures », *Le Devoir*, 4 juillet 1967.
67. « Monarchy in Quebec », *Wikipedia*, http://en.wikipedia.org/wiki/Monarchy_in_Quebec, accédé le 12 septembre 2012.
68. Claude Ryan, « Le passage d'Elizabeth II au Québec », Éditorial, *Le Devoir*, 27 juillet 1976, 4.
69. « Elisabeth II au Peuple canadien – la grandeur du Canada réside dans l'entente entre ses deux peuples », *Le Devoir*, 6 juillet 1976, 4.
70. Claude Ryan, « Le passage d'Elizabeth II au Québec », Éditorial, *Le Devoir*, 27 juillet 1976, 4.
71. Serment d'allégeance, Article 128, *loi constitutionnelle de 1867*.
72. Charles Lynch, "Bloc Québécois: Members make oaths of office seem ridiculous," *Ottawa Citizen*, 29 juillet 1990.
73. Jean-Marc Salvet, « L'assermentation en privé », *Le Soleil*, 20 septembre 2012, 12.
74. Quoique selon certains, une telle initiative évite d'impliquer le représentant du Souverain dans des débats partisans en l'obligeant à lire une prose trop politique.
75. *Hodge v. The Queen* [1883], 9 A.C. 117 (J.C.P.C.); *Liquidators of the Maritime Bank v. Receiver General of New Brunswick*, [1892], A.C. 437 (J.C.P.C.).
76. Robert Dutrisac, « Québec renonce à réclamer des pouvoirs – mais le gouvernement Marois exigera le transfert de milliards dépensés par Ottawa », *Le Devoir*, 10 octobre 2012, A1, A10.
77. Allocution de Sa Majesté la Reine Elizabeth II suivant la Proclamation royale de la Loi constitutionnelle du Canada (1982), citée dans Gilles Paquin, « La Reine a déploré l'absence du Québec », *La Presse*, 19 avril 1982.

78. *The Virgin Islands Daily News*, "Ottawa Governor to Visit Caribbean," 14 février 1969. Lord Willingdon avait visité les États-Unis en 1927 et Lord Tweedsmuir en 1937.
79. La Souveraine effectua quatre visites pendant les neuf années du gouvernement Mulroney et trois visites pendant les dix années du gouvernement Chrétien.
80. J.J. Granatstein and Robert Bothwell, *Pirouette: Pierre Trudeau and Canadian Foreign Policy* (Toronto, University of Toronto Press, 1990), 336.
81. Ibid., 337.
82. Il y eut aussi le projet de loi C-60 déposé en 1978, qui amplifiait le rôle et la visibilité du gouverneur général, le qualifiant de «Premier Canadien ».
83. Christopher McCreery, "Myth and Misunderstanding: The Origins and Meaning of the Letters Patent Constituting the Office of the Governor General, 1947," dans Jennifer Smith et D. Michael Jackson, eds., *The Evolving Canadian Crown* (Montreal & Kingston: McGill-Queen's University Press, 2012), 46 et ss.
84. Thomas S. Axworthy et Pierre Elliott Trudeau, *Les années Trudeau : la recherche d'une société juste* (Montréal, Le Jour Éditeur, 1985), 397, n. 16.
85. Mark Lovewell, "The Inconvenient Crown," *Literary Review of Canada* 20, No. 5 (2012), 26-27.
86. Pierre Elliott Trudeau, avec la collaboration de Ron Graham, *Trudeau: l'essentiel de sa pensée politique* (Montréal, Le Jour Éditeur, 1998), 132.
87. Katherine L. Morrison, "The Only Canadians: Canada's French and the British Connection," *International Journal of Canadian Studies / Revue internationale d'études canadiennes* 37 (2008), 177-194.
88. Canadian Press, « la Reine a rendu hommage au biculturalisme du N-B, » *L'Évangéline*, 16 juillet 1976, A2.
89. Expression utilisée par le premier ministre Mulroney à l'élection de 1984. C'est son ami, l'avocat et futur Sénateur Jean Bazin, qui lui a suggéré d'utiliser l'expression. Voir Brian Mulroney, *Mémoires*, 369.
90. Denis Lessard, « Élisabeth II revint au Québec après 23 ans », *La Presse*, 22 octobre 1987, A2.
91. Exposition Lire Bourassa - allocution de M. Robert Bourassa le 22 octobre 1987, émission archives.
92. *L'Actualité* révéla, dans son édition du 15 novembre 1996, alors que Roux était étudiant en médecine à l'Université de Montréal pendant la guerre, qu'il avait dessiné une croix gammée sur la manche de son sarrau.
93. Québec, Assemblée nationale, *Débats*, 20 novembre 1996; « Bouchard Tables Motion to Abolish Lieutenant-Governor Position », *The Gazette* (Montréal), 15 novembre 1996, A18.
94. La Presse Canadienne, « Immunité réclamée – Lise Thibault porte sa cause en appel », *Le Devoir*, 11 septembre 2012, A3.
95. Robert Dutrisac, « Motion pour l'abolition du « vice-roi », *Le Devoir*, 8 novembre 2012, A7.
96. *Le Devoir*, « Cloutier s'oppose désormais au choix du « vice-roi » par l'Assemblée », 21 janvier 2013, A3.
97. Patrick Taillon, « Projet de loi sur la succession au trône d'Angleterre – Une occasion de sauver ce qui reste du veto du Québec! » *Le Devoir*, 2 février 2013.

98. Jean Chrétien, *Dans la Fosse aux Lions*, 195-197.
99. Peter Donolo, directeur des communications du Premier ministre Chrétien, « Liberals considering break from monarchy », CBC, 18 décembre 1998.
100. Jean Chrétien, *Passion Politique* (Montréal, Boréal, 2007), 274.
101. Jim Fox, "Quebec dredges up monarchy issue once again," *St. Petersburg Times*, 6 mai 2007, http://www.sptimes.com/2007/05/06/Worldandnation/Quebec_dredges_up_mon.shtml, accédé le 12 septembre 2012, rapportant les déclarations du ministre provincial Benoit Pelletier (Libéral) : il n'est « pas impossible que nous ayons à reconsidérer le rôle du monarque » (it is «not impossible that we might have to reconsider the role of the monarch»).
102. *The Globe and Mail*, 24 août 1996, D6; Déclaration du vice premier ministre du Canada John Manley à la veille de l'arrivée de la Reine pour la visite marquant le Jubilé d'or en 2002. Chris Wattie, « Manley calls for end of monarchy », *National Post*, 5 October 2002; Michael Bliss, « Is it Time for Canada to Cut its Ties to the Monarchy? Yes » , *The Toronto Star*, 15 septembre 1997, A16 ; « L'idée de rompre le lien avec la monarchie divise le Caucus libéral », Radio-Canada avec La Presse Canadienne, 11 janvier 2012 ; Aussi, les députés Pat Martin et Nathan Cullen: Chris Plecash, « Monarchy a defining trait of government's cultural policy », *Hill Times*, 26 mars 2012 ; Au congrès biennal du Parti Libéral du Canada, tenu à Vancouver du 13 au 15 janvier 2012, une proposition présentée par l'aile des jeunes Libéraux à l'effet de former un comité d'étude pour préciser une alternative au régime de monarchie constitutionnelle est défaite aux deux tiers des voix : Ariana Fiocca, « Cannabis and the Crown », *The Brock Press*, Brock University, 23 janvier 2012 ; Radio-Canada / La Presse canadienne, « L'idée de rompre le lien avec la monarchie divise le caucus libéral », 11 janvier 2012 ; Katherine L. Morrison, "The only Canadians: Canada's French and the British Connection", 177: "Does Canada's continued adherence to the British monarchy keep Canada divided and prevent a sense of common nationalism?"
103. Notes on Polls on the Monarchy, Michael Dewing, Parliamentary Information and Research Service, 2 June 2010, "Recent polls show that more Canadians would prefer replacing the monarchy with an elected head of State than would prefer retaining monarchy. However, one fifth to one quarter of Canadians do not feel it matters one way or the other."
104. Philippe Lagassé, "Crown discussion should go beyond Harry's adventures," *Ottawa Citizen*, 29 août 2012.
105. Myriam Revault d'Allonnes, *Crises sans fin* (Paris, Seuil, 2012).
106. Rhéal Séguin, « Marois sees the Queen as symbol of federal imposition on Québec », *The Globe and Mail*, 8 août 2012, A4.
107. Renvoi relatif à la sécession du Québec, [1998] 2 R.C.S. 217.
108. Katherine L. Morrison, "The only Canadians: Canada's French and the British Connection," 177-194; Biz – Québec 101 – Éditions Caractère, Collection *Les Incollables* (jeu éducatif), Montréal, Octobre 2011.
109. Claude Couture, « Révisionnisme, américanité, postcolonialisme et minorités francophones », *Francophonie d'Amérique*, 26 (Les Presses de l'Université d'Ottawa et le Centre de recherche en civilisation canadienne-française, 2008), 53-54.
110. Jocelyn Letourneau et David Northrup, « Québécois et Canadiens face au passé : similitudes et dissemblances », *The Canadian Historical Review* 92 (2011),

193; Jocelyn Letourneau, *Le Québec entre son passé et ses passages* (Montréal, Fides, 2010).

111. Louis Cornellier, « Le retour du nationalisme conservateur », *Le Devoir*, 1er et 2 septembre 2012, F6.
112. Pierre Côté, *Québécois 101- Notre portrait en 25 traits* (Montréal, Éditions Québec/Amérique, 2012), 124. Voir aussi l'article de Lysiane Gagnon, « Hargne et vulgarité », *La Presse*, 16 mars 2013, A31 : « [...U]n rapport à l'Église complexe et malsain, le fait d'un peuple malheureux qui n'en finit plus de régler ses comptes avec ses origines, comme un homme déboussolé encore hanté, à l'âge adulte, par le besoin de haïr sa mère ».
113. « Motion sans préavis » adoptée le 22 mai 2008, Procès-verbal de l'Assemblée nationale (N° 87), 1ère session, 38e législature, 840; "Christian guiding principles were contained in a motion adopted unanimously by all parties in the National Assembly yesterday in its first response to the report," *The Montreal Gazette*, 23 mai 2008 (Rapport Bouchard-Taylor, 52-53 et 271, pour la recommendation 63). Déclaration de Pauline Marois à Jean-Michel Demetz, *L'Express*, Fr, 16 novembre 2012 : « il [le crucifix] restera car c'est notre patrimoine et notre histoire ».
114. Arrêté ministériel du gouvernement de René Lévesque du 11 mai 1977 : le 24 juin devient officiellement le jour de la Fête nationale du Québec.
115. C'est le 20 novembre 2002 que le gouvernement du Québec proclame par décret la *Journée nationale des Patriotes*. Fête fériée et chômée au Québec, elle est célébrée le lundi qui précède le 25 mai de chaque année et le fut pour la première fois en mai 2003.
116. Bob Hepburn, "Harper's love of all things British," *Toronto Star*, 27 septembre 2012, A23.
117. Entretien du philosophe Marcel Gauchet et Gyulaine de Monjou (France Inter), Émission *Euromag*, Radio-Canada, 31 mars 2012.
118. Jean-Pierre Issenhuth, « En quête d'un art de vivre », *Liberté*, 175, 30, no. 1 (1988), 6-7.
119. Henri Hauser, « Le principe des nationalités, ses origines historiques », *La Revue politique internationale*, Vol. V (jan.-juin 1916) (Paris, F. Alcan), 122, cité par Maurice Lemire, *Les Grands Thèmes nationalistes du roman historique canadien-français* (Québec, PUL, 1970), 227.
120. Éric Desrosiers, « Le mythe du pauvre francophone mis à mal par le Conference Board », *Le Devoir*, 11 octobre 2012, B1.
121. Eric Hobsbawm, *Nations et nationalisme depuis 1780*, 237.
122. Elizabeth Renzetti, "Royal double standard: exceptional when it suits them, normal folk when it doesn't," *The Globe and Mail*, 20 octobre 2012, A2.
123. Jean-Marc Piotte et Jean-Pierre Couture, *Les nouveaux visages du nationalisme conservateur au Québec* (Montréal, Québec-Amérique, 2012); Louis Cornellier, « Le retour du nationalisme conservateur », *Le Devoir*, 1er et 2 septembre 2012, F6.
124. Gérard Bouchard, « Une nouvelle Révolution tranquille? », *La Presse*, 22 septembre 2012, A39.

3

Commentaire : la Couronne au Québec, de credo rassurant à bouc émissaire commode

Linda Cardinal

The author comments on Senator Joyal's chapter on the monarchy in the history of French-speaking Canada. She questions why the monarchical idea is not given much thought in Quebec history, especially given Quebecers' interest in constitutional debates. She observes a lack of understanding about the monarchy in Quebec and argues that minimizing this heritage will not help people to think through the issue.

Le chapitre du sénateur Joyal sur la monarchie dans l'histoire du Canada francophone est foisonnant d'idées; il est aussi fort intrigant. Il relate beaucoup d'événements, dont les passages de la Reine au Québec. Par contre, ces événements qu'il décrit sont-ils si importants pour mériter autant d'attention? S'ils font partie de la mémoire, force est de reconnaître qu'ils ne sont pas passés à l'histoire. La monarchie serait-elle un impensé dans l'histoire du Québec?

Il nous paraît utile de situer la réflexion du sénateur sur la monarchie dans le contexte des débats historiographiques sur le Québec d'avant les années 1960, afin de faire la lumière sur la place qu'y occupe la monarchie. Ces débats ont donné lieu à des remises en question importantes de la supposée nature rétrograde du Québec d'avant les années 1960. Dans ce cadre, la question de la place à accorder aux idées libérales et républicaines dans l'histoire de la pensée politique au Québec a été déterminante.[1] Or, qu'en est-il de la monarchie dans ces débats?

Le chapitre du sénateur repose sur l'hypothèse selon laquelle la Couronne au Québec a été, historiquement, un credo rassurant qui serait devenu un bouc émissaire commode. Il affirme que traditionnellement, les Canadiens français avaient la fibre monarchique. De la Nouvelle-France à l'Empire britannique, le Québec a toujours vécu sous une monarchie, une situation dont les Québécois semblent s'être bien accommodés. En soi, cette information nous paraît renversante.

À force de penser l'histoire du Québec sur le mode de la rupture, les historiens et les sociologues semblent avoir négligé de se pencher sur le fait que la monarchie continue de faire partie des dimensions qui définissent son régime politique. Les événements relatés par le sénateur Joyal invitent ainsi à revenir sur la question du lien des Québécois avec leur passé monarchique. Nous ne pouvons pas rendre justice à l'ensemble des propos du sénateur dans ce court texte, mais sa réflexion et les éléments d'analyse qu'il propose ne peuvent pas laisser le lecteur indifférent. Ce bref commentaire tentera de proposer un début d'éclairage sur l'idée monarchique dans l'historiographie québécoise à la lumière du texte du sénateur Joyal.

La monarchie et l'historiographie du Canada français

Le sénateur Joyal rappelle des faits et des événements qui lui permettent de penser que la monarchie au Québec devrait occuper une place de choix dans les représentations des Québécois. Il y aurait une histoire à écrire sur la question au Québec. Or, jusqu'à présent, les commentateurs, sociologues, historiens et politologues, sauf exception, ont été peu soucieux de la place de la monarchie dans l'histoire sociale, institutionnelle et constitutionnelle du Québec. Entre autres, nous retenons du texte du sénateur que le monarque attribuait une grande importance à la diversité linguistique du Canada et qu'il comprenait bien le rôle clé du Québec dans la protection de l'héritage canadien-français, de la langue et de la culture françaises dans les Amériques. Le monarque reconnaissait la légitimité du nationalisme canadien-français / québécois et que la préoccupation des francophones envers leur langue et leur culture constituait à la fois une grande source de fierté ainsi qu'un enjeu de tous les jours. Ainsi, le sénateur Joyal veut nous inviter à revoir la croyance populaire et nationaliste selon laquelle la monarchie ne serait pas compatible avec les aspirations du peuple canadien-français. Pourquoi, donc, les Québécois auraient-ils fait de la monarchie un bouc émissaire? Selon le sénateur Joyal, la cause réside dans le nationalisme québécois revanchard. Ce nationalisme cherche à exorciser des Québécois ce vieux démon associé à la Conquête, à la colonisation et au projet d'assimilation de Lord Durham. Il est aussi fondé sur l'idée que Québec, par le passé, était une société traditionnelle, ancienne, passéiste, conservatrice, ethnique, raciste, xénophobe. Pour sa part, le nationalisme québécois aspire à une société plus moderne, ouverte sur le monde et libérée de son passé de colonisé[2]. Alors que pour le sénateur Joyal, le Québec d'avant les années 1960 fait partie d'un monde impérial, il ne fait pas de doute qu'il constitue une société ouverte sur le monde. Or, la doxa veut que la société québécoise à cette époque vive dans une Grande Noirceur plus qu'elle ne participe à un monde qui donne accès à deux grands empires, français et anglais.

Cette image du Québec d'avant les années 1960 comme une société rétrograde n'est pas que le propre d'une certaine historiographie québécoise. Elle a été consacrée dans l'imaginaire canadien au point de rendre impossible toute référence au passé autre que dans les termes de cette orthodoxie. En effet, le sénateur Joyal n'en parle pas dans son texte, mais le *chromo* selon lequel le Québec est une société historiquement traditionnelle et nécessairement conservatrice, passéiste et rétrograde se reproduit formidablement dans les médias canadiens-anglais. En fait, il nous paraît constituer le principal filtre à partir duquel la vie sociale et politique au Québec est interprétée. Est-ce aussi l'effet du nationalisme québécois « revanchard »? Certains journalistes du *Maclean's* nous invitaient, en 2011, à penser que ce *chromo* ferait même partie de l'ADN social des Québécois – nous pensons ici au dossier spécial du magazine sur la corruption au Québec. Si ces propos frôlent la caricature, un regard impressionniste sur les courriers des lecteurs ou les blogues auxquels ont accès les internautes viennent souvent confirmer ces préjugés. Le passé du Québec est aussi un bouc émissaire commode. L'attaquer permet de mobiliser les passions et d'associer les comportements des Québécois à une forme de pathologie sociale et individuelle. Pire, en dépit de sa Révolution tranquille, ses pathologies ne cessent de la hanter. Or, comment expliquer ce consensus presque parfait entre les nationalistes québécois revanchards et certains interprètes canadiens-anglais de la vie sociale et politique au Québec? À vrai dire, le chapitre du sénateur Joyal ne porte pas sur cette question. Au contraire, le conservatisme du Québec dont témoigne le sénateur, dans son texte, n'est pas en porte à faux avec une certaine ouverture de la société québécoise sur le monde. Le Québec populaire qu'il nous présente est fièrement attaché à ses héritages français et britannique. Comment expliquer ce contraste? De toute évidence, l'historiographie québécoise et les préjugés auxquels s'abreuve un certain Canada de langue anglaise font l'impasse sur la nature du conservatisme d'avant la Révolution tranquille au Québec. L'originalité de la démarche du sénateur Joyal est qu'elle vise à reprendre le débat sur la nature de la société québécoise et, de façon particulière, sur son conservatisme d'avant les années 1960. Chez ce dernier, ce conservatisme est d'abord et avant tout monarchiste.

Le texte du sénateur Joyal propose une chronologie des principales étapes qui auraient conduit au changement d'attitude des Québécois envers la monarchie, au tournant des années 1950 et 1960. Il suggère qu'en refusant de penser la monarchie le Québec a perdu une part importante de son âme. Il s'est défait de sa capacité de comprendre son passé. Il se serait coupé de repères qui pourraient l'aider à mieux guider son présent.

Jusqu'à présent, si le débat historiographique a tenté de renouer avec le passé libéral et républicain des Québécois, certains travaux plus récents ont aussi souhaité sortir la tradition de pensée conservatrice des greniers de la pensée politique au Québec, afin de lui redonner sa place dans la république des idées. Nous pensons ici aux efforts dans ces travaux de revoir l'historiographie moderniste afin d'y situer les thèses d'acteurs d'allégeance conservatrice importants au Québec d'avant les années 1960[3]. Un débat plus idéologique fait rage depuis quelques années au sujet du statut à accorder au conservatisme dans l'échiquier des idées politiques contemporaines[4]. Toutefois, si le texte du sénateur Joyal cadre mal avec ce débat, force est de constater que les nouveaux interprètes du conservatisme font aussi l'impasse sur la question de la monarchie.

Parmi les historiens francophones contemporains dont les travaux pourraient être mis en dialogue avec ceux du sénateur Joyal, mentionnons le récent ouvrage de Claude Couture et Paulin Mulatris, *La nation et son double*[5]. Dans ce très bel essai, Couture et Mulatris se proposent d'insérer l'histoire du Canada français dans le contexte du XVIIIe siècle britannique. Or, les auteurs ne sont pas tendres envers la Couronne et les gouvernements britanniques qui se succèdent à l'époque. Cette monarchie qui, pour le sénateur Joyal, protège les Canadiens français jette, chez Couture et Mulatris, les bases d'une modernisation et d'une expansion de son empire – vers le Canada, mais également vers les Indes et l'Afrique, qui sont caractérisées par la corruption, le favoritisme et l'exploitation. Malgré ses pratiques peu recommandables, le monde anglo-britannique se représente pourtant comme une société supérieure et singularise l'Autre comme étant inférieur. Il « orientalise » l'Autre, pour reprendre l'expression d'Edward Saïd[6]. Il hiérarchise les cultures selon une logique binaire lui permettant de se retrouver du côté des peuples supérieurs, cela va de soi. Chez Couture et Mulatris, ce mécanisme de représentation de l'Autre fait partie de l'ADN social du Canada et permet d'expliquer le rapport trouble du Canada anglais avec le Québec. En d'autres mots, en restituant le Canada anglais dans l'histoire du monde anglo-britannique, celle du XVIIIe siècle, d'une part on s'aperçoit qu'il s'est également coupé de son passé et qu'il a un rapport tout aussi amnésique avec ce dernier que les Québécois avec le sien. D'autre part, en se coupant de la relation symbolique avec son passé au sein de l'Empire britannique, le Canada fait l'impasse sur ses difficultés à reconnaître le Québec comme une société « normale », dont la spécificité est d'être à la fois de tradition française et nord-américaine.

S'il faut renouer avec le passé monarchiste des Canadiens français au sein de l'historiographie canadienne et québécoise, le sénateur Joyal pourrait devoir répondre aux thèses postcoloniales de Couture et de Mulatris. Ces dernières n'ont rien du nationalisme revanchard dans lequel le sénateur Joyal puise une part de sa critique. Au contraire, Couture et Mulatris ne semblent pas attachés au nationalisme. Ils étudient le Québec dans son contexte plus large, celui du monde atlantique et anglo-britannique. Ainsi, à l'instar du sénateur, mais d'une perspective foncièrement distincte, ils cherchent à penser la continuité du Québec et du Canada anglais avec le monde « ancien ».

Selon une perspective radicalement différente de Couture et de Mulatris ou du sénateur Joyal, Gérard Bouchard fait aussi partie de la minorité d'historiens à se demander comment aborder cette difficile question. Il a consacré une part de ses travaux à expliquer aux Québécois que s'ils ont un passé qui n'est pas l'expression d'une grande noirceur, il n'en demeure pas moins caractérisé par des rendez-vous manqués avec l'histoire. Comme il le souligne dans son ouvrage *La pensée impuissante*,[7] les Québécois ont été incapables d'une véritable rupture avec l'ordre canadien. Plus volontariste que Couture et Mulatris, l'approche de Bouchard, déjà esquissée dans son autre ouvrage marquant, *Genèse des nations et cultures du Nouveau Monde*,[8] tient pour acquis que les Québécois devraient se couper de leur passé monarchiste. Cette impuissance à devenir un peuple souverain mine sa capacité d'action.[9]

La monarchie et le régime politique canadien

Sur le plan de la science politique plus classique, approfondir la question de la continuité du Québec avec son passé monarchiste pourrait se révéler pertinent pour mieux comprendre les fondements de sa vie institutionnelle et politique. Selon Eugene Forsey, que cite le sénateur Joyal, le monarque est un garant de la constitution et est un rempart contre tout abus de pouvoir. La Reine ou son représentant sont des gardiens de la démocratie constitutionnelle du Canada. Forsey semble avoir bien compris toute la complexité qui caractérise le régime politique canadien. Comment un monarque peut-il être le gardien de la démocratie?

On a longtemps affirmé dans les débats historiographiques et politiques que les Canadiens français ne comprenaient rien à la démocratie et que ce fut grâce au régime britannique qu'ils ont appris à devenir des démocrates. Or, dans ses récents travaux, Marc Chevrier soutient que dès la Nouvelle-France, les Canadiens français témoignent d'un esprit qui n'est pas sans faire penser à une certaine idée démocratique.[10] Or, il est aussi vrai que depuis 470 ans, ils ont accordé leur loyauté à un monarque, sauf que ce dernier a toujours été absent. Ils n'ont jamais vraiment eu de liens directs avec le monarque. De fait, cette démocratie dont les Canadiens français étaient apparemment dépourvus a été gagnée grâce à leur engagement envers le gouvernement responsable, le principe électif, le suffrage universel et la lutte à la corruption. Ce comportement n'est pas inné. Il vient d'une expérience historique bien particulière des Canadiens français en Amérique du Nord qui, pour plusieurs, ferait d'eux des républicains plus que des monarchistes. Il faudrait donc s'abstenir d'une approche naturaliste de la monarchie aux dépens de l'histoire des luttes des Canadiens français pour la démocratie.

Dernière remarque

L'absence de travaux sur la question de la monarchie au Québec est une réalité difficilement compréhensible lorsque l'on connaît l'intérêt des Québécois pour les débats constitutionnels. À ce chapitre, le gouvernement du Québec, les fédéralistes réformistes de l'époque des années 1960, en l'occurrence, ont raté des occasions de transformer l'ordre constitutionnel canadien. À titre d'exemple, en 1968, au lieu d'abolir la chambre haute au Québec, il eût été indiqué de lui donner un nouveau rôle, plus démocratique. Il est vrai que les autres provinces n'ont pas fait mieux. De plus, le Québec sera la dernière province à se défaire de sa chambre haute. Or, en maintenant cette dernière, le gouvernement québécois à l'époque aurait pu souhaiter redéfinir la fonction de lieutenant-gouverneur. Rappelons qu'à ce moment, Trudeau était premier ministre du Canada. Il avait souhaité faire du gouverneur général le premier Canadien afin de poursuivre l'œuvre de « canadianisation » de la Couronne. Or, le Québec aurait pu réussir là où le Canada a échoué et ainsi marquer sa différence. En abolissant la chambre haute, le Québec a peut-être manqué une chance d'influencer l'ordre constitutionnel canadien de façon durable, au lieu de banaliser le statut du lieutenant-gouverneur en pensant qu'il ne s'agit que d'un symbole d'un ordre ancien et vétuste. En fait, cet ordre ancien constitue un impensé malheureux dans la vie institutionnelle du Québec. C'est mal comprendre l'importance de la monarchie ou de la Couronne dans l'histoire du Québec et les scénarios actuels afin de minimiser cet héritage nous paraissent peu utiles à l'avancement du débat.

Notes

1. Parmi les travaux sur le libéralisme et le républicanisme au Québec, voir Marc Chevrier, « L'idée républicaine au Québec et au Canada français – les avatars d'une tradition cachée, » dans *L'idée républicaine dans le monde, XVIII*[e] */ XXI*[e] *siècles*, Paul Baquiast et Emmanuel Dupuy, dir., Vol. 2. (Paris : L'Harmattan, 2007); Marc Chevrier, *La République au Québec, une idée suspecte* (Montréal : Boréal, 2012); Gilles Paquet et Jean-Pierre Wallot, *Un Québec moderne, 1760-1840* (Montréal : Hurtubise HMH, 2007); Yvan Lamonde, *Histoire des idées sociales au Québec, 1760-1894* (Montréal : Fides, 2000); Leslie Choquette, *De Français à paysans : modernité et tradition dans le peuplement du Canada français* (Montréal et Paris : Les Éditions du Septentrion et Presses de l'Université de Paris-Sorbonne, 2001); Louis-George Harvey, *Le printemps de l'Amérique française* (Montréal : Boréal, 2005); Fernande Roy, *Histoires des idéologies au Québec au XIX*[e] *siècle* (Montréal : Boréal, 1993).
2. Cette représentation du nationalisme québécois n'est pas spécifique au texte du sénateur Joyal. Elle occupe une place importante dans l'imaginaire québécois et canadien-anglais. Pour une synthèse du nationalisme au Québec selon l'approche traditionnelle, voir Michael Behiels, *Prelude to the Quiet Revolution:*

Liberalism vs Neo-nationalism (Montréal: McGill-Queen's University Press, 1985).

3. Pour une synthèse des thèses conservatrices, voir Linda Cardinal et Jean-Michel Lacroix, dir., *Le conservatisme : le Canada et le Québec en contexte* (Paris : Presses Sorbonne Nouvelle, 2009) et Frédéric Boily, *Le conservatisme au Québec. Retour sur une tradition oubliée* (Québec : Les Presses de l'Université Laval, 2011).
4. Cheldy Belkhodja, « Une sensibilité conservatrice? La critique du multiculturalisme chez les nouveaux penseurs de la droite au Québec, » *Études ethniques canadiennes/Canadian Ethnic Studies* 40, n° 3 (2009), 79-100.
5. Claude Couture et Paulin Mulatris, *La nation et son double* (Québec : Les Presses de l'Université Laval, 2012).
6. L'approche de Couture et Mulatris est en partie inspirée de la thèse d'Edward Saïd sur l'orientalisme. Saïd est considéré comme un des pères de l'approche postcoloniale. Voir Couture et Mulatris, *La nation et son double,* et Edward Saïd, *Orientalism* (London : Vintage, 1977).
7. Gérard Bouchard, *La pensée impuissante* (Montréal : Boréal, 2004).
8. Gérard Bouchard, *Genèse des nations et cultures du Nouveau Monde* (Montréal : Boréal, 2002).
9. Or, pour Couture, si les Québécois sont si impuissants, ils ont pourtant bien réussi à devenir une des sociétés les plus modernes et libérales en Amérique du Nord. Voir Claude Couture, « Révisionisme, américanité, postcolonialisme et minorités francophones, » *Francophonies d'Amérique* 26 (2008), 41-62.
10. Chevrier, « L'idée républicaine au Québec et au Canada français – les avatars d'une tradition cachée ».

4

The Crown and the Media

Phillip Crawley and John Fraser in Conversation

John Fraser, maître du Massey College et toujours journaliste, et Phillip Crawley, éditeur et chef de la direction du Globe and Mail, *proposent un échange informel sur les rapports entre les médias et la Couronne. Ils évoquent les liens historiquement ambivalents qui unissent les deux institutions, tour à tour marqués au coin du respect, du mépris et d'une instrumentalisation réciproque. Ils abordent aussi l'évolution récente mais potentiellement décisive du phénomène désormais confirmé du recul du journalisme traditionnel face à l'essor des médias sociaux, qui a jusqu'ici profité à la Couronne en permettant aux membres de la famille royale et à leurs homologues vice-royaux de toucher directement le public sans passer par la presse généraliste.*

At the conference "The Crown in Canada: A Diamond Jubilee Assessment" in Regina in October 2012, John Fraser and Phillip Crawley had a conversation about the role the media plays in reporting and commenting on the Crown. Both Fraser and Crawley have been working journalists for most of their professional lives, and to some extent still are, but today Fraser is the master of Massey College at the University of Toronto and Crawley is the publisher and chief executive officer of the *Globe and Mail*, Canada's national newspaper. The discussion was amiable and anecdotal. Although the two men do not see eye to eye on everything, they are both supporters of the status quo for the Crown as it functions in Canada, with Crawley being the more practical of the two and Fraser the more romantic.

Fraser began the discussion by asking Crawley whether or not the *Globe and Mail* was still as "confused" about the role of the Crown as it had been a few years ago. Crawley responded with a laugh and an interesting account of the shifting editorial viewpoints of various editors:

> When Richard Doyle and Norman Webster were editors, the newspaper followed a traditional and enthusiastic line of support for the Sovereign.

> But [William] Thorsell argued that the Crown was something left over from colonialism and suggested that the head of state of Canada should be chosen, or elected, by the Companions of the Order of Canada, which was—shall we say—an adventurous suggestion. Since then, however, the *Globe and Mail* has returned to a straightforward position of supporting the constitutional status quo.

Crawley asked Fraser about his own days of royal and vice-regal coverage in Canada, which elicited a couple of anecdotes featuring the Queen Mother and Governor General Georges Vanier, but then the discussion became a little more serious as they scrutinized the role of the media. Both men agreed that the media and the Crown were hopelessly intertwined, the Crown needing the media to get its message across to a wider public than it could reach on its own, and the media using the Crown to engender reader or viewer interest, whether for ill or for good. Crawley made the point that the media does not have to apologize for covering peripheral members of the Royal Family who occasionally misbehave, because this is perceived as genuine news. Fraser reiterated the familiar point that the British press were deferential to a fault during the notorious period of events leading to the abdication of King Edward VIII.

Both men observed a decline in deference toward traditional sources of respect, not only in the media but throughout Western societies, but neither was comfortable blaming the media as chief culprit. The traditional defence of giving the public what it wants made a few appearances, but then the discussion became earnest when the British hacking scandal entered the agenda. Both men deplored what it said about the "low end" of contemporary journalism and gave their own perspectives on the scandal.

Fraser said the worst of the hacking scandal emerged as he was writing his best-selling book, *The Secret of the Crown: Canada's Affair with Royalty.* He reported that corruption, particularly among journalists working at the British *News of the World*, had become so pervasive that some members of the Metropolitan Police, assigned to protect members of the Royal Family, actually supplied cellphone numbers to journalists knowing that private conversations would be hacked. He also told the story of a young psychiatrist, now working in Toronto, who was doing his residency in a London hospital during the early 1990s under a famous psychiatrist when he received a phone call from a journalist at the *News of the World* asking him to check his supervisor's appointment book to see if the Princess of Wales was a patient. When he declined, he was threatened with exposure of deeds he had not committed and told that the truth of the accusations would not matter as the *News of the World* assumed he "wouldn't have the means to disprove them."

This anecdote brought out a rueful observation from Crawley, who had a friend from his younger journalism days deeply implicated in the scandal and facing the possibility of a significant jail term. It was quite a moving moment as the publisher of the *Globe and Mail* talked about the responsibility of a free press and its duty to avoid going down the road of abusing its power to bully people or subvert the law.

Both men also discussed what needed to be done to improve coverage of Crown events in Canada, from royal visits to vice-regal functions. Fraser noted that the national broadcaster, the Canadian Broadcasting Corporation, was among the more problematic media players in that it still reflected a sentiment that the Crown in Canada was on the decline, whereas CTV—sometimes in startling contrast—simply followed the public mood. When William and Kate came to Canada, Fraser noted, CTV caught the mood, while CBC reported the tour as if it were a visit from a foreign head of state. Crawley pointed out that his own newspaper took a straightforward approach to the tour and, while the exuberant gushing of past years and past royal tours was gone, there nevertheless was a residue of affection and respect that was duly noted by journalists who covered the events. But, he noted, that did not mean the *Globe and Mail* would shy away from difficult stories that were justified on the basis of solid research and commentary from legitimate observers.

Both men agreed that the federal government's championing of the Crown after many years of neglect had made a huge difference, not only in restored respect but also in renewed questioning of the institution. That, said Fraser, was always going to be the case. No institution in the country can escape public scrutiny, and journalism is the most obvious tool for such scrutiny. Crawley concluded the discussion by saying that the new generation of royals and the increased profiles of vice-regal figures in the provinces and at Rideau Hall signal a general renewal in the institution.

5

Educating Canadians on the Crown – A Diamond Jubilee Challenge

Peter H. Russell

La méconnaissance du public quant au rôle de la Couronne dans notre régime parlementaire a de sérieuses incidences pratiques. Pour bien mesurer ce rôle, il est indispensable aux Canadiens de comprendre pourquoi, dans une démocratie parlementaire, les fonctions de chef d'État et de chef de gouvernement sont des charges distinctes exercées par des titulaires différents. Une fois ce principe établi, on voit plus clairement l'intérêt d'avoir à la tête du pays un monarque plutôt qu'un chef d'État républicain. L'autre défi consiste à faire connaître le pouvoir de réserve de la Couronne s'agissant de protéger la démocratie parlementaire, ce qu'elle fait en dressant un compte rendu officiel et accessible des principes, pratiques et conventions de notre régime parlementaire. La troisième et la plus urgente des mesures à prendre pour éduquer les Canadiens consiste à combler le vide observé dans les programmes scolaires d'instruction civique au sujet du fonctionnement des gouvernements parlementaires et du rôle de la Couronne.

The Canadian monarchical story is a colourful and fascinating part of Canada's heritage, and should be much better known. My hat is off to people such as Garry Toffoli and Arthur Bousfield at the Canadian Royal Heritage Trust for being sturdy and indefatigable custodians of that history, and writers such as John Fraser[1] for bringing that history alive and making it accessible to the Canadian public. Important as the work of these historians of the Canadian Crown is, it does not address the knowledge gap about the Crown that has the most serious practical consequences for the operation of parliamentary democracy in Canada. That gap is the Crown's constitutional role in Canada's parliamentary system of government. The great majority of Canadians have scarcely a clue about this function of the Crown.

As Nathan Tidridge shows,[2] the textbooks used in high school civics courses teach young Canadians that the representatives of the Crown in Canada are nothing more than figureheads. They fail to explain that, though the Crown no longer rules, those vested with its authority continue to hold powers that can play a vital reserve role in the operation of our parliamentary system of government. The purpose of that role today, far from being to interfere with parliamentary democracy, is to secure responsible government from being changed into a system of unaccountable, prime ministerial government.

The Crown's Constitutional Role in Parliamentary Democracy

Canadians generally know that the Queen and her representatives from time to time turn up in Parliament to perform some ceremonial duty—in particular, reading the speech from the throne at the opening of Parliament. When the Queen, the governor general, or a lieutenant governor intones the cheery banalities of the throne speech, the public fully realizes that the royal representative is reciting the ideas of politicians who head up the government. Some members of the public also know that before a bill passed by a provincial legislature or by both houses of the federal Parliament becomes law, it must receive royal assent, and they expect that assent to be given automatically.

But what the public generally knows little about is that the Crown exercises powers that are vital to the life and death of Parliament. It is the Crown that summons, prorogues, and dissolves Parliament. Although in the vast majority of cases, the Queen and those exercising her powers in Canada perform these functions on the advice of prime ministers whose ministries command the confidence of the House of Commons, there are occasions when they must be guided by their own independent judgment. This right—nay, this duty—of the Crown to exercise independent judgment in performing a function of crucial importance to parliamentary democracy falls under the category of reserve powers of the Crown.

In the democratic age in which we like to think we live, it will not do to have a person who is unelected—and even worse—who inherited an office perform any function of government that is substantively important. That is why, in order to survive into the age of democracy, the British monarch acquiesced in exercising nearly all of the powers formally vested by law in the Crown only on the advice of ministers accountable to a democratically elected legislature. Monarchs in other parliamentary countries survived by making the same accommodation with democracy.

But in the United Kingdom and in other countries that adopted the Westminster model of parliamentary democracy, a small reserve of real power and responsibility remains in the hands of the Crown. It is most essential for the public to understand why this residue of discretionary royal power remains and what principles should govern its exercise.

Duality at the Top of Parliamentary States

The crucial point for citizens of parliamentary democracies to understand is that the head of government cannot also be the head of state. In a parliamentary democracy, it is the legislature that decides who will be prime minister and head up the government. Most of the time, elections make it clear which party's leaders have majority support in the Parliament the people have elected. But there may be occasions when it is not clear, and then someone other than the incumbent prime minister must decide who should be asked to form a government. In a constitutional monarchy, it is the monarch as head of state, or a vice-regal official acting with the Sovereign's delegated authority, who may have to exercise independent judgment in deciding who should be invited to be prime minister in those relatively rare situations where it is not clear who has the support of a majority in the elected chamber of Parliament.

Why should it not be up to the incumbent prime minister to decide whether to remain prime minister after an election? That was precisely what one of Prime Minister Stephen Harper's former advisors, Tom Flanagan, argued should be the case in a real democracy.[3] Flanagan advanced this argument in January 2009, after the prorogation of Parliament allowed the Harper government to avoid a likely vote of non-confidence. It was Flanagan's contention that if that non-confidence motion had carried against the government, Prime Minister Harper would have had the right to demand that the governor general dissolve Parliament and hold an election—even though less than three months had elapsed since the last election and there was strong evidence that the leader of the opposition could form a coalition government that could hold the confidence of the House of Commons.

Flanagan argued that Canada has moved beyond "the antiquated machinery of responsible government from the pre-democratic age." In the democratic age, the choice of who should lead the government should be made directly by the people rather than indirectly by members of Parliament. Flanagan did not stipulate whether the people's choice should be determined by whose party gets the most votes or the most seats in the House of Commons. But in either case, Canada's parliamentary democracy should now be one in which the will of the people was the predominant factor in deciding who governs. Flanagan argued that elections should be held to change governments because "Canada changed from a constitutional monarchy to a constitutional democracy."[4]

A group of constitutional scholars (of which the author was one) published a rebuttal of Flanagan, arguing the case for the Crown's reserve power, in certain circumstances, to refuse a prime minister's request for dissolution.[5] Although the scholars argued their case well, it did not seem to resonate with the general public, in particular the majority of Canadians who, according to survey data, believe that the prime minister of Canada is directly elected.[6] What members of the public do not understand is why direct election of the head of government will not work well in a parliamentary system of government. The problem—and indeed the educational challenge—is that they do not understand or recognize how parliamentary democracy differs from the American presidential/congressional government, whose politics many Canadians follow as closely as their own. In the American system, there is no duality at the top. The president is directly elected by the people and is both the head of state and the head of government. In parliamentary systems, the people elect a Parliament which in turn determines who will head the government. The head of government is not the head of state. The head of state's role is to ensure that government is directed by members of Parliament who command the confidence of the Parliament the people have elected.

If people can grasp this fundamental difference between parliamentary government and presidential/congressional government, they can understand the difficulty in having the people directly determine who should be prime minister. If the leader of the party that gets the most House of Commons seats automatically becomes prime minister and remains prime minister until the electorate gives another party a plurality of seats, it may be very difficult for government to function. If the prime minister does not have a majority in the House of Commons, the government may soon lose a confidence vote, in which case it would call another election—which might produce much the same result as the previous election. A system in which only the prime minister can call an election, and only new elections can determine who is prime minister, could produce a steady diet of elections, which, as Eugene Forsey pointed out years ago, would be the death of democracy.[7]

Canada could, of course, abandon responsible government and adopt the American presidential/congressional system. That would require a huge constitutional change for which there seems to be little support in Canada. Nor is the idea of directly electing the prime minister all that practical or appealing. The only country I know of that has this arrangement is Israel, where the prime minister is elected in an election separate from the one that elects the Parliament or Knesset. The prime minister must lead the government even if opposition parties are in a majority in the Knesset. Such a system would be a very hard sell in Canada. I should add that Israel as a parliamentary system has duality at the top. An indirectly elected president as head of state provides some stability in the event that the parliamentary system breaks down.

Parliamentary Republics versus Parliamentary Monarchies

In our parliamentary tradition, it is the monarch as head of state, or his or her vice-regal representative, who protects parliamentary democracy and possesses reserve powers to intervene on those rare occasions when it is unclear who holds the confidence of the House of Commons. But this function need not be performed by a monarch or vice-regal representative. Indeed, the majority of parliamentary democracies have non-monarchical, republican heads of state. Pretty well all of the newer parliamentary democracies in the Commonwealth and in the former Soviet Bloc countries of Eastern and Central Europe are republics. But monarchy predates democracy. The monarchies that have survived were successful in accommodating democracy, or, as in Spain, helping to restore democracy. Many Commonwealth countries became parliamentary republics because of the British Crown's association with imperial rule, not because they thought a republican head of state would better serve their parliamentary democracy. In Canada, republican sentiment is fuelled mostly by nationalist sentiment—the view that our head of state should be a Canadian. I have not heard Canadian republicans argue that a republican head of state would be better equipped to secure parliamentary democracy.

It is at this point in facing the educational challenge that we need to assess the value of our monarchical arrangements for parliamentary democracy. For modern parliamentary democracies, monarchy is not the most obvious form for the head of state. Nowadays, parliamentary republics do not contemplate becoming monarchies, whereas virtually all parliamentary monarchies face a republican challenge. The burden of proof, so to speak, rests with the advocates of constitutional monarchy.

The Merits of Monarchy

The clearest benefit of monarchical heads of state for parliamentary democracies is the Crown's independence of partisan politics. On those rare occasions in which the head of state may have to intervene and make a judgment as to which party leader has the best chance of commanding the confidence of the elected house of the legislature, it is an advantage to have a head of state who does not owe her office to the support of any political party. By way of contrast, heads of state in modern parliamentary republics have come to office through either direct election by the people or indirect election by the legislature. In either case, their electoral success will have been facilitated by partisan support. In modern democracies, elections cannot be won without some partisan support. So the republican president will come to office with some partisan colouring and will lack the political neutrality of the monarch or non-partisan vice-regal representative. In the 1990s, when the *Globe and Mail* was supporting republicanism, it proposed that partisanship could be avoided by having a new Canadian head of state chosen by Companions of the Order of Canada. But the chances of selling this proposal to Canadians are virtually nil, as would be the chances of insulating the internal politics of the Order from partisan politics.

As David E. Smith notes in his contribution to this book, this built-in advantage of the monarchical head of state may be undermined in Commonwealth countries where appointed vice-regal officials exercise the monarch's powers in relation to local parliaments. Once Commonwealth prime ministers took over the power of selecting governors general, they were tempted to select political colleagues who had served in their governments. This, I believe, was a serious mistake. Fortunately, the last three Canadian governors general have not had the clear partisan alignments of a number of their predecessors.

A parliamentary system with a monarchical head of state also averts the danger of having the duality at the top of a parliamentary democracy—president and prime minister—occupied by two leaders who both claim to have a popular mandate. The risk here is of having two sheriffs in town, and the one who is supposed to be mainly a figurehead not being content with such limited power. The risk is greatest when the president is directly elected, and as recent Australian history so clearly demonstrated, once the people smell a republic coming, they are unlikely to settle for anything less than a president they elect. The 1999 Australian referendum rejected a constitutional convention's proposal for a republican head of state indirectly elected by the federal Parliament because most Australians favoured direct election.[8]

In terms of the personal qualities one looks for in a good parliamentary head of state, the institutional argument for monarchy is less strong. Nonetheless, I think it can be said that monarchs and their vice-regal representatives are at least as likely as presidents to have the requisite quotients of knowledge of public affairs, decency and good judgment, love of country, and personal charm and energy. Indeed, my impression of the track record of monarchical and republican heads of state is that, on the whole, the stronger performers have been on the monarchical side. Commonwealth monarchies, in their head of state arrangements, get the glitter and glamour of the royals combined with the local sensibilities and accessibility of governors general and lieutenant governors. I doubt that presidential replacements could match this combination.

Finally, there is one other advantageous feature of the personal side of monarchy that we are reminded of, as we and all the world follow with intense interest the birth and early days of a possible future sovereign. Our head of state is grounded in family relations that make the institution so utterly human and close to our own life experiences. This invests our head of state with a humanity republicans can only envy.

Writing It All Down

Whether monarchical or republican, there is the question of knowing what should guide the head of state on those rare occasions when intervention to maintain parliamentary democracy may be necessary. This is the second part of the educational challenge.

In monarchical systems such as ours the answer has been "constitutional conventions"—so-called unwritten constitutional rules, practices, and principles. In recent years here in Canada, and elsewhere in the Westminster parliamentary world, faith in the efficacy of unwritten constitutional conventions has worn rather thin. I am one of those who have lost faith. In *Parliamentary Democracy in Crisis*, reflecting on the difficult position the governor general was in when she was advised by Prime Minister Harper in December 2008 to prorogue Parliament, I wrote:

> This situation suggests that the time has come to bring those spooky unwritten constitutional conventions down from the attic of our collective memory and try to see if we can pin them down in a manner that is politically consensual and popularly accessible.[9]

Since then, there has been growing support for Canada's emulating New Zealand and Great Britain in developing a succinct, publicly accessible document, which in those countries is called a *Cabinet Manual*.[10] These cabinet manuals set out many of the agreed-upon practices of parliamentary and cabinet government and the principles that underlie them. Some scholars and commentators press further and advocate "writing it all down" so that there are precise-enough rules that the need for the monarch or vice-regal officer to exercise discretion in heeding the advice of elected officials is completely eliminated.[11] Though I remain a strong supporter of a Canadian cabinet manual along the lines of New Zealand's and the UK's, I would like to stress the limits of what can be written down. It is misleading to think of such a manual in terms of a detailed rule book, like the rules of baseball, designed to cover every possible situation and eliminate any exercise of judgment on the part of the umpire. Even the rules of baseball—and other games—do not go that far. And we can never get anywhere close to those rule books in codifying the principles, practices, and rules of parliamentary / cabinet government.

Consider a couple of examples: first, the role of the Crown when the electorate returns a "hung parliament." Both the New Zealand and UK manuals stress the point that the main responsibility of sorting out who should be asked to form a government after such an election rests with the parliamentary leaders, not the Crown. Indeed, the politicians should try to avoid calling upon the governor general or the Sovereign by taking time to work out which party or combination of parties has the best chance of commanding the confidence of Parliament. Acceptance of this practice by all party leaders does not forever eliminate the possible exercise of Crown discretion in the formation of government, but makes it much less likely to be called into play. I should add that political consensus on this point would ensure that Parliament, not the party leader with the most seats, decides who should govern.

A second example is caretaker governments. Since it is a fundamental principle of parliamentary democracy that the government commands the confidence of the elected house of Parliament, the powers of government should be restricted when it cannot be known whether the government has that confidence. When might that be? The New Zealand and UK manuals identify three such occasions: the period after Parliament is dissolved up to the election of a new Parliament; immediately after an election if no party has a majority in the House; and following the loss of a confidence vote. The manuals also contain rules that restrict government activities under the caretaker convention: no major policy initiatives or long-term commitments or senior appointments should be made during these periods. There is also provision for emergency situations in which government must take an important initiative. It should be noted that these rules are expressed in fairly general terms, leaving room for judgment on the part of the Crown—for instance, in making appointments.

Some rules relating to the Crown's reserve powers could be written down more firmly than in a cabinet manual. An example is the summoning of Parliament after an election. The New Zealand and Australian constitutions both have sections prescribing the maximum time that can elapse after an election before the new Parliament is summoned by the Crown (six weeks in New Zealand and a month in Australia). The UK has a well-established practice of the Sovereign being asked to summon Parliament no later than three weeks after an election. But in Canada we have no provision or established practice on this matter, and we have had the experience of prime ministers waiting for nearly five months before asking the governor general to summon Parliament. I have advocated inserting a thirty-day requirement in our written Constitution.[12]

Some other matters relating to the Crown-in-Parliament, such as whether a request to prorogue Parliament should require a majority vote in the House of Commons and what constitutes a vote of non-confidence, would be more appropriate for Parliament to regulate by its rules and procedures than through a cabinet manual. The Canadian Parliament and many provincial legislatures have endeavoured to reduce the uncertainty about when the Crown should dissolve Parliament by passing fixed-date election laws. The federal Parliament did so in 2007. In 2009, Justice Shore of the Federal Court rejected a challenge to Prime Minister Harper's calling a snap election in 2008 on the grounds that in passing the fixed-date election law, Parliament did not intend to bind the advice a prime minister gives to the governor general because that would be tantamount to binding the Crown. That decision should not go unchallenged because it completely subverts Parliament's intention to prevent snap elections.

So, while not every aspect of the Crown's role in parliamentary government can or should be covered in a Canadian cabinet manual, achieving as much as New Zealand and the United Kingdom have done with their cabinet manuals would be a remarkable step forward in civic education in Canada. That is the greatest benefit of a cabinet manual. It will not remove the possibility of disputes and crises arising over the conventional part of our Constitution. But by describing in good, plain language how the different parts of our parliamentary/cabinet system of government work—including the role of the Crown—a cabinet manual would serve as a citizens' textbook for parliamentary principles and practices that are not set down authoritatively anywhere else.

Taking Up the Education Challenge in the Classroom

Let me conclude with a few words about addressing the educational challenge in the classrooms of the nation.

Canadian political scientists, notably Henry Milner and Paul Howe,[13] have demonstrated through penetrating empirical research something that many of us suspected was the case. Their research shows a marked decline in civic literacy among young Canadians. That decline is evident in falling voter turnout among the youngest voters. This civic illiteracy extends to all aspects of government and politics and most certainly to the role of the Crown in our parliamentary democracy. If most of our older citizens have at best the shakiest of ideas on the role of the Crown, we can imagine how this subject must be a deep black hole for our citizens-to-be.

Nathan Tidridge, an award-winning Ontario secondary school teacher, has written an excellent book to support teaching young Canadians about Canada's constitutional monarchy.[14] In 2012, Tidridge wrote to Ontario's education authorities pointing out that the role of the Crown is not addressed in history or civics courses in our schools, urging them to remedy this situation. He backed up his submission to Ontario's Ministry of Education with a memorandum analyzing the inaccuracies and inadequacies of the "Trillium List" of textbooks approved by the ministry for use in Ontario schools. Tidridge argues that these approved textbooks are riddled with misleading and erroneous statements.[15] For example, one states that the prime minister is the leader of the party with the most seats in the House of Commons, without any mention of the need to command the confidence of the House. The Crown fares even worse: one text implies that the Queen is nothing more than a British connection, and another highlights the "republic of Canada" in the "Fight for Responsible Government."

The Churchill Society for the Advancement of Parliamentary Democracy strongly supported Nathan Tidridge's submissions to the Ontario Ministry of Education. Drawing from the literature on civic education, Tidridge and I proposed a format that might be used to teach about the Crown's role in Parliament. Henry Milner, among others, advocates the use of simulation as the most effective methodology in civics education. Pedagogical research shows that students learn and retain more when classroom teaching is supplemented by participation in a simulated situation—be it a press conference, a parliamentary debate, or an election. We proposed a simulated constitutional crisis involving the governor general or lieutenant governor, to be tried on an experimental basis in a small sample of Ontario schools.

Conclusion

To sum up, I urge a three-pronged approach to meeting the challenge of educating Canadians on the Crown.

First is filling the most fundamental gap in Canadians' understanding of the role of the Crown in Canada's Westminster system of government. Citizens need a better grasp of the key structural difference between parliamentary democracy and presidential/congressional systems: in parliamentary systems the head of state and the head of government are different offices held by different people, whereas in presidential/congressional systems the directly elected president is both head of state and head of government. Once people grasp the duality at the top of parliamentary states, they will more easily understand why some reserve of power must be left in the hands of the head of state in a parliamentary democracy, be it a republican president or a monarch. And in turn, the advantage of the head-of-state role being performed by a person untainted by partisan politics, which are necessarily involved in getting elected (directly or indirectly) as president, becomes more evident.

Second is educating people about the conventions that pertain to the proper exercise of the Crown's constitutional powers in a parliamentary democracy. In Canada, up to now, these conventions have remained "unwritten" in that there is no authoritative document describing them. New Zealand and the United Kingdom have recognized the need in the contemporary era for a well-written, succinct, and publicly accessible description of the agreed-upon principles and practices of parliamentary democracy. That is what their cabinet manuals provide. Canada would benefit greatly from producing a similar document that, among other things, would educate the public on the Crown's role in our system of responsible government.

Third, there is an urgent need to prepare tomorrow's citizens for participation in our parliamentary democracy. Civics education in Canadian schools today ranges from the non-existent to the inadequate and erroneous. We are systematically denying young Canadians the opportunity of understanding the distinctive nature of our parliamentary democracy, including the important role of the Crown in securing its integrity.

For those of us who understand and respect the role of the Crown in our system of government, taking up the three prongs of this educational challenge is a fitting assignment following our monarch's Diamond Jubilee.

Notes

1. John Fraser, *The Secret of the Crown: Canada's Affair with Royalty* (Toronto: House of Anansi Press, 2012).
2. Nathan Tidridge, "Ontario Civics Textbooks and Their Errors concerning the Canadian Crown," presented at the conference "The Crown in Canada: A Diamond Jubilee Assessment," Regina, October 2012.
3. Tom Flanagan, "Only Voters Have the Right to Decide on the Coalition," *Globe and Mail,* January 9, 2009, A13.
4. Ibid.
5. "What Happens Next If PM Loses Vote on Coming Budget?" *The Star*, January 23, 2009, AA6.
6. "In Wake of Constitutional Crisis, New Survey Demonstrates That Canadians Lack Basic Understanding of Our Country's Parliamentary System," *Ipsos.com*, December 15, 2008, http://ipsos-na.com/news/.
7. Eugene Forsey, *Freedom and Order* (Toronto: McClelland & Stewart, 1974).
8. See Steve Vizard, *Two Weeks in Lilliput: Bear-Baiting and Backbiting at the Constitutional Convention* (Ringwood, Victoria: Penguin, 1998).
9. Peter H. Russell, "Learning to Live with Minority Parliaments," in *Parliamentary Democracy in Crisis*, ed. Peter H. Russell and Lorne Sossin (Toronto: University of Toronto Press, 2009), 148.
10. Cabinet Office, Department of the Prime Minister and Cabinet, *Cabinet Manual, 2008* (Wellington: New Zealand Government, 2008); Cabinet Office, *The Cabinet Manual: A Guide to Laws, Conventions and Rules on the Operation of Government* (London: Cabinet Office, 2011).
11. See, for example, Peter Aucoin, Mark D. Jarvis, and Lori Turnbull, *Democratizing the Constitution: Reforming Responsible Government* (Toronto: Emond Montgomery Publications, 2011).
12. Peter H. Russell, *Two Cheers for Minority Government: The Evolution of Canadian Parliamentary Democracy* (Toronto: Emond Montgomery Publications, 2008), 147.
13. Henry Milner, *The Internet Generation: Engaged Citizens or Political Dropouts* (Medford, MA: Tufts University Press, 2010); Paul Howe, *Citizens Adrift: The Democratic Disengagement of Young Canadians* (Vancouver: University of British Columbia Press, 2010).
14. Nathan Tidridge, *Canada's Constitutional Monarchy* (Toronto: Dundurn, 2011).
15. Nathan Tidridge, see note 2 above.

Part 2

Crown and Constitution

6

The Crown in Canada Today: How Dignified, How Efficient?

David E. Smith

Parle-t-on trop ou trop peu de la Couronne dans le Canada d'aujourd'hui ? Comment le savoir vraiment puisqu'on ne peut déterminer sur quelles bases répondre à la question. Mais peut-être est-il malvenu de s'interroger sur l'importance (ou l'inutilité) de la Couronne. Plutôt, soutient l'auteur, mieux vaudrait se demander ce que signifie pour les Canadiens et leurs pratiques administratives le fait que leur pays soit une monarchie constitutionnelle dont le souverain réside dans un autre pays.

Il y a 145 ans, dans The English Constitution, *Walter Bagehot établissait une distinction entre les éléments de cette constitution qui relèvent de la « dignité » et de l'« efficacité ». La dignité émanait ainsi de la Couronne et de la Chambre des lords, l'efficacité revenant au cabinet et à la Chambre des communes. Dans le Canada d'aujourd'hui, avance ici David Smith, la Couronne elle-même incarne ces deux aspects : le premier, fondé sur le comportement solennel et royal de la reine, et le second, fondé sur l'action gouvernementale et politique de ses représentants. L'une et l'autre de ces dimensions ont peu à peu gagné en importance dans la vie politique canadienne, conclut l'auteur, qui examine les raisons de cette dichotomie nationale relativement récente.*

In the year of Confederation, British journalist Walter Bagehot, then editor of the *Economist*, published a series of political essays under the title *The English Constitution*.[1] In the nearly century and a half since its appearance, the book has served as a primer on constitutional monarchy in British-styled parliamentary systems. This is the guide the Queen, Prince Charles, and Prince William have read to prepare for the role fate has assigned them. Presumably—although I am less confident of this than I used to be—their first ministers have read it, too. While the scope of his investigation is broader than the following comment might convey, it is true that Bagehot remains the master interpreter of the royal part of the Constitution, which, it needs stressing, is the same in principle in its relationship to Parliament at Ottawa or Regina, Canberra or Wellington, as it is at Westminster. By contrast, practice in a country such as Canada, where sections 9 through 16 of the Constitution Act, 1867 entrench the Crown as the executive power, is not so easily stated. Constitutional monarchy requires interpreters—for example, Bagehot on one side of the Atlantic, Eugene Forsey on the other—because there are few statutes that circumscribe monarchy, except perhaps those dealing with matters such as succession. Its place in Canada's Constitution is generally accepted as being based on convention, that is, widely shared understandings about how the institution works. I could have written "how the *system* works," but that would be wrong. Constitutional monarchy is not a *system* of government, such as provided in the constitutions of the Fifth Republic in France or the United States. It stands alone and, indeed, for much of English history, apart from Parliament. The Glorious Revolution of 1688, which saw Parliament invite William and Mary to ascend the throne, marked the beginning of devolution of monarchical power to politicians that has continued to this day, and indeed is not yet complete.

I apologize for this lugubrious introduction to a chapter occasioned by a rare and joyous event—the sixtieth anniversary of the Sovereign's accession. Elizabeth II now surpasses George III, who became King a year after the battle of the Plains of Abraham, and trails Victoria by four years as the longest reigning monarch in British history. Together, the three—George III, Victoria, and Elizabeth II—have ruled for 184 years of Canada's 252-year history. Whatever one's constitutional sympathy, and with Canadians it really is difficult to tell (Are they closet republicans, phlegmatic monarchists, or just congenitally passive about this subject as with every other subject except hockey?), it is rather hard to ignore such regal persistence. Indeed, the current government of Canada has promoted the royal presence, as evident in the reinstitution of the designation "royal" for the Canadian navy and air force, and in the edict from Ottawa that the Sovereign's photograph be prominently displayed in chancelleries abroad and in government offices at home.

As important as the visual image may be, it is the intellectual concept of the Crown that is the focus of this chapter. For this reason, it is useful to return to Bagehot. His famous work provides an explanation of the relationship between the different parts of the Constitution: Cabinet to Commons, Commons to Lords, and the three of them to the Crown. In the twenty-first century, it is difficult to appreciate the originality of this interpretation, since we have long accepted this view as self-evident. Yet before he wrote, the parts of the Constitution had scarcely more coherence than scenes from a historical drama on *Masterpiece Theatre*: a king here, a prime minister there, an archbishop in the background, dynastic intrigue, patrician Whigs, countrified Tories, and beyond the walls of Parliament, yeoman farmers and sharp-eyed shopkeepers. What did it all mean? The order Bagehot imposed on this political kaleidoscope was as follows: there were efficient or active institutions (the Commons and the

Cabinet) that did things; and there were dignified or passive institutions (the Crown and the Lords) that personified the state, symbolized morality, and represented society. The use of the Crown lay not in what it did so much as in what it meant to people. The Crown *was* its subjects. This interpretation Bagehot thought to be self-evident. Everyone understood what Queen Victoria was there for. Moreover, she lived a resplendent life (even in mourning): church, family, army, navy, estates, and except for the occasional churlish Irish republican, adoringly loyal subjects in all parts of the globe painted pink. Everyone loved a show, and this was as good as it got. In 1867, Great Britain was the most prosperous and stable country on earth, and its political institutions universally admired.

Bagehot's main object was to explain the role of the House of Commons in the Constitution, a subject in need of elaboration if Gilbert and Sullivan's contemporaneous depiction of peers and princes in *Iolanthe* and *The Mikado* was any indication of public appreciation of governmental matters. The year *The English Constitution* appeared saw the second, and this time massive, expansion of the franchise for men; the first had been in 1832 and the third would be in 1885. For political observers, the important question was how these tens of thousands of new male voters would be accommodated in British politics. From Bagehot's perspective, the Crown had an essential part to play in this acculturation—as a focus of allegiance or, more crudely put, as a pacifier. In this endeavour in the last half of the nineteenth century, the Crown and the people were joined in a mutually dependent but beneficial relationship, one that never existed in Canada, in large part because the franchise here was conferred at the outset *en masse* on men.

The extension of the franchise is one of several instances in British history where the personal bond between monarch and people was overtly articulated in a manner seldom seen in Canada, except perhaps within the context of the imperial-colonial relationship (Sir Robert Borden's invocation during the First World War of "One Empire, One Flag, One Navy" being a notable example of the exception).[2] I say this while recognizing that in 2012 in Niagara-on-the-Lake, where I live, every second lamppost flew a Union Jack, and every fifth able-bodied male on weekends donned the redcoat of a British regular and invariably routed the American invader, who never seemed to learn that he was destined to lose. Still, I treat such contradictory evidence to my generalization as aberrant behaviour destined to disappear after 2014. There is no Canadian Shakespeare and, more to the point, no Henry V as conceived by Shakespeare: "For he today that sheds his blood with me shall be my brother." This is not to depreciate the strength of loyalty Canadians, of British origin or not, may hold for their Sovereign (especially in the decades before the Second World War), but it draws a contrast between the mother country and Canada—strength of the personal tie to the Crown in the former, its tenuousness in the latter. That contrast is central to understanding the place of the Crown in Canada today. For in this country, the Crown is about *both* form and substance. If Bagehot categorized institutions as dignified and efficient, in twenty-first century Canada the Crown itself is similarly divided, between the pomp and circumstance of ceremony and the uninspiring reality of grey-suited government.

When I began teaching Canadian politics half a century ago—before the arrival of the Internet—I did what young professors usually did: kept a clipping file on, among other topics, parliamentary institutions, interest groups, political parties, and federalism. I also had one on the Crown. I discovered that, while the other folders expanded, the one devoted to the Crown remained ever thin. Few people wrote about the Crown, and the few who did usually said the same thing: the Crown was a unifying institution; it symbolized all that was good about Canada; and it offered a dramatic contrast to the configuration of political life in the United States (our neighbour being for political, as for most purposes, the "significant other"). I found these assertions unconvincing, particularly as Canada in the last half of the twentieth century moved, under direction of the Liberal Party, toward a national, non-royal identity depicted through distinctive flags, anthems, educational curricula, and even stamps and money, and through the transformation of the office of governor general into a "Canadianized" institution—although we never went as far as some European countries to rename thoroughfares (Victoria Avenue in Regina is still Victoria Avenue and not the Avenue of the Constitution Act, 1982). The more Mr. Diefenbaker railed against the loss of royal insignia, the more antique and niche-like the topic became: a carapace of the *ancien régime*. Nonetheless, while the Crown as an emblem of monarchy seemed to be evaporating, the Crown as an instrument of government assumed new form and prominence.

Although the Queen as a model of the modern monarch remained ever popular but seldom present, the visibility of the Crown in public life seemed to grow daily, if on occasion in contradictory ways. Canada's commitment to United Nations peacekeeping, along with the unification of the military services in the late 1960s, contributed to a decline in public perception of the military (think regiments and armouries) as an historic arm of the Crown in Canada. Yet, at almost the same time, the identification of the Crown as protector of First Nations, along with references, for example, to the Royal Proclamation of 1763 (from year three of George III's reign), began to appear with regularity in mainstream media, as First Nations exerted treaty and land claims through challenges in law and in the (Queen's) courts. Again, and also contemporaneously, there was the development of an array of civilian honours, first nationally (the Order of Canada, 1967) and then in the provinces (for example, the Saskatchewan Order of Merit, 1985), which at one and the same time shared their provenance with the Crown (they are awarded by the Crown's representative in Ottawa and in the provincial capitals) but recognized "on behalf of

Canadians" the achievements of Canadians, both nationally and in the province.[3]

From my own perspective, and this may result from being a professor of politics, the primary development that has affected, moulded, or framed Canadian views of the Crown—but not monarchy—is the rise of the administrative state. Already before the Second World War, there was a growing concern (expressed far more trenchantly in the United Kingdom than in Canada) about government by the unelected. The title of Lord Hewart's book *The New Despotism* (1929) captured the alarmed tone of the critique.[4] Canada's War Measures Act, passed in 1914, which provided the basis for government during the two World Wars, accentuated this concern as wartime powers continued well into the 1950s. Much of the governing that resulted appeared as administration in the form of delegated legislation under various names (for example, orders-in-council or statutory instruments). The issue came to public prominence during the "pipeline debate" of 1956 and the general election the following year, which saw the Liberals, in power for nearly three decades, finally collapse before the Progressive Conservatives, now led by John Diefenbaker. In the words of Denis Smith (Diefenbaker's biographer), "The Conservative message that Liberal cabinets had usurped the House's powers—and thus, perhaps the country's liberties—struck popular chords."[5]

In Parliament for fifteen years, Diefenbaker had made a career out of criticizing abuse of administrative powers, among which cases were internment of Japanese Canadians in 1942, the Russian spy drama involving Igor Gouzenko in 1946, and the Jehovah's Witnesses' cases from Quebec of the 1950s. Together, these saw federal and provincial governments deny or abuse traditional civil liberties. Among many other influences, to be sure, these abuses lay behind Diefenbaker's commitment to introduce a Bill of Rights, realized in 1960. What has this to do with the Queen, already on the throne five years when Diefenbaker became prime minister? Nothing personally, it may be said, but everything to do with perceptions of the Crown as an instrument of government. If there is a theme in academic literature and media coverage of government in the last half-century, it concerns the concentration of executive power and the enfeeblement of Parliament. In Canada, cabinet, a committee of the Privy Council, is by tradition deemed "the government," but the concept of an executive, separate from Parliament, comprising the prime minister and, since the days of Pierre Trudeau, the prime minister's office, has been slowly emerging. A political reorientation was given a great boost by Preston Manning's affection for congressional government as a limitation on what he liked to call unchecked executive power in Westminster-styled parliaments.

All prime ministers labour under the indictment that they are dictators or autocrats. Maybe the charge possesses a scintilla of truth, although to my mind we have never had a Gaddafi in Ottawa. Invariably, however, claims to support the case cite one of two pieces of evidence: either use of delegated power (conferred by statute on a minister), which by definition is at one remove from Parliament, or use of prerogative power, which, also by definition, is completely removed from Parliament because it remains with the Crown, which in Canada is embodied in the Sovereign's representative, the governor general. Examples of the prerogative in action include the vast number of gubernatorial appointments made on the advice of the first minister, but not, it needs to be stressed, the appointment of senators or superior court judges, where the appointing authority is constitutionally entrenched, by sections 24 and 96 respectively, in the executive in the person of the governor general. Similarly, the conduct of foreign and military affairs is based in the main either on prerogative power or on statute, although Philippe Lagassé has convincingly argued that section 15 ("the command-in-chief of the land and naval militia") vests constitutional powers in the executive and for that reason may *not* be supplanted by statute.[6]

In recent years there has been much talk—but no action—about the need to reform and democratize government. It is worth observing that, often as not, when this subject arises what is really at issue is taming the Crown's prerogative power. When Stephen Harper first became prime minister, one of his commitments was to establish an appointments committee to vet nominations to public bodies in order to limit partisanship as the sole determinant of the selection. Implementation of that promise met with controversy, as has every public discussion of the subject: recall the election debate in 1984 between Brian Mulroney and John Turner over Turner's acceptance, when he became prime minister, of the patronage appointments Trudeau had made of individuals deemed irredeemably Liberal to positions high and low. If this, or other exercises of the prerogative, rested with Parliament and not the Crown, as some reformers have suggested they should, doubtless matters would be different since, when it came to appointments, authority would be shared; whether the quality of appointments would be better is less certain.

Some prerogative power—dissolution and prorogation of Parliament or the selection of the prime minister, for example—is not automatically exercised on advice. This so-called reserve power is used at the discretion of the Crown's representative. I will not analyze the prorogation controversies of 2008, except to note what to my mind was their most important consequence: to focus attention on the governor general. Although the attention was neither sustained nor the criticism always well-informed, in contrast to the past the focus of comment was constitutional in nature: absent was the ceremonial talk that so often had enveloped and clouded discussion of the Crown.

The most significant feature of the prorogation episode was the consensus among the public and in the media that the governor general had a central—or, in the words of this chapter's title, an efficient as opposed to a dignified—role to play in resolving the controversy. At no time did the subject of the utility of constitutional monarchy as Canada's form of government enter the debate. Indeed, quite the reverse: political scientist Tom Flanagan advanced the argument that "only voters have the right to decide on the proposed Liberal-NDP coalition [the proposal that had set the whole episode in motion]," while maintaining that it was "the Governor General, as protector of Canada's constitutional democracy, [who] should ensure the voters get [that] chance."[7] Throughout the prorogation controversy, the positions taken by participants were defined by where they sat in the House of Commons. Among the ranks of the public, partisan allegiance was almost as predictable an indicator of support or opposition to the prime minister's request. In contrast, the governor general was perceived by the public and politicians alike as impartial—almost the quintessential officer of Parliament—a genre that includes the auditor general and commissioner of official languages.

Here was a made-in-Canada controversy that took its form and found its resolution (how satisfactory depended on the observer) in the context of *Canada's* Crown. Nothing like it has happened in Great Britain, nor is it likely to happen. British politicians are scrupulous in shielding the Sovereign from the necessity of making any debatable use of the prerogative. If ever there was such constitutional sensitivity in Canada, that is no longer the case. The greater frequency of minority governments here than in the United Kingdom may be one explanation, since the pressure of governing increases when legislative majorities disappear. Yet discussions among party leaders in the United Kingdom following the general election in May 2010, where no party won a majority of seats, did not involve the Queen, until the prospective prime minister was invited to Buckingham Palace. The aura, experience, and independence of the Sovereign from government in London contrasts with the absence of these characteristics for the governor general in Ottawa. The visibility of the Sovereign is one of her strengths—just being there is enough. Arguably, the more visible Canada's governor general, the more vulnerable he or she appears. Governors general must *do* something—charity, sports, arts, the North, the disadvantaged—to anchor themselves in the public's mind and in public life. Laudable as good works may be, how do they contribute to the constitutional order?

There has been a depreciation of the stature of the Crown in Canada, and its representative, in every significant respect. Canadian governors general are appointed for a comparatively short term: at five or six years, their tenure in office is less than that of the auditor general of Canada, the chief electoral officer, or the commissioner of official languages. If Bill C-7, "An Act Respecting the Selection of Senators and Amending the Constitution Act, 1867 in Respect of Senate Term Limits," which imposes nine-year-term limits on senators, becomes law, then the governor general will have a shorter term than the senators he or she appoints. It will also be less than that of most governments.

Liberal governments from Mackenzie King onward made promotion of Canada's autonomy in the Empire and then the Commonwealth a priority. The St. Laurent papers in the National Archives have many files labelled "national status," including such subjects as the creation of Canadian citizenship, search for a distinctive flag and anthem, and more. Pearson made a distinctive flag a reality, and Trudeau brought home the Constitution with its Byzantine amending formula. Along the way he strove to Canadianize the office of governor general. There was much to celebrate in this march to nationhood, and the Liberals were masters at organizing these celebrations. There was a cost associated with this civic triumphalism, however—to the party itself, but more importantly, to the Crown in Canada. The more autonomous the Canadian polity and Constitution became from Great Britain, the more autonomous (yet exposed and vulnerable, too) was the Canadian Crown. Arguably, actions by the present (Harper) government have aggravated the problem: on the one hand they elevate the Sovereign, in contrast to policies of former Liberal and Progressive Conservative governments, while on the other hand they utilize the Sovereign's surrogate, the governor general, for what is seen in some quarters as political purposes.

When the subject of the Crown arises as symbol, or in activities separate from Parliament, the current government demonstrates a regard and a heightened concern some of its recent predecessors lacked. Paul Martin's treatment of Adrienne Clarkson or Pierre Trudeau's of Ed Schreyer come to mind.[8] This is not true of the current government when the subject is the Crown-in-Parliament, however. Consider, for instance,

> the fixed election date fiasco, the questionable use of prorogation to avoid defeat, the misuse of the confidence convention by *both* the Martin and Harper governments ... the nonsensical debate over the legitimacy of coalitions and the disingenuous musings over whether a party must have the most seats to be called upon to form a government.[9]

How is one to reconcile protestations of loyalty to the Crown, which under constitutional principles established as long ago as 1688 means the Crown-in-Parliament, with exhortations to Conservative supporters that the "party must fight ... against ... attacks on our *democratically elected government*" (emphasis added) or radio advertisements asserting that "[Dion] thinks he can take power without asking you, the voter. This is Canada. Power must be earned, not taken"?[10]

The first principle of the Canadian Constitution is that there is no constituent power outside of Parliament. Nonetheless, politics today increasingly pits the people against Parliament, or more precisely, against the opposition in Parliament—to the opposition's disadvantage, it might be said, since the opposition is less "elected" than the government and, by inference, less legitimate on that account. Of course, only the minority of Canadians know that governments are not elected. The extra-parliamentary dimension has always been an important part of Canadian politics, as a history of political parties makes clear. But it has never been as pervasive as now. Reasons external to Canadian developments may be cited for this change, the transformation in political communication one obvious example. That is a bigger topic than can be discussed here, but I do not want to ignore it and thereby suggest that what is happening in Canadian politics is solely the result of action by government. Still, there is a homegrown reason that helps explain the advent of the people. That is the extraordinary organizational activity that accompanied the creation of the Conservative Party of Canada. Its success at establishing a mass membership base and the financial security this has provided are familiar topics in the media, in part because of the edge they give the Conservatives over their competitors. Phrases like the "permanent campaign" and "the arms race that never stops" convey the sense of an external force propelling politics from outside of Parliament. How many times have MPs been told that bills before them "were part of the Conservative election platform" or that the majority government has "a clear mandate." Now that argument is coming from the other side of the House as well: on potential changes to Old Age Security, the opposition parties complained in 2012 that the prime minister "did not raise the issue in the last election and [that] he lacks a mandate to change the system."[11]

In a vast society like Canada's, built on immigration and settlement, whose Constitution is rooted in another land, the Crown could never be more than an august symbol. For much of the country's history, the Sovereign's surrogate, the governor general, represented the Sovereign to the people. After 1952, the policy of successive governments to Canadianize the Crown—one could perhaps use the Canadian neologism "patriate"—led to a change in emphasis in the relationship. Periodic royal visits continued, but the quotidian and practical world of monarchy became gubernatorial. It would be misleading to view that transition as devaluing or limiting the Crown in Canadian life. Quite the reverse, since governors general subsequently played a visible role in the quest for national unity and now are being used to transform Canada's parliamentary into an electoral democracy. Under Bill C-7, the prime minister will continue to recommend to the governor general individuals for appointment to the Senate, while at the same time promoting as nominees winners of provincially-based senatorial elections. The prime minister and the governor general can do no other without discrediting the integrity of the Crown. The Senate of Canada is being more than reformed—it is being transformed, by statute rather than constitutional amendment, out of recognition from the institution the Fathers of Confederation provided for, after longer debate than on any other topic, in the constitutional settlement of 1867. As improbable as it may seem, the Crown is now the key to democratizing Canadian legislative institutions. How efficient is that? How puzzling, too? In the emerging constitutional scheme of things, what is the place of the Crown when authority is said to rest with the people?

On the occasion of the Queen's Diamond Jubilee, the Crown in Canada occupied a significantly different political space than it did at the time of her accession. In 1952, the ceremonial and constitutional Crowns were indisputably united as one. That is no longer true. There is a ceremonial Crown that may be Canadian in its activities and deportment but which remains British in derivation and associations, and there is a constitutional Crown that, for want of imagination at coining a better description, is in essence domestic.

This is beginning to sound rather like a latter-day *Tale of Two Cities*: order in one capital, anarchy in the other. Still, the point needs to be made that what is at issue here is a reservoir of real power beneath the pomp of ceremony. When Stephen Harper sought a candidate to replace Michaëlle Jean as governor general, he was reported to have established a "secret committee to search for candidates" who would possess constitutional knowledge and be non-partisan. C. E. S. Franks, a constitutional authority, praised the "new" process and "recommended that it be made permanent in law."[12] How that might be accomplished, he did not specify. Yet there was the sense that a precedent was being established and that henceforth the nomination of individuals with close partisan attachments to the government of the day would no longer be tolerated. That was not always the case; for instance, between 1984 and 1999 three successive governors general—Jeanne Sauvé, Ramon Hnatyshyn, and Roméo LeBlanc—were former cabinet ministers (in Hnatyshyn's case, a cabinet minister defeated at a general election one month before his appointment). I was not acquainted with Sauvé or LeBlanc, but I did know Hnatyshyn well and had great respect for him as MP, cabinet minister, and governor general. Nonetheless, the partisan linkage distorted the public's perception of the office. But potential partisanship now seems an antique worry. The last three governors general have not held elected office, and if the new selection process becomes the norm, which appears that it has with the creation of a new permanent committee on vice-regal appointments, no future governor general will likely have either. At the same time, the process raises the efficient while it reduces the dignified dimension of the position, an adjustment the government's elevation in Canadian life of royalty and "Britishness" reinforces. The presumption of Michaëlle Jean in describing the governor general (herself) as Canada's head of state was peremptorily and publicly rejected by the Harper government in 2009. In the matter of the executive, the government is adamant about who is agent and who principal: the first lives in Ottawa and the second in London.

The relationship between formal and political executives has altered, as may happen in a country where conventions matter, and in a manner quite different from countries where that relationship is regulated by statute law. At the same time that Canada's new governor general was being designated, Germany chose a new president through a "secret" election by a college of electors composed of members of the federal Parliament and of state representatives. Despite the institutional separation intended to discourage partisan influence, the presidential vote, according to the *New York Times*, was a "test [for] Merkel's Ailing Coalition," one that the coalition survived: "Merkel's Pick Wins German Presidency," said the *Times*.[13] No one in Germany appears to find this manner of selecting the president problematic for the intrusion of partisan politics it permits, but then, German presidents possess few of the prerogative powers that rest in the hands of Canada's governors general.

I hope that in making these remarks about the Crown, I will not suffer the same fate as Lord Altrincham, who criticized the cost of the coronation in 1953 and later described the Queen's voice as shrill. He had his faced slapped by a man on the street and was banned from appearing on the BBC. Attitudes may have changed in Great Britain, but elsewhere criticism of monarchy can still get one into trouble. In 2012, in Morocco, a magazine editor was jailed and his publication closed over an opinion poll that asked the question: "Do you approve of the King?" Ninety percent of respondents answered "yes." Prosecutors argued that his action constituted a criminal offence, since "monarchy cannot be judged." They won, he lost.

Notes

1. Walter Bagehot, *The English Constitution* (London: Oxford University Press, 1961. First printed 1867).
2. Carolyn Harris's chapter in this volume offers another example of bonds that might have existed between Canadians and members of the Royal Family in the past.
3. Christopher McCreery, *The Canadian Honours System* (Toronto: Dundurn, 2005).
4. Rt. Hon. Lord Hewart, *The New Despotism* (London: E. Benn, 1929).
5. Denis Smith, *Rogue Tory: The Life and Legend of John G. Diefenbaker* (Toronto: MacFarlane Walter and Ross, 1995), 217.
6. Philippe Lagassé, "The Crown's Powers of Command-in-Chief: Interpreting Section 15 of Canada's Constitution Act, 1867," *Review of Constitutional Studies* 15, no. 3 (2013).
7. Tom Flanagan, "Only Voters Have the Right to Decide on the Coalition," *Globe and Mail*, January 9, 2009, A13.
8. Adrienne Clarkson, *Heart Matters: A Memoir* (Toronto: Viking, 2006), 192 and 195; Robert Sheppard and Michael Valpy, *The National Deal: The Fight for the Canadian Constitution* (Toronto: Fleet Books, 1982), 1-5.
9. Paul Benoit and Gary Levy, "Viability of Our Political Institutions Being Questioned," *The Hill Times*, May 25, 2011, 15.

10. Tim Naumetz, "Conservatives 'Lay Track' to Attack Media, Real Opposition Party in New Parliament," *The Hill Times*, June 13, 2011, 1 and 6. See too, "Tories Begin Battle against Coalition," *CBC News*, December 2, 2008, http://www.cbc.ca/canada/story/2008/12/02/harper-coalition.html.
11. Mark Kennedy, "PM Says OAS Changes Being Considered," *Leader-Post* (Regina), February 4, 2012, A5.
12. Bill Curry, "Secret Committee, Seeking Non-Partisans: How Harper Found New G-G," *Globe and Mail*, July 12, 2010, 1 and 4.
13. Nicholas Kulish, "Presidential Vote Tests Merkel's Ailing Coalition in Germany," *New York Times*, June 26, 2010, A5; "Merkel's Pick Wins German Presidency," *USA Today*, July 1, 2010, 7A.

7

Commentary "Inefficient Efficiency": The Use of Vice-Regal Reserve Powers

Robert E. Hawkins

Dans son chapitre du présent ouvrage, David Smith soutient que la Couronne canadienne joue un rôle gouvernemental plus visible et plus actif que son équivalent britannique. À l'appui de son hypothèse, il cite le rôle du gouverneur général dans l'évolution du Canada vers le statut de nation, la quête d'unité nationale du pays, le fréquent usage des prérogatives royales et la proposition voulant que le gouverneur général nomme uniquement des sénateurs élus. Or, lui répond ici Robert Hawkins, la Couronne canadienne joue certes un rôle utile ou « efficace » au sein du gouvernement, mais il s'agit d'une forme « inefficiente » d'efficacité. En temps normal, la Couronne a ainsi pour rôle de ne rien faire. Et c'est demeurant un arbitre impartial que le gouverneur général peut assurer qu'en période exceptionnelle de menace contre la démocratie, la Couronne puisse faire entendre la voix du peuple. D'excellentes raisons empêchent de codifier pareilles circonstances, parmi lesquelles ont citera tout de même les menaces à la légitimité de la Constitution, la subversion de l'institution parlementaire, l'inexécutabilité du système électoral, l'incapacité de pourvoir un poste soudainement inoccupé au Cabinet du premier ministre et la paralysie induite par les activités illégales du pouvoir exécutif.

As Walter Bagehot suggests, there are two kinds of institutions that make up the English constitution: the "dignified ones" which, in Bagehot's words, win loyalty by "excit[ing] and preserv[ing] the reverence of the population," and the "efficient ones," which use that authority to make government work.[1] The dignified, but inefficient, British Crown gains the homage of the subject; the efficient, but not so dignified, British politicians employ the power created by that homage to govern.

David E. Smith, arguing that the Canadian Crown has evolved differently than the British one, turns Bagehot on his head. Except for the occasional royal tour, we "phlegmatic monarchists" have not bonded with the Crown in the same way as subjects in the Sceptred Isle. We have transformed our Crown from a dignified institution into an efficient one, that is to say, from one that "personifie[s] the state, symbolize[s] morality, and represent[s] society" into one that has a central, or active, role to play in our "grey-suited" government.[2]

Dr. Smith suggests several reasons why the Canadian Crown is perceived as having a more visible role in governing Canada than its counterpart in Britain. These reasons include the way in which Canada has evolved from colonial to national status, the Canadianization of the office of the governor general, the governor general's role in Canada's quest for unity, the centralization of executive authority in Canada with its increasing resort to the prerogative power for making a "vast number of gubernatorial appointments" and for running the administrative state, and the frequent use of prerogative powers in Canada, possibly triggered by a succession of minority governments, in matters such as prorogation. Because the vice-regal representative lacks the "aura, experience, and independence of the Sovereign," and because our politicians, unlike British politicians, have failed to shield him or her from, in David Smith's words, the "debatable use" of prerogative, our "active" governor general has become more visible, and so more exposed and more vulnerable.

The problem is not just one of exposure. David Smith also suggests that the rise of sentiment in favour of direct democracy poses a challenge. At the time of the prorogation controversy in December 2008, Harper government allies appealed to "the people," the "extra-parliamentary dimension," to "fight against attacks on our democratically elected government," under threat from the opposition coalition's invitation to the governor general to call on them to form a new government. The "advent of the people," stoked by the government's "permanent campaign—the arms race that never stops," constituted "an external force propelling politics from outside of Parliament." In Dr. Smith's view, these populist cries represented not only a misunderstanding of the first principle of the Canadian Constitution, that there is no constituent power outside of Parliament, but also a threat to the principle of Crown-in-Parliament, and so to the Crown itself.

David Smith warns of worse. At the same time that the government was fanning populist flames that menaced the Crown, it was also using the Crown as "the key to democratizing Canadian legislative institutions." The government proposed an elected senate in which the prime minister would have the governor general appoint only individuals chosen at the ballot box. How clever; how nefarious. In his peroration, Dr. Smith rhetorically asks, "In the emerging constitutional scheme of things, what is the place of the Crown when authority is said to rest with the people?"

We have been cautioned. Radical democratization risks transforming our system of Crown-in-Parliament into a system of "We the People." The Jacobins are at the gates.

Fear not. The Jacobins got through the gates some time ago, and the City has not crumbled. I agree with David Smith that the Crown has an active, or efficient, role in Canada, in the sense that it plays a visible part in making our machinery of government work. But there is a paradox in this. What makes our Crown efficient is not its efficiency, but its very inefficiency. This "inefficient efficiency" can be placed alongside the other oxymorons that convention embeds in our Constitution, oxymorons like loyal opposition, liberal democracy, and constitutional monarchy itself.

The Queen's representatives in Canada act by "not acting," do by "not doing." This recognizes the fact that the Sovereign and her representatives are unelected elements in a constitutional monarchy. How can such inefficiency be efficient? By exercising the art of "not doing," the Queen's representative safeguards his or her neutrality—deliberately, insistently, and resolutely—so that in moments of genuine constitutional crisis, he or she can take on the important and active role of constitutional arbiter. Vice-regal neutrality is a powerful sword to be wielded only when the Gordian knot tightens in a way that threatens the unwritten democratic principle that Canada's Supreme Court has given constitutional force. Perhaps it is ironic that an undemocratic actor in our system of government is cast in the role of the ultimate defender of our democracy.

A genuine constitutional crisis, as distinct from one puffed up through political posturing, cannot be resolved through the operation of normal democratic processes—by Parliament or at the ballot box. Such crises will be few and far between, in part because politicians who precipitate them will ultimately have to answer to their electors, and in part because the Charter requires that the electorate, or its representatives, be consulted in a timely fashion in order to maintain the working of representative and responsible government.[3] The governor general's role in times of crisis is to ensure that normal democratic discourse can resume.

I am reluctant to list examples of genuine constitutional crises in which normal democratic processes become blocked for fear of seeming to codify the governor general's reserve powers. Such a codification would be unconstitutional unless it was adopted in accordance with the Constitution's unanimous amending formula.[4] Such a codification would also be unworkable. Apart from the impossibility of anticipating all eventualities, its operation would risk drawing the governor general further into the political fray, while exposing the reserve powers to judicial review. Further, such a codification is unnecessary. The reserve powers are governed by convention, evolving through precedent and consensus, much as the common law evolves, without becoming an ossified body of rules.[5]

Without purporting to formulate a code, it is nonetheless possible to cite several examples of democratic constitutional failure necessitating the intervention of an impartial arbiter.

1. *The authority of the Constitution is overturned:* One thinks of King Carlos of Spain thwarting an attempted military coup in February 1981 by announcing on television his support for the legitimate democratic government.
2. *The operation of Parliament is subverted:* The prime minister refuses to summon a prorogued House within the *constitutionally* mandated time limit, or refuses to resign or recommend dissolution after losing a confidence vote in Parliament, or seeks to govern for an extended period of time using special warrants in place of having Parliament vote supply.
3. *The functioning of the electoral system is frustrated:* The prime minister refuses to call an election that is *constitutionally* due, refuses to resign or meet the House within a reasonably short period following electoral defeat, or seeks dissolution and a second election immediately following defeat at the polls in order to avoid meeting the new House. Further, in the case of a hung election, where the prime minister is unable to command a stable majority in the House, and no other party, or combination of parties, can do so either, intervention may be required.
4. *The first minister's office is abruptly vacated* and his or her party caucus is unable to designate a successor able to command the confidence of the House.
5. *The executive is implicated in illegal activity* that impairs the functioning of the state.

It has to be stressed again just how limited the "efficient" aspect of the governor general's role is in the workings of government. The intervention must be to preserve democracy, the crisis must be genuine and unambiguous, and the operation of the Constitution must be blocked such that nothing short of vice-regal intervention will restore the democratic process. Faced with a genuine threat to the Constitution, if no valid alternative exists, the governor general has the power to dissolve the House and call an election.

So, while I agree with David Smith that the Crown in Canada is an "efficient" part of the Constitution, I want to suggest that it owes its efficiency to its inefficiency. In ordinary times, the proper role of the Crown in government is inactivity. That very inactivity, however, means that in dangerous times there exists one neutral actor, with great power, able to restore constitutional order by making the democratic voice of the people heard. David Smith sees the Jacobins as a threat to the Crown; I see the Crown as their protector.

May I end on a personal note? I have read much of what David Smith has written and have had the great privilege of being his colleague in the Johnson-Shoyama Graduate School of Public Policy at the University of Regina. His chapter in this book, in its breadth of knowledge, in its originality and in its expository elegance, is entirely typical of Dr. Smith's extensive body of scholarly thought. He has mentioned Eugene Forsey in the same breath as Walter Bagehot. I would like to conclude by saying that David Smith is, in every measure, in every constitutional insight, our generation's Eugene Forsey.

Notes

1. Walter Bagehot, *The English Constitution* (London: Oxford University Press, 1961. First printed 1867), chap. 2. http://www.gutenberg.org/files/4351/4351-h/4351-h.htm#chap01.
2. Unless otherwise cited, quotations in this commentary are from David E. Smith's chapter in this volume, "The Crown: How Dignified? How Efficient?"
3. Section 4 of the Charter requires that an election be held once every five years; section 5 mandates that Parliament sit once every twelve months.
4. *Conacher v. Canada (Prime Minister)*, 2009 FC 920 (FC), par. 53; upheld on other grounds, 2010 FCA 131 (FCA); leave to appeal to the Supreme Court of Canada refused, 2011 Can Law II 2101 (SCC).
5. Eugene Forsey wrote, "To embody them [the reserve powers] in an ordinary law is to ossify them. To embody them in a written constitution is to petrify them." Quoted in Peter Boyce, *The Queen's Other Realms: The Crown and Its Legacy in Australia, Canada, and New Zealand* (Sydney: Federation Press, 2008), 61.

8

The Law of Succession and the Canadian Crown

Ian Holloway

La loi concernant l'accession au trône après le décès d'un souverain régnant repose sur certains des principes les plus simples et les plus explicites de tous ceux qui fondent notre structure constitutionnelle. Ils n'en demeurent pas moins incompris et ont été notoirement faussés il y a quelques années par un parlementaire canadien ayant proposé une moyen « tout simple » de rompre le lien unissant le Canada à la Couronne. Ce chapitre traite des principes juridiques régissant l'accession au trône et fait valoir qu'aucun d'entre eux ne supprime l'exigence pour un Canada qui désirerait devenir une république d'obtenir le consentement unanime du parlement fédéral et de chacune des dix provinces du pays, conformément à l'article 41 de la Loi constitutionnelle de 1982.

Introduction – The Age of Faithlessness

Ours is the age of faithlessness. Our grandparents might have been able to take heart in the sincere belief that, to use the words of the old parliamentary prayer, Divine Providence would continue to bless our country. But since the second half of the twentieth century—and particularly from the mid-1960s onwards—Canada has been on a seemingly relentless march toward secularism. Rather than providing succour, notions like "Divine Providence" and "blessing" today attract ridicule in mainstream society. Morality may remain a part of our civil discourse, but it is a morality grounded almost exclusively in the prejudices of the present, rather than in any view about enduring truths.

One supposes that as a matter of philosophy, this is a respectable, if arguable, view. Indeed, one could argue that far from being a creature of Yorkville and the Summer of Love, today's moral secularism is in keeping with an intellectual tradition that dates back three centuries or more, to the Age of Enlightenment. The problem, though, is that in its Canadian guise at least, secularism has now begotten a deep stream of anti-historicism. Less and less are we willing to accept the past as a yardstick against which to measure acceptability in the present. Instead, we expect things to be justified only by what we believe today, with little or no regard for yesterday or tomorrow. We mightn't actually use the term itself, but to borrow from John Ralston Saul, we seem to revel in having become Voltaire's "bastards."[1]

The perniciousness of this becomes critical in a constitutional system like Canada's, which depends to a significant extent on principles that are grounded neither in written formulation nor in a present-day version of rationality, but rather in history. In such a system, faithlessness and anti-historicism can be positively toxic to the rule of law. The rule of law can only flourish where there is broad public support for the premises of the legal system itself. The rub is that ours is a system born almost a millennium ago out of the conditions of a feudal and agrarian society. If people are not willing to accept this as a matter of foundational principle—if they are not willing to accept as authoritative the historical foundations of the rule of law—then our constitutional structure looks quite rickety indeed.

The Efficient and Dignified Parts of the Constitution

In his classic work, *The English Constitution,* which was first published in the same year as Canada's Confederation, Walter Bagehot, the great nineteenth-century essayist and editor (and failed lawyer) famously wrote of the "efficient" and "dignified" aspects of the British Constitution. The former, he said, are those parts that actually set out the rules by which governmental power operates. In the Canadian setting, this includes (perhaps most contentiously in our history) sections 91 and 92 of the Constitution Act, 1867, which distribute power between the federal and provincial governments; sections 96–101, which set out the provisions by which the superior courts operate; and sections 17–57, which speak to the exercise of legislative power at the federal level. Importantly for believers in the system of constitutional monarchy, one other "efficient" feature of the Constitution is section 9 of the Constitution Act, which vests executive authority in the Queen.

In contrast, Bagehot described the dignified parts of the Constitution as "those which excite and preserve the reverence of the population."[2] In his assertion, these were as critical to the success of constitutionalism as the efficient parts. Without constitutional dignity, efficiency was impossible: "There are two great objects which every constitution must attain to be successful.... Every constitution must first *gain* authority, and then *use* authority; it must first win the loyalty and confidence of mankind, and then employ that homage in the work of government."[3] Later, he made the same point in a slightly different formulation: "The dignified parts of Government are those which bring it force—which attract its motive power. The efficient parts only employ that power."[4]

And the Mystical

Writing as he was in the middle decades of the nineteenth century, Bagehot can hardly have been expected to anticipate the anti-historical faithlessness of the present age. But from our vantage point today, it might seem that there is a third part to the British constitutional model that is just as real, and just as essential, as the efficient and dignified parts. This is what one might call the "mystical" part—those doctrines and practices that are grounded in the mists of history and the social dramas of bygone ages. These practices might not make sense according to our present lights but remain central to the way our Constitution operates, both in law and in fact, even in the twenty-first century.

It is apparent to even the most unengaged observer that one of the most commonly heard complaints about Canada's constitutional structure concerns its mystical elements. As noted, the efficient parts of the Constitution make plain the centrality of the monarchy to our constitutional structure. In vesting executive authority over Canada in the Queen, section 9 of the Constitution Act, 1867 could not be more clear. But those who advocate a change to a republican form of government for Canada typically argue that our system of constitutional monarchy involves both a "democratic deficit" (because we do not elect the head of state) and "systemic discrimination." The system discriminates, they claim, on the basis of religion (because of the provisions of the Act of Settlement, 1701, which forbid the monarch from being in communion with the Roman Catholic Church) and gender (because of the laws of primogeniture, through which the throne passes to sons before daughters). Taken together with the fact that the Queen makes her habitual residence in the United Kingdom, these objections form a kind of secular-age holy trinity of anti-historical condemnation of the Constitution. As *Globe and Mail* columnist Margaret Wente once put it, the monarchy "embodies the triumph of inheritance over merit, of blood over brains, of mindless ritual over innovation."[5] In a vulgarly expressed nutshell, that is the case for republicanism in Canada.

The De Facto Impossibility of Removing the Queen from the Canadian Constitution

Most of the more pragmatic Canadian republicans accept that there is a tremendous wellspring of affection for Queen Elizabeth. So they often pin their hopes on the move to a republic to the moment of her passing. Typical is the spirit expressed by Jeffrey Simpson in 2009, at the beginning of a visit to Canada by the Prince of Wales, when he wrote of the Queen, "God bless her, and long may she reign over us—after which Canada should cut its ties to the British monarchy."[6] The problem, though, is that this runs up against proscriptions set out in section 41 of the Constitution Act, 1982 as follows:

> An amendment to the Constitution of Canada in relation to the following matters may be made by proclamation issued by the Governor General under the Great Seal of Canada only where authorized by resolutions of the Senate and House of Commons and of the legislative assembly of each province:
> (a) the office of the Queen, the Governor General and the Lieutenant Governor of a province;
> ...
> (e) an amendment to this Part.

Whether the credit for this should go to Prime Minister Pierre E. Trudeau as a closet monarchist (which one doubts), most observers have assumed that section 41 would be a significant barrier to any move toward a Canadian republic. The Citizens for a Canadian Republic suggest that "the degree of difficulty in obtaining provincial approval is overrated,"[7] but section 41's requirement of unanimity among the ten provinces is something that constitutional pragmatists, even of the republican variety, acknowledge is politically unlikely ever to be achieved—barring a truly national catastrophe, which would make the impetus for changing the form of government seem like small beer.

"The McWhinney Solution"

Section 41's requirement of unanimity has led some to seek alternative avenues for change. Perhaps the most ingenious of these came from Professor Ted McWhinney, a former Liberal MP for the constituency of Vancouver Quadra. After his retirement from Parliament, he published a book entitled *The Governor General and the Prime Ministers* in which he argued that all it would take to end the link with the Crown would be simply "to [fail] to proclaim any legal successor to the Queen in relation to Canada."[8] He continued, "The 'office of the Queen' would thus remain but remain inactive, and like very many other 'spent' sections of the Constitution Act, *presumably* wither away and lapse by convention."[9] He offered as a successful example of such an arrangement the Hungarian regency period from 1920 to 1944, when the country was ruled by Miklos Horthy, a "regent" who exercised authority in place of the Hapsburg kings who had been deposed after the First World War.

Apart from proposing the anti-Semitic dictatorship of Admiral Horthy—surely Canada deserves better than that—there are two problems with McWhinney's argument. The first is that it shows contempt for the Canadian Constitution and its purposes. Whether Professor McWhinney likes it or not, the philosophy underlying Confederation was to establish Canada as a functioning constitutional monarchy. Section 9 makes this clear, as does the preamble to the Constitution Act, 1867 when it sets out the basis for the constitutional structure of the new union: "Whereas the Provinces of Canada, Nova Scotia and New Brunswick have expressed their Desire to be federally united into One Dominion *under the Crown of the United Kingdom of Great Britain and Ireland, with a Constitution Similar in Principle to that of the United Kingdom …*" (emphasis added). With all respect to republican sensibilities, it is hard to see how Canada as we know it can be considered anything *other than* a monarchy. And this is not merely a quaint nineteenth-century vision of what it meant to be different from the United States. As part of the patriation process, the decision was taken, through the adoption of section 41 of the Constitution Act, 1982, actually to *deepen* the entrenchment of the monarchy in the constitutional scheme of things. For the government to do what McWhinney urges, however clever it might seem on paper, would be contrary to the plain purpose of those who framed our system of government.[10]

The second flaw with the McWhinney argument is that it glosses over the legal principles that govern succession to the throne. The common law regarding succession was set out in Calvin's Case, a judgment of the English Court of King's Bench in 1608.[11] The case involved the question of the legal status in England of people born in Scotland after the so-called union of the crowns in 1603. The crucial legal issue was the status of King James VI of Scotland upon the death of Queen Elizabeth I of England. Of course, he became James I of England, but at what stage? Was it only after some positive action by the English Parliament? This is how Sir Edward Coke, the Lord Chief Justice, answered that question:

> [T]he title [to the Throne of England] is by descent; by Queen Elizabeth's death the Crown and kingdom of England descended to His majesty, and he was fully and absolutely thereby King, without any essential ceremony or act to be done *ex post facto*: for coronation is but a Royal ornament and solemnization of the Royal descent, but no part of the title.[12]

To buttress his argument, Chief Justice Coke went on to note that Henry VI was not formally crowned until the eighth year of his reign,[13] yet "he was as absolute and complete a King, both for matters of judicature, as for grants, etc, before his coronation, as he was after."[14] As the first edition of *Halsbury's Laws of England* put it, "On the death of the reigning sovereign the Crown vests immediately in the person who is entitled to succeed, it being a maxim of the common law that 'the King never dies'. The new Sovereign is therefore entitled to exercise full prerogative rights without further ceremony."[15] Of course the same point can be made about the present Queen's reign. She became Sovereign upon the death of her father in February 1952, but her formal coronation did not take place until the summer of 1953. Yet no one disputes that she was lawfully the Queen during that sixteen-month period.

The Place of the Proclamation

In fact, the McWhinney solution has already been put to the test in the United Kingdom. In 1994, Tony Benn, a noted socialist (and republican) and former MP, suggested that on the death of Queen Elizabeth, he would object to the summoning of the Privy Council to proclaim a new Sovereign. Tony Newton, MP, the Lord President of the Council, responded that whether or not the Privy Council convened was of no legal relevance to the succession because the Prince of Wales "would succeed immediately and automatically to the Throne on the death of the Sovereign."[16]

It is true, as both Benn and McWhinney noted, that the new monarch is proclaimed—in the United Kingdom by the Privy Council and in Canada by the Queen's Privy Council for Canada—as soon as practicable after the death of the old sovereign. But this proclamation does not *make* someone the monarch. Rather, it simply declares what has already taken place by operation of the common law. One need only examine the wording of the Canadian proclamation upon the death of King George VI and the accession of Queen Elizabeth: "The High and Mighty Princess Elizabeth Alexandra Mary is now *by the death of Our late Sovereign of happy and glorious memory* become our only lawful and rightful Liege Lady Elizabeth the Second" (emphasis added).[17]

In other words, it is the death of the monarch that triggers succession. And the succession is instantaneous. It does not depend upon the positive action of either the Privy Council or Parliament. That is why the old saying, "The king is dead; long live the king!" represents an accurate statement of the law. Barring any amendment to the Constitution, the fact of succession is guaranteed by the common law. Upon the demise of Queen Elizabeth, she will automatically be succeeded by the heir to the throne. And by virtue of section 9 of the Constitution Act, 1867, executive authority over Canada will then be fully vested in the new king. The "McWhinney solution" is no solution to anything. It is simply a canard.

Altering the Rules of Succession

Having said this, one should not assume that it would be impossible to alter the rules of succession so as, for example, to allow Roman Catholics to ascend to the throne, or to change the law of primogeniture so that the eldest child of a reigning monarch becomes heir apparent, regardless of gender. All it would take is an amendment to the Act of Settlement, 1701. But to accomplish this would require a tremendous degree of political will—and an even greater measure of political skill. For it would have to involve near-simultaneous change in the law among all of the Queen's realms across the world. Moreover, the Act of Settlement has been held in Canada to enjoy constitutional status, which complicates amendment even further.[18]

Looking at this issue from a Canadian perspective, the preamble to the Constitution Act, 1867 makes it clear that *our* monarch must be the same person as the monarch of the United Kingdom. This was a point made by former prime minister Louis St. Laurent in the debate on the royal titles bill in 1953: "Her Majesty is now Queen of Canada but she is the Queen of Canada because she is Queen of the United Kingdom.... It is not a separate office ... it is the sovereign who is recognized as the sovereign of the United Kingdom who is our Sovereign."[19] In other words, it would not be possible, at least under the current constitutional framework, for the United Kingdom to have the Prince of Wales succeed Queen Elizabeth but for Canada instead to opt for the Duke of Cambridge. For good or ill—but because of history—the current law that determines succession to the throne of the United Kingdom, and hence to the throne of Canada, is the Act of Settlement, 1701.

The Act of Settlement was born out of the century of near-constant constitutional tumult that existed in England between the Reformation and the Glorious Revolution of 1688. As wrong as it seems to our present sensibilities, one consequence of the Reformation, and the Tudor and Stuart periods that followed it, was that Roman Catholicism came to be associated with a fear of insurrection and civil unrest. That is why, when the last reigning Stuart, James II, who had had ambitions to re-Catholicize England, fled the kingdom, Parliament resolved to invite two Protestants, William of Orange and his English wife, Princess Mary,[20] to assume the throne. When it became apparent that their successor, Queen Anne, would die without leaving any surviving children, Parliament moved to codify the rules of descent to ensure that the monarch would henceforth have allegiance only to the domestic church, the Church of England. This remains the law today regarding succession to the throne—including the throne of Canada.

There was within living memory an illustration of the political complexity of changing the succession. In 1931, the Imperial Parliament passed the Statute of Westminster, in which it said that it would thereafter legislate for "the dominions"—then understood to include Canada, Australia, New Zealand, South Africa, Ireland, and Newfoundland—only at the dominions' request. London was not surrendering its imperial sovereignty through the Statute of Westminster; rather, it was signalling a spirit of partnership among certain senior members of the British Empire.

The abdication crisis of 1936 gave play to the provisions of the Statute of Westminster in a way, and with an urgency, that one assumes the drafters of the statute had never contemplated. For the crisis was not only played out in the corridors of Belvedere Castle and Whitehall, but also in the Centre Block in Ottawa, and in Canberra, Wellington, Pretoria, and Dublin.[21] That is because as a matter of law, the British government had to obtain the assent of the dominions to alter the succession from Edward VIII to his younger brother, Prince Albert (who became King George VI), and eventually to his daughter, Princess Elizabeth, our current Queen. Accordingly, when the British Parliament passed His Majesty's Declaration of Abdication Act, 1936, it did so with the explicit request from Ottawa (to consider the matter from our perspective) that the statute apply in Canada as well. The next year, Canada and South Africa passed their own statutes in the same vein, but these were symbolic Acts only.[22] The legal change had been effected by the British legislature. The critical point, though, is that the British government acknowledged through the way it handled the legal aspects of the abdication crisis that the succession was a shared matter of concern for all of the king's self-governing realms.

In 2011, at the Commonwealth Heads of Governments Meeting in Perth, Australia, the leaders discussed proposals to amend the law of succession both to alter the primogeniture laws and to remove the ban on people in the line of succession marrying Roman Catholics (though the heirs to the throne themselves would still be required to be in communion with the Church of England). There was general agreement to the proposals, and in December 2012 the British government introduced a Succession to the Crown Bill.[23] But things have become legislatively more complicated since the days of the abdication crisis. In 1936, the British Parliament (wearing its Imperial Parliament hat) had retained a right to legislate for the entire Empire, limited in the case of the dominions only by the requirement in the Statute of Westminster for the dominions to request the legislation. Since 1982 in Canada's case, and 1986 in the case of Australia, Britain has formally surrendered all of its residual legislative authority over the two countries.[24] Similar provisions exist now in most of the Commonwealth countries. This means that most of the Queen's realms will have to pass their own legislation to change the succession. In April 2013, the British Parliament passed the Succession to the Crown Act, 2013. The Canadian counterpart is entitled the Succession to the Throne Act, 2013; interestingly, it received royal assent *before* the British legislation. But it remains to be seen whether the Canadian legislation is constitutional. A challenge to the constitutionality of the Act has been filed in the Superior Court of Quebec, arguing that any change to the succession needed to comply with the provisions of section 41 of the Constitution Act, 1982. Ultimately, this issue will have to be played out in the courts.

Conclusion

For believers in the current form of the Canadian constitutional structure, the future looks brighter than it has in many years. The present government of Canada, which now enjoys a majority, has been acting robustly to remind Canadians of the place of the Crown in our society, and all of the royal tours to Canada in recent years have been popularly received. Moreover, the law remains clear—Canada is a constitutional monarchy, and barring any constitutional change, the succession is guaranteed by the common law.

Yet, while there is reason for reassurance, there is also reason to be concerned. For one thing, the proposal for changing the rules of succession has the potential to become procedurally sticky. Another, perhaps more worrying, factor is the strand of anti-historicism that seems now to be so entrenched in our society. It has long been fashionable to decry the lack of civics education in the public school system. But the real challenge goes deeper than that. Of course, we need to teach young Canadians about political parties and the importance of voting and the like. But we have an equally pressing need to institute history as a part of the curriculum throughout all grades. And it cannot simply be the history of Canada from 1867 onward. When it comes to law and government, Canadian history did not begin at Confederation. Rather, it began in 1066—the same year that English legal and constitutional history began. The Battle of Hastings remains a watershed event in Canadian history, as do Magna Carta and the Black Death and the Reformation and the Glorious Revolution and every other event that helped shape the British Constitution—to which our Constitution must be similar in principle.

Likewise, it is ridiculous to think that events in Canada took place divorced from what was going on in Canberra, Wellington, Capetown, and New Delhi. The point is that we are our own fully independent nation now, but our history is so intertwined with the history of Great Britain and the British Empire that it is impossible to understand how law and government in Canada works without a real understanding of how—and why—they developed elsewhere. Canadian nationalists will be aghast to see it put this way, but the real road to deepening understanding of, and consequently respect for, our institutions and laws is to increase the degree of British and Commonwealth history in the public education system. In our system, historical understanding is the *sine qua non* for real and enduring respect for the rule of law. Monarchy or republic, queen or president, without understanding and respect for history, we will never be able to say that our constitutional fabric is truly strong.

Notes

1. Borrowing from the title of his 1992 book, *Voltaire's Bastards: The Dictatorship of Reason in the West* (London: Penguin Books).
2. Walter Bagehot, *The English Constitution*, Fontana Library ed. (London, 1963), 61.
3. Ibid. Emphasis in original.
4. Ibid.
5. Margaret Wente, "A Royal Pain: Take My Queen—Please!" *Globe and Mail*, February 7, 2002.
6. Jeffrey Simpson, "No Offence Prince but Our Ties to the Monarchy Should End," *Globe and Mail*, October 30, 2009.
7. Citizens for a Canadian Republic, "Frequently Asked Questions," updated May 26, 2012, http://www.canadian-republic.ca/faq.html. One can only assume that the Citizens for a Canadian Republic did not follow the debates over the Meech Lake and Charlottetown Accords.
8. Edward McWhinney, *The Governor General and the Prime Ministers* (Vancouver: Ronsdale Press, 2005), 125.
9. Ibid. Emphasis in original.
10. This is a point I have written about before. See "Liberal Stalking Horse for Stealth End of Monarchy," *Canadian Monarchist News*, Spring 2005, 2.
11. 77 ER 377, 7 Co Rep 1a.
12. 77 ER, 389.
13. Reigned 1422–1461.
14. 77 ER, 390.
15. The Earl of Halsbury, ed., *The Laws of England*, vol. 6, *Constitutional Law* (1909), 325.
16. Quoted in Vernon Bogdanor, *The Monarchy and the Constitution* (Oxford: Clarendon Press, 1995), 45.
17. The full proclamation was as follows:

    WHEREAS it hath pleased Almighty God to call to His Mercy Our Late Sovereign Lord King George the Sixth of blessed and glorious memory by whose decease the Crown of Great Britain, Ireland and all other His late Majesty's dominions is solely and rightfully come to the High and Mighty Princess Elizabeth Alexandra Mary, Now Know Ye that I, the said Right Honourable Thibaudeau Rinfret, Administrator of Canada as aforesaid, assisted by Her Majesty's Privy Council for Canada do now hereby with one voice and consent of tongue and heart, publish and proclaim that the High and Mighty Princess Elizabeth Alexandra Mary is now by the death of Our late Sovereign of happy and glorious memory become our only lawful and rightful Liege Lady Elizabeth the Second by the Grace of God, of Great Britain, Ireland and the British Dominions beyond the Seas Queen, Defender of the Faith, Supreme Liege Lady in and over Canada, to whom we acknowledge all faith and constant obedience with all hearty and humble affection, beseeching God by whom all Kings and Queens do reign to bless the Royal Princess Elizabeth the Second with long and happy years to reign over us. Given under my Hand and Seal at Arms at Ottawa, this Sixth day of February, in the year of Our Lord one thousand nine hundred and fifty-two, and in the first year of Her Majesty's reign.

18. See *O'Donohue v. Canada* (2003) 102 CRR (2d) 1; appeal by O'Donohue dismissed March 11, 2005.
19. *Hansard*, February 3, 1953, 1566.
20. Princess Mary was also the eldest daughter of James II. Domestic life among the higher classes was infinitely more complicated in those days!
21. Newfoundland had surrendered its dominion status in 1933.
22. The Succession to the Throne Act, 1937 and His Majesty King Edward the Eighth's Abdication Act, 1937, respectively.
23. http://www.publications.parliament.uk/pa/bills/cbill/2012-2013/0110/cbill_2012-20130110_en_2.htm#l1g1.
24. By virtue of the Canada Act, 1982 and the Australia Acts, 1986, respectively. The New Zealand equivalent is the Constitution Act, 1986, but that was an Act of the New Zealand Parliament, not the British Parliament.

9

A Case for the Republican Option

John D. Whyte

Le Canada est un État démocratique libéral peuplé de citoyens qui ne sont pas des sujets aux intérêts simplement protégés par des structures constitutionnelles, mais bien des participants qui collaborent aux processus d'autonomie gouvernementale en jouant un rôle politique majeur et non seulement procédural. Des citoyens qui agissent en vertu des conditions d'autonomie indispensables de liberté et de traitement équitable, lesquelles sont remplies dans un État démocratique libéral par des structures de polyarchie et de responsabilité largement prescrites dans la Constitution canadienne. L'une de ces structures de séparation, à tout le moins dans certaines circonstances politiques, doit être la charge de chef d'État, ou une quelconque forme de distinction entre les fonctions de politique et de légitimité, même entendues au sens large.

Mais si le républicanisme est aujourd'hui l'essence de la gouvernance canadienne, quel mal y a-t-il à préserver une forme d'autorité politique ancrée dans la divinité, la succession par sang royal et l'allégeance ? Sans doute aucun, les formes anciennes pouvant répondre à des besoins modernes. Peut-être la royauté, par exemple, qui a historiquement et fortement contribué à la création des nations, peut-elle encore favoriser une solidarité communautaire et l'adhésion à un idéal national. Mais est-ce vraiment le cas ? Car on peut aussi soutenir qu'elle en est venue à occuper l'espace politique réservé au chef de l'État sans avoir la moindre résonance culturelle ou, plus sérieusement, la moindre capacité de contester la détention ou l'exercice du pouvoir politique.

Introduction

From constitutional and governmental perspectives, in Canada the Crown is the embodiment of the state, and the personal manifestation of the Crown—the Sovereign—is Canada's head of state. The Sovereign is not only the Canadian head of state but the head of state for each of the provinces. Heads of state are the highest office-holders of sovereign nations. The notion of head of state is a trope for state authority, either through creating the myth that all power flows from the offices of heads of state or is exercised in their name, or through adopting the idea that heads of state embody the spirit and identity of the nation. If a state can be said to be governed according to a general will, the office of the head of state is the locus of that will.

The head of state is not normally a purely ceremonial office. The office carries specific, often highly significant political functions, at least at the level of formal role, though it has little actual political discretion. In Canada, one of the head of state's functions is to approve bills passed by legislative bodies. In fact, in Canada, the Crown is a constituted element of Parliament or of the provincial legislatures. Bills, in other words, must receive royal assent before they become statutes and have the force of law. In addition, a large proportion of the formal powers exercised by executive governments in Canada, that is, by cabinets, is done in the name of the head of state, and a great proportion of the orders emanating from cabinets must be approved by the head of state before becoming effective. The Crown, as the office of the Canadian head of state at both the federal and provincial levels, also possesses a range of prerogative powers. Among these powers is extending mercy to, or pardoning, convicted offenders, although now by federal legislation the cabinet has been assigned the power to exercise the mercy prerogative instead of the Sovereign or vice-regal representative. There is, however, one significant class of prerogative powers that relates to the responsibility of Canadian heads of state. This is to sustain the integrity of responsible government and, in particular, to maintain the principle that the first minister and his or her government must enjoy the confidence of the houses of Parliament, federally, or legislative assemblies, provincially.

These descriptions are not to suggest that the significance of the Canadian Crown in the person of the Sovereign (currently the Queen) is limited to these constitutional roles. All nations value their heritage, even when that heritage bears only distant relation to current values, practice, and national identity. Many Canadians believe that forming government under a monarchy gives this nation distinctiveness, a sense of historical rootedness and continuity; that it gives specific content to national spirit and endows the greyness of public government with a degree of ceremonial panache.

Preserving the head-of-state function in the specific form of monarchy, however, has little significance for the operation of our constitutional order. This is because the place of the Sovereign in the operation of the Canadian state has been taken over almost entirely by the Canadian governor general and provincial lieutenant governors. The Letters Patent 1947 issued by King George VI, as well as later letters patent and other formal agreements made between the Sovereign and the Government of Canada, put into effect a comprehensive, although not total, delegation to the governor general of the Crown's prerogative powers that are relevant to the federal order of government.[1] Although letters patents and agreements empowered the governor general to exercise most of the powers and responsibilities that are constitutionally held by the Queen, these powers were not formally, or finally, devolved. This delegation of powers could, theoretically, be revoked by the Sovereign, thereby restoring the role of the Sovereign as set out in the Constitution Acts, 1867 to 1982. However, there is no possibility that this will ever occur. Such a breach of Canadian self-determination, and deviation from now well-established constitutional practice, is inconceivable. No Canadian government could accede to the reversion of the head of state's responsibilities to someone who, while in a formal sense is Canadian, is in general perception in Canada and elsewhere, another nation's monarch.[2] Canada's powers as a sovereign nation, including those held by the Crown, are, with very few exceptions, exercised through those holding constitutional and political offices within Canada.

In light of these developments, the idea of monarchism in Canada, in the sense of a nation being under the ultimate authority of a ruler holding power through heredity, is both irrelevant to its political operation and misleading with respect to the actual source of state legitimacy. On the other hand, in the absence of an alternative account of state authority, the role of the Crown as a symbol for describing an ultimate location of state power is vital and convenient, both morally and functionally. The Crown, and the ancient idea of the sovereign as the root source of the state's authority, also solve the moral problem of what historical fact gives warrant to state coercive authorities, or gives entitlement to the exercise of control over the lands that constitute the state's territory. Functionally, the idea of the Crown justifies the powers of supervision and consent (even though, now, only notional powers) over the governing acts of those who claim to act for the citizenry. It also grounds the vital authority to determine which persons and political parties represent the will of the citizenry and, therefore, who is entitled to formulate and administer the laws of the state.

Not only is the notion of the Crown a solution to basic moral conditions for governing, the actual historical practices guiding the relationship between the sovereign and the governors gave birth to a form of common law that describes how this relationship will effectively work. If the structure of a sovereign acting as head of state were abandoned, we might be concerned over losing normative understandings about the underlying relationship between head of state and government. As a result, we would not know for sure what governmental power is based on, or how it can be made accountable in terms of it following democratically determined preferences. On the other hand, constitutional conventions relating to the functioning of the head of state would hardly disappear if the sovereign were to be replaced by a head of state appointed to the office through a process based on political will or popular will.[3] The nature and functioning of royal prerogative powers are reasonably clearly understood and are generally accepted as subject to constitutional conventions that act as a guide to their exercise. There has been little sense that the relationship between the head of state and the government is not governed by constitutional understanding or convention, although recent exercises of head-of-state discretion relating to the prorogation of Parliament and the prorogation of one provincial legislative assembly have generated controversy. Furthermore, in some Commonwealth countries there is a movement to codify the exercise of head-of-state powers, and that development could be a model for Canada. The codification of the head of state's power over preserving responsible government matches exactly the liberal democratic precept of rule of law, or the notion that governmental powers must be exercised according to clear standards. Significant head-of-state functions need not be placed in jeopardy by the de-monarchization of this office.[4]

If there is no *essential* reason why Canada must remain a monarchy, the concomitant question is whether there is any *good* reason why Canada should become a parliamentary democracy under a republican form of state authority and with republicanism serving as the basis for state legitimacy. With respect to this question, I shall make five claims.

First, there is reason to question the fit between the political value of monarchy and Canada's constitutional culture. This claim rests on very general conceptions of Canadian statecraft, namely, ideas about the source of political authority and the appropriate relationship between state power and mechanisms of accountability. The question of fit with constitutional culture does not include consideration of social values, or social dissonance produced through the symbolism of hereditary monarchy and entitlement to political office. This chapter does not attack constitutional monarchy for its social character or its reification of political privilege.

Second, if we aspire to create, and be governed through, statecraft that reflects and reinforces the way in which the Canadian democratic state pursues the notions of justice, legitimacy, accountability, and political stability—and these must certainly be the underlying aspirations of the good state—republican ideas about ultimate political authority provide a more coherent basis for the political organization that we are governed by.

Third, civic republican theory captures better than monarchy the concepts of the Canadian state as expressed in the Canadian Constitution. In other words, as the focus moves from general ideas that underlie our state organization to the specific substantive provisions and commitments of the Constitution, there is a close functional relationship between those terms and republican ideas.

Fourth, notwithstanding the established and highly valued relationship between the Crown and Aboriginal peoples expressed through the Royal Proclamation of 1763 and subsequent treaties, it is possible that the basic claims of Aboriginal Canada for political recognition are better advanced and defended through civic republican theory than through the political structure of monarchy. While this claim carries the risk of appearing to prescribe for Aboriginal peoples their best interests (hardly a politically tolerable practice), its purpose is only to suggest different conceptions of the source of Aboriginal political authority with a view to exploring their efficacy.

Fifth, civic republicanism, better than a political structure based on monarchy, matches the chief moral imperatives governing the Canadian political community in this age, in this time and place, with the social and political implications of the pluralism that now defines us.

The Monarchy Culture and Canada's Constitutional Culture

Monarchy's claim to legitimacy as a political structure is not groundless. Nor has it been pursued without sound political purpose, or simply for reasons of exploitation and aggrandisement. Monarchy arose as a form of authority for the highest of political goals—as a response to the need to establish political stability. Stability in power depends on both effective control and a legitimate basis for authority. In the great struggle to create nations out of tribes and baronies, monarchy had an advantage over despotism, which was subject to constant challenge by force, and over theocracy, which was subject to constant challenge by superior revelation. Monarchy sought to find a more certain and more legitimating condition for holding power through generating fealty based on the apparently intrinsic qualities of spirituality and heredity. The monarch was seen to be anointed by God. And the inherent instability of succession, whether of power or estate, was controlled through heredity. Perhaps more controversially, monarchy was preferable to its chief rival, confederacy or treaty or compact, because it materialized myths of common experience, common identity, and common purpose—better currencies for sustaining territorial integrity and the security of holdings. Whatever today's reservations about monarchy may be, it is clear that for a very long period of human history there was little question about the effectiveness, or the legitimacy, of single rulers.

The success of monarchy in creating political order, therefore, rests on divinity, succession, and fealty. Rendering of rulers as divinely chosen, or even as divine, is a common strategy behind monarchical authority. Clear succession is valuable, because conflict over succession harms authority and disrupts the social and economic exchanges that allow societies to flourish. Fealty is the continuing theatrical sign that a monarchy is stable, as manifested both in reassuring signs of political success and in warnings to dissidents of the risks that flow from rebellion.

But, of course, none of these qualities of monarchy any longer reflect the values that today we ascribe to political authority. God has left the political arena as we have adopted a role for divinity that is less determinate, sullied, partisan, and exclusionary. Aristocratic succession has become absurd in a world that values merit, flexibility, and efficiency over certainty. Liberty is valued over fealty, perhaps because dynamism produces better social dividends than fixity, or perhaps because the claims of humanism and freedom have rendered fealty obsolete. As noted by J. G. A. Pocock, the royalist claim is that "kings ruled by a right intelligible to human reason" but also "independent of human consent."[5]

This dissonance does not, of course, mean that monarchy is finished. Monarchy carries other attributes—stability, efficiency, and political sanction—that can serve to sustain it. These qualities are hardly exclusive to monarchy, but they seem to be considered good enough to carry on with the way things are, at least in Canada. Stability arises from the continuing avoidance of political debate—possibly intense political debate—over what methods should be used to identify the nation's head of state and over exactly what powers should fall to that newly constructed office. Not only would these questions be contested, the answers arrived at might be inefficient if unintended consequences were to result. Therefore, we might prefer monarchy because we know what it means in the operation of the presently constituted state. Finally, political acceptance tells us that monarchy is serving an existing set of political interests, although interests that are more symbolic than structural or distributional. Naturally, this fact should not suppress criticism and reform, so long as it is managed through negotiation and the use of instruments of constitutional continuity—that is, through constitutional amendment. This is the way that sovereign, self-governing political communities choose to act. The impetus for amendment, however, is blunted by repeated and unequivocal political sanctioning of an arrangement that seems, in the words of David E. Smith, "congenial to its environment."[6]

Of course, we have already experienced a great deal of monarchical change without actually ending monarchy[7]—Magna Carta, the 1689 Bill of Rights, the modern Parliament, the limitations on royal prerogative powers within the normative strictures of constitutionalism, the indivisible Crown made divisible and, in Canada, the transfer of the Sovereign's authority to the Canadian representatives of the head of state. In fact, there is no real statecraft argument against the complete domestication of our heads of state. We can, in fact, make major constitutional changes without warfare, and without unbearable uncertainty. The chief uncertainty is how to create a new form of head of state that would not lead to the assumption of too much power, a risk that arises whenever political office is filled through competition and successful striving, rather than through fate—or grace. As yet, there is no consensus over a method for appointing a non-monarchical head of state. Of course, constitutional convention has already established a domestic process that is, as a matter of practice, unchecked either by monarchical authority or by any form of contemporaneous political accountability. However, that method of appointment, appointment by the prime minister of both the federal and the provincial heads of state, lacks political legitimacy and would generate far too much democratic stress—and too much federalism stress—to be entrenched as the purely domestic process for the appointment of the Canadian head of state. Ironically, Canadian monarchy's strongest claim for continuation is based on its most suspect characteristic—an established form of succession through heredity.

Monarchy's essential political attributes no longer have relevance in the modern liberal democratic state; and its secondary attributes, including the claims that certainty is to be preferred to uncertainty and that continuation is preferable to change, are hardly powerful. The barrier to ending the Canadian monarchy owing to a lack of mechanism for appointment that would both guarantee political neutrality and forestall the temptation to assume the power of ruling may not be sufficient to forestall the end of monarchy if the imaginary of royalty has all but left the station. It may soon become necessary to face the issue of an appointment method for a purely domestic head of state.

Monarchy and the Foundations of the Canadian State

In Canada, we have adopted a complex structure of public government. However, behind the specific arrangements and relationships of responsible government—the division of legislative powers in a federal arrangement, the branches of government and separation of powers, the development of parliamentary officers and instruments to assist with legislation and parliamentary control, minority community rights, and the constitutionalization of individual and group rights—are more basic conceptions of liberal democracy that are designed to make public government stable and just. These are democratic consent, and constitutionalism and the rule of law. With respect to the latter, Canada, like many liberal democratic states, ensures that the powers of the branches and agencies that comprise the state are limited: the government is accountable to Parliament, and its power is subject to constitutional and legislative grants of authority. Legislatures are accountable to electorates and subject to constitutional limits. Courts are constrained by the internal restraints of applying established law and the discipline of legal reasoning and judicial restraint. All Canadian political bodies are bound by the terms of the federal structure and the specific protections provided by constitutional rights. The theme of our Constitution is the protection of interests, both because these protections are thought to keep the actions of the state just and because the protections reflect ideas of fairness conducive to political stability. These systems and standards for accountability ensure that those exercising power do so within the prescribed conditions and substantive limits on political power.

But where does the concept of monarchy fall in relation to these fundamental constitutional ideas? There are two basic answers to this question. First, as noted, the state is founded on two clusters of ideas—the idea of constitutionalism and the rule of law, and the idea of representative government. The two normative conceptions that relate to these ideas are citizenship and democracy. The fundamental point behind these conceptions is to have a state that is bound to the citizen in both a normative sense and a procedural sense. The normative condition of this state is that it is most definitely not a site of unquestioned and unmediated loyalty. In a word, a state based on citizenship and democracy cannot be said to be composed of subjects, but citizens. This distinction is often taken as the line of demarcation not just of democracy but of republicanism. Exactly what a citizen is owed by the state and, in turn, what a citizen owes the state and fellow citizens is certainly up for discussion, and that is why there are so many different notions of what republicanism is. Some versions of republicanism demand a high degree of citizen investment in the process of co-governing. Some versions focus less on civic participation and more on the state's guarantee of certain conditions of freedom, or on state protection against domination. Another version of republicanism declares that the relationship between state and citizen is based on state solicitude for the capacity of citizens to engage on more-or-less-equal terms in public government and political debate.[8] It is sometimes asserted that the republican state is marked, first, by the triumph of public decision-making and public debate over private, or closed, deliberations with respect to state aims and, second, by the indispensability of virtue (e.g., selflessness, search for a common good, and moderation in advancing preferences) in public life. At this point, it is not essential to name the precise conception or precise virtue of republicanism that our Constitution most clearly reflects, but rather to note simply that our Constitution's fundamental ordering conceptions are based on citizenship; that is, our Constitution is based entirely on the interests of citizens.

Thomas Paine defined republicanism as a sovereignty of justice, not a sovereignty of will no matter how acquired. In the modern context of constitutional monarchy, however, a distinction between sovereign will and legal restraint on political power is too blunt. Generally, the ideas of citizen engagement, citizen liberty, and citizen capacity all fit the elements of the Canadian Constitution, and the fact of monarchy does not alter that except at the level of the abstraction that still resides in oaths of office and in the identity of state authority. The ideology of republicanism tracks Canada's large political themes and relates imperfectly to monarchy. In particular, republicanism takes a firm stand against political privilege arising from status, or from office or majority. Republicanism is hostile to any spectre of domination and is committed to the protection of citizens individually or in groups who become vulnerable through unpopularity or dissidence or numbers.

Another feature of republicanism is that the virtue of the state is not located in the virtue and honour of the Crown. It arises from the power of citizen engagement with the means and ends of political power and political judgment.[9] Constitutional monarchy, while now neither tyrannical nor dominating, stems from a culture of obeisance and compliance, and this metaphor of the state continues. While it is not clear that these distinctions have large functional significance, they reflect paradigm differences.

The second answer to the question of monarchy's fit with constitutional precepts is less tied to theories of republicanism. It draws on the Constitution's fundamental premises that all political power must be accountable, and therefore the head of state is to be seen as part of a complex of relationships that check and balance each other. The general structural integrity of both responsible government and the constitutional rule of law rests on the principle of holding power accountable. Notionally, checking abuses of power is a function assigned to Canadian heads of state—the Queen, the governor general, and lieutenant governors. Canadian surrogates of the Sovereign are assigned what appears to be a significant checking function through the power to grant assent to proposed legislation and sign governmental orders. However, these offices have, in Canada, come to have virtually no real independent power with respect to the instruments by which substantive government policy is implemented.

But the head of state retains significant influence in two areas. The first relates to political succession. State stability is most at jeopardy when an incumbent must cede governing power, since such power usually comes with great effort and holding it is, in many ways, immensely gratifying. Power is not surrendered happily—although often graciously, to be sure—by those who hold it. In parliamentary democracies, decisions that power should be surrendered and to whom are the responsibility of the head of state and are to be exercised prudently and in accordance with an established practice. Since change of governmental power is representative democracy's most fraught moment, respect for and acceptance of that power are democracy's most vital conditions. This power, however, does not amount to a check on substantive governmental policy formation; although it is a strong power, it is a limited one. But policy is not the head of state's only point for creating substantive state value. Procedural conditions and restraints also represent a substantive influence on the state. Process has an intrinsic moral worth that reflects and shapes a state's values, and hence, its purposes. A commitment to orderliness and neutrality in difficult political moments expresses a substantive idea about the good state and generates confidence and acceptance. It can also produce in citizens an equal commitment to peaceable resolution, just as tyranny can produce the death of altruism and public spiritedness.[10]

The second of the head of state's checking functions is the power to force articulation of the reasons for governmental action, to seek justification and to urge reconsideration. The head of state in our system has the right "to be consulted, to encourage and to warn."[11] In Canada, as far as we know, this head-of-state function was not always appreciated by first ministers, and there has not been a firmly established pattern of consultation.[12] In the United Kingdom, however, as a matter of firm precedent, consultation with the Queen takes place on a weekly basis.[13] This is clearly a form of separation of powers, although one that is marked by a power imbalance. Yet misgivings of the head of state over a measure that he or she must endorse should normally represent some check against questionable government policy. And weight of experience carries a persuasive effect except on the dangerously wilful. However, to the extent that a head of state is treated as ornament, or the population relates to that person through the currency of celebrity and adulation, or believes that the head of state is all privilege and lacks independent political merit, or sees no personal authority but only the power assigned by a distant ruler to a surrogate, then this role for the head of state—this process of accountability, as soft and as tenuous as it may be—will be empty of force or function. It is always the case that powers that have been rendered soft will fail when confronted by hard rulers. This has been close to the situation in Canada.

Liberal democracy is not a strong instrument at any time. Elections are infrequent, and the mechanisms of parliamentary accountability (and parliamentary officer accountability) can be snubbed or neutered by governments. Likewise, the head of state can hardly forestall determined tyranny. It would, however, enhance the practice of Canadian democracy if heads of state were effective in causing government leaders to reconsider the advice that is tendered to them. The supposition behind this claim is that the slight degree of separation of powers that it would require to produce a checking effect would take root better if the domestic heads of state were no longer to be representatives of the Queen, but rather representatives of the people of Canada or the people of a province. Even more, the influence of these offices would gain greater traction if Canada were to adopt a method of selection that reflected broad political concurrence in appointments, such as ratification of appointments by legislative majorities or legislative super-majorities. While generating increased political legitimacy for the head of state carries its own risks of refusal and political deadlock, it seems likely that the features of both the popular election of governments and the government's extensive executive apparatus, neither of which the head of state would enjoy, would serve to hold the head of state's powers to seeking justification and soft persuasion.

Government in Canada can doubtlessly be prey to executive control, and we should seek to strengthen, even minimally, the restraints on executive authority that can arise from the constitutional separation of the functions of policy initiation and non-partisan assessment. It is exactly the effectiveness of these sorts of structures on which liberal democracy depends.

The Constitution's Republican Themes

The Canadian Constitution reflects republican ideas of the state. As has been noted, it is not perfectly settled what ideals of statecraft republicanism entails, but it clearly refers to a system of government that rests on self-governance, or the right of self-determination of "we the people," and on the idea of political non-domination of persons and groups. According to some theorists, this last tenet is what distinguishes republicanism from liberal democracy.[14] The conditions for self-governance are citizen engagement and responsibility, citizen liberty, and citizen capacity. The condition for self-determination and non-domination is that the state not adopt unjustified preferences for some citizens or groups—preferences that are not relatable to the public good. Republicanism, with its dependence on effective citizen agency, is hostile to disempowerment, exclusion, and domination. A republic typically embraces the normative idea that a national majority should not get its way at the expense of the vital interests of groups in politically identified conditions and regions or with politically identified community features and identities.

The Canadian Constitution, matching the republican theory of fair treatment of all, carries the republican features of rights, federalism, and the protection of minority rights, as well as legal protection against unconstitutional or oppressive governmental action provided by a judiciary with constitutional independence from government. Each of these constitutional features expresses the ideas of non-interference with citizen capacity and non-domination of people and groups, and requires a functional ability to marshal instruments for opposing the will of majorities, most particularly national majority governments. Once again, political value is located in both the substantive content of the Constitution and the processes of government it prescribes. The central condition of constitutionalism, that there is an independent branch of government—the judiciary—to enforce the promises of the Constitution, means that policy preferences are subject to reasoned deliberation (at least at the point of review by courts, although republican theory also expects a high level of legislative consciousness of the interests of diverse communities), generalized justification with respect to the public good served by laws, and liberty to challenge politically legal ordering that ignores identity and vital condition. It is this review function that provides one avenue of a republican democratization of governmental power (and guarantees governmental non-domination) through equal government-citizen contestation over the state's actions of legislating, regulating, and administering.[15]

Beyond the goals of justice, fairness, and due process that ground constitutional rules of law and find expression in the imposition of justifiable regulatory burdens on citizens, there is constitutionalism's more general project of human dignity. This project is reflected in the idea that constitutional protection of basic interests and communities speaks to the protection of core human interests and values. At the core of human interest is the capability to form, express, and pursue life purposes. In this light, the underlying purpose of the republican state may be to give effect to the entitlement of everyone—individuals and collectivities—to pursue their chosen redemptive strategies and to do so under conditions of relative effectiveness.

The constitutional instrument of self-determination is democracy—the principle under which power flows from the preferences of individuals. Ultimately, therefore, the governed are the governors. It follows that, for the democratic state, voters must have the capacity to participate fully, deliberate wisely, and choose autonomously. Further, the Canadian Constitution confers recognition and entitlements aimed at sustaining the identity and integrity of groups, both for specific minority communities and as a general principle of associational life. Behind the idea that distinct identity is deserving of protection is the recognition that securing the dignity and worth of groups and the capacity of individuals who comprise those groups is a vital feature of freedom and resistance to domination. Core fundamental freedoms—speech, religion, and assembly—are constitutionally protected because they allow citizens to express individual interests and to work with others to enhance their personal influence. These freedoms speak to constitutional concern for political and social capacity.

In this way, the Constitution can be seen as mandating state intervention to alleviate the worst forms of suffering and domination. The goals of human dignity and human capacity referred to here are reflected in our existing constitutional concepts such as fundamental justice, liberty, security of the person, prevention of cruel and unusual treatment, equal protection, and group rights. These claims are also implied in constitutional precepts about human entitlement and human capacity to live and serve as a citizen.[16]

The other constitutional location for the Canadian state's commitment to people's capacity to participate in public life and to resist domination is found in the provisions of the Constitution Act, 1867, in which governmental powers are federally allocated to the national government and provincial governments. The regulatory powers of governments that are empowered under the federal structure in the Canadian Constitution strongly suggest the idea that governmental responsibility includes social support and care for citizens.[17] These jurisdictional authorities may not mandate the modern activist state, but they contemplate its agenda.

Canadian constitutionalism in all aspects, except, of course, for the grounding of the Canadian state's authority on the Crown, rests on republican notions of state purpose and legitimacy.

Aboriginal Perspectives on the Crown

In Canada we are seeking healing from the ravages of the colonization of Indigenous persons, and political reconciliation between Aboriginal Canada and non-Aboriginal Canada. To achieve healing and reconciliation, three political conditions must be met. The first is the freedom of each of Canada's Aboriginal peoples to act on their own collective will and the right to govern their own political communities.[18] The second condition is political equality between Aboriginal political communities and the various public governments in Canada.[19] The third condition is the creation of, and commitment to, coordinating principles and agencies that represent the spirit of reconciliation and equality—awareness that the harms of colonialism need redressing through the recognition of Indigenous peoples' rights exercised within the bounds of modern statecraft's imperative for mutual accommodation.[20]

At the core of liberty, equality, and the overcoming of both colonial and Canadian oppression and destruction is the recognition of Aboriginal self-government. This concept means politically structured autonomy that will frequently need to be exercised through neutral instruments for reconciling competing and mutually impacting policies. The chief feature of the Canadian challenge in this regard is embracing a constitutional novelty that will recognize Aboriginal regimes based on Aboriginal nationality and Canadian citizenship. These are regimes that cannot continue to be tied to political structures and constitutional principles—such as parliamentary sovereignty, exhaustive legislative authority, a third order of government under the current federalist structure, or possibly, the Crown as the root of state authority—that would defeat the effect of self-government.[21]

Of course, new constitutional orders can be (and have been) produced, when we have the political will, without altering the offices of the Queen, the governor general, and lieutenant governors. But to do so presents a problem. The problem is that, unless we create a third aspect of the divided Crown—the Queen of Aboriginal Canada—the Crown as the current hallmark of state authority will appear to be absent from Aboriginal government, as indeed it is in those instances in which Aboriginal self-government agreements have been negotiated. The idea of the Queen of Aboriginal Canada will not actually work, except as a purely abstract or de-materialized symbol of Aboriginal governments' head of state, because Aboriginal self-government does not translate into a single Aboriginal political community. The problem of Crown source for political authority could, presumably, be solved by casting Aboriginal governments as subordinate agencies empowered through federal and provincial legislation. But such a device would defeat the central notion that Aboriginal government is an existing right that is implemented, and not created, through legislative recognition.

The Queen metaphor for the source of political authority is, in any event, misleading. As new forms of government are recognized and placed within national structures of governance, the actual and functional hallmark of Canadian state authority will be the consent of the people of Canada—Aboriginal and non-Aboriginal—acting through political representatives. Of course, we have all been living under this conflicted situation of the state's core identity, but it will be the development of constitutionally based Aboriginal self-government that will most clearly underscore this irreconcilability.

It would be a mistake to be unmindful of the significance of the Crown, both as concept and as person in the form of the Queen, in Aboriginal claims for the vindication of human rights, inherent Indigenous rights, international law rights, constitutional rights, Crown proclamation rights, and treaty rights, and in the pursuit of a mutually respectful relationship between peoples who share this land. It is true that this belief in a personal royal duty—or in a personal royal responsibility—that transcends national boundaries and constitutional developments was undermined by Lord Denning in the English Court of Appeal decision in *R. v. Secretary of State for Foreign and Commonwealth Affairs, ex parte Indian Association of Alberta* in 1982.[22] Lord Denning dismissed the First Nations argument that treaty obligations entered into in the name of the Queen bind the British Crown, not the Canadian federal Crown.[23] Their aim was to use these continuing treaty obligations as a bar to patriation of the Canadian Constitution by the Constitution Act, 1982. Lord Denning concluded that the concept of the indivisible Crown had, by usage and practice, disappeared and that it was now divisible by nation and by jurisdiction: "None [of the obligations to which the Crown bound itself] is any longer binding on the Crown in respect of the United Kingdom."[24] However, those seeking to break the nexus between the monarchy and the political grounding for Aboriginal claims must concede that this legal decision, correct in its day and in its context, is not final enough or legitimate enough to shatter the treaty relationship between First Nations and the Crown. The decision, after all, speaks only to the relationship with the British Crown.

The formation of treaties is only one aspect of the personal relationship between First Nations and the Queen, but is clearly the most potent instance of the relationship. Treaties are not contracts so much as covenants. A covenantal relationship is a living relationship; it is not exhaustively defined in writing. Its breach—and breaches are inevitable because the making of a covenant is surrounded by so much harmony and such deep representations of integrity that lapses are bound to occur—cannot break the relationship. A covenant is a promise to live in a relationship through accepting failures and redressing them in processes of healing and restoration. A covenant's force is not found in exact words but in principles and general terms of intersocietal accommodation. The world's dynamism does not render a covenant irrelevant; it only invites adaptation and renewal by the parties. Finally, covenants cannot be purely institutional; they are based on personal commitments, ideally personal commitments sworn before God, because the promises create a moral binding—not just legal obligation—that institutions cannot adequately bear. In reading the treaty-making record with First Nations in Canada, the element of personal commitment from both sides is startling. From the side of the Canadian government, with respect to the numbered treaties, the personhood that matched the personal weight of First Nations chiefs was the Queen. Her personhood was accentuated by casting her not as ruler but as mother, an image that carries a moral commitment to caring and sustaining that is as powerful as humankind can devise. It is not the least surprising that monarchy carries inertial weight in the Canadian Aboriginal / non-Aboriginal relationship.

The question is whether this symbolism is matched by functionality. If not, tragedy ensues. When the symbols of a relationship disguise its reality, the relationship is marked by repeated disappointment, a sense of betrayal and deep barriers to constructing a positive basis for the relationship. But, in truth, there is no certain answer to the expendability of the Crown in the development of Canadian Aboriginal / non-Aboriginal relations. The republican constitutionalist will surely maintain that the relationship that needs to be built is between Aboriginal peoples and the rest of Canada, and that this relationship is not based on personal undertakings. It is a constitutional relationship that we are shaping, and it needs to be built on the consent of peoples. The very specific relationship created through treaty-making is no longer a force of modern political reconciliation.

On the other hand, Sákéj Henderson has argued that Aboriginal and treaty rights reflect a deep structure of legal pluralism that British colonialism conducted in the name of its Sovereign and that became embedded in the Sovereign's continuing constitutional duty.[25] It is the making of treaties that most clearly assumes Aboriginal sovereignty. That treaties are the promises of the monarch serves to create a special duty—or a burden of honour—that should not slide away to an obligation of mere governments, with governments' inevitable attenuation of promises for reasons of political exigency. The idea of an Aboriginal peoplehood, separate and protected, that lies behind treaties is the opposite of oppression and colonialism, and the fact of the Sovereign's commitment to this idea should not be removed.

In Every Riven Thing

American poet Christian Wiman, in his poem, "Every Riven Thing,"[26] suggests that with our great intelligence we see difference and distinctiveness everywhere. Creation is a collage, a composite, and we never cease trying to grasp its reality through grasping its parts. With this human mind we distinguish and classify; we see structures and arrange orders of being. But creation's oneness (in Wiman's terms, God's oneness) is broken by this process of reason and so is our sense of belonging to this world, being nurtured by this world and being made whole as the world is made whole.

> Belonging, to every riven thing he's made,
> means a storm of peace.
> Think of the atoms inside the stone
> Think of the man who sits alone
> Trying to will himself into a stillness where
> God goes belonging.

What is true for all of creation is true also for its human part, and so in order to live at peace and in trust with complexity, difference, and pluralism everywhere, we need to see and experience the unity of every part of our life, not just the shadow reality of "rivenness" and the separation of everything. We all know this unity to be true. The human experience on this planet has only one chance and that is to acknowledge differences, but to love everything as if all were one, and our fate joined. The condition for receiving enrichment from diversity is seeing our common condition and common fate. Pluralism is our world, but oneness our salvation. In the great endeavour to reach through pluralism to trust, is it not relevant to consider the weight on our consciousness of the way that we organize the state?

Royalty, especially the royalty of parts of the Commonwealth, is certainly a symbol of a common community. And, when it comes in the form of Queen Elizabeth II, it seems to be the part of our political order over which we do not descend into factions and difference. But Canadian royalty hides the commonality of the human struggles that bring people into a single nation with a common hope. The Canadian Crown comes from a very specific narrative of discovery and a distinct course of colonialism when, in fact, there are multiple stories of Canada's formation. It comes from a specific national identity when there are so many national origins and ethnic communities that are joined together in making Canada. Our monarchy comes from the saga of a few families when there are so many ways to nurture and encourage, to instil distinction, to deserve recognition, and to gain the privilege of leading. It comes out of a political narrative that explains one nation's political struggles, but there are many other national stories, including our Canadian stories of many political initiatives—the stories that have shaped Canada.

In our search to be one nation of many parts, a nation of differences and distinctions joined by trust and belonging to a common political identity—a common destination—monarchy may be a totem that can reach the soul of only some. We are not bound to our political community through royalty but through its gifts of opportunity, safety, justice, and belonging—the products of self-rule and the rewards of active citizenship. Can we not, one wonders, construct a head for our nation that confirms our hope for the spirit of unity and trust in diversity?

Notes

1. For a detailed discussion of the Letters Patent, 1947, as well as later delegations of the Sovereign's constitutional and prerogative powers, see Christopher McCreery, "Myth and Misunderstanding: The Origins and Meaning of the Letters Patent Constituting the Office of the Governor General, 1947," in *The Evolving Canadian Crown,* ed. Jennifer Smith and D. Michael Jackson (Montreal and Kingston: McGill-Queen's University Press, 2012), 31.
2. In any event, the constitutional amending rules set out in Part V of the Constitution Act, 1982 most likely militate against unilateral federal action with respect to the existing arrangements. Initiatives to alter the offices of the Queen, the governor general, or the lieutenant governors would require the consent of the federal Senate and House of Commons and all the provincial legislative assemblies.
3. Popular choice and popular consent with respect to the office of Sovereign is not a novel concept. For most monarchies, including the English kings, during most of history the question of who shall be accepted as Sovereign has been fiercely contested, and the capacity to gain support largely determined who prevailed.
4. Although it is difficult to see how codification of head-of-state powers would add to uncertainty (or not decrease popular mystification), some have warned against its ill effects. See, for example, Robert E. Hawkins, "Written Reasons and Codified Conventions in Matters of Prorogation and Dissolution," in Smith and Jackson, *The Evolving Crown*, 99.
5. J. G. A. Pocock, *The Ancient Constitution and Feudal Law: A Study of English Historical Thought in the Seventeenth Century* (New York: W.W. Norton & Co., 1967), 150.
6. David E. Smith, *The Republican Option in Canada: Past and Present* (Toronto: University of Toronto Press, 1999), xx.
7. For an account of radical change in the power of the Crown, see Philip Corrigan and Derek Sayer, "'This Realm of England Is an Empire': The Revolution of the 1530s," in *The Great Arch: English State Formation as Cultural Revolution* (Oxford: Basil Blackwell, 1985), 43-54. Corrigan and Sayer trace the course in the sixteenth century of imposing parliamentary control over the Sovereign's spiritual and temporal authority.
8. For a historical review of republican theory, see Joyce Appleby, *Liberalism and Republicanism in the Historical Imagination* (Cambridge, MA: Harvard University Press, 1993). Appleby notes that "classical republicanism made civic virtue—the capacity to place the good of the commonwealth above one's own—the lynchpin of constitutional stability and liberty-preserving order." For a description of the connection between the American republican ideas in

favour of liberty and against destructive factionalism and the constitutional goal of providing citizens with real capabilities to participate and act and be free from debilitating indigence and exclusion, see Martha C. Nussbaum, "Constitutions and Capabilities: 'Perception' against Lofty Formalism," *Harvard Law Review* 121, no. 5 (2007): 46-53.

9. See, for example, James Madison, "The Utility of the Union as a Safeguard against Domestic Faction and Insurrection," *The Federalist No. 10,* November 22, 1787 (http://www.constitution.org/fed/federa10.htm), in which he demonstrates that republican government can meet the challenge of self-interest: "Complaints are everywhere heard from our most considerate and virtuous citizens ... that our governments are too unstable, that the public good is disregarded in the conflicts of rival parties, and that measures are too often decided, not according to the rules of justice and the rights of the minor party, but by the superior force of an interested and overbearing majority, ... [by] a number of citizens ... who are united and actuated by some common impulse of passion, or of interest, adversed to the rights of other citizens, or to the permanent and aggregate interests of the community" (paras. 1-2).
10. George Kateb, "Remarks on the Procedures of Constitutional Democracy," in *Constitutionalism* (Nomos XX), ed. J. Roland Pennock and John W. Chapman (New York: New York University Press, 1978), 215.
11. To cite the oft-quoted statement by Walter Bagehot in *The English Constitution* (1867).
12. The current prime minister is evidently meeting regularly with the governor general. This is a positive development, but this practice seems to have been triggered by a new level of comfort between the prime minister and the current governor general. It is hardly a victory for improved constitutional relationships when developments are based purely on personal comfort and preferences. The practice in provinces undoubtedly varies, but it seems that a pattern of first minister consultations with lieutenant governors is growing stronger.
13. A vivid, though imagined, rendition of weekly meetings between the Queen and the British prime minister is dramatized in the recent play by Peter Morgan, *The Audience* (London: Faber & Faber, 2013). The structure of the play—representations of the interchanges between the Queen and the twelve prime ministers who have served as her first minister—is based on an actual process. Form determines substance to a considerable degree, and since these meetings actually took place, the serious conversations in the play likely bear some relation to the actual events.
14. See Philip Pettit, "Before Negative and Positive Liberty," chap. 1 in *Republicanism: A Theory of Freedom and Government* (Oxford: Oxford University Press, 1997).
15. Hoi Kong, "Towards a Civic Republican Theory of Canadian Constitutional Law," *Review of Constitutional Studies* 15 (2011): 241.
16. There is no denying the controversial nature of both the basis for human rights and the content of rights. Amartya Sen addresses both questions in *The Idea of Justice* (Cambridge, MA: Belknap Press of Harvard University Press, 2009), 357-70. He notes that the republican basis for rights is less a matter of state protection (since the state's constant interest is in suppressing criticism) and more a matter of ensuring that the liberties and abilities of

citizens are not dependent on the will of others. Sen states that the viability of state-protected human rights is closely linked to the presence of agencies of "impartial scrutiny" (385).

17. See John D. Whyte, "The Obscure Moon Lighting an Obscure World: Looking at the Unwritten Constitution," *Journal of Parliamentary and Political Law* 6 (2012): 431.
18. Article 3 of United Nations Declaration on the Rights of Indigenous Peoples (General Assembly Resolution 61/295) states: "Indigenous peoples have the right of self-determination. By virtue of that right they freely determine their political status and freely pursue their economic, social and cultural development."
19. See James Tully, "Constitutionalism in an Age of Cultural Diversity," in *Strange Multiplicity: Constitutionalism in an Age of Diversity* (Cambridge: Cambridge University Press, 1995), 183-212, in which he argues that contemporary constitutionalism has rendered the ideas of singular identity, uniform sovereignty, comprehensive and exclusive authority, and canonical structure otiose. These ideas have been replaced with diverse nationalism, members' life-giving cultural identities, and a nation's just peace grounded in the processes of mediated peace. Tully concludes, "If this [contemporary] view of constitutionalism came to be accepted, the allegedly irreconcilable conflicts of the present would not have to be the tragic history of our future" (211).
20. The principle of coordinated political authorities is reflected in The Nisga'a Final Agreement (April 27, 1999), http://www.nnkn.ca/files/u28/nis-eng.pdf.
21. See *Campbell v. Attorney General (British Columbia) and Nisga'a Nation*, 2000 BCSC 1123 (July 24, 2000). The decision of Williamson, J. rejects all arguments that the First Nation government negotiated in the making of the Nisga'a Final Agreement violated the structure of the Constitution of Canada. Hence, the constitutional concepts that seem to be non-inclusive of First Nations self-governments are not a bar to their creation or recognition.
22. (1982) Q.B. 892 (Court of Appeal).
23. See J. R. Miller, *Compact, Contract, Covenant: Aboriginal Treaty-Making in Canada* (Toronto: University of Toronto Press, 2009), 157-59. Canadian government representatives would, no doubt, conceptualize their rhetoric as speaking *for the Crown*, but they explicitly identified their principal as the Queen.
24. *Supra* note 22, at 917.
25. James (Sákéj) Youngblood Henderson, "The Perspectives of Aboriginal Peoples of Canada on the Monarchy: Reflections on the Occasion of the Queen's Golden Jubilee," *Constitutional Forum Constitutionnel* 13 (2003): 9. Henderson states that "Elizabeth II's [Coronation] Oath constitutionally assured Aboriginal peoples in Canada that the Crown would respect their Aboriginal birthrights" (10).
26. Christian Wiman, "Every Riven Thing," in *Every Riven Thing* (New York: Farrar, Strauss and Giroux, 2010), 24-25.

Canada's Diamond Jubilee portrait of Queen Elizabeth II, by Toronto artist Phil Richards, was unveiled by the Queen in 2012. It is located in the ballroom of Rideau Hall.

The Diamond Jubilee Window, located above the Senate (east) entrance to the Centre Block on Parliament Hill. The window was a gift from the Senate to Her Majesty Queen Elizabeth II in celebration of the 60th anniversary of her reign. It depicts both Queen Elizabeth and Canada's first reigning monarch to reach her diamond jubilee, Queen Victoria, Her Majesty's great-great grandmother. The window was created by Goodman Zissoff Stained Glass Studio of Kelowna, British Columbia, and was dedicated in February 2012.

Photo credit: The Senate of Canada

The calendar in the Senate Chamber, commissioned in 2013 in celebration of the Diamond Jubilee of Her Majesty Queen Elizabeth II. The calendar was created by Manuk Inceyan of the Montreal firm Barocco in consultation with Paul Maréchal and Dominion Sculptor Phil White. It was paid for by subscription from senators and Senate officials, whose names are inscribed in a plaque affixed to the base.

Photo credit: The Senate of Canada

The Queen's personal Canadian flag is flown on Parliament Hill on Accession Day, February 6, 2012, marking the Diamond Jubilee of Queen Elizabeth II.
Photo credit: The Canadian Press / Sean Kilpatrick

Part 3

The Crown in Practice

10

The Provincial Crown: The Lieutenant Governor's Expanding Role

Christopher McCreery

En leur qualité de membres de la suite vice-royale, les lieutenants-gouverneurs ont de plus en plus emprunté au rôle de sensibilisation du public joué par les gouverneurs généraux depuis le mandat de Jeanne Sauvé. Ils ont néanmoins trouvé un meilleur équilibre entre l'application du concept de « mandat personnel », désormais lié au rôle moderne du représentant de la reine, et leur fonction traditionnelle de valorisation de la Couronne canadienne et de l'identité provinciale. Lors des périodes où la Couronne et la souveraine ont été marginalisées au niveau fédéral, les lieutenants-gouverneurs ont en effet persisté à faire valoir cet aspect de leurs devoirs, se permettant même d'innover en certaines occasions.

Cet examen de l'évolution des fonctions des lieutenants-gouverneurs des quarante dernières années offre un aperçu du rôle de la Couronne provinciale, de ses constantes comme de sa vulnérabilité. Car bien que cette charge n'ait plus rien à voir avec son mandat d'origine de délégué fédéral au sein des capitales provinciales, certaines ambiguïtés et incohérences continuent d'entraver la capacité des lieutenants-gouverneurs d'agir comme membres à part entière de la suite vice-royale du Canada.

> "In several Provinces there is public talk of doing away with the Lieutenant-Governors as an economy. Personally, I see little use in having nine Lieutenant-Governors as well as a Governor-General."
>
> —Lord Bessborough to Sir Clive Wigram, April 18, 1934

As his vice-regal tenure drew to a close, the Earl of Bessborough, fourteenth governor general of Canada, wrote to the King's private secretary, Sir Clive Wigram, of his opinion that the lieutenant governor's role was of marginal value, fraught with complexities local in nature and imbued with personality conflicts of a provincial nature. The governor general was not alone in his feelings about the position and usefulness of the Crown's provincial surrogates. Nevertheless, throughout the constitutional negotiations that would preoccupy the national and provincial capitals in the 1940s and again from the 1960s to 1990s, there was no serious discussion of abolishing these representatives of the Sovereign.[1] Over the past two decades there has not even been muted discussion of abolishing the state office at the apex of each province's system of government. Indeed, the utility and presence of the lieutenant governors have expanded and increased over the past forty years in a manner that few could have foreseen in Bessborough's time.

Discussion of the Crown in post-Confederation Canada has tended to focus on its federal incarnation, with the provincial Crown left aside, viewed as a miniature version of Ottawa.[2] R. MacGregor Dawson reflected in his foreword to John T. Saywell's seminal work on the office of the lieutenant governor, "Many people with orderly minds tend to see the office and function of the lieutenant governor simply as a copy in essential of what they profess to find at Westminster and Ottawa. The truth is that no very exact parallel between the two major governments can be drawn."[3] Today, this assessment warrants a re-examination, especially in light of the expansion of the role of the lieutenant governor in many areas and the near extinction of the prospect that the federal power of reservation or disallowance regarding provincial legislation will be exercised. Since the end of the Second World War, the provincial Crown has evolved in tandem with its federal counterpart in many areas, and in a few instances has proven to be more dynamic and robust, even in the face of indifferent governments of all stripes and jurisdictions. There is some utility in beginning with a review of precisely who the lieutenant governors are and how their position has transformed since Confederation.

The provincial Crown is largely manifested and promoted through the person and office of the lieutenant governor. While the position of lieutenant governor is secured in the Constitution Act, 1867 and the Constitution Act, 1982—with matters touching upon the Crown exceedingly difficult to amend since patriation—the lieutenant governors have never had an easy time of discharging their duties as representatives of the Sovereign. Scarcely a decade after their offices were established, Prime Minister Alexander Mackenzie suggested that it was time to "terminate the regal splendour, so entirely out of keeping with actual circumstances"[4] of their position. Mackenzie had little time for the role, and aspired for the lieutenant governors to be little more than ceremonial judges minding affairs on behalf of Ottawa. A number of governors general believed that the role of their provincial counterparts was narrow, hindered by a lack of resources and encumbered by lack of independence from their provincial governments. As Bessborough wrote to King George V via Sir Clive Wigram in 1934,

> In several Provinces there is public talk of doing away with the Lieutenant-Governors as an economy. Personally, I see little use in having nine Lieutenant-Governors as well as a Governor-General. They have no personal contact with Your Majesty whatever. Though most respectable and patriotic men, they have no training, no background, and are too well-known locally to be able to impress themselves on the population as being really personal representatives of the Crown. Not one of the existing Lieutenant-Governors can afford the great expense of touring their Provinces, where they could really do useful work in encouraging patriotic fervor in little visited isolated districts.... I do not think the doing away with the Lieutenant-Governors would, for the reasons I have given, in any way diminish the prestige of the Crown in the Dominion.[5]

Despite Bessborough's reflections on the position and role of lieutenant governors, none of his concerns would resonate today. Concerning his lament that lieutenant governors have "no training," one cannot help but wonder what sort of training Bessborough envisioned. Certainly, even he would accept that a modestly distinguished career in public or private service was sufficient. This is something that present-day lieutenant governors have all brought to the office, as the partisan tinge so often linked to the appointment has dissipated.

Non-partisanship is a characteristic that was formally employed in the 2011 selection of the governor general and most recently by the Advisory Committee on Vice-Regal Appointments.[6] This is not an insignificant achievement when one considers that from Confederation until 1988, 65 percent of lieutenant governors had previously served as elected politicians.[7] The propensity to appoint individuals with strong partisan background remained significant from 1988 to 2005 when 72 percent of appointments (twenty-three of the thirty-two) were given to former politicians or senior party officials. Of the seventeen lieutenant governors appointed since Stephen Harper became prime minister, only two have had strong partisan backgrounds—a negligible 11 percent. The partisan colouring of these office holders has largely faded to beige over the last eight years.

Today, lieutenant governors are also devoid of the long-lingering silhouette as agents in the capitals responsible for overseeing provincial affairs on behalf of the federal government. Polling suggests that the governor general and lieutenant governors are viewed as being bipolar in a positive manner[8]—representing the Crown while also representing all of the people within the province, politically beige and able to connect with a myriad of communities, thus furthering the Crown's unifying capacity.

By examining developments in the role of the lieutenant governor over the past four decades, we can better gauge the effectiveness of the role as a focal point for the Crown in the provinces. This chapter uses

Walter Bagehot's paradigm of the efficient and dignified elements of the Sovereign's role to illuminate the constitutional and ceremonial role of lieutenant governors in both federal and provincial spheres.

Sovereign's Delegate in the Provinces: Efficient and Dignified Aspects

While the role of the governor general and the lieutenant governors, whom Governor General David Johnston has frequently referred to as "Canada's vice-regal family,"[9] is to serve as the Queen's representatives and function as constitutional heads of their respective jurisdictions, the delineation of roles and responsibilities is not neatly covered in a single document. For the governor general, the broad role and office are delineated in the Letters Patent Constituting the Office of the Governor General, 1947, with a few references included in the Constitution Act, 1867. Conversely, the role of the lieutenant governors takes up ten sections of the Constitution Act, 1867, and precious little is left for inclusion in the Commission and Letters of Instruction issued to lieutenant governors upon appointment. The existence of the office and person of a governor general prior to Confederation is cited as the reason why there was no need to fully define the role in the Constitution Act,[10] while the birth of lieutenant governors as federal officers with Confederation explains their extensive inclusion in sections 58–67 of the Constitution Act, 1867.

The wording of the Commission appointing lieutenant governors has remained largely unchanged since Confederation; similarly, the Letters of Instruction do little to illuminate the reader as to the role of the officer trusted with their discharge. Standardized letters of instruction were not issued to lieutenant governors until 1887, two decades after the office came into being. As Saywell observed, "the federal government obviously placed little stock in the value of formal instructions."[11]

The present iteration of the Letters of Instruction dates from 1976 and is a near carbon-copy of its antecedent that was issued in 1952.[12] A laconic document in comparison with the Letters Patent, 1947, the Letters of Instruction, 1976 outline the appointment of the lieutenant governor; the requirement for taking certain oaths; the ability to administer oaths; the ability to reserve bills for the signification of the governor general-in-council (along with explanation for the reservation); the requirement to transmit within six months of prorogation of the provincial legislature a copy of each act that has been granted royal assent to the minister of Canadian Heritage; and the requirement to follow direction of the governor general-in-council disallowing acts and proclaiming the disallowance. Lastly, the lieutenant governor may not leave or "quit the province" without having informed the minister of Canadian Heritage nor leave Canada in an official capacity without receiving leave through the same minister.

A read of these documents makes it appear as though the lieutenant governor's efficient role is little more than a cipher and post office for the federal government. It is only when juxtaposed to the ruling of the Judicial Committee of the Privy Council, *Liquidators of the Maritime Bank v. the Receiver General of New Brunswick, 1892*, that the status of lieutenant governors as representatives of the Sovereign is fully revealed: "A Lieutenant Governor, when appointed, is as much the Representative of Her Majesty for all purposes of provincial government as the Governor General is for all purposes of Dominion Government."

This single statement has long served as the battle cry of provincial autonomy and the legal proof that lieutenant governors are not mere federal agents but representatives of the Queen in right of their province. In 1948, the Supreme Court of Canada went further in clarifying the lieutenant governor's relationship with the federal government. The court unanimously found that the office of the lieutenant governor is purely provincial in disposition:

> The nature of the federal and provincial legislative and executive powers is clearly settled and the Lieutenant-Governor, who "carries on the Government of the Province" manifestly does not act in respect of the Government of Canada. All the functions he performs are directed to the affairs of the Province and are in no way connected with the Government of Canada.[13]

The provincial efficient role of the lieutenant governor mirrors that of the governor general in federal jurisdiction in most aspects: granting royal assent; approving orders-in-council; summoning, dissolving, and proroguing the legislature; selecting a head of government; and swearing in ministries. Even with the adoption of fixed-election-date legislation federally and in eight provinces, the vice-regal role has not been significantly altered, in large part because the wording of these acts assiduously avoids trampling on the Crown's prerogative to dissolve the legislature.

We should also not underestimate the effect that regular meetings between the lieutenant governor and the premier can and often do have. In at least six provinces there is a tradition of regular meetings in which the two principles discuss a variety of matters—all in camera, rarely with a formal agenda prepared, no minutes of meetings, and no staff present—often to the annoyance of the political and bureaucratic *apparatai*. On these occasions, the lieutenant governor exercises his or her right to be consulted, to encourage, and to warn. We are not privy to the actual details of the discussions—nor would it be advisable for such things to be made public until years after. But it would be difficult to justify taking an hour or two out of the very active schedules of the premier and the lieutenant governor if the discussions were limited to the weather and the next NHL draft.

The lieutenant governor's role differs in other respects from that of the governor general, notably the lingering powers of reservation and disallowance. Bill C60, introduced by Pierre Elliot Trudeau's government in 1978 following the release of the white paper "A Time for Action," would have expunged the powers of reservation and disallowance; however, both remain, covered in sections 55 to 57 of the Constitution Act, 1867. A number of scholars have questioned why these powers were not expunged "in the major constitutional reforms of 1981–82 if it was generally agreed that they were constitutionally obsolete."[14] Reservation was last exercised in 1961 in Saskatchewan, much to the annoyance of the Diefenbaker government, which disavowed the action with great alacrity.[15] In many respects the courts have assumed the lieutenant governors' power of reservation in that they have the ability to place legislation into a state of stasis pending further review.[16]

At the first conference of the governor general and lieutenant governors, held at Rideau Hall in 1973, Eugene Forsey delivered an important treatise on the modern position of lieutenant governors. On the subject of disallowance, he reflected that the power is "now widely but perhaps prematurely, considered to be constitutionally obsolete. It is certainly not legally obsolete."[17] But it is highly unlikely in an era of permanent provincial autonomy that any federal government would consider, much less employ, the old power of disallowance, which has not been used in generations. David E. Smith notes that "disallowance was a failing remedy in the 1870s";[18] it can hardly be viewed as a viable mechanism for imposing the will of the federal government in the modern era. Such actions would return the lieutenant governor to nothing more than a federal agent, instantly politicize the Crown in a detrimental manner, and foment a high level of national discord. The prospect of a lieutenant governor being instructed by the governor general-in-council to issue a proclamation disallowing a piece of legislation ranks with the likelihood of the Sovereign withholding royal assent. We should remember that it is the governor general-in-council who instructs disallowance, not the lieutenant governor; in such instances the lieutenant governor is reduced to an automaton.

The lieutenant governors, unlike the governor general, have no formal role in military affairs or extraterritorial relations. The governor general acquired a military role in 1905 when the Sovereign delegated the position of commander-in-chief, and an extraterritorial role in 1917 through Resolution IX at the Imperial War Conference. The resolution, which permitted the Government of Canada to conduct extraterritorial relations without reference to the British government, would lead to the governor general being able to venture overseas on behalf of the Canadian government.

So what of the lingering federal role? Peter Hogg notes that once "an appointment is made the lieutenant governor is in no sense an agent of the federal government: he or she is obliged by the conventions of responsible government to act on the advice of the provincial cabinet."[19] Yet this does not preclude lieutenant governors from carrying out duties that are federal in nature within the confines of their province. The lieutenant governors' dignified role as promoters of identity and the Crown is not limited to "provincial" matters. Over the past forty years, the dignified aspects of the lieutenant governors' role have blurred across federal and provincial jurisdictions. Through the multifaceted nature of the Crown, lieutenant governors promote provincial identity while also advancing national cohesion and membership in the broader Canadian family. They may be the penultimate personifications of the Crown in each jurisdiction, but they also discharge a duty federal in scope by promoting certain elements of the dignified federal state.

While the efficient role has remained largely unchanged, the dignified aspect, both provincial and federal in scope, has expanded well beyond the Commission and Letters of Instruction. Much of the expanded role has come in relation to the federal aspect of representing the Crown and Canada writ large. These high-profile activities have brought many more citizens into contact with the Queen's representatives as personifications of both the federal and provincial Crown. Indeed, we can best describe the dignified federal role of lieutenant governors as that of representing the provinces to themselves and representing Canada in the provinces. Thus, in the dignified realm they are symbolic agents for the promotion of province and nation—not nefarious federal constitutional interlopers.

While the lieutenant governors are representatives of the Queen in right of their respective provinces, they continue to carry out duties on behalf of the Crown in right of Canada. It is in these dignified areas of cross-pollination that the effectiveness and influence of the lieutenant governors as representatives of the Crown have been enhanced. This has been greatly aided by expansion of the Canadian honours system and involvement in citizenship swearing-in ceremonies, the Caring Canadian Award program, and commemorative events such as jubilees and national anniversaries. These comparatively recent developments have been added to lieutenant governors' pre-existing roles of serving as provincial patrons for various organizations, presenting awards and according recognition, touring their provinces, and undertaking various events at the community/grassroots level. In essence, the lieutenant governor is serving as the constitutional head of a province, while simultaneously acting as its "promoter-in-chief." The level of citizen engagement, and the role of the lieutenant governor as a fellow citizen who aids in highlighting the good works of others, have broadened greatly.

Throughout the Queen's Diamond Jubilee year, lieutenant governors were principally involved at the grassroots level in celebrations and recognition functions, with more than 450 events held or attended by lieutenant governors in relation to the Jubilee. While this is nothing new (witness their involvement in the 1897 Diamond Jubilee of Queen

Victoria), the grassroots focus—beyond stiff formal dinners and military parades—is further evidence of the depth to which the lieutenant governors can reach into communities. The involvement of lieutenant governors in the Diamond Jubilee built upon the 2002 Golden Jubilee celebrations and will certainly be considered in plans for the 150th anniversary of Confederation in 2017.

Two other aspects of the dignified federal role can be found in the relationship the Crown has with First Nations and the Canadian Forces. Even prior to the installation of Canada's first Aboriginal lieutenant governor in 1974, when Ralph Steinhauer was appointed in Alberta, many lieutenant governors have had a special relationship with the First Nations of their provinces. This relationship has grown extensively over the past decade, notably in British Columbia, Alberta, Saskatchewan, Ontario, New Brunswick, and Nova Scotia. The appointment of Aboriginal lieutenant governors in Ontario (2002), British Columbia (2007), and New Brunswick (2009) has helped to enhance the connection. Native leaders have consistently viewed the lieutenant governor as a representative of the Queen[20] and as a direct connection to the Crown with which they have treaties—even if these treaties are administered through the Government of Canada.

The connection to the Canadian Forces enjoyed by lieutenant governors is revealed in a few areas: service of some lieutenant governors as honorary colonels in the Canadian Army and Royal Canadian Air Force and as honorary captains in the Royal Canadian Navy, and voluntary services performed by honorary aides-de-camp. At present, three lieutenant governors hold honorary appointments in the Canadian Forces; this number has been as high as six. Whether or not they serve in honorary positions, lieutenant governors in every jurisdiction have an involvement with the Canadian Forces. This connection can be traced to pre-Confederation times, when a number of governors served as commanders-in-chief.

Within provincial jurisdiction, the dignified aspect of the lieutenant governor's role has similarly expanded. By the time the Order of Newfoundland and Labrador was established in 2001, every province had created an order of merit with the lieutenant governor serving as chancellor (except Quebec, where the premier presents the honour).[21] These programs have drawn the lieutenant governors further into the field of honours beyond the presentation of national exemplary service medals, commemorative medals and, on certain occasions, the Order of Canada. Their involvement has come from two sources: the desire of provincial governments to afford their new provincial honours the legitimacy that the Crown affords such distinctions, and the desire of lieutenant governors to expand their role in recognizing exemplary citizenship on behalf of the Crown, be it in its federal or its provincial manifestation. A 2012 Ipsos Reid poll found that among the key activities Canadians wanted their vice-regal representatives to carry out, 68 percent believed that presenting awards and recognizing citizens were important. The promotion of provincial heritage and identity ranked third, with 72 percent of respondents citing it as important. Also highly valued was working on community projects to protect the environment at 73 percent or to help the disadvantaged at 76 percent.[22]

The International Sphere

Counter-intuitively, one area in which the lieutenant governor's role has expanded is that of provincial missions abroad; these visits have emulated the governor general's overseas role in certain aspects. The outward international role played by governors general since Vincent Massey's address to the United States Congress in 1954 and Roland Michener's visit to the Benelux countries in 1971 has expanded to become a regular aspect of the governor general's duties. Although these missions are largely goodwill affairs, successive federal governments have viewed them as important tools in promoting Canada's interests overseas. Such visits help to further diplomatic relations between friendly states and forge new links with countries that Canada does not have a deep connection with. In the international sphere, the governor general is viewed as being at the level of a head of state, well beyond that of a federal cabinet minister or diplomat. Successive governments would not have seen fit to invest the requisite resources, personnel and budgetary, into these visits were they not highly useful tools of outreach and amity.

Following a trade mission visit to West Germany made in 1964 by Nova Scotia's lieutenant governor, Major-General E. C. Plow, the department of the Secretary of State reminded all lieutenant governors that their appointments did not include any extra-provincial role. The following year, Plow embarked upon yet another trade mission, this time to Japan; however, on this occasion he formally consulted the Government of Canada.[23] When lieutenant governors travel unofficially outside their province, they do so as regular citizens, with no honours, salutes, flags, or other courtesies extended to them as in their home province.

As the number of provincial trade missions overseas expanded in the 1990s, there was a sort of delayed reaction and lieutenant governors began to be included in these international goodwill ventures seeking to enhance commercial, cultural, and educational relationships. Most recently, the lieutenant governor of Manitoba accompanied his premier on missions to China. The former lieutenant governor of New Brunswick, Herménégilde Chiasson, also went on a mission to China. While in office in Ontario, Hilary Weston made a visit to Ireland, the Vatican, and Russia.[24] Even on the national stage, lieutenant governors have occasionally been called upon to play a role beyond the provincial scope. One of the most prominent examples occurred in 2010 during the Winter

Paralympic Games, when Lieutenant Governor David Onley of Ontario was included in a variety of events, even though the games were taking place outside his province. Onley was similarly called upon to serve as part of the Canadian delegation at the 2012 summer Paralympic Games in London, this time with assistance from his own provincial government.

As some provinces have come to employ their lieutenant governors in overseas endeavours, there is a likelihood that even the more nonplussed provincial governments will come to see them as useful tools of diplomacy and goodwill, seeking to achieve a level of engagement overseas that is routinely part of the lieutenant governors' role at home. It has taken fifty years for the federal government to become indifferent to these sorts of missions, and it is only in the last decade that a few provinces have begun to employ their lieutenant governors in such a fashion.

Promoting the Crown

Lieutenant governors have been much less prone to minimizing their role as representatives of the Crown than has been the case federally. A number of federal governments and some former governors general sought to reduce the vice-regal connection to the Crown, while trumpeting the governor general's authority as that of Canada's head of state. In what can politely be termed the "cult of the governor," these incumbents focused their tenure entirely on a set grouping of themes and interests, none of which included promoting or even acknowledging their role as the Queen's representative or their constitutional role in government.

During periods when the role of the Queen and Crown was significantly underplayed by the governor general of the day, notably during the Clarkson and Jean tenures, lieutenant governors remained stalwart promoters of the Crown. This was revealed through installation speeches, routine addresses, websites, use of the royal salute and the royal anthem at ceremonies, and even such obvious gestures as displaying a portrait of the Queen in public locations within their offices. More importantly, lieutenant governors actively promoted the Crown by honouring their place within our system of government, acting as neutral constitutional arbiters, and articulating their role as one of convivial citizen engagement and interaction.

The active promotion of the Crown by lieutenant governors can be traced to the 1970s when the federal government began to "Canadianize" the Crown. The Canadianization of the 1970s and 1980s typically reduced the prominence of the Queen and marginalized the appertaining symbols, which were viewed as "British" by mandarins struggling to deal with Quebec nationalism.[25] Lieutenant governors felt it increasingly necessary to explain their role as constitutional heads and ceremonial promoters of their respective provinces, and this mandate dovetailed naturally with the promotion of the Crown and the role it plays within our democratic system. Lieutenant governors have conveyed this message through speeches and public engagements, through books, pamphlets, and tours and, within the last decade, through a robust presence on the Internet.

This is not to suggest that this support for the Crown and constitutional monarchy is solely on account of a personal interest that lieutenant governors have taken in promoting the institution. While many lieutenant governors have shown personal attachment to the Sovereign, their support for the Crown is also tied to the nature of their position in the provinces. There is an inherently reflective aspect to the role of the lieutenant governor, in that their status is entirely derived from their constitutional position as the Queen's representatives. Being a representative of the Queen bestows "instant symbolism."[26] It is difficult for incumbents to eschew the benefits of this connection without greatly diminishing the status of the provincial vice-regal office; this has been proven especially true in provinces that have modest populations. Unlike the governor general, lieutenant governors have relied heavily upon the reflective prestige of the Crown for their own authority and status. Governors general may sideline the reflective nature of their office because of the pomp and circumstance accorded them by Ottawa in fulfilling their national, international, military, and honours / recognition roles. The governor general is also usually imbued with a national persona by the press, something that only some lieutenant governors have been able to achieve, notably Sir Eugène Fiset, George R. Pearkes, Lincoln Alexander, David Lam, Lois Hole, Margaret McCain, Pauline McGibbon, Hilary Weston, John Crosbie and, within the francophone world, Herménégilde Chiasson.

Support and Vulnerability

Lieutenant governors have always been the most vulnerable of the Queen's representatives when it comes to dealing with fluctuating levels of support. Canadian history is replete with examples of arbitrary budget reductions and administrative decisions made in an effort to punish the Crown's representative, usually on account of some decision by the federal government. The most obvious byproduct has been the reduction or closure of Government Houses as residences and ceremonial homes in half of the provinces: New Brunswick (1890), Ontario (1937), Alberta (1937), Saskatchewan (1944), and Quebec (1999). Today only Ontario and Quebec remain without Government Houses; however, of the three reopened Government Houses only New Brunswick's is used as both a residence and ceremonial home. While the façade of seeking a fiscal saving has often been used, it has never been employed without a degree of discord between the premier and the federal government of the day.

Provincial budgets and administrative support have also been known to fluctuate when tension develops between a lieutenant governor and the provincial government.

The penchant for provincial governments to treat their governors in this way has transpired with similar frequency and under comparable circumstances in the Australian states. These instances highlight the need for adequate financial resources and administrative support to prevent the office from returning to a position that could be effectively discharged only by individuals of substantial means, capable of supplementing provincial and federal support with their own funds.

Moreover, provincial governments have at times been "provincial" in the pejorative sense of marginalizing or ignoring the office of lieutenant governor. Especially in Quebec under the various Parti Québécois administrations, the lieutenant governor has been sidelined. There is no question that the lieutenant governor of Quebec has the most challenging role of all his Commonwealth realm colleagues in discharging his dignified functions. The tendency to blatantly sideline the lieutenant governor can be traced to the premiership of Maurice Duplessis. His government followed what can be described as the "de Valera approach"[27] of secluding the Crown and its representative at every opportunity while continuing to rely upon the lieutenant governor's constitutional functions—a sort of schizophrenic relationship of dependence on the legal authority but disdain for the symbolic and ceremonial duties. Quebec's attitude is ironic given the part played by the provincial Crown in securing provincial autonomy and independence in so many areas within the federal state.[28]

Provincial governments have near limitless latitude to impinge upon the independence and arm's-length relationship that the office and person of lieutenant governor is supposed to have with their governments. This is a relationship not delineated in any formal document or act; rather, it should emulate how other arm's-length officers interact with provincial governments. For example, provincial chief justices and federally appointed judges rely upon support from provincial governments yet are treated as arm's-length entities for budgetary, operational, and human resources purposes. A similar arrangement would ensure the independence and neutrality of the lieutenant governors and their offices; however, it remains elusive. For fear of trampling on provincial rights or causing a needless federal-provincial imbroglio, the federal government has assiduously respected the provinces' right to treat—some might say abuse—their respective lieutenant governors as they see fit, undermining the larger role, both dignified and efficient, that lieutenant governors are supposed to play.

By contrast, it is more difficult for the federal government to marginalize the governor general, given the national presence and scope of the role. Moreover, it is not in the federal government's interest to leave the representative of the head of state cloistered, homeless, and unsupported.

While there have been instances of fluctuating administrative and budgetary support, when compared with what has transpired in some provinces over the past seventy years incursions into Rideau Hall's independence have been infrequent.

While there remain varying degrees of support for the lieutenant governors beyond a very modest annual grant from the federal government, over the past two decades there has been a professionalization and modest expansion of the offices that serve lieutenant governors in most provinces. In every province save Prince Edward Island, the lieutenant governor's office now employs a chief of staff, often styled private secretary or principal secretary, some at the level of assistant deputy minister.[29] Until the late 1980s, most lieutenant governors were served by an administrative assistant, a correspondence secretary, a driver, and a few honorary aides-de-camp, the latter offering their services on a voluntary basis. The exception to this formula has been the larger provinces—British Columbia, Ontario, and Quebec—and Newfoundland and Labrador.[30]

Angels Dancing on the Head of a Pin? Administrators, Symbols, Styles, Salutes, and Tours

There are a number of matters, both dignified and efficient in nature, that hinder the ability of lieutenant governors to fully discharge their role as the Sovereign's surrogate in their respective provinces. On the surface, many of these points could be viewed as trivial or only necessary in the most unusual circumstances. Over the past five years, the Canadian public has learned a great deal about how unusual political circumstances can greatly heighten the significance of the royal prerogative in determining the duration and viability of a government, and so there is a renewed interest in the constitutional fire-extinguisher role that the Crown's representatives can discharge. Nor should we ignore the importance of the symbolic and ceremonial elements of the lieutenant governors' role, for it is the constant public side of their function that is most frequently encountered by the citizenry—constitutional crises being mercifully rare.

While the courts long ago determined that the lieutenant governors are equal to the governor general,[31] there has been great reluctance on the part of federal authorities to acknowledge this in the dignified aspect of the lieutenant governors' role. As for the efficient responsibilities, lieutenant governors have been left to their own devices. All this is despite the fact that many of these issues have been discussed openly for the past century, dating back to the 1913 Interprovincial Conference.

From the efficient side, the lieutenant governors and the constitutional functioning of the provinces are incredibly vulnerable when a lieutenant governor dies in office.[32] Unlike the Sovereign, or even the governor general, when a lieutenant governor dies in office the entire executive apparatus of the state comes to a grinding halt. "The King is dead, long live the King" does not apply; rather, "the lieutenant governor is dead, we need a new lieutenant governor immediately" is the mantra when it comes to the continuance of a provincial government's ability to exercise executive authority.[33]

This is because an administrator's ability to act on behalf of a lieutenant governor evaporates upon the death of a lieutenant governor. The legal capacity of the administrator (usually the chief justice of the province) is directly tied to the commission of an individual lieutenant governor, not to the office. By contrast, when a governor general dies in office, the administrator can act in the governor's place. When the lieutenant governor of Alberta, Lois Hole, died in 2005 it took two weeks for a replacement to be identified, secured, vetted, and installed. For two weeks in Alberta no orders-in-council, no instruments of advice, no royal assent could be given. At the time of publication, three serving lieutenant governors are over the age of 73, and one, aged 82 years, recently retired; statistically the average life expectancy for a Canadian male is 78 years. Few consider the death of a lieutenant governor to be an issue—save the lieutenant governor personally—until it occurs, but then it is a crisis because it paralyzes government.

The development of the Advisory Committee on Vice-Regal Appointments, announced in 2012 by the prime minister's office, is an excellent step toward formalizing the appointment process. To highlight the role of lieutenant governors as representatives of the Sovereign, there would be some advantage to having the prime minister forward the names of proposed lieutenant governors to Her Majesty for consideration in advance of their appointments.

All of the provincial tables of precedence rank lieutenant governors as senior officers, aside from Saskatchewan where the Queen is placed at the head of the table. Federally they rank ninth, immediately after members of the federal cabinet and Leader of the Opposition—so in reality they rank fortieth or fiftieth if they are in the presence of members of the federal cabinet and heads of Commonwealth and foreign missions accredited to Canada. This has been the case since 1939, when lieutenant governors were demoted at the direction of Prime Minister Mackenzie King in advance of that year's royal tour. From Confederation to 1939, lieutenant governors had ranked after the governor general in the federal table of precedence,[34] ahead of the prime minister and members of the federal cabinet. Successive prime ministers, dating back to Sir John A. Macdonald in 1886, had contemplated demoting lieutenant governors within the table of precedence. The federal government viewed lieutenant governors as mere federal officers who held patronage plums; indeed, at the time such appointments were largely filled by retired, defeated, and failed politicians.[35] But the motive was largely partisan: the prime minister wanted maximum visibility during royal visits and state visits.

A similar pattern holds for the provinces. Since the 1964 royal tour, premiers have replaced lieutenant governors as hosts during royal tours. Again, the motive was greater visibility for elected officials. The provincial government rubric—that he who pays gets the visibility—has trumped a tradition dating from the 1860 royal tour of the Prince of Wales. This tour showed that it was important, especially in the provinces, for the representative of the Crown to be closely associated with the royal personage making a visit.

The titles and honours afforded to lieutenant governors are a source of confusion to many people, and this confusion may hinder the full discharge of the office. Lieutenant governors are addressed as "Your Honour," a designation most often associated with judges. Matters are further convoluted when governors in other realms are styled "Excellency." Indeed, lieutenant governors prior to Confederation were styled in this fashion, a form of address that is also accorded to high commissioners and ambassadors accredited to Canada. For the student of the ceremonial aspects of the role, it is well known that lieutenant governors are given a fifteen-gun salute,[36] while the governor general receives a twenty-one-gun salute, an honour that was raised from a nineteen-gun salute in 1949.

The more cumbersome issue of the designation *lieutenant* governor is not so easily addressed, as changing the office to "governor" would require an amendment to the Constitution Act, 1867. Even the most ardent defender of the institution would agree that this is a non-starter, at least not as a stand-alone alteration; the benefits of such a change are minute in relation to the potential debate that would ensue. Similarly, the occasional proposal that lieutenant governors simply be styled "governors" in all official documentation is problematic. Nevertheless, in both Newfoundland & Labrador and Nova Scotia the colloquial "governor" continues to be used in referring to the lieutenant governor, due to historical precedents.[37]

The administrative subordination of lieutenant governors to the minister of Canadian Heritage and his department is another Macdonald-era holdover. Like reservation, this is a "reminder of colonial status which the modern provincial governments dislike,"[38] as J. R. Mallory described it, although it is doubtful today that provincial governments even consider the threat of reservation as being viable. Prior to the Second World War, the secretary of state had significant latitude in dealing with the various provincial secretaries, who have almost entirely disappeared from the world of interprovincial relations. Ideally, there should be a small vice-regal secretariat in the Privy Council Office, as a stand-alone office co-located with Rideau Hall or through the Canadian secretary to the Queen, that could serve all vice-regal representatives regardless of jurisdiction. The dispatch of acts of the legislature should ideally be ended altogether, or at the very least be transmitted through a less lowly mechanism than the Department of Canadian Heritage.

A number of these anomalies have been noted by scholars and commentators over the years, notably John T. Saywell, Andrew Heard, and, most recently, D. Michael Jackson and Lynda Haverstock. Some of these items could be rectified with the stroke of a pen and an order-in-council under the direction of the minister of Canadian Heritage. The present governor general's collegial approach to the vice-regal family has eliminated one of the principal obstacles to imbuing the lieutenant governors with greater symbolic equality as personal representatives of the Queen within their jurisdictions. The weightier issue of the demise of a lieutenant governor and mechanism for appointment of an administrator is more problematic, as it would require a constitutional amendment.

An Expanded Role

The growth of the lieutenant governors' role over the past forty years, while largely limited to the dignified aspect of their duties, has enhanced the scope and effectiveness of the provincial Crown. The expanded role that has been assumed by lieutenant governors is the result of the Crown stepping in to fill a vacuum in certain dignified areas, and to a lesser degree the necessity for keeping partisan officials out of institutions such as provincial honours. The continuance of the efficient role of regular meetings with premiers and the soft sort of authority or advice that can be exercised behind closed doors perpetuates the role of the lieutenant governor as more than a ceremonial actor alone.

The developments have been incrementally dynamic, which is to be expected given the nature of an institution rooted in history and tradition. Not becoming entangled in contretemps over federal and provincial jurisdiction when it comes to the dignified aspect of the role has been an important element of the successes achieved over the past three decades. The concept of the Canadian vice-regal family, what MacKinnon termed a "team of governors," is increasingly important. While a uniform approach will never work in a country as expansive and diverse as Canada, there is much to be gained by the various representatives of the Crown continuing to sharing best practices and experiences in citizen engagement and grassroots involvement, serving not only as constitutional heads of their respective jurisdictions but also as cheerleaders-in-chief for the achievements and endeavours of the citizens they serve on behalf of the Queen.

Certainly there are areas where existing practices vis-à-vis the lieutenant governors' relationship with the federal government should be altered to better reflect their position as the Queen's representatives in the provinces; however, most of these changes would constitute housekeeping matters. The lieutenant governors and the provincial Crown have proven to be resilient and active in seizing opportunities to promote both provincial and federal identity while maintaining a close connection with the citizenry through patronage, recognition, ceremonies, and other collective endeavours. As promoters-in-chief and chief executive officers of each province, lieutenant governors continue to uphold the dignity of the Crown, fostering voluntary service and outreach to both traditional constituents and marginalized communities, while advancing provincial identity and achievements on the local and provincial stages. That they have found an enhanced role in promoting the dignified aspects of the federal state and also delved into the international arena demonstrates the capacity of lieutenant governors to serve Crown, province, and country in an increasingly fluid and rapidly changing society.

Notes

1. John T. Saywell, "The Lieutenant-Governors," in *The Provincial Political System, Comparative Essays*, ed. David Bellamy, Jon Pammett, and David Rowat (Toronto: Methuen, 1976), 307.
2. The 1892 ruling of the Judicial Committee of the Privy Council in *Liquidators of the Maritime Bank v. Receiver General of New Brunswick*, that the lieutenant governor represented the Queen in a province just as the governor general did federally, confirmed the co-sovereign status of the provincial Crown in Confederation.
3. R. MacGregor Dawson, foreword to *The Office of Lieutenant-Governor: A Study in Canadian Government and Politics*, by John T. Saywell (Toronto: Copp Clark Pittman, 1986), vii.
4. Alexander Mackenzie to Sir Oliver Mowat, January 29, 1876, Mackenzie Papers 5, Queen's University Archives.
5. Lord Bessborough to Sir Clive Wigram, April 18, 1934, Bessborough Papers, West Sussex Record Office.
6. Prime Minister's Office, "New Advisory Committee on Vice-Regal Appointments," November 4, 2012, http://www.pm.gc.ca/eng/media.asp?id=5142.
7. From 1867 to 1988, 138 of 211 lieutenant governors had campaigned for or served in elected office federally or provincially. See Jeffrey Simpson, *The Spoils of Power* (Toronto: Harper Collins, 1989), 309-10; and Peter Boyce, *The Queen's Other Realms* (Sydney: Federation Press, 2008), 96.
8. Ipsos Reid, "The New Canada and Its Regal Relevance: A Historic Role in a Dynamic Time," June 2012.
9. The Right Honourable David Johnston, speaking at a luncheon for lieutenant governors and territorial commissioners, October 2, 2011.
10. Andrew Heard, *Canadian Constitutional Conventions: The Marriage of Law and Politics* (Toronto: Oxford University Press, 1991), 16.
11. Saywell, *Office of Lieutenant-Governor*, 172-73.
12. Order-in-Council PC 1976-2593, October 21, 1976. The previous Letters of Instruction differed only in the requirement that acts be transmitted to Ottawa within ten days of prorogation of the provincial legislature.
13. *The King v. Caroll* [1948] SCR 126, 130-31.
14. David E. Smith, *The Invisible Crown: The First Principle of Canadian Government* (Toronto: University of Toronto Press, 1995), 43.

15. The governor general subsequently granted royal assent to the bill reserved by the lieutenant governor of Saskatchewan; see Order-in-Council PC 1961-675, May 5, 1961; and J. R. Mallory, "The Lieutenant Governor's Discretionary Powers," *Canadian Journal of Economic and Political Science* 27 (November 1961): 518-22.
16. Fred Burke, "The Office of Lieutenant Governor," in *Provincial Government and Politics,* ed. Ronald C. Rowat (Ottawa: Carleton University, 1973), 130.
17. Eugene Forsey, "Notes on the Constitutional Position and Powers of the Lieutenant Governor" (talk delivered at Rideau Hall, 1973), 20.
18. Smith, *Invisible Crown,* 150.
19. Peter W. Hogg, *Constitutional Law of Canada,* 2nd ed. (Toronto: Carswell, 1985), 91.
20. It is worth noting that lieutenant governors are "representatives of the Queen" and not "personal representatives of the Queen," in that they perform a constitutional function on behalf of the Crown. However, they do not personally represent the Sovereign as would someone such as the Duke of York, who served as the Queen's personal representative at the funeral of Pierre Trudeau in 2000, while then governor general Adrienne Clarkson served as the Queen's representative in right of Canada.
21. There is no chancellor of the *Ordre national du Québec,* and the lieutenant governor plays no formal role in the Order.
22. Ipsos Reid, "New Canada."
23. Privy Council Office, *Manual of Official Procedure of the Government of Canada,* vol. 1, prepared by Henry F. Davis and André Millar (Ottawa: Government of Canada, 1968), 308.
24. Weston visited the Vatican and Russia with the agreement of the premier of Ontario; her Russia visit was in conjunction with the Toronto bid for the 1996 Summer Olympics.
25. Peter Boyce, *The Queen's Other Realms,* 70-76.
26. Frank Mackinnon, *The Crown in Canada* (Calgary: McClelland & Stewart, 1976), 94.
27. As president of the executive council of the Irish Free State, Eamon de Valera introduced the Executive Authority (External Relations) Act, 1936. This act abolished the office of the governor general and effectively removed the Crown from most of the dignified and efficient roles.
28. Smith, *Invisible Crown,* 166.
29. In Prince Edward Island, the lieutenant governor is served by an executive assistant. In Nova Scotia, the position of private secretary, which was re-established in 2009 following a lengthy absence, has been filled on a temporary basis.
30. Although not a large province, the newest province in the federation has the longest track-record of employing a full office staff, dating back to its days as a dominion. These offices have demonstrated an indefatigable dedication to representing the Crown even in periods when provincial support has been withdrawn or greatly reduced.
31. Heard, *Canadian Constitutional Conventions,* 107.
32. Constitution Act, 1867, section 67.

33. In 1872 the federal government attempted to circumvent this problem by appointing administrators as "temporary lieutenant governors"; however, this was found to violate section 59 of the Constitution Act, 1867.
34. From 1867 to 1905 they ranked immediately after the general officer commanding the British Army in Canada.
35. It is worth noting that in Australia the state governors continue to rank immediately after the governor general and ahead of the Commonwealth prime minister, as had been the case in Canada until 1939.
36. This was, not coincidentally, the same number of guns fired for a salute to the lieutenant governor of an Indian state. The Viceroy of India received a thirty-one-gun salute, as did other members of the Royal Family, while the King Emperor received a 101-gun salute.
37. Given that Newfoundland had a full governor until 1949, this is somewhat understandable, especially when coupled with the fierce sense of identity that is a hallmark of the province. Conversely, Nova Scotia has not possessed a full governor since 1786, but its history of representative and responsible governments may explain provincial attachment to the designation.
38. J. R. Mallory, *The Structure of Canadian Government* (Toronto: Macmillan Press, 1971), 329.

11

THE SPEECH FROM THE THRONE AND THE DIGNITY OF THE CROWN

RICHARD BERTHELSEN

Le fait qu'un gouverneur général ou un lieutenant-gouverneur ouvre une session parlementaire ou législative en prononçant un discours du trône rédigé par le gouvernement au pouvoir sème-t-il dans la population une certaine confusion quant à la neutralité ou la partialité du représentant de la Couronne ? Certains discours débordent-ils le cadre des projets législatifs de la session en se transformant en manifestes politiques ou en cherchant à marquer des points contre d'autres gouvernements ou des partis d'opposition ? Quelles pratiques s'appliquent actuellement aux discours du trône, au Canada et dans d'autres royaumes ? Pourrait-on mieux remplir ce devoir constitutionnel en vue d'accroître la dignité de la Couronne et de ses représentants ?

L'auteur analyse ici des discours du trône prononcés au Canada et dans d'autres royaumes du Commonwealth, retrace leur évolution et compare les pratiques en usage. Il s'attarde notamment au changement d'approche observé au Québec, où l'exercice est partagé entre le lieutenant-gouverneur et le premier ministre. Il examine enfin comment les discours du trône peuvent compromettre la dignité des représentants de la Couronne et propose des solutions de rechange qui permettraient, au sein du présent cadre constitutionnel, de renforcer la nature apolitique des postes de gouverneur général et de lieutenant-gouverneur.

"I greet you as your Queen. Together we constitute the Parliament of Canada. For the first time the representatives of the people of Canada and their Sovereign are here assembled on the occasion of the opening of Parliament. This is for all of us a moment to remember."

—Speech from the Throne, 23rd Parliament of Canada,
1st session, October 14, 1957

"Regularly, in Ottawa a great ceremony takes place—a time honoured scene, a moment of splendour. It is the opening of Parliament."

—Jacques Monet, *The Canadian Crown*[1]

The opening of Parliament in a Commonwealth realm manifests the Crown-in-Parliament and Crown-in-Council simultaneously. Bagehot described it as a moment born of the symbolic, "dignified" part of the Constitution, but one that also demonstrates the "efficient" part, that is, the way in which government actually works.[2] In the Crown Commonwealth, only the Queen or her representatives can "declare the causes for summoning parliament" by reading the speech from the throne.[3] The speech is drafted by ministers, their staff and civil servants, but the Crown's representative reads it to parliamentarians. There is an inherent contradiction in this exercise, given the parliamentary and ceremonial grandeur around the throne speech and its use as a vehicle for outlining and advocating the government's policies and legislative plan for the new session. The speech is also the only public statement delivered by a governor general, governor, or lieutenant governor that steps into the policy or political realm and where the Crown speaks for the government of the day as opposed to the state.

The wording of the speech from the throne in various parliaments has evolved considerably over recent decades, with jurisdictions borrowing characteristics from one another. In many Commonwealth parliaments, throne speeches have developed into political manifestos. Some attempt to settle scores with previous governments or with opposition parties, while others identify provincial perspectives on federal government policy. The pronouns employed in throne speeches can be befuddling. In Canada the traditional term "my government" has become "the government"[4] or "your government," and recently "our government." There is an increasing use of "we" to describe actions by governments in some speeches, which could lead listeners to question both the Crown's impartiality and whether it is an active part of the executive. The shift in these pronouns and the use of the speech as a political statement increasingly appear to infringe upon the dignity of the Crown. Given the increasing public expectation, particularly in Canada, that vice-regal representatives speak for all citizens and avoid political issues, the speech from the throne can confuse members of the public as to the objectivity or partisanship of the Crown's representative.

In his 1989 article "Depoliticizing the Speech from the Throne," former federal cabinet minister Mitchell Sharp suggested that the speech had "been converted from its original purpose into a vehicle of government propaganda." He brought attention to trends, in terms of length and partisanship, that undermined the Crown and the purpose of this parliamentary event.

Sharp noted that the speech from the throne was delivered by "a political neutral [who] has to read words like these with as little emotion as possible, thus robbing them of any inspirational impact." Notwithstanding his own attempts as a minister in two governments to shorten the throne speech, Sharp concluded that it had become much longer over time and that as a public relations exercise it was "a dud, an overnight celebrity, quickly forgotten." He also measured the length and graded the content of twelve recent Canadian speeches. He considered whether they provided a "factual, non-argumentative description of impending policies and legislation" and whether the speech would have been better delivered by the first minister or a cabinet member. The average length of the speeches was 4,244 words. Four speeches received a grade of B and seven received Cs. The only speech to receive an A came, perhaps surprisingly, from Quebec. Not only did it have the most benign content, but it was also the shortest speech, at just under 3,000 words.[5]

This chapter examines how the speeches have evolved since Sharp wrote his critique. My review of recent federal and provincial throne speeches almost a quarter-century later has found that, while the average number of words per speech remains around 4,300, Quebec now makes do with less than 900 words. A number of excerpts given in this chapter suggest that the issues raised by Sharp have become more pronounced over the past twenty years. While I did not rate or grade the speeches according to Sharp's scale, I did note a troubling variety of approaches on the use of pronouns (e.g., my, our, your) and the use of "we" by the Crown to refer to the government, as well as the incorporation of practices drawn from the American president's address to Congress on the State of the Union. I also identify other issues that have presented challenges to governors. My review considers the most recent throne speeches in the Parliaments of all other Commonwealth realms in addition to the Canadian bodies (save Tuvalu, where the throne speech is not available), as well as parliamentary websites that describe the procedures around the opening of Parliament.

The chapter will review recent throne speeches in Canada and other realms, with particular attention paid to issues that have arisen in Ontario and Quebec. These two provinces are highlighted because Ontario appears to be the first jurisdiction in Canada to have demonstrated more partisanship in the text, and many believe that Quebec no longer has a throne speech. I also consider how the increasingly partisan nature of throne speeches is infringing on the dignity of the Crown. Finally, I propose remedies that can be used to protect the dignity of the Crown and vice-regal actors, and discuss approaches used in other jurisdictions that may be more effective.

Canada

The Queen has opened the Parliament of Canada on two occasions. The difference in the length and text of her speech on these occasions is tell-ing. On her first visit as Queen in 1957, Her Majesty was presented with a speech of 1,314 words that included simply constructed sentences:

> My Ministers will place before you a measure to ensure that those working in industries under federal jurisdiction will receive annual vacations with pay. You will be asked to approve bills relating to certain railway branch lines, amendments to the Canadian and British Insurance Companies Act, and, insofar as the other business before you permits, to several other statutes.[6]

During her Silver Jubilee in 1977, the Queen was asked to read 2,950 words and give voice to rather more ambitious statements:

> The Government will also be placing before Parliament, and in this way before the people of Canada, later in this Session, a measure that will contain a number of proposals relating to the Constitution of Canada, which it believes will be of particular importance for the future of the country. The proposals will be concerned, among other matters, with the essential nature of the Canadian federation and its objectives, with certain fundamental rights and freedoms which the Government feels should be enjoyed by all Canadians as being essential to Canada's continuing existence as a free and democratic society, and with certain elements of the framework of the Canadian federation that are important to its effective functioning. It is the hope of the Government that these proposals will stimulate a process of constitutional review in which all governments in Canada will share and in which Canadians generally will have an opportunity to express their views.[7]

In 1996, Governor General Romeo LeBlanc chose to stand at a podium to deliver the speech (introducing a ministerial tone to the proceedings), a practice later adopted by some vice-regal colleagues elsewhere. He explained his role in rather stark terms:

> On the opening of the second session of this Parliament, and on behalf of the Government of Canada, I make the following brief statements of government policy. The Prime Minister and Ministers will expand on this in coming days. Legislation and other administrative measures will follow.[8]

By 2006, the newly elected Conservative government included members of the Canadian Armed Forces as prominent guests in the Senate chamber.[9] Writing in the *Globe and Mail*, columnist Jane Taber noted that "the Harper Government chose to emulate the way Americans deliver their State of the Union addresses by inviting Canadian heroes rather than filling the chamber with old politicians."[10] During the throne speech one year later, the governor general spoke directly to military personnel seated in the chamber:

> I would like to address the first words in this chamber to the members of the Canadian Forces, some of whom are present here today. Their commitment and courage in the name of justice, equality and freedom—whose benefits are not accorded to all peoples in the world—are worthy of our utmost respect. [11]

By 2011, the throne speech had unambiguously merged government and campaign communications lines:

> Canadians have expressed their desire for a strong, stable national government in this new Parliament. With this clear mandate, our Government will deliver on its commitments.
>
> Our Government's plan builds on five years of hard work to create the right conditions for growth and job creation: a stable, predictable, low-tax environment; a highly skilled and flexible workforce; support for innovation and new technologies; and wider access to markets abroad. This approach has allowed Canada to meet the challenges of the global recession. The next phase of our Government's plan is designed to help us stay on track during the recovery. Since 2006, Canadians have benefited from significant, broad-based tax cuts.[12]

Some aspects of the American ritual of the State of the Union, including partisan statements, exhortations to all citizens, and the appearance of members of the audience to emphasize a point, appear to have worked their way into Canadian speeches from the throne not only in Ottawa but also in the provinces.

Quebec and Ontario: Divergent Practices

In the "discours du trône" at the opening of the third session of the twenty-eighth legislature of Quebec in 1968, the lieutenant governor stated, "The time has come to reform our parliamentary institutions and make of them a modern and effective instrument to serve the Quebec community."[13] The statement was reflective of the Quiet Revolution's influence on government structures and legislative mechanisms, but it also signalled that Quebec, of all the provinces, was most willing to attempt parliamentary innovations to reflect social realities. The creation of the National Assembly of Quebec to succeed the bicameral legislature in 1969 was accompanied by the francization of legislative terms, renaming and ultimately shortening the speech from the throne, and abolishing the gowns worn by the Speaker and table officers. Quebec nationalist antipathy toward the Crown and a desire to modernize parliamentary practices led to the diminution of the lieutenant governor's profile and opening ceremonial.

In February 1970, the "Discours inaugural" read by the lieutenant governor noted the following objectives of the Union Nationale government of Jean-Jacques Bertrand (reproduced in the language as read):

> Le gouvernement désire manifester de nouveau sa ferme intention de continuer à placer les travaux parlementaires sous le signe de l'action et de l'efficacité. Déjà, l'an dernier, le discours inaugural a changé de ton et de caractère. On ne saurait arrêter d'avance le programme d'une session entière à une époque où l'Assemblée nationale doit être en tout temps au service du Québec et où l'élaboration des lois exige une participation croissante et continue des commissions parlementaires et du public.
>
> Since the last session, when you broke with an outmoded formalism, you have been undertaking to free our parliamentary system of certain customs which no longer suit today's aspirations and needs.
>
> Without prejudice to what might be done at the opening of a new Legislature, it has seemed fitting this year to further simplify the ceremonies which mark the opening of the session.[14]

The Union Nationale government cut the length of the speech from an average of a few thousand words to approximately 300 words in 1970; this trend continued through the next legislature under Robert Bourassa. Lengthier speeches and a more traditional approach to outlining government legislative intentions returned in 1973 and lasted until the arrival of the Parti Québécois government of René Lévesque in 1976. During this period, parliaments were opened by a "discours inaugural du lieutenant-gouverneur," but the government's program was to a greater extent laid out by the first minister following the departure of the lieutenant governor from the assembly. Ultimately, this became the "discours d'ouverture" given by the premier and the subject of the first confidence vote in the assembly.

From 1976 until the return of Bourassa as first minister in 1985, speeches averaged 300 words and were renamed the "allocution d'ouverture." One very short speech of 50 words was given in 1980 that specifically outlined the nature of emergency legislation to be passed the same day.

In his 1989 review, Sharp noted that the Quebec speech was "relatively brief, factual and politically neutral" and "consisted in the main of a simple description of the legislation to be put before the National Assembly."[15] This observation was still true in 1996:

> Le gouvernement vous proposera au cours de cette session plusieurs législations dans les domaines socioéconomique et culturel. Vous aurez alors l'occasion de faire valoir vos opinions sur chacune d'elles, et je suis

convaincu que vous rechercherez à faire triompher, dans ces échanges, la règle du droit, dans le meilleur intérêt de notre population.[16]

From 1999 onward, however, the speech began to refer less and less to government business and instead stuck to congratulations for newly elected members, statements of sorrow on the deaths of former colleagues, and recognition of parliamentary and provincial celebrations and anniversaries. Since 1999 the speeches have been no more than 1,500 words. For the opening of the national assembly in 2012, the lieutenant governor was given 897 words to read, which are excerpted below:

> Je veux tout d'abord féliciter tous les membres de l'Assemblée nationale qui ont obtenu l'appui de leurs commettants respectifs lors des élections générales du 4 septembre dernier. La population vous a accordé sa confiance, et je suis convaincu que vous vous acquitterez des responsabilités qui vous sont dévolues avec honneur et dévouement.
>
> Les travaux de cette séance, comme le stipule le règlement de l'Assemblée, seront réservés exclusivement à la présentation par la première ministre de son programme de gouvernement.
>
> Je note en effet avec une grande satisfaction que les femmes représentent maintenant près du tiers des élus.
>
> Nos concitoyens ont également ouvert les portes de l'Assemblée nationale à un grand nombre de nouveaux élus. Sur ces banquettes, on compte en effet 40 nouveaux députés, auxquels je souhaite la bienvenue. Parmi eux se trouve le plus jeune député jamais élu au Québec; je veux bien sûr parler du député de Laval-des-Rapides, M. Léo Bureau-Blouin.
>
> Face aux nombreux défis auxquels le Québec est confronté et alors qu'une nouvelle législature commence, je voudrais avant tout vous transmettre un message de confiance. Le Québec est une grande démocratie. Notre Parlement est l'un des plus anciens au monde, et nous en sommes très fiers. En même temps, la société québécoise participe pleinement à la modernité et à la construction du futur. Dans de nombreux domaines, nous nous situons à l'avant-garde de ce qui se fait de mieux sur la planète. Le Québec a tous les atouts pour poursuivre son développement, et vous en êtes les premiers artisans. Concrètement, vous êtes les responsables d'un travail législatif dont la vocation est d'améliorer la vie de l'ensemble des Québécois, et je sais que cette mission vous tient tous à coeur.[17]

There is little doubt that this speech is conspicuously non-partisan. While it is respectful of the democratic process, it does not purport to speak for the government. The Crown, in the person of the lieutenant governor, opens the session but does not describe the forthcoming legislative program. While some may feel that Quebec does not have a throne speech, the "allocution d'ouverture" preserves the lieutenant governor's neutrality in a Parliament and in a province where the monarchy is, at least to some, unwelcome and unwanted. It reflects the unique approach to the throne speech that has evolved in the national assembly over the past four decades.

Interestingly, the speech could be seen as a return to earlier times in which the lord chancellor laid the agenda before Parliament after the Sovereign opened it. Ironically, in Canada's least monarchical jurisdiction, the lieutenant governor has never been asked to mouth words that are overtly partisan or promotional of the government's agenda. This is not so elsewhere.

Ontario's throne speeches have evolved over the years from a position of greater dignity and neutrality to being increasingly partisan. The election of a Conservative government in Ontario in 1995 saw the introduction of "your government" rather than "my government" and "my ministers."[18] This attempt to identify the government with its citizens rather than its constitutional master has been adopted in the federal Parliament and several provinces. A recent example by the Liberal government in Ontario abides by the notion that the lieutenant governor speaks to and for the entire populace:

> That's why—for the next four years—your government will focus its efforts on strengthening Ontario's economy and creating jobs. At the same time, it will continue to protect the gains Ontarians have made, together, recognizing that quality hospitals, good schools and strong public services are the foundation of a strong economy and a great quality of life. To that end, your government will implement the plan it campaigned on—and Ontarians elected it to carry out—as a strong, steady government. Where there are good ideas, your government will adopt them. Where members are willing to work together to strengthen our economy and create jobs, your government will welcome the opportunity to work with them. Your government rejects the politics of division and rancour and will oppose measures that do not serve to move Ontarians forward, together.[19]

The speech in November 2005 replaced the varying formulaic conclusion "God bless Canada, God bless Ontario, God save the Queen" with the proletarian exhortation "Let's get to work." Throne speeches in Ontario have, on occasion, borrowed the American practice of seating individuals in the chamber and mentioning their names and support, as in the State of the Union address. Given the neutrality of Hansard-like television coverage of the proceedings that focus only on the speaker, this strategy may not have had the desired effect. Speeches became so political in some instances that the lieutenant governor has had to suffer heckling from the opposition benches during the reading of the speech.[20]

Ontario also experienced one of the most serious breaches of throne speech tradition in Canada, when the 1998 speech named a parent who had written in support of the government's strict discipline programs for young offenders. This inadvertently—and illegally—revealed the identity of the young offender in question and generated a firestorm of criticism and calls for a police inquiry. The solicitor general and minister of correctional services resigned the next day and offered an apology in the assembly to the lieutenant governor.[21]

Other Canadian Provinces

Throne speech writers in other Canadian provinces have taken note of developments in the Canadian and Ontario parliaments. The speeches in other parts of the country are growing in length and are increasingly partisan in the ways in which they refer to previous ministries, promote the current government, draw attention to federal-provincial tensions, and criticize the legal system. Some recent examples:

> *New Brunswick.* Throughout this legislative session, ministers will provide more information on the initiatives and legislation outlined in this Speech from the Throne. Your government will also provide details on other programs and policies of importance to all New Brunswickers. As Premier David Alward said earlier this year, innovation will be the rocket fuel for our economy.[22]
>
> *Nova Scotia.* My government is sticking to its plan. The plan is on track. The plan is working. Even as it has had to build a sustainable, balanced financial foundation for the province from the structural deficit it inherited, my government is also implementing significant change that is making life better for families now and into the future.[23]
>
> *British Columbia.* Following an exciting and unifying playoff run by the Vancouver Canucks, the Stanley Cup riot was a dark stain on our province.
>
> This breakdown in civil order requires that justice be done, and that it also be seen to be done. A dedicated team of Crown Counsels is in place to swiftly process all Stanley Cup riot charges and ensure that justice is served. The government also respectfully asks and has requested Crown Counsel to advocate for television and radio access to the courts during proceedings for those charged in relation to the Stanley Cup riot.[24]

> *Newfoundland and Labrador.* We urge the Government of Canada to take full advantage of our strengths by investing in defence infrastructure and initiatives at key centres such as 5 Wing Goose Bay, 9 Wing Gander and Canadian Forces Station St. John's on our country's easternmost flank. Canada has a responsibility, not only to ensure the security of our nation's coasts, but also to ensure the safety of those who travel them. Whether it is fishers sailing the seas in boats or rig workers skimming the seas in helicopters, people are not unjustified in expecting the Government of Canada to provide the resources to enable Coast Guard and Search and Rescue personnel to respond promptly and effectively to emergencies.[25]

Alberta has, from time to time, organized legislative business such that the premier gives a speech in the assembly on the first day of the fall sitting, referred to as the "State of the Province" address (the session having opened earlier in the calendar year with a speech from the throne). In this address, the first minister outlines the government program for the fall sitting.

The Canadian Territories

The three territories are evolving constitutionally, and their commissioners have been instructed to conduct themselves as provincial lieutenant governors, notwithstanding their role as representatives of the federal government rather than the Crown.[26] As a result, the opening address by commissioners in the assemblies now resembles the throne speech in the provinces. In fact, Yukon now refers to the event as a throne speech. In Nunavut, in 2011 the commissioner read the opening address entirely in her dialect of Inuinnaqtun, surely a first in the Commonwealth for an indigenous language! Recent examples show that the territories are following provincial trends in speech length, political content, and references to territorial ambitions within the federation.

> *Yukon.* It is worthy to note that my government is the only government since the inception of party politics in 1978 to achieve a third mandate. This indeed is historic and clearly demonstrates that the people of the Yukon continue to want political stability, continuity and prosperity.[27]

> *Northwest Territories.* My speech today marks a departure from the Commissioner's address this Chamber has become used to. It is not the customary ceremonial welcome. Commencing today it is much more similar to other Canadian jurisdictions. My address adopts the practice of laying out your government's agenda for the coming months, while touching on recent accomplishments and looking forward to future development challenges.[28]

The United Kingdom

There is no equal to the ceremonial associated with The Queen's Speech[29] or to the antiquity of the ritual in London. The traditions and their evolution since the late fourteenth century could easily be the subject of another chapter. In earlier times, the monarch would often speak briefly before asking the lord chancellor to outline the legislative agenda, but since the mid-seventeenth century it has been the norm for the Sovereign to read the speech (with the exception of George I, due to lack of fluency in English, and Victoria, because of ongoing mourning for the Prince Consort). The ceremony as it unfolds today dates from the mid-nineteenth century.[30] The rise of responsible government in the UK and its self-governing colonies meant that the speech had to be written by ministers rather than reflect the monarch's views. From the reign of Edward VII, the Sovereign has almost always read the speech in the manner and splendour that we now recognize.[31] The speech consists of two clear parts: executive actions based on the royal prerogative (foreign affairs, economic and defence issues) and legislative priorities (specific bills to be introduced).

The Queen's Speech, which is now given in May or after a general election,[32] is usually less than one thousand words and is often delivered in approximately ten minutes.[33] It is a model of brevity and keeps fairly close to its purpose:

> My Government's legislative programme will focus on economic growth, justice and constitutional reform. My Ministers' first priority will be to reduce the deficit and restore economic stability. Legislation will be introduced to reduce burdens on business by repealing unnecessary legislation and to limit state inspection of businesses.[34]

While Westminster does not seem immune to hints of government agenda-setting, The Queen's Speech alone respects the form in its brisk listing of upcoming legislation. But even in London there can be concern over the words written for the Queen. In a recent presentation at TEDxHouses of Parliament, Lord Hennessy of Nympsfield noted, "Now endless initiatives are rolled out going forward. Even our dear Monarch has to endure this when she reads out The Queen's Speech at the beginning of each session of parliament. I don't know how she does it. Unendurable."[35] Compared to the speeches put forward to Her Majesty's representatives to read elsewhere, though, the Sovereign has little to quibble with in length or jargon at Westminster.

It is interesting to note that the devolved legislatures of Scotland, Northern Ireland,[36] and Wales have not adopted the tradition of the throne speech. While the Queen has spoken at the opening of multi-year sessions of the Scottish and Welsh assemblies, she has only spoken in general or reflective terms and has not outlined the legislative programs of the devolved administrations. These speeches bear far more resemblance to the kind of speech now delivered by the lieutenant governor of Quebec.

New Zealand and Australia

The Queen has opened the New Zealand Parliament on five occasions, more than any other Commonwealth realm.[37] The first line of the speech is now delivered by the governor general in Maori. New Zealand throne speeches are given at the beginning of a three-year Parliament, but the prime minister delivers a statement about the government's program for the next twelve months to the House at the beginning of each calendar year.

Her Majesty has opened the Australian Commonwealth Parliament three times[38] and that of New South Wales twice,[39] as well as once each for Tasmania, Victoria, Western Australia, and South Australia. Queensland has not had the honour.[40] Australian parliamentary openings are occasions for visible ceremonial. Most parliaments in Australia have adopted single-session parliaments, either through standing orders or through practice, considerably reducing the number of throne speeches and prorogations. To emphasize the role of Crown-in-Council, in the state of Victoria a meeting of the executive council is held on the governor's arrival, at which the speech is formally approved by a minute of council before it is delivered.

Most federal and state speeches now include recognition that legislators are on Aboriginal lands, a practice started in the Commonwealth Parliament in 2008. For example, the throne speech in Victoria in 2010 began, "I would like to acknowledge the traditional owners of the land on which we gather, the Kulin nation."[41] In Canberra and in most states, an Aboriginal welcoming ceremony is given equal prominence to military honours on the governor's arrival. Australian throne speeches exhibit some of the characteristics found in Canada in the ways in which they attempt to speak to all citizens, discuss topics of social and cultural importance, and promote what might be considered overly ambitious political agendas.

> *Australia.* I also acknowledge the remarkable circumstance of our nation having its first female Governor-General and first female Prime Minister. This historic conjunction should be an inspiration not only to the women and girls of our nation but to all Australians. Rather, it is the Government's hope that through its strong leadership, combined with goodwill and consensus, even more can be achieved to the benefit of our people and the advancement of our Commonwealth in the term that lies ahead.[42]

> *New South Wales.* The Government's *100 Day Action Plan* delivers key elements of the Five Point Action Plan.[43]

> *Queensland.* The state of Queensland's finances has been exposed, and the current position is unsustainable with our debt headed for unprecedented levels. It is only by reining in Government spending, waste and duplication that my Government will, over time, be able to address Queensland's budgetary issues. My Government is committed to growing a balanced four pillar economy as it looks to the future to restore hope and opportunity, and to build a better Queensland.[44]

The state of Western Australia offers a different approach. There, the throne speech makes clear that the governor is being *advised* of the government's plans and policies, and the formula "The Government has advised me..." appears many times. This distances the governor from the actions of the government and dissociates him or her from future ill will or partisan backlash. It also does not confuse the actions of the governor with those of the elected politicians:

> The Liberal National Government has advised me of its commitment to improving the health sector across the state, particularly regional health services through providing additional support to the Royal Flying Doctor Service (RFDS) and the Patients Assisted Travel Scheme (PATS).[45]

The Americas

The Queen's Caribbean and Central American realms organize traditional ceremonies for the openings of their parliaments. A cursory Internet search returns many examples of governors general arriving wearing their civil and military uniforms and inspecting guards of honour. Although these throne speeches still employ the use of "my government," they are also among the longest in the Commonwealth and show signs of increasing partisanship. Some recent examples:

> *Jamaica.* The Government places priority on preparing and passing an Act to establish Jamaica as a Republic, within the Commonwealth of Nations. The Government will be proceeding in this regard through consensus and dialogue with the Opposition.[46]

> *St Vincent & the Grenadines.* Mr. Speaker, it is heartening that my Government remains fully committed to serving the public interest having won the trust and goodwill of Vincentians for a third Parliamentary term in December 2010.[47]

> *Belize.* It is customary in a speech of this kind to outline the Government's projects, plans and priorities over the next five years. While much has been achieved during the last term of office, my Government will continue the

> focus on economic and social programs, infrastructure and physical development, national security and public safety and the delivery of Government services. We will pursue all these and more under the principles of good governance, honesty and transparency.[48]

South Pacific parliaments have produced some contentious and lengthy speeches from the throne. A recent example in Papua New Guinea refers to the parliamentary crisis that took place there in 2011 and 2012:

> I was confronted with legal issues as to who to recognize as Prime Minister and where I should get advice from. Just a short distance from my residence at the entrance of Government House, I watched two different police factions fight over power and we know all too well how many of us tried extremely hard to find solutions to the problem. There was confusion and fear and there were scary and uncertain times.
>
> Thankfully Mr. Speaker, in all of this the ordinary citizens of Papua New Guinea stood firm and resolute. They could have taken to the streets to express their anger as we so often see in many countries. They could also have taken sides along tribal, provincial or regional lines and take on each other, but they did not. Instead they displayed patience and understanding and they left the political events to take their own course.[49]

Solomon Islands takes the prize for the longest speech in the Crown Commonwealth in recent years—more than 12,000 words, notwithstanding its population of half a million. Throne speeches there are often a compendium of individual island and government agency plans. In the 2008 throne speech, the governor general admonished those departments that had not submitted items to him:

> Before making my concluding remarks please permit me to register my profound displeasure over a very serious negligence of duty by Permanent Secretaries. I was given a 67-page draft speech on Wednesday 12 March 2008 with the expectation that I should condense or reduce the draft to the content now before the Legislature to my dissatisfaction. Certain permanent secretaries have not made their submissions to Cabinet Office thus their ministries do not appear in the speech. The Government House, may I humbly submit is not the place where Permanent Secretaries should give their incomplete work to be done by the Governor General and staff.[50]

Discussion

This review has found many similarities among contemporary throne speeches throughout the Crown Commonwealth, but Westminster and

Quebec stand out from the rest. The Westminster and Quebec speeches are the least controversial and non-partisan and are consistently brief. There, however, the similarities between the two end. The speech at Westminster is delivered by a very experienced constitutional actor and is written by politicians and civil servants who work within a framework of tradition and respect. In London, the speech does not bring the Sovereign into the political arena, which cannot be said to be the case in other realms and jurisdictions. Ironically, in Quebec, the election of separatist governments with little affection for the Crown has led to minimalist throne speeches that totally avoid the political issues of the day and protect, perhaps accidentally, the lieutenant governor's role and neutrality.

The three devolved legislatures that have recently been created (or re-created in the case of Scotland and Northern Ireland) have given the first minister the role of setting the agenda for the session. Only in Scotland and Wales are the assemblies addressed by the Sovereign in a manner more like that of Quebec. Unlike the Quebec national assembly, however, these speeches are not part of the opening legislative procedures but are separate ceremonial occasions.

Without rating the speeches for their adherence to a constitutional norm, little if nothing has improved since Mitchell Sharp concluded his investigations. In fact, the observance of proprieties has declined. The speech writers do not appear to consider the distinct voice that the Crown's representative brings to the occasion, nor the suitability of some content. For many governments throughout the Crown Commonwealth, the speech has become an uninspiring laundry list of policies and promises that not even the most efficient Parliament could deliver. Future studies on throne speeches could consider what role they have in creating a feeling among the electorate that the workings of Parliament are neither explicit nor comprehensible: Do speeches create unrealistic expectations among voters, and do they suggest a belief that the Crown plays a role in creating government policy?

Among the first elements apparent in reading the speeches is the use of the pronoun to describe the government. This seemingly minor issue can have great significance. While some traditionalists may hold that the constitutional relationship is better represented by the phrase "my government" or "my ministers," the use of "the government" can suggest a greater distance between the reader and the government of the day. There is strong evidence to suggest that the use of "the government" began in Quebec in the 1960s and has spread throughout the Commonwealth over the past four decades. This phrase is usually employed in jurisdictions that seek to downplay the Crown, but it has its advantages in placing distance between the governor and legislative and policy promises. The use of "your" or "our" government in various parliaments across Canada seems to be an attempt to encourage a greater feeling of ownership by listeners and to suggest that voters should see themselves reflected in the government's policies. In this context, the use of "we" (as in "We will reduce the size of Manitoba's public service by 600 over three years"[51]) leads to great confusion, seeming to directly involve listeners and the Crown in policy and government action. Drafters of the throne speech should steer clear of "we."

Those involved in writing the speech, that is, staff largely centred in the communications operations supporting first ministers and their cabinets, might consider whether the length and word choices are effective. While governments may believe that the throne speech is an opportunity to put their case to the populace without interruption, the major policy and legislative initiatives could be accomplished by a shorter, more focused speech and one that is more appropriate for the Crown to give. Alternatively, the Quebec example has much to recommend it. The speech opens the work of the Parliament but leaves the prime role for policy to the first minister. The New Zealand and Australian Parliaments offer another variation: a multi-year single-session Parliament that provides the first minister with an opportunity to speak on the agenda in subsequent calendar years. A "session" thus runs for the entire electoral term. This option has some attractive elements: it emphasizes the ceremonial importance of the first opening of Parliament following an election, and reduces or eliminates prorogation. The antipodean openings also honour Aboriginal peoples prominently in the text and in the ritual. This model of acknowledging land title during throne speeches and arrival ceremonies could have some applicability to Canadian parliaments, as well as other realms where there is a distinct indigenous history and heritage.[52]

Government communications are now highly sophisticated and involve different techniques and platforms, but the throne speech merits special consideration of its characteristics. The dignity of the occasion, the voice of the reader, and the purpose of the event suggest a more sober approach in keeping with the non-partisan nature of the Crown. Pronouns like "your" and "our" must be used with care when speaking on behalf of the Crown. Advocacy of a policy or the offerings of self-congratulations to governments for their re-election or policy successes seem out of place coming from the throne. There are many opportunities to place these views on the record in a parliamentary cycle, not the least of which is the address-in-reply debate.

Perhaps the best advice comes from an individual who has likely read more throne speeches throughout the Commonwealth than anyone could ever want to. Her Majesty, during her historic attendance at a British cabinet meeting in December 2012, is reported to have expressed the hope that next year's speech would be "on the shorter rather than longer side."[53] Her subjects can surely agree that this is, at the very least, a good starting point for enhancing the dignity of this parliamentary occasion.

Acknowledgements

The author is grateful for sharp-eyed editing by Geoffrey Little at Concordia University, who provided invaluable advice on the text, in addition to the research guidance of Sherry Smugler, government publications librarian, Robarts Library, University of Toronto.

Notes

1. Jacques Monet, *The Canadian Crown* (Ottawa: Clarke, Irwin & Company, 1979), 9.
2. Walter Bagehot, *The English Constitution*, 2nd ed. (London: Henry S. King and Company, 1867).
3. Privy Council Office, *Manual of Official Procedure of the Government of Canada*, prepared by Henry F. Davis and André Millar (Ottawa: Government of Canada, 1968).
4. Throne speeches began to refer to "the government" rather than "my government" in 1969.
5. Mitchell Sharp,"Depoliticizing the Speech from the Throne," *Parliamentary Government* 8, no. 4 (1989): 16-18.
6. Speech from the Throne, Canada, October 14, 1957.
7. Speech from the Throne, Canada, October 18, 1977.
8. Speech from the Throne, Canada, February 27, 1996.
9. In recent years, the guest list for the speech has reduced invitations for certain categories from the table of precedence such as the diplomatic corps, lieutenant governors, and privy councillors and included more discretionary guests. As senators' desks are no longer removed, there is reduced space available for seating. The chief of the defence staff as well as several aides-de-camp to the governor general have always attended the speech.
10. Jane Taber, *Globe and Mail*, April 5, 2006, A6.
11. Speech from the Throne, Canada, October 16, 2007.
12. Speech from the Throne, Canada, June 3, 2011.
13. Official Debates, Legislative Council of Quebec, February 20, 1968.
14. Official Debates, National Assembly of Quebec, February 24, 1970.
15. Sharp, "Depoliticizing the Speech," 17.
16. Official Debates, National Assembly of Quebec, March 25, 1996.
17. Official Debates, National Assembly of Quebec, October 31, 2012.
18. Speech from the Throne, Ontario, September 27, 1995.
19. Speech from the Throne, Ontario, November 22, 2011.
20. Hilary Weston, *No Ordinary Time: My Years as Ontario's Lieutenant-Governor* (Toronto: Whitfield Editions, 2007), 46. Even the Queen suffered minor heckling from members of the House of Lords on November 24, 1998, when Her Majesty read that the Lords would be reformed to become more democratic and representative.
21. Weston, *No Ordinary Time*, 49.
22. Speech from the Throne, New Brunswick, November 27, 2012.
23. Speech from the Throne, Nova Scotia, March 29, 2012.

24. Speech from the Throne, British Columbia, October 3, 2011.
25. Speech from the Throne, Newfoundland and Labrador, March 5, 2012.
26. *Commissioners of the Territories* (Ottawa: Minister of Public Works and Government Services Canada, 2000).
27. Speech from the Throne, Yukon, December 1, 2011.
28. Speech from the Throne, Northwest Territories, May 23, 2012.
29. Also referred to as "Her Majesty's Most Gracious Speech" or the "Gracious Address."
30. The rebuilding of the Palace of Westminster in 1852 and the architecture of the building contributed to the ceremonial as we now know it.
31. H. S. Cobb, "The Staging of Ceremonies of State in the House of Lords," in *The Houses of Parliament: History, Art, Architecture* (London: Merrell, 2000).
32. The adoption of The Fixed Term Parliament Act, 2011 changed this from the traditional date in November.
33. On May 17, 2005, the Queen read the speech from the throne in London and flew to Canada, still managing to undertake several engagements on arrival in Regina.
34. Queen's Speech, May 9, 2012, House of Lords, London, UK.
35. Lord Hennessy of Nympsfield at TEDxHouses of Parliament, July 26, 2012, http://www.tedxhousesofparliament.com/speakers/peter-hennessy.
36. There was a tradition of a throne speech in the Parliament of Northern Ireland (1921–1972), but the Northern Ireland Assembly (1998–) does not incorporate this practice. The executive instead publishes a Northern Ireland Programme for Government.
37. In 1954, 1963, 1970, 1974, 1977, and 1990.
38. In 1954, 1974, and 1977.
39. In 1954 and 1992.
40. Unlike Australia, the Queen is not part of the legislatures of Canadian provinces, and it has never been the practice for Her Majesty to perform a parliamentary function in a province. She has given ceremonial speeches in the legislatures of Quebec (1964), Saskatchewan (1987), and Alberta (2005).
41. Speech from the Throne, Victoria, December 21, 2010.
42. Speech from the Throne, Commonwealth of Australia, September 28, 2010.
43. Speech from the Throne, New South Wales, May 3, 2011.
44. Speech from the Throne, Queensland, May 16, 2012.
45. Speech from the Throne, Western Australia, November 6, 2008.
46. Speech from the Throne, Jamaica, May 10, 2012.
47. Speech from the Throne, St. Vincent and the Grenadines, January 14, 2013.
48. Speech from the Throne, Belize, March 21, 2012.
49. Speech from the Throne, Papua New Guinea, August 21, 2012.
50. Speech from the Throne, Solomon Islands, March 17, 2008.
51. Speech from the Throne, Manitoba, November 19, 2012.
52. The Ontario speech from the throne delivered on February 19, 2013, opened with an acknowledgement of the traditional territory of the Mississaugas of the New Credit, likely the first time Aboriginal title was referenced in a Canadian throne speech.
53. *Daily Mail*, December 18, 2012.

12

Cabinet Manuals and the Crown

James W. J. Bowden and
Nicholas A. MacDonald

Dans une monarchie constitutionnelle fondée sur la convention de gouvernement responsable, le principe voulant que les ministres assument la responsabilité de toutes les actions de la Couronne revêt une importance primordiale. Or il arrive souvent que la population, les médias, la classe politique et même les spécialistes comprennent mal le rapport entre les gouverneurs et leur premier ministres. Les manuels de Cabinet peuvent toutefois favoriser une meilleure compréhension des travaux du gouvernement et un débat factuel plus équilibré sur le pouvoir exécutif en apportant un éclairage sur les précédents historiques et les usages courants. Les auteurs examinent ainsi la nature des conventions et principes constitutionnels tout en les distinguant des coutumes en la matière. Et ils s'appuient sur le Manual of Official Procedure of the Government of Canada *de 1968 pour illustrer la fonction d'« officialisation » exercée par les manuels de Cabinet.*

À l'aide d'exemples actuels, ils font aussi valoir qu'un meilleur accès au savoir constitutionnel aurait profité au public, aux médias et aux spécialistes. En fait, une meilleure connaissance du Manual *précité aurait pu façonner le débat, estiment-ils, car les manuels de Cabinet préservent en définitive la neutralité politique des gouverneurs en détournant de leur pouvoir discrétionnaire les critiques des médias et du public pour les recentrer vers leur juste cible : les ministres responsables et le bien-fondé de leurs recommandations. Ce faisant, les manuels de Cabinet viennent clarifier le cadre constitutionnel canadien et désigner où réside vraiment l'obligation de rendre compte.*

Considerable academic discussion has arisen over "cabinet manuals" in the Commonwealth realms,[1] and the idea of such a manual in Canada has attracted much interest.[2] In these debates, one document, the *Manual of Official Procedure of the Government of Canada*, has been largely unknown, ignored, or dismissed—often on the grounds that it is a "very technical document" and "too bulky and too dense to serve the purposes of a cabinet manual."[3] Admittedly, the Canadian manual was designed for practitioners (decision-makers in government) and is thus quite technical in nature. But to dismiss the *Manual* on the basis that it is too complex is curious logic—one would hardly discard tomes on parliamentary procedure on such grounds. Despite its perceived shortcomings, the *Manual* offers considerable insight on constitutional practices in Canada and the rationales underlying those practices.

This chapter will explore the use of cabinet manuals in navigating Canada's complex constitutional framework; specifically, it will expand on the role such manuals play in clarifying the role of the Crown, the Queen, and her representatives in Canada vis-à-vis first ministers, in a system predicated on the conventions of responsible government. The chapter begins with a discussion of constitutional conventions, the political norms that cabinet manuals are meant to describe. We then explore how cabinet manuals "officialize" these norms. Third, we examine the *Manual of Official Procedure of the Government of Canada* as an effort to officialize constitutional conventions in Canada. Finally, we examine instances in Canada where a cabinet manual could have been used by the media and academics to clarify the nature of certain Crown prerogatives, and the impact that an authoritative source may have had on shaping academic and public discourse about these powers.

Constitutional Principles, Conventions, and Customs

Cabinet manuals serve to document the use of constitutional conventions. To understand the purpose of these manuals, it is first necessary to appreciate what conventions are and how they operate.[4]

Constitutional conventions are unwritten, politically enforceable norms. These norms evolve from practices and customs that complement and contextualize laws or the written constitution. Norms imply exceptions, and more broadly allow for exemptions. In practical terms, conventions help decision-makers determine how they should act in any given situation.[5]

In contrast, customs do not hold such a degree of suasion. They exist as hallmarks of older times. Indeed, as Andrew Heard has put it, customs refer to "symbolic traditions or pleasing rituals whose observance or absence has no substantial impact on the operation of constitutional rules and principles."[6] For example, it is only by custom that the governor general does not enter the House of Commons.

More fundamentally, constitutional conventions are the manifestations of constitutional principles. These principles underpin conventions and provide their normative justification. When a convention no longer conforms to its corresponding principle, it loses its purpose and is called into question.[7]

Decision-making of a constitutional nature thus amounts to the application of conventions; in other words, the adaptation and adjustment of precedents and norms to the circumstances of a current situation.

Conventions allow Westminster parliaments to adapt organically when necessary in order to strike an effective balance between continuity and change.

Equally important, the validity or soundness of a convention may be ascertained based on whether it conforms to constitutional principles. The viability of the Westminster system depends upon the adaptability of convention and its ability to ensure that its constitutional conventions continue to serve, rather than contradict, the fundamental principles found in the constitution. The Supreme Court of Canada recognized this in the *Patriation Reference*, stating that:

> While they are not laws, some conventions may be more important than some laws. Their importance depends on that of the value or principle which they are meant to safeguard. Also they form an integral part of the constitution and of the constitutional system.... That is why it is perfectly appropriate to say that *to violate a convention is to do something which is unconstitutional* although it entails no direct legal consequence.[8] [emphasis added]

Unwritten principles and conventions, it should be recognized, can be more powerful and persuasive than written rules. Codified sets of rules rely upon the coercive force of law; convention encourages proper behaviour through self-restraint and a sense of duty to respect the Constitution, Parliament, and the Crown.

This approach to constitutionalism stands in stark contrast to the principles that underpin the American constitution, which embodies the idea that "ambition must be made to check ambition," as James Madison famously described in the *Federalist Papers*.[9] He added,

> The interest of the man must be connected with the constitutional rights of the place. It may be a reflection on human nature that such devices should be necessary to control the abuses of government. But what is government itself but the greatest of all reflections on human nature? If men were angels, no government would be necessary. If angels were to govern men, neither external nor internal controls on government would be necessary.[10]

The Westminster system trusts that the government restrains itself and requires that Parliament will hold it to account when it does not; the American system presumes the self-interest and ambition of the political actors and therefore codifies institutional checks and balances in order to constrain and contain their excesses.

It is important for the effective functioning of a system like constitutional monarchy, which relies so much on convention, that there be a widely accepted political ethic and understanding of the "proper behaviour" that convention entails. When some conventions are misunderstood or misinterpreted or ignored, a cabinet manual may serve a useful purpose in reminding political actors of how constitutional conventions are meant to work.

Cabinet Manuals and Officialization

Cabinet manuals, or handbooks, as with any non-justiciable interpretive references, are not designed to prescribe specific solutions to future and unknowable constitutional crises. Nor are they designed to serve as exhaustive lists.[11] Handbooks instead serve as guidelines and statements of general principles that can exert suasion on political actors and clarify their roles through a shared ethos. One way handbooks do so is by "officializing" conventions. Officialization refers to the government's endorsement of a particular interpretation of convention, which it then uses as a point of reference in constitutional and procedural decision-making. The government's officialization should not be construed as the only possible interpretation or an exhaustive list, particularly because subsequent governments may revise and update it.

An alternative to preserving the organic nature of conventions would be to "codify" them, thereby converting conventions into statutory or constitutional law in order to coerce adherence to constitutional principles and responsible government by the force of law. This approach would move issues from the political to legal realm, from Parliament and the electorate to the courts.

In 1990, Eugene Forsey took a strong stance against the codification of constitutional conventions and vigorously defended the Westminster tradition of unwritten constitutional conventions:

> Conventions are essentially, and intensely, practical. They rest ultimately on common sense. They are, accordingly, flexible, adaptable. To embody them in an ordinary law is to ossify them. To embody them in a written Constitution is to petrify them.[12]

Codification thus does not merely "ossify" or "petrify" politically enforceable constitutional convention—it eliminates the constitutional character of convention altogether. Indeed, with codification, conventions would cease to develop organically to the extent that they become law. Codification eliminates the politically enforceable character of convention altogether by converting these political norms into justiciable law.[13]

But transforming constitutional conventions into justiciable law comes at a price. For instance, the electorate can hold governments to account when they fail to respect constitutional conventions, but they cannot throw out of office a court with whose decisions they disagree.

If former conventions are codified in statute or in the written constitution, they become subject to judicial review and interpretation. For example, Prime Minister Trudeau's Constitutional Amendment Bill of 1978 (which failed) would have both preserved the executive power of dissolution and codified the prime minister's and governor general's respective roles in the event that the government lost the confidence of the House of Commons.[14] The courts could potentially have ruled upon the legality and constitutionality of dissolutions, and thus the results of elections themselves, and in turn which party or parties would form a government. In this way, codification can empower the courts at the expense of both the Commons and the electorate. In 2007, the Parliament of Canada passed legislation that sets out fixed elections every four years, though the law deliberately bypasses, and does not purport to amend, the written constitution through a non-derogation clause that preserves the governor general's power to dissolve Parliament.[15] However, this issue was still brought before the courts after the early dissolution of the 39th Parliament in 2008. While both the Federal Court and Federal Court of Appeal rejected the application, the courts would not be able to dismiss so easily a case that refers to a strict, codified provision of the written constitution.[16]

Cabinet manuals officialize, rather than codify, conventions. The officialization of constitutional conventions into handbooks of all types generally preserves the flexibility of the Westminster system and can serve as educational guidance for the media, parliamentarians, and the general public. Moreover, having manuals that officialize instead of codify averts the possibility of involving the courts in political matters.

Ultimately, it is best for elected officials to sort out disagreements over different interpretations of convention among themselves and let the electorate assess the wisdom of their decisions. But a politically enforceable handbook—a guide, but not an arbiter—can encourage constitutional actors to better understand their responsibilities. In turn, the media might report more accurately on issues involving constitutional conventions, particularly those that tend to arise during minority parliaments. With a manual providing better information to the media, one could then hope that the public would better understand when and how to hold their elected representatives to account for their adherence to, or deviation from, Canadian constitutional conventions. In Canada, such a manual was created, but it was not made public and it has not been updated. Nonetheless, this manual remains a valuable officialization of Canada's constitutional conventions, one that can still be used to gauge how the decisions of recent governments accord with current conventions.

The *Manual of Official Procedure of the Government of Canada*

The Privy Council Office (PCO) produced the *Manual of Official Procedure of the Government of Canada* between 1964 and 1968 at the behest of Prime

Minister Lester Pearson and under the direction of Gordon Robertson, Clerk of the Privy Council.[17] Henry F. Davis and André Millar are credited as the primary researchers and authors of the *Manual*. In his foreword, Pearson explained that the *Manual* "fills a long-recognized need for quick and thorough guidance on the many constitutional and procedural issues on which the Prime Minister, individual ministers or the Government must from time to time exercise discretion and judgement."[18] Pearson added,

> The *Manual* examines the principal elements of government, states the legal position in given situations, and identifies the considerations relevant to decision and discretion in particular circumstances. Precedents are described and evolution outlined. Administrative procedures are defined and representative documents are included as sources or examples.[19]

Political and constitutional issues tend to arise suddenly and require immediate attention. In a system built upon on convention and custom, ministers and officials must be fully informed of all the relevant precedents and procedural considerations before making decisions. The *Manual* fulfils this need and, in Pearson's words, "obviate[s] the requirement for urgent research on courses of action whenever a situation arises."[20]

The United Kingdom and New Zealand refer to their equivalent references as cabinet manuals, perhaps because they deal exclusively with the executive. However, the *Manual of Official Procedure of the Government of Canada* far exceeds the scope of the British and New Zealand documents, because it also includes extensive material on the House of Commons, the Senate, and Parliament as a whole.

PCO classified the *Manual* as "confidential," printed one hundred copies, and distributed them to the office of each minister and deputy minister, the governor general and the governor general's secretary, and the chief justice and the executive secretary of the Supreme Court.[21] Government House forwarded a copy to Buckingham Palace.[22] Each copy was numbered, in order to be able to "recall them for amendment" and "to revise the *Manual* periodically in order to reflect changes in law and practice."[23] In a draft letter to cabinet ministers, PCO reiterated Pearson's foreword that the government had "long felt the need for authoritative guidance on the law and procedures in the operation of the federal executive."[24] The *Manual*, like other cabinet manuals, provides a concise officialization of conventions and customs but does not codify them. This type of guidebook is made for the executive by the executive.

Pearson ended his foreword by dedicating the project to future prime ministers: "I am confident that it will be of valuable assistance to any successors in the office of Prime Minister and to all those directly responsible for the process of government in Canada."[25] Pearson also affirmed that "the *Manual* is designed to be expanded to cover additional areas of interest and new practices arising from changes in law or custom."[26]

The *Manual of Official Procedure of the Government of Canada* (volume 1) and its *Appendices* (volume 2) consist of over 1,500 pages and 17 chapters, each of which breaks down the subject into five sections: Position, Background, Procedure, Ceremonial, and Appendices. The Position section "describes the situation where decisions may have to be taken or discretion exercised in stated circumstances."[27] The Background describes the historical precedents that "led to the present position," and the Procedure prescribes the administrative action necessary to implement a decision and identifies those responsible for such action."[28] Volume 2 is a compilation of templates and historical documents that support the content of volume 1.

The chapters cover the following topics, in order of appearance: ambassadors, high commissioners, and consuls; cabinet; elections; funerals and memorial services; government; governor general; honours and awards; House of Commons; judges; lieutenant governors; ministers; Parliament; prime minister; Privy Council; Senate; Sovereign; and visits by foreign dignitaries.

Each chapter breaks down the subject yet further. For example, the chapter on government contains five subtopics: resignation of government, formation of new ministries, restraints on business which may be transacted by governments in certain circumstances, considerations relating to minority governments, and access to records of other administrations. The chapter on the governor general contains the greatest number of subheadings, including the "appointment and extension of term," "removal," and "death." It also covers the choice of prime minister; the summoning, prorogation, and dissolution of Parliament; consultation with the governor general; and the "prerogative of mercy."

The Trudeau government largely abandoned the *Manual*, including the final French-language version,[29] and focused on the drastic constitutional questions arising from the late 1970s and the patriation of the Constitution. Subsequent governments were preoccupied with efforts to pass the Meech Lake and Charlottetown accords, referenda on the secession of Quebec, onwards to the Clarity Act in 2000—by which time thirty years had passed since the *Manual* was drafted.

In addition to constitutional debates, the sheer bulk of the *Manual* may explain why it has never been revised or updated.[30] In response to media inquiries during the federal election of 2011, the Privy Council Office prepared a memorandum on the *Manual*. While sources have noted that the *Manual* is considered by PCO to be dated in its interpretation of some conventions, it is still consulted from time to time as a reference.[31]

The Canadian practice may have also been to shift away from single-reference sources altogether, focusing instead on more specific guidelines such as *Accountable Government: A Guide for Ministers and Ministers of State* (2008 and 2011); *Guidance for Deputy Ministers* (2003); *Accounting Officers: Guidance on Roles, Responsibilities and Appearances before Parliamentary*

Committees (2007); *Guidelines on the Conduct of Ministers, Secretaries of State, Exempt Staff and Public Servants during an Election* (2008); and *Responsibility in the Constitution* (1977).[32]

Nonetheless, it becomes apparent that in more recent contexts the *Manual of Official Procedure of the Government of Canada* would have provided useful information not only on the more controversial uses of the executive powers of prorogation and dissolution, but also on various other powers of the Crown and aspects of responsible government that have received media attention.

The Prorogation of 2008

Prime Minister Stephen Harper's prorogation of December 4, 2008, generated lively scholarly and public controversy over the role of the governor general under responsible government and the executive prerogative powers of the Crown.[33] Yet this prorogation episode offers a good example of where officializations can prove useful. Indeed, from the start reference to the *Manual* would have clarified the respective constitutional roles of the prime minister and governor general and the crucial differences between prorogation and dissolution. It would have explained the government's traditional position on the use of prorogation: "The Governor General accepts the Prime Minister's advice on summoning and proroguing Parliament."[34] Further, "the Governor General does not retain any discretion in the matter of summoning or proroguing Parliament, but acts directly on the advice of the Prime Minister."[35] Indeed, "the decision to prorogue is the Prime Minister's."[36]

At the time of the prorogation controversy, Brian Topp was a senior advisor to the leader of the New Democratic Party, Jack Layton, in coalition negotiations with the Liberal Party. Topp anticipated the use of prorogation as a tactic by the prime minister to avoid the impending vote of no confidence in the government.[37] But he also admitted that, upon learning of the existence of "a manual drafted in the 1960s by the Privy Council Office" from one of his "Conservative correspondents," trying to persuade the governor general to deny the prime minister's request for prorogation was a "forlorn hope."[38] From his own account, Topp understood, and accepted, that the *Manual* "directs the governor general to grant a prorogation of the house to the prime minister, unconditionally and in every case."[39]

Governor General Michaëlle Jean prorogued the first session of the 40th Parliament on and in accordance with Prime Minister Harper's advice on December 4, 2008. Though this was done after obliging the prime minister to wait in Rideau Hall for two hours so that she could consult constitutional scholar Peter Hogg,[40] upon the expiration of her mandate in 2010 Jean explained that she kept Harper at Rideau Hall "not to create artificial suspense" but rather "to send a message … that this [prorogation] warranted reflection."[41] This, of course, was an act within her rights to be consulted, to advise, and to warn.

By constitutional convention, "it is custom for Parliament to be on summons and therefore it is always prorogued to a certain stated date."[42] In fact, the governor general issues two instruments "by and with the advice and consent of the Prime Minister": the first proclamation prorogues the current session, and the second pro forma proclamation summons the next session after forty days for "despatch of business."[43] The prime minister may then advise the governor general to extend the duration of the intersession through a separate proclamation.[44] Every prorogation of the Parliament of Canada, from 1867 to the present, has adhered to this convention.

On December 4, 2008, Prime Minister Harper assured the governor general that he would not advise a subsequent extension of the prorogation and pledged that his government would meet the Commons in January 2009. Harper thus conformed to the standard pro forma proclamation that accompanies prorogation of the Parliament of Canada. Previous prime ministers have advised extensions. For instance, Prime Minister Chrétien advised Governor General Clarkson to prorogue Parliament on November 12, 2003, and to recall it on January 12, 2004.[45] Chrétien resigned, and Governor General Clarkson swore in Paul Martin as prime minister on December 12, 2003.[46] On January 12, 2004, Martin advised Clarkson to extend the prorogation to February 2.[47]

Some commentators also objected when Harper advised Jean to appoint eighteen senators during the intersession and variously claimed that Harper did not possess, or should not have possessed, the legal-constitutional authority to tender that advice during the intersession.[48] But, as will be further explained, the ministry's powers and authorities derive from the Crown, not from Parliament,[49] which means that cabinet still carries on all executive functions when Parliament is adjourned, prorogued, or dissolved.

Other Contemporary Applications

The 2008 prorogation of Parliament provides one example of an incident where the availability of information on the exercise of Crown prerogatives could have clarified contentious issues to the media, academics, and the public. In this section we turn to three contemporary uses of Crown prerogative that caused some confusion in the media and academia, and that serve as examples of where officializations could have provided valuable insights.

The first is the caretaker convention, more properly "the principle of restraint," and its use during the 2011 federal election when Canada committed to participate in the Libya mission. The second is the use of state funerals, with the example of Jack Layton, the late leader of the New Democratic Party in August 2011. The final example is the use of the royal prerogative of mercy to pardon farmers in the summer of 2012.

The Principle of Restraint (or the Caretaker Convention) and Nature of the Government's Authority

As the *Manual* emphasizes, the nature of the government's authority is such that "a Government receives its authority from the Crown and is responsible to Parliament for the exercise of that authority."[50] As a result, cabinet carries out all executive functions whether Parliament is sitting, adjourned, prorogued, or dissolved.

During an election, the legislature is dissolved and thus ceases to exist altogether. While members of the legislature thus lose their offices, ministers of the Crown remain in office and continue to govern. The government possesses full legal powers and authorities for the duration of its tenure, but it may exercise self-restraint and limit itself to the routine and necessary, because the House of Commons cannot fulfil its core function of holding the government to account and of scrutinizing spending during the writ.[51] As the *Manual* makes clear,

> As long as a Government is in office its legal authority is unimpaired and its obligation to carry on the government of the country remains, whether Parliament is dissolved or not. The necessity to account to Parliament for the exercise of this authority does impose restraints in certain circumstances. The extent of these restraints varies according to the situation and to the disposition of the Government to recognize them.[52]

In addition, the tenure of the prime minister determines the term in office of his or her ministry, which means that his or her resignation or death results in the automatic resignation of all other serving cabinet ministers and the end of that ministry.[53] The governor's first constitutional duty is to ensure that there is always a first minister and cabinet in office.[54]

In 2008, the PCO produced a directive entitled *Guidelines on the Conduct of Ministers, Secretaries of State, Exempt Staff and Public Servants during an Election*. This document provides an official interpretation of the principle of restraint:

> During an election, a government should restrict itself – in matters of policy, expenditure and appointments – to activity that is: a) routine, or b) non-controversial, or c) urgent and in the public interest, or d) reversible by a new government without undue cost or disruption, or e) agreed to by the Opposition (in those cases where consultation is appropriate).[55]

By way of example, during the federal election of 2011, Foreign Affairs minister Lawrence Cannon consulted with opposition leaders on Canada's participation in a NATO-led mission in Libya before travelling abroad to hold meetings on the subject.[56] These international meetings pertaining to Canada's participation in Libya required the attendance of a minister of the Crown and were both "urgent and in the public interest" and "agreed to by the Opposition."

State Funerals

On August 22, 2011, Jack Layton died only two months after the previous general election, when he became leader of Her Majesty's Loyal Opposition. The Government of Canada arranged for a state funeral in his honour. The *Manual* provides some guidelines on state funerals that indicate the rationale and process behind this decision.[57]

> There is no accepted definition of what constitutes a State funeral in Canada. It should be regarded as being a funeral which merits official participation at the highest level, organized and financed by the State even though the extent of actual Government involvement in each area, participation, organization and finance, may vary greatly according to the circumstances and the wishes of the family. A State funeral is justified on the ground that the State is a "co-bereaved" because of the position of the deceased.[58]

It also explains that current and former governors general and prime ministers, and current cabinet ministers "have been regarded as entitled to State funerals." In addition, "there is no regular pattern for Government participation in funerals of senators ... [or] members of Parliament."[59]

However, the prime minister also possesses the personal discretion to offer a state funeral to any Canadian. The prime minister "decides whether a State funeral should be proposed and ascertains the wishes of the family of the deceased."[60] In such cases, the prime minister also "determines, in consultation with the family, and with the Cabinet if he so wishes, what the Government's involvement should be, in particular what the Government representation will be."[61] Prime Minister Harper conformed to this protocol; he offered a state funeral to the Layton family and they accepted the honour.[62]

Royal Prerogative of Mercy

On August 1, 2012, the law repealing the Canadian Wheat Board's monopoly entered into force. The same day, Prime Minister Harper announced that his government had invoked the royal prerogative of mercy in order to issue full pardons to farmers who had violated the criminal prohibition against breaking the Wheat Board's monopoly while it still held the force of law.[63] The Harper government considered the previous criminal prohibition unjust and believed that these farmers should not carry criminal records for having committed a crime that no longer existed.[64]

The *Manual* contains some guidance on the royal prerogative of mercy, although this section would require extensive revisions because Parliament has since abolished capital punishment and passed the Criminal Records Act, which codifies procedures used by the Parole Board in seeking applications for clemency. Indeed, although the relevant provisions of the Criminal Code have changed, the *Manual* recognizes the effect of the Criminal Code on the prerogative in a non-derogation clause that explicitly preserves the royal prerogative of mercy: "Nothing in this Act in any manner limits or affects Her Majesty's royal prerogative of mercy."[65]

> The prerogative of mercy delegated to the Governor General in the Letters Patent and enunciated in the Criminal Code are one and the same. The procedure has been to take action with reference to the statutory provisions of the Code although the prerogative would continue to exist, as set out in the Letters Patent, even if the Criminal Code were silent on the subject.[66]

In other words, the executive power of mercy remains a prerogative power and is also a statutory power simultaneously. Parliament chose to place the statutory power alongside the prerogative power, yet the statute does not supplant the prerogative.

The *Manual* focuses mostly on the historical development of the royal prerogative of mercy, which the Sovereign has delegated to the governor general through Letters Patent. It explains that prior to the Letters Patent, 1878, the governor general exercised *personal* discretion; thereafter, the governor general exercised the maximum limit of the Bagehotian rights to be consulted, to advise, and to warn with respect to any clemency for capital crimes.

> While the prerogative of mercy is now only exercised on advice, the Governor General is nevertheless expected to reach a personal judgement for which purpose he is given full background information. He is free to express any concerns he may have about the advice offered and may even ask for it to be reconsidered.[67]

However, a further paragraph clarifies, "In non-capital cases it is usual for the Governor General to accept the recommendation laid before him."[68]

Thus in 2012, the Harper government acted on the authority of the prerogative power, which the statutory power has not displaced. While the governor general grants an "ordinary pardon" under the royal prerogative of mercy on and in accordance with the advice of the minister of public safety, whose responsibilities include the Parole Board of Canada, in this case the Prime Minister's Office took the initiative and first contacted the farmers.[69] Some opposition MPs criticized the Harper government's decision; Liberal leader Bob Rae even accused the government of having "corrupt[ed] the process."[70] Yet it was generally misunderstood that the prerogative of mercy exists alongside the statutory process contained in the Criminal Records Act.

Cabinet Manuals: Clarifying the Role of the Crown

Unwritten convention, precedent, and history form the foundation upon which Canada's constitutional framework rests and from which it derives its authority and legitimacy. This principle of the importance of history and convention means that we must apply historical precedents and the existing body of knowledge to contemporary situations. The contemporary cases we have discussed demonstrate that the Government of Canada has followed proper constitutional practice, as found in the *Manual*. Importantly, the government does not need to endorse these references publicly in order to abide by them. Officializations are therefore useful in analyzing the government's actions and decisions, but their utility might increase if they were publicly acknowledged and if the media referred to them in doing research for political reporting.

In other words, the *Manual* and other officializations can "obviate the requirement for urgent research on courses of action whenever a situation arises,"[71] not only with respect to the federal executive itself, but also for political journalists who analyze and disseminate this information to the public. In this way, cabinet manuals may assist in educating those in Parliament, the media, academia, and citizens on how some of the internal mechanics of government work, in much the same way as the Canadian House of Commons procedural authority—*House of Commons: Procedure and Practice*—has served to educate people on the role and procedure of Parliament.[72] In addition, the *Manual* provides a solid academic foundation upon which scholars can base their research as to the nature, state, and existence of certain conventions, customs, and procedures. Scholars could ground their research in how the system operates, thereby eliminating the need to speculate.

For our purposes here, the importance is ensuring the integrity of the Crown, specifically, emphasizing that ministers of the Crown take responsibility for all acts of the Crown; that the Queen and her representatives are above politics and do not as a matter of course exercise personal discretion; and that calls for political accountability must be directed to politicians.

The tapestry of laws, principles, and conventions that governs the Canadian constitutional framework and the relationship between its constituent parts are remarkably complex. Officialization serves to clarify the system and provides for greater understanding as to where accountability properly lies.

Notes

1. See Cabinet Office, Department of the Prime Minister and Cabinet, *Cabinet Manual* (Wellington: Her Majesty the Queen in Right of New Zealand, 2008). First produced in 1979, this manual is now on its eighth edition. While it does not delve into historical precedents, at 180 pages it presents succinct descriptions of the machinery of government on a range of issues like the formation of governments, the governor general's reserve powers, and the caretaker convention. See also Cabinet Secretariat, Department of the Prime Minister and Cabinet, *Cabinet Handbook*, 6th ed. (Canberra: Commonwealth of Australia, 2009). First produced in 1983, at 40 pages it focuses on descriptions of the conventions and practices relating to collective and individual ministerial responsibility. See also Cabinet Office, *The Cabinet Manual: A Guide to Laws, Conventions and the Rules on the Operations of Government* (London: Crown Copyright, 2011). At 110 pages, the first edition resulted from the publication in December 2010 of a draft cabinet manual, which the Brown government originally authorized in anticipation of a hung parliament; the Cameron government subsequently agreed to allow the manual to undergo extensive consultation with Parliament. The production of this manual followed a 2009 study entitled *Making Minority Parliament Work: Hung Parliaments and the Challenges for Westminster and Whitehall*, authored by scholars of the Constitution Unit at University College London.
2. See "Government Formation in an Age of Hung Parliaments: Background Paper," *Public Policy Forum* (February 2011); "Government Formation in Canada: Ottawa Roundtable," *Public Policy Forum* (March 21, 2011); and Peter H. Russell and Cheryl Milne, *Adjusting to a New Era of Minority Government: Report of a Workshop on Constitutional Conventions* (Toronto: University of Toronto, David Asper Centre for Constitutional Rights, 2011).
3. Peter H. Russell, "Principles, Rules and Practices of Parliamentary Government: Time for a Written Constitution," *Journal of Parliamentary and Political Law* 6, no. 2 (2012): 362.
4. Portions of this section are excerpts or modifications to the authors' work "Writing the Unwritten: The Officialization of Constitutional Conventions in Canada, the United Kingdom, New Zealand, and Australia," published in the *Journal of Parliamentary and Political Law* 6, no. 2 (2012).
5. Bowden and MacDonald, "Writing the Unwritten," 367.
6. Andrew Heard, "Constitutional Conventions and Parliament," *Canadian Parliamentary Review* 28, no. 2 (2005): 20.
7. Bowden and MacDonald, "Writing the Unwritten," 368.
8. Reference re Resolution to Amend the Constitution, [1981] SCR, paras 883-84.
9. Alexander Hamilton or James Madison, "The Structure of the Government Must Furnish the Proper Checks and Balances between Different Departments," *The Federalist Papers*, No. 51, reprinted from the *New York Packet*, February 8, 1788.
10. Ibid.
11. Sir Gus O'Donnell, "The New Cabinet Manual" (address to the Institute for Government, London, United Kingdom, February 24, 2011), accessed May 29, 2011, http://www.ucl.ac.uk/constitution-unit/events/public-seminars-10-11/cabinet-manual.

12. Eugene Forsey, "The Present Position of the Reserve Powers of the Crown," in *Evatt and Forsey on the Reserve Powers* (Sydney: Legal Books, 1990), xc.
13. Bowden and MacDonald, "Writing the Unwritten," 372-73.
14. Privy Council Office, *The Constitutional Amendment Bill* (Ottawa: Her Majesty the Queen in Right of Canada, 1978), 19-20.
15. Parliament of Canada, "An Act to Amend the Canada Elections Act," Bill C-16, 39th Parliament, 1st Session, 2006-2007 (Ottawa: Her Majesty the Queen in Right of Canada, 2007). Royal assent, May 3, 2007.
16. *Conacher v. Canada (Prime Minister)*, 2009 FC 920, para. 75-78; *Conacher v. Canada (Prime Minister)*, 2011 4 F.C.R., para. 13.
17. Privy Council Office, "Draft Letter to Cabinet Ministers," June 17, 1968, Ottawa. However, the *Manual* was only distributed in June 1968 under Prime Minister Pierre Trudeau. Intriguingly, the correspondence between Robertson and Davis suggests that Pearson regarded the *Manual* as a tool for prime ministerial centralization.
18. Privy Council Office, *Manual of Official Procedure of the Government of Canada*, prepared by Henry F. Davis and André Millar (Ottawa: Government of Canada, 1968), iii.
19. Ibid.
20. Ibid.
21. Privy Council Office, "Memorandum for the Prime Minister: *Manual of Official Procedure of the Government of Canada*," March 18, 1968, Ottawa.
22. Privy Council Office, letter from Henry F. Davis to the Secretary to the Governor General, March 17, 1969, Ottawa.
23. Privy Council Office, "Draft Letter to Cabinet Ministers," June 17, 1968, Ottawa.
24. Ibid.
25. *Manual of Official Procedure*, iii.
26. Ibid.
27. Ibid., iv.
28. Ibid.
29. Privy Council Office, "Memorandum for Mr. Robertson: Manual of Procedure," Henry F. Davis, January 23, 1969, Ottawa.
30. Privy Council Office, "*Manual of Official Procedure of the Government of Canada:* Qs and As," Ottawa, 2011.
31. Privy Council Office, "Memorandum for Rachel Curran: Access to Information Request for the *Manual of Official Procedure of the Government of Canada*," Ottawa, 2011.
32. Privy Council Office, *Guidance for Deputy Ministers* (Ottawa: Her Majesty the Queen in Right of Canada, 2003); Privy Council Office, *Accounting Officers: Guidance on Roles, Responsibilities and Appearances before Parliamentary Committees* (Ottawa: Her Majesty the Queen in Right of Canada, 2007); Privy Council Office, "Responsibility in the Constitution," accessed June 15, 2011, http://www.pco-bcp.gc.ca/index.asp?lang=eng&page=information&sub=publications&doc=constitution/table- eng.htm.
33. See Nicholas A. MacDonald and James W. J. Bowden, "No Discretion: On Prorogation and the Governor General," *Canadian Parliamentary Review* 34, no 1 (2011): 7-16. See also Peter Russell and Lorne Sossin, eds., *Parliamentary Democracy in Crisis* (Toronto: University of Toronto Press, 2009); Peter Hogg,

"Remarks on the Governor General's Discretionary Powers" (address to the Spring Seminar on the Role of the Governor General of the Canadian Study of Parliament Group, Ottawa, March 26, 2010); Peter Hogg, "The 2008 Constitutional Crisis: Prorogation and the Power of the Governor General," *National Journal of Constitutional Law* 27 (2010); "Dates and the Expansion of the Governor General's Power" (address to the University of Ottawa's Faculty of Common Law's Forum on "Canada's New Governor General: The Challenges Ahead," September 28, 2010); Barbara J. Messamore, "Conventions of the Role of the Governor General: Some Illustrative Historical Episodes," *Journal of Parliamentary and Political Law* 4 (December 2010); Henri Brun, "La monarchie réelle est morte depuis longtemps au Canada," *La Presse*, December 4, 2008; Guy Tremblay, "La gouverneure générale doit accéder à une demande de prorogation ou de dissolution," *Le Devoir*, December 4, 2008.

34. *Manual of Official Procedure,* 149.
35. Ibid., 150.
36. Ibid., 401.
37. Brian Topp, *How We Almost Gave the Tories the Boot: An Inside Story behind the Coalition* (Toronto: James Lorimer & Company, 2010).
38. Ibid., 156.
39. Ibid.
40. Peter Hogg, *Constitutional Law of Canada,* 5th ed. supplemented (Toronto: Thomson Reuters, 2011), 9-37.
41. Alexander Panetta, "Governor-General Had Hidden Message in Prorogation Crisis," *Globe and Mail*, September 28, 2010. "You have to think about it. You have to ask questions. The idea wasn't to create artificial suspense. The idea was to send a message—and for people to understand that this warranted reflection," said Ms. Jean.
42. *Manual of Official Procedure,* 401. While this is the convention at the federal level, the provinces do not necessarily follow this convention. For example, in Ontario, section 5 of the Legislative Assembly Act stipulates that "it is not necessary for the Lieutenant Governor in proroguing the Legislature to name a day to which it is prorogued, nor to issue a formal proclamation for a meeting of the Legislature when it is not intended that the Legislature shall meet for despatch of business."
43. Ibid.
44. Ibid. The *Canada Gazette* publishes all proclamations and speeches of prorogation. (The governor general normally promulgated prorogation through a speech from the throne in the Senate until the 1940s, when the deputy governor general did so. By the 1960s, the governor general promulgated prorogation by proclamation.)
45. "Proclamation Proroguing Parliament to January 12, 2004," *Canada Gazette,* November 14, 2003; "Proclamation Summoning Parliament to Meet January 12, 2004 (Despatch of Business)," *Canada Gazette,* November 14, 2003.
46. Privy Council Office, "Guide to Canadian Ministries since Confederation."
47. "Proclamation Summoning Parliament to Meet February 2, 2004 (Despatch of Business)," *Canada Gazette*, January 12, 2004.
48. Lorraine Weinrib, "Prime Minister Harper's Parliamentary Time Out," in *Parliamentary Democracy in Crisis,* ed. Peter H. Russell and Lorne Sossin (Toronto: University of Toronto Press, 2009), 64.

49. *Manual of Official Procedure*, 93; R. MacGregor Dawson, *The Government of Canada*, 5th ed., revised by Norman Ward (Toronto: University of Toronto Press, 1970), 174-75.
50. *Manual of Official Procedure*, 89.
51. Bowden and MacDonald, "Writing the Unwritten," 379.
52. *Manual of Official Procedure*, 89.
53. Ibid., 77-79.
54. Department of Canadian Heritage, *Ceremonial and Protocol Handbook* (Ottawa: Government of Canada, 1998), G.4-2.
55. Privy Council Office, *Guidelines on the Conduct of Ministers, Secretaries of State, Exempt Staff and Public Servants during an Election*, 1.
56. Campbell Clark, "Cannon Leaves Hustings to Attend Second Round of Libya Crisis Talks," *Globe and Mail*, April 11, 2011.
57. James W. J. Bowden and Patrick Baud, "Jack Layton and the Prime Minister's Prerogative to Offer State Funerals," *iPolitics*, September 3, 2012.
58. *Manual of Official Procedure*, 61.
59. Ibid., 61-62.
60. Ibid.
61. Ibid., 65.
62. Tim Naumetz, "PMO Says Harper Non-Partisan in Making Statement on Layton," *The Hill Times*, August 23, 2011.
63. Douglas Quan, "Wheat Board Pardons from Harper Could Open the Door to Abuse, Critics Charge," *Vancouver Sun*, August 2, 2012.
64. Department of Public Safety, "Questions and Answers: PM's Announcement of Royal Prerogative of Mercy," Ottawa, 2011. One question read, "Why did the government pardon these individuals?" The answer from the Minister's Office was: "Western Canadian farmers asked for freedom of choice in their own business decisions. They protested the restrictions imposed by the CWB and were charged by the Liberal government. When they won in court, Ralph Goodale had the Liberal government unilaterally change the law to recriminalize their actions. Canadians object to injustice and farmers continued to fight for freedom. When they did, they were punished with unwarranted and unjustified Customs charges. It is time for the injustice to be corrected."
65. Canada, Criminal Code (R.S.C., 1985, c. C-46), section 749.
66. *Manual of Official Procedure*, 166.
67. Ibid., 167.
68. Ibid.
69. Parole Board of Canada, "Fact Sheet: Royal Prerogative of Mercy," November 4, 2008, accessed March 14, 2013, http://pbc-clcc.gc.ca/infocntr/factsh/man_14-eng.shtml; Quan, "Wheat Board Pardons from Harper."
70. Quan, "Wheat Board Pardons from Harper."
71. Privy Council Office, "Draft Letter to Cabinet Ministers," June 17, 1968, Ottawa.
72. Audrey O'Brien and Marc Bosc, *House of Commons Procedure and Practice*, 2nd ed. (Ottawa: House of Commons and Yvon Blais, 2009).

13

Confidant and Chief of Staff: The Governor's Secretary

Christopher McCreery

Les origines du poste de conseiller principal des représentants du souverain au Canada remontent à l'arrivée du premier gouverneur à Port Royal, en 1603. Collectivement désignés sous le nom de « secrétaires vice-royaux », le secrétaire du gouverneur général et les secrétaires privés des lieutenants-gouverneurs servent donc de collaborateurs des représentants de la Couronne depuis bien avant la Confédération. Sur le plan administratif, ils accomplissent une tâche particulièrement méconnue du rôle de la Couronne en assurant le premier contact entre les gouverneurs et la classe politique, les titulaires de charge et le grand public. Outre ce rôle consultatif qu'ils jouent en qualité de chefs de cabinet, de nombreux secrétaires sont aussi responsables d'une résidence vice-royale et officielle, avec toutes les tâches d'un chef de service en matière de logistique, de budget et de dotation en personnel.

Tenu à plus de subtilité qu'un fonctionnaire chargé de la gestion d'un simple bureau, le secrétaire vice-royal exerce les fonctions uniques de conseiller à la fois principal et personnel du gouverneur lors des activités constitutionnelles et solennelles de la Couronne. De la Confédération à ce jour, l'auteur examine le rôle des secrétaires en soulignant l'ampleur et l'évolution de leurs tâches.

> "To my mind the private secretary is nearly as important as the person of the Governor."
>
> —Sir Ralph Williams, Governor of Newfoundland 1909–1911

The position and role of the secretary to the governor general and private secretaries to the lieutenant governors—what we will collectively style the vice-regal secretaries—is one of the most veiled aspects of the Crown's role in an administrative sense; yet the position serves as an important interface between the Crown's representative and the outside world. Well beyond acting as a bureaucratic functionary, a chief of staff, and an administrative head of the vice-regal household / office, the secretary serves as the governor's principal official conduit, acting as gatekeeper and guardian of access to the Crown's representative. Perhaps more importantly, the secretary serves as confidant, advisor, arbiter, and often friend—what Sir Shuldham Redfern, long-serving secretary to the governor general, described as "adviser on all matters of policy, though in no sense a rival to the governor general's political advisers."[1] This function is, furthermore, essential to the relationship between the representative of the Sovereign and the head of government and extends beyond the confines of government circles.

The position of secretary to the governor is one of the oldest in the Canadian state, predating Confederation and even the attainment of responsible government. The first secretary, Jean Ralluau, arrived in 1604 with the landing of Pierre du Gua de Monts, who served as the first governor of Acadia.[2] With the passage of more than four hundred years, the role of the secretary has evolved in tandem with that of the governor, although the advisory and administrative role remains largely unaltered.[3]

This chapter focuses on the development of the secretary's position into what are known today as the secretary to the governor general and the private secretaries to the lieutenant governors. The continuity of the role dating back to the French regime is of more than just peripheral interest, given that the core functions have survived the evolution of the Canadian federal state. The chapter begins with a brief examination of the role played by the private secretary to the Queen and the Canadian secretary to the Queen, as well as an overview of the position of secretaries in Australia. We then delve into the history of vice-regal secretaries in Canada and their position in the pre- and post-Confederation periods. Given the differences—often subtle—between the role of the secretary to the governor general and the secretaries to the lieutenant governors, we examine the functions undertaken by these two types of vice-regal secretaries separately.

The Royal Secretaries

Vice-regal secretaries mirror much of the role and function of their counterpart in London. We therefore begin with an examination of the role played by the private secretary to the Queen and the significant independence and influence of that position.

Counterintuitively, the post of private secretary to the Sovereign is of a more recent vintage than that of the vice-regal secretaries. It was only in 1805 that the position developed, largely "in an unplanned and unnoticed way, almost indeed by accident."[4] Prior to this, the home secretary was responsible for most of the duties that are now discharged by the private secretary to the Sovereign. Private secretaries to the Sovereign are personal appointments, although they must be acceptable to the prime minister and the civil service.[5] As Vernon Bogdanor notes,

> The private secretary and his assistants are the only people who are solely concerned with the interests of the sovereign.... A private secretary may have to suggest to the sovereign that he or she exercise prerogatives in a way that the government might not like; he might, for example, have to suggest that the sovereign refuse a dissolution. Therefore, he cannot be a government appointee.[6]

Although there are some undeniable parallels between the role of the Sovereign's private secretary and that of the Canadian vice-regal secretaries, there are also some important differences. While the Sovereign tends to remain on the throne for decades and is consequently served by several private secretaries in succession, her vice-regal representatives serve for a period of approximately five years and are each usually served by a single secretary over the course of their terms. The Queen and Royal Family embody the continuity and institutional memory of the Palace. Conversely, governors draw the institutional memory from the broader bureaucracy and from secretaries—especially in the provinces—who have served multiple governors. The Sovereign's private secretary is responsible for liaising with the Queen's representatives in her fifteen realms and sixteen national governments, a role that has expanded greatly since the adoption of the Statute of Westminster, 1931.[7] The vice-regal secretaries, by contrast, have more limited scope and influence. "The lesser status reflects ... the derivative nature of the vice-regal office."[8] No vice-regal office is as "administratively independent of the political executive as Buckingham Palace."[9]

The position of the Canadian secretary to the Queen is of a relatively recent vintage. The position was first held by Lieutenant-General Howard Graham, who served as coordinator for the 1959 royal tour.[10] It was the Queen who decided that Graham should be styled as her Canadian secretary for the duration of the tour. Since this time, a succession of officials have been appointed as Canadian secretaries to the Queen for the purpose of coordinating specific tours; all have been appointed on the advice of the prime minister following informal consultation with the Queen. Until 1996, the appointments were specific to each tour. The last person appointed under this method was Major-General Gus Cloutier, Sergeant-at-Arms of the House of Commons, in 1994; he became the first indeterminate appointment in 1998. Cloutier held both positions until his death in 2005. Kevin MacLeod, Usher of the Black Rod in the Senate, succeeded him as Canadian secretary in 2009. In 2012, MacLeod resigned as Usher of the Black Rod and was appointed the first full-time Canadian secretary to the Queen by Order-in-Council 2012-1481. The position, beyond coordinating royal tours and chairing the newly formed vice-regal appointments committee, continues to develop.

Independence of Office: Australia and Canada

In the Queen's realms, the governor general's office in Australia enjoys the most significant degree of independence, through amendments to the Governor General Act, 1974 made in 1984, which transferred full financial and management responsibilities to the office of the secretary.[11] Prior to 1984 the office was, in an administrative sense, staffed by personnel seconded from the prime minister's department. These changes emanated in large part from the experience of Sir David Smith, the long-serving official secretary to the governor general of Australia (1973–1990). Smith endured the 1975 Australian constitutional crisis that saw Governor General Sir John Kerr dismiss Prime Minister Gough Whitlam. Smith would later reflect upon the awkward position in which both he and the office of the governor general were placed following the dismissal of Whitlam. Former colleagues in the public service complained about his role in the affair:

> Their complaint was that I had failed to keep "my" prime minister and "my" department head informed about what the Governor-General was thinking and planning. For my part, I was of the view that my total loyalty and commitment were to the Governor-General, and no-one else, and I found the notion that I should have acted otherwise to be grossly offensive and quite improper. It was then that I resolved to secure some independence for myself, my office and my staff.[12]

Few statements better illustrate the tension that vice-regal secretaries can face in discharging their duties. Smith's experience also illustrates the necessity to militate against there being even an appearance of undue influence over the independence of the governor and his office by the political executive, lest they be seen as tools of the party in power, thereby robbing the Crown of its perceived neutrality and representative nature.

The offices of the governors of both Queensland and Tasmania also enjoy a significant degree of autonomy, not unlike that in place at the federal level in Australia. In Tasmania, the appointment of an official secretary and other officers is covered under the Governor of Tasmania Act, 1982. The state's annual report notes the position of the office within government: "As an independent entity, the Office of the Governor provides personal, administrative and logistical support enabling the Governor to exercise the constitutional powers and responsibilities of office.... The autonomous nature of the Office is consistent with the Governor's role to function with political neutrality."[13]

In Canada, the office of the secretary to the governor general enjoys nominal independence, but is treated as a "department" of the federal government under the Financial Administration Act. In the provinces, no lieutenant governor's office is established as a separate entity through legislation. Ontario's lieutenant governor's office, however, is regarded as a separate agency of the government and thus enjoys the greatest degree of independence. Quebec's bureau du lieutenant-gouverneur also has a significant degree of autonomy. In every other province, the office of the lieutenant governor is attached to a government department for budgetary purposes. The degree of nominal and real independence from the political executive varies greatly, as the vice-regal offices report through a government department.

In theory at least, the Crown's representative and the office supporting him or her must have a sufficient degree of autonomy to fulfill the governor's role as the Sovereign's representative and neutral arbiter within the political system. To preserve the autonomy of the governor's office, the staff must be accountable to the governor. They should not report to a government official or minister, because doing so could expose the vice-regal office to undue political influence. A minister could exert this influence in a myriad of ways, reduction in budgetary resources or human resources being the most obvious. There is a necessity for an arm's-length relationship between the vice-regal office (including the person of the governor) and the government of the day and the wider bureaucracy. However, this does not mean that the proverbial arm is severed: a balance is required between autonomy and oversight.

A minister is ultimately responsible for securing the appropriation to support the office of the governor and thereby accepts political responsibility for the governor. This is why vice-regal offices are required to adhere to labour regulations, treasury board rules, and other policies related to the operation of government and disbursement of funds. There is obviously a razor's edge that must be traversed to ensure that the political executive does not trespass on the governor's constitutional responsibilities; at the same time, the governors and their offices must be answerable for their actions, especially the use of public funds. Federally in Canada and Australia and at the subnational level in Queensland and Quebec, this is why the vice-regal secretary, and not a minister, appears before legislative committees to explain the expenditures made by the vice-regal office. For these reasons, the governor's involvement in selecting a secretary, albeit in the modern context usually from a pool of public servant candidates, is relevant to our understanding of the role and function. The level of independence and method of appointment of the secretaries across Canada will be more fully examined in the second half of this chapter.

The Historical Administrative Landscape

In the two decades straddled by the attainment of responsible government, the private secretary to the governor was at the apex of power. The secretary coordinated the administration of the colony and advised on the dispensation of patronage and other matters of policy that would eventually pass into the hands of the responsible legislature, members of the executive council, and the clerk of the executive council / secretary to the cabinet. This concentration of authority briefly transformed the position of "secretary / private secretary" into the position of "civil secretary."

The role of the secretary began as that of principal assistant to the governor. The secretary aided in the preparation of dispatches to officials in the home country, served as emissary to the general populace, and on occasion acted as a stand-in for the governor.[14] As the complexity and magnitude of colonial administration expanded, so too did the roles of the governor and the secretary. Nowhere was the growth of the office greater than in the province of the United Canadas, the largest jurisdiction in British North America. Here, the position of the secretary morphed into the transitional post of civil secretary that had attached to it, beyond the role of private secretary, the responsibility for heading up the administration of the colony. (In the modern context, this is most similar in function to that of the clerk of the executive council.)

As historian John Hodgetts observed, "the office of the Governor's Secretary followed the rise and decline of the personal powers of the Governor."[15] The achievement of responsible government in the 1850s, which reduced the governor's role, required that the civil secretary revert to his previous station as private secretary and advisor to the governor. Meanwhile, the positions of the clerk of the executive council and the provincial secretaries were enhanced in authority and scope.

Sydenham and Stanley: The Two Models of Appointment

The appointment of a secretary has historically been the personal choice of the governor; certainly this was the case from the arrival of Ralluau in the early seventeenth-century until the mid-1840s, when a second model developed. The appointments of secretaries to the various governors of British North America were announced in the *London Gazette* and later in the respective government *Gazettes* in Canada. These appointments were viewed as Crown offices of moderate significance, not unlike purchased officers' commissions that headed up the list of War Office appointments.

WAR OFFICE, 7 January 1792
NOVA SCOTIA

> James M. Freke Bukley, Gent[leman] to be Secretary to the Lieutenant-Governor of Nova Scotia, vice Richard Bulkely, who resfigns.[16]

Lord Sydenham, the first governor general of the Province of the United Canadas and tasked with implementing the *Durham Report*, firmly believed that the secretary should remain a personal appointment to the governor, one that would expire upon the governor's departure from office. Sydenham worried that a permanent secretary would raise the ire of colonial politicians and be seen as too powerful an official, in competition with local civil servants who were more pliable. Indeed, in a few instances this became an issue publicly debated in the legislature and quietly mentioned in the corridors of power.[17]

Lord Stanley, on the other hand, believed that the secretary should be a permanent appointment to provide for continuity and stability. As the secretary of state for War and the Colonies in 1833–34 and again in 1841–45, he viewed the position of secretary to the governor in the same vein as the principal private secretaries and permanent secretaries who served members of the British cabinet. Stanley wanted the secretary to be "dependent for the continuance in office on the pleasure of the Queen and not a mere attaché of the Governor."[18] He noted that the "secretary in Canada, as you are now well aware, is practically the Chief office of the Executive Government, next after the Governor."[19] Stanley was no doubt concerned about the relatively short tenure of governors general in Canada, which, from the turn of the eighteenth century until the appointment of Sydenham in 1839, had averaged just over two-and-a-half years. From 1837 to 1847, four governors served in rapid succession. With the deaths of Sydenham and of his successor, Charles Bagot, in office, there would also be lengthy periods when the vice-regal throne was vacant, making the presence of an able and knowledgeable advisor to the ersatz governor all the more important in a tumultuous period. Like the governors, secretaries were almost invariably drawn from British officialdom and very rarely had a connection—via birth or prior experience—with the jurisdiction to which they were appointed to serve.

Sydenham worried that a permanent vice-regal secretary would come to be extremely powerful within the colonial civil service and a focus of controversy. This reality was borne out in 1847 during Lord Elgin's tenure as governor general, when the legislature attempted to abolish the office of civil secretary.[20] Sydenham observed, "It is evident that the officer who is and always must be the confidential servant of the Governors and whose tenure of office should therefore terminate with the Governors, can never on his first arrival, and scarcely indeed at any time, profess the intimate local knowledge which is necessary to carry on … the whole internal arrangements of the Province."[21] Unfortunately for Sydenham, his tenure as governor was cut short by a fatal riding accident; nevertheless, his views on the appointment of secretaries continue to have relevance to this day.

Sir Charles Bagot, who served as governor from 1841 to 1843, was bound to follow the direction of the colonial office. He commissioned the first secretary under what would come to be known as the "Stanley model" of permanent appointment. In seeking out a qualified candidate, Bagot outlined his requirement for "a heaven-born Secretary":

> He should be ready, very laborious, very phlegmatic – very courteous – thoroughly master of all forms and technicalities and terms of office correspondence – and without any latent design of being *Vice-Roi* over me. He should speak French *tout bien que mal*, and have the patience of Job.[22]

With this, the Colonial Office sent forward Rawson W. Rawson, who would serve as the secretary to the governor general from 1842 to 1844. A graduate of Eton, he had entered the service of the Board of Trade[23] as private secretary to Charles Poulett Thompson (later Lord Sydenham) and the future prime minister, William Ewart Gladstone.[24] Bagot had already employed his son, Captain H. Bagot, to serve as private secretary, and from 1842 to 1846 both a civil secretary and a private secretary were employed. The precise division of labour is not known; however, it appears that the civil secretary dealt with the larger issues of policy and interdepartmental relations with the governor, while the private secretary managed Government House, personal correspondence, and appointments.

It was to be a short-lived experiment, with the "Sydenham model" of quasi-personal appointment ultimately triumphing until well into the next century in both federal and provincial jurisdictions. Lord Elgin, who had such an indelible influence on Canadian affairs, shared the Sydenham view of the secretary as a position appointed by the serving governor for the duration of that governor, and not a permanent fixture of the office.[25]

The Sydenham model continues to be widely employed. In the provinces, the secretaries are selected by the respective lieutenant governors. With a few exceptions, the secretaries have been members of the provincial public service and not plucked from outside government. In Ottawa, a pure form of the Sydenham model survives, whereby each new governor general selects his or her secretary and, aside from two secretaries since the end of the Second World War, the tenure of each secretary has lasted roughly the duration of the governor.

Confederation

The advent of Confederation resulted in another signal change for the vice-regal secretaries, as the role of lieutenant governors in the colonies was augmented. While the lieutenant governors continued to represent the Crown, they took on the additional role of serving as federal officers in the new provinces. Commensurate with this, the position of secretary in the provinces was reduced. The role of the secretary to the newly established Dominion governor general, which had been curtailed as responsible government took hold and the extensive influence of the civil secretary was trimmed, saw an increase in importance in the post-1867 period. The secretary to the governor general and secretaries to the lieutenant governors have much in common, although of course the latter do not have the roles of interface with Buckingham Palace, the Canadian honours system, and deputy of the governor general. Moreover, the influence of secretaries in the provinces has fluctuated, while that of the secretary to the governor general has been maintained.

Secretary to the Governor General

The position of secretary to the governor general combines what were at various times three different offices: civil secretary, private secretary, and military secretary. The pre-Confederation position of civil secretary in the Province of the United Canadas as a senior deputy minister is one of the principal reasons that the secretary to the governor general is not styled "private secretary." The designation "civil" was dropped when Viscount Monck was appointed governor general in 1861, and since then the senior personal advisor to the governor general and administrator of his affairs has been called the "secretary to the governor general." Until 1922, the governor general was additionally aided by a military secretary and periodically by a private secretary. While the military secretary had a degree of independence and was not a subordinate of the secretary to the governor general, the private secretary was very much junior to the secretary to the governor general. The secretary and military secretary were British officials seconded to Rideau Hall, but the private secretary was usually a Canadian civil servant—providing the continuity of memory and administrative prowess that Lord Stanley so desired to be instilled in the office.

The position of the military secretary to the governor was of cursory importance. It emerged following the British taking control of Quebec. As the designation suggests, this largely forgotten councillor served as an advisor to the governor on military matters and as a liaison between the governor and the commander-in-chief of the military or naval forces stationed in the jurisdiction. Prior to 1867, under certain circumstances the power of the commander-in-chief, a position held by a senior British military or naval officer, trumped the position of the governor in relation to military matters.[26]

With Confederation and the creation of the provinces, the only military secretary position to survive was that attached to the governor general. The role of the military secretary began a lethargic demise with the withdrawal of British troops from Canada in November 1871, following ratification of the Treaty of Washington. In 1905, the Letters Patent Constituting the Office of the Governor General were amended to vest the Sovereign's role as commander-in-chief (as outlined in section 15 of the Constitution Act, 1867) in the person of the governor general.[27] The military secretary continued to liaise with the department of militia and defence, and the general officer commanding the Canadian army, until the end of the Great War. As the commander-in-chief role of the governor general was transformed into a symbolic and ceremonial post, the role of the military secretary was merged with that of the secretary to the governor general, a change that came about in 1922. This change was not entirely new: since Confederation there had been times when the two posts had been held simultaneously by the same person.

The Government House *Green Book*,[28] penned by Sir Alan Lascelles, secretary to the governor general from 1931 to 1934 and who would go on to be private secretary to King George VI and later Queen Elizabeth II, is certainly the most detailed description of the role of secretary. Much of the treatise continues to define the role of the vice-regal secretaries in both federal and provincial jurisdictions:

> He has, in Canada the courtesy rank of a Deputy-Minister.… Apart from his routine work, the Secretary must always be prepared to furnish the Governor-General with information, and advice, when required to do so, on any subject; or, if he is not able to give it himself, to get such information or advice from the right quarter, and it is his special business to assist His Excellency in keeping in touch both with current events and current public opinion. He must also make himself thoroughly familiar with the constitutional position of the Governor-General, its duties and limitations; he must see to it that due regard to the position is paid by others; on him falls the onus of acting as a buffer between the Governor General and the importunate and undesirable; and he is ultimately responsible for the maintenance of the proper traditions of Government House.[29]

He is not only His Excellency's chief liaison-officer with the outer world, but also responsible for seeing that other members of the staff understand their duties and discharge them satisfactorily.

> It is impossible to classify exactly and in watertight compartments all of the Secretary's routine duties; the following categories are, however, comparatively exhaustive: --
>
> (a) The administration of the Governor-General's Office.
> (b) The submission to His Excellency, in their proper form, of all State papers requiring His Excellency's signature or attention.
> (c) The handling of His Excellency's correspondence.
> (d) The maintaining of contact between Government House and Buckingham Palace, and between Government House and the Prime Minister of Canada's Office.
> (e) The submission to His Excellency of all invitations, public or private, that may be addressed to him; the arrangement of all engagements that His Excellency decides to undertake; and the issuing to the Staff of orders in connection with such engagements.

(f) The arrangement of personal interviews with His Excellency – especially interviews with the Prime Minister and other officials.
(g) The arrangement for all formal and ceremonial functions.
(h) The arrangements in connection with the appointment of an Administrator, or Deputy Governor-General, when required.
(i) The administration of His Excellency's Honorary A.D.C's [aides-de-camp].
(j) The preparation of material for His Excellency's speeches, messages and replies to formal Addresses.
(k) The maintenance of Etiquette and Precedence.
(l) The general control, through the A.D.C's Office, of the Government House invitation-list.
(m) Relations with the Press.
(n) The arrangement of railway-transportation when His Excellency travels.
(o) The organization of His Excellency's official tours and visits.
(p) The administration of the Orderlies.
(q) The administration of the Governor-General's Patronage.
(r) Decisions on questions of Dress.
(s) Personal attendance on the Governor-General when required.[30]

This extensive list of responsibilities was further refined by Lascelles' successor, Sir Shuldham Redfern, who described the secretary as "the interpreter of [ministerial] advice, and the director of the means of carrying it out."[31] Redfern came to office with unique experience, having served as governor of a province in the Anglo-Egyptian Sudan prior to his appointment as secretary to the governor general. He also emphasized the role of the secretary as the governor general's confidential advisor, the one official in whom the King's representative could confide and with whom he could be entirely frank without fear.[32] This was, of course, a reciprocal relationship, in that the secretary could also speak with alacrity and unvarnished honesty when issues arose.

Upon his appointment as governor general in 1946, Lord Alexander insisted on having a Canadian serve as secretary (see Table 1).[33] Major-General H. F. G. Letson served as Alexander's secretary throughout his tenure as governor general. Hitherto, all secretaries had been brought from Britain by various governors general. There was one exception to the parade of British secretaries who served the Sovereign's representative in Canada: Arthur Sladen. Immigrating to Canada in 1887 at the age of 21, Sladen joined the staff of the office of the secretary to the governor general in 1891 and from 1923 to 1926 served as secretary to the governor general. Despite his short period of service as secretary, it is of some importance that Sladen, a Canadian and highly experienced Ottawa civil servant, served as Lord Byng's chief advisor during the King-Byng Affair. Sladen's career was mirrored by that of a younger colleague, Frederick Periera, who joined the office in 1898 and became the first Canadian to hold the penultimate position in the office as assistant secretary.[34]

TABLE 1
Secretaries to the Governor General since the Appointment of the First Canadian as Secretary

Secretary	*Service*	*Governors General Served*
Arthur Sladen, CMG, CVO	1923–1926	Lord Byng (1921–1926)
Richard Osborne	1926–1927	Lord Willingdon (1926–1931)
Sir Eric Miéville, GCIE, KCVO, CSI, CMG *	1927–1937	
Sir Alan Lascelles, GCB, GCVO, CMG, MC †	1931–1935	Lord Bessborough (1931–35)
Sir Shuldham Redfern, KCVO	1935–1946	Lord Tweedsmuir (1935–1940) Earl of Athlone (1940–1946)
Major General H.F.G. Letson, CB, CBE, MC, ED, CD	1946–1952	Lord Alexander (1946–52)
Lionel Massey (Secretary) & J.F. Delaute (Secretary Administrative)	1952–1959	Vincent Massey (1952–1959)
Esmond Butler, CVO, OC	1959–1985	General Georges Vanier (1959–1967)
		Roland Michener (1967–1974)
		Jules Léger (1974–1979)
		Edward Schreyer (1979–1984)
Léopold Amyot, CVO	1985–1990	Jeanne Sauvé (1984–1990)
Judith LaRocque, CVO	1990–2000	Ramon Hnatyshyn (1990–1995)
		Roméo LeBlanc (1995–1999)
Barbara Uteck, CVO	2000–2006	Adrienne Clarkson (1999–2005)
Sheila-Marie Cook, CVO	2006–2010	Michaelle Jean (2005–2010)
Stephen Wallace	2010–	David Johnston (2010–

Notes:
* Served as private secretary to Willingdon as Viceroy of India (1931–1936 and 1946–1948) and as assistant private secretary to King George VI (1936–1945).
† Served as private secretary to King George VI and Queen Elizabeth II (1943–1952).

The appointment of the first Canadian-born governor general in 1952 brought about a temporary change to the secretary's post. Vincent Massey requested that the single position of secretary be divided into two: secretary to the governor general, which was to be filled by Massey's son Lionel, and secretary (administrative), which was filled by J. F. Delaute, who had served as assistant secretary to the governor general since 1947. While Delaute was a civil servant paid out of the federal treasury, Lionel Massey was paid by his father and not out of public funds.[35]

Georges Vanier's arrival at Rideau Hall brought this arrangement to an end; the two positions were again merged into the single job of secretary, and the position of assistant secretary was restored. Following a minor contretemps with Prime Minister John Diefenbaker, the tradition of the governor general personally selecting his secretary was further entrenched. Since the appointment of Esmond Butler in 1959, prime ministers and their offices have been loath to attempt to directly influence the appointment of the secretary to the governor general; it has been treated as a senior arm's-length post within the federal public service. Despite its official status as a public service job, to this day it is recognized that the "appointment of the Secretary was made on the recommendation of His Excellency himself."[36]

Esmond Butler, a veteran of the Royal Canadian Naval Volunteer Reserve who had served in the Second World War and gone on to work with United Press in Switzerland, had joined the staff of Vincent Massey in 1955 following a series of negative press stories about Massey and the vice-regal household. In essence, Butler became the first vice-regal press secretary in the Commonwealth. During the 1957 royal tour of the Queen and the Duke of Edinburgh, he was approached by Sir Michael Adeane, private secretary to the Queen, to undertake similar duties at Buckingham Palace. In this role, Butler became the first press secretary to the Sovereign and did so with some success, gaining experience at the highest level. He would go on to become the most influential secretary to the governor general in the history of the office.[37]

Diefenbaker had his own candidate for the position of secretary to the governor general; however, Vanier had knowledge of this and was fearful that a secretary imposed by the political executive would diminish the independence of the Crown.[38] In his saintly manner, Vanier put forward his own candidate, who had been suggested by both Massey and the Queen's private secretary. To prevent any questioning of his decision, in advance of broaching the topic with Diefenbaker, Vanier sought the advice of Adeane, who said that Butler came on the recommendation of the Queen. This made it impossible for Diefenbaker—the consummate monarchist—to refuse Vanier's request. Unable to take his frustrations out on the governor general directly, Diefenbaker turned on the new secretary and had cabinet reduce his salary from $12,000 to $10,000 per annum.[39]

Butler would remain as secretary for twenty-five years, playing a significant role in the transformation of the office, the orientation of five governors general, and the establishment of the Canadian honours system. His departure, following a short period of service with Jeanne Sauvé, was not of his own choosing; however, he left, true to form, as a loyal courtier, without public comment or complaint.[40] Few people better understood the reality that the secretary serves at the pleasure of the governor. Butler was widely viewed to be the only vice-regal secretary in the history of the Commonwealth to come close to "paralleling the influence of a private secretary at Buckingham Palace."[41] His departure witnessed the return of the Sydenham model of quasi-personal appointments of secretaries to the governor general. All subsequent incumbents have been drawn from the Canadian public service,[42] appointed by commission under the great seal of Canada, and, aside from Judith LaRocque, all have served in tandem with the governor general who recommended their appointment, with brief overlaps during the period of transition from one governor general to another.

The *Green Book* continued to be used until the departure of Butler. His successor, Léopold Amyot, introduced the *Management Manual*, which provided a more detailed, and bureaucratic, set of policies and procedures. This primarily reflected the change in the structure and atmosphere at Rideau Hall from that of a household to a small government department. It was at this time that the positions of assistant secretary and comptroller were replaced by a deputy secretary, director of hospitality, and chief of administration.

Elements have been added to the role of the secretary to the governor general beyond what Lascelles outlined in the *Green Book*. In 1905, the Letters Patent Constituting the Office of the Governor General had been amended to allow an official in the office of the secretary to the governor general to sign certain classes of documents, primarily land grants, on behalf of the governor general. This responsibility was later expanded to include warrants of election, writs of election for the election of members of the House of Commons, and commissions of appointment. Most recently, in 2011, the secretary to the governor general, as deputy of the governor general, has been endowed with

> all the powers authorities and functions vested in and of right exercisable by me as Governor General, saving and excepting the powers of dissolving, recalling or proroguing the Parliament of Canada, or appointing members of the Ministry and of signifying Royal Assent in Parliament assembled.[43]

This recent development places in the hands of a senior public servant, albeit one personally selected by the governor general, the ability to exercise an extraordinary vice-regal authority in his or her absence or incapacity. Canada is the only realm where a secretary is vested with such a significant authority; furthermore, no provincial vice-regal secretary is so empowered.

The secretary is able to grant royal assent via written declaration;[44] however, unlike the justices of the Supreme Court, the secretary is not permitted to preside over a royal assent ceremony before Parliament assembled, or recall or prorogue Parliament. The commissions granted to justices of the Supreme Court of Canada enable them to act as deputies of the governor general, limited only from "the power of dissolving the Parliament of Canada."[45] Over the past decade, a number of justices have expressed concern about the potential for their judicial impartiality and independence to be impugned by litigants appearing before the Supreme Court, should a case arise in relation to a bill to which a justice has granted royal assent or a regulation which they authorized by an order-in-council in their executive capacity as deputies of the governor general. Concern about the role of justices of the Supreme Court in granting royal assent has come from other quarters as well, notably Senator Hugh Segal, who has suggested that assent not be granted "by senior judges but by a designated commissioned series of officers specifically assigned for that purpose."[46]

Another addition to the secretary's role came in 1967 with the establishment of the Order of Canada and the appointment of the secretary to the governor general as secretary general of the Order of Canada and later as secretary general of the Order of Military Merit (1972) and the Order of Merit of the Police Forces (2000). The secretary to the governor general also serves as herald chancellor of the Canadian Heraldic Authority, a position created in 1988 when the authority was established. The symbolic and legal scope of the secretary's role has thus been thoroughly enhanced since 1967; undoubtedly, the most significant change has been the new-found power to grant royal assent.

Secretaries have occasionally been drawn into the spotlight and required to defend their principals' interests in the public realm. The most recent example of this occurred in 2004, when parliamentarians criticized international travel being undertaken by then governor general Adrienne Clarkson. Appearances by the secretary before House of Commons committees are not unusual as part of the estimates process; however, the situation of explaining the governor general's travel was unprecedented. The secretary, Barbara Uteck, appeared before the House of Commons Standing Committee on Government Operations and Estimates to explain the expenditures and defend the governor general, who had been sent on the international tour at the behest of the Government of Canada.[47] Awkwardly, it was left to the lone secretary to defend not only the governor general, but also a decision taken by the prime minister and the minister of foreign affairs, who were both largely silent on the matter.[48] The principle that ministers of the Crown must defend the Crown's representative is one often forgotten by politicians in power. In an extraordinary move, Clarkson herself appeared on a national current affairs show to explain her travel expenses.[49]

The Secretaries in the Provinces

It is important to recall that the lieutenant governors are representatives of the Crown by judicial fiat, not constitutional design, and this has meant that their offices have been treated quite differently than their counterpart in the federal sphere, in the other realms, and in the Australian states. The closest cousins to the provincial secretaries are the official secretaries to the governors of the Australian states, where vice-regal establishments are larger and have a higher degree of independence and insulation from the political aspects of the bureaucracy.

There can be a great deal of ambiguity surrounding the role and function of the secretaries to the lieutenant governors. This is especially true in provinces where the position has not enjoyed a universal or consistent presence in the various Government Houses or vice-regal offices. Indeed, in some jurisdictions the employment of a secretary has been sporadic, patronage-based, or simply filled with a clerical functionary who principally acted as a stenographer and junior gatekeeper for the viceroy.

In writing about the role of the Crown in Australia, New Zealand, and Canada, Australian political scientist Peter Boyce touched upon the role of the secretaries in the Canadian provinces, noting that "although in several provinces the lieutenant governor's senior assistant has assumed an increasingly influential role, the office of secretary has never acquired the system-wide status that it has enjoyed in the Australian states." [50] Historically, this was true in the case of most provinces, save Quebec, Newfoundland, and British Columbia, where the administrative structures and supports afforded to the offices of the lieutenant governor and the secretaries that serve them have been the most robust. In Alberta, Saskatchewan, Manitoba, Ontario, and Nova Scotia, the position of private secretary was for a time reduced to that of assistant or executive assistant. The vacuum was filled in an ad hoc manner by senior/chief honorary aides-de-camp who served over the tenure of multiple lieutenant governors. Aides-de-camp, usually at or above the rank of commander, lieutenant-colonel, or wing commander, came to fulfil an element of the ceremonial and outreach role that was traditionally played by the private secretary.

Just as the administration of Canadian courts went through a process of transformation and professionalization in the 1970s,[51] so have the provincial vice-regal offices since the early 1990s. As with most developments in Canada's structures of governance, there has been a somewhat uneven evolution from province to province. Not surprisingly, this professionalization has followed—in a lagging fashion—the growth and expansion of the lieutenant governor's role over the past forty years, a matter examined more thoroughly in Chapter 10.

Twenty years ago, it was certainly true that in the provinces "there was no able confidant like Esmond Butler, instead, usually a lone secretary who periodically might appeal to the governor general's secretary for guidance."[52] Today the state of affairs has changed: the paucity of experience and lack of stature within provincial bureaucracies have become the exception and not the norm. It would be naïve to suggest that the secretaries now embody the same institutional memory that is exemplified in the Queen's household at Buckingham Palace and to a lesser degree at Rideau Hall or the offices that serve the Australian governors; however, the growth of the lieutenant governor's role has, by its very nature, necessitated a degree of professionalization and formalization of practice. This process has been furthered by biennial meetings of the provincial private secretaries, which grew naturally out of the conference of the governor general and lieutenant governors inaugurated by Roland Michener in 1973.

Most of the responsibilities outlined by Lascelles in the *Green Book* apply to provincial private secretaries, but their role and function is not as broad as that of their counterpart in Ottawa. Thus provincial private secretaries do not serve as deputies of the governor; their interaction with Buckingham Palace is invariably through Rideau Hall; and they do not serve as heads of large households or honours administrations. On the other hand, the provincial vice-regal secretaries are deeply involved in areas where their counterparts in Ottawa and London are not, notably the management and interaction with volunteers, be they honorary aides-de-camp, assistants, docents, and even gardeners.

The most significant role of provincial vice-regal secretaries is in communications. Where Buckingham Palace and Rideau Hall have extensive communications secretariats, the provincial vice-regal secretaries are very much on their own, despite the higher demand for and profile of lieutenant governors over the past four decades. The secretaries serve as communications directors, writing speeches, developing website content, and interacting with the press as key spokespersons. In a number of jurisdictions there are also Government House charitable foundations in which the secretaries play a key role. It is, however, at the grassroots and community level of events that the provincial secretaries are most deeply entrenched, largely as a result of the modest size of the provincial vice-regal offices across Canada. Offices are served by two to four administrative staff and, in provinces where there is a functioning Government House, by a household staff of four to eight. It is at this level and through the growth of these interactions with communities and a myriad of patron organizations—the average lieutenant governor serves as patron of forty-two groups—that the role of lieutenant governors, and their secretaries, has significantly expanded over the past forty years. There are also functions and traditions purely regional in nature that the secretaries perform which are well beyond the sphere of involvement of their non-provincial counterparts.

A detailed study of the precise nature of the individual role exercised by each provincial secretary would become mired in elements local in complexion and be of marginal use beyond the curiosity of an interjurisdictional analysis. However, by examining the method of appointment used to employ private secretaries, we can gain some understanding of the level of autonomy enjoyed by the offices.

No lieutenant governor's office is established as a separate entity or agency within government through legislation. The broader office exists by virtue of the Constitution Act, 1867 and by the convention that every lieutenant governor since Confederation has been served by at least a modest staff who assist in the duties of the Crown's representative. As already noted, the office of the secretary to the governor general is regarded as an independent agency (treated as a department) of government that employs public servants, uses certain government services, and is subject to the Financial Administration Act. In the provinces—apart from Ontario and Quebec, where the office of lieutenant governor enjoys significant autonomy—the office is nominally attached to a government department for budgetary purposes. The most frequent home department is the executive council office, although in Manitoba and Prince Edward Island it is the department of transportation and infrastructure, in British Columbia the department of finance, and in Nova Scotia the department of intergovernmental affairs. The level of contact that each office and secretary has with their home department varies; however, in most jurisdictions the contact is primarily in the use of the department as a corporate services unit.

In every province save Prince Edward Island, a secretary is employed at the level of senior manager, and in three or four jurisdictions assistant deputy minister, drawing a provincial salary as part of the lieutenant governor's office or Government House administration. Designations vary, although the most ubiquitous remains "private secretary," which is used in all provinces except New Brunswick, Prince Edward Island, and Quebec.[53] Hyphenated designations are not uncommon, with "executive director" or "chief of staff" included with some job descriptions. In Quebec, the secretary is styled secrétaire général, a designation first adopted in 1957 but replaced in 1974 with the title "executive secretary and senior aide-de-camp." Quebec recently returned to secrétaire général, which is seen to fully reflect the office's independent status. Following the Sydenham model, the secretary is only appointed with the approval of the lieutenant governor, except in British Columbia where the lieutenant governor is not involved in the selection process. Secretaries are also subject to removal at the request of their lieutenant governor, a not unprecedented occurrence.

Conclusion

The vice-regal secretary, be it in the federal or provincial sphere, is a highly nuanced position, one that, although rooted in an ancient office, continues to develop and evolve in tandem with the role of the Crown's representatives. The role is multifaceted as confidant, advisor, and arbiter. Often the individual who helps to brief and orient a new governor, along with exercising the administrative and household functions, plays an influential part in the duties and public face of the Crown's representatives.

The office that serves the governor must be treated as separate from the operation of the broader government to preserve the governor's persona as neutral arbiter, able to resist the request of the political executive when it is constitutionally and conventionally correct to do so, without fear of reprisals. Similarly, the secretaries must be able to offer advice and have access to competent authorities—both inside and outside government—in order to counsel the Crown's representative without concern that their position, or the viability of their office, will be assaulted by the government of the day or the bureaucracy.

Within the broader public services that operate throughout Canada, very few positions discharge functions similar to the vice-regal secretaries. The chiefs of staff who serve heads of government are similar, in that they are personally selected by their principal and are responsible for providing highly sensitive advice and criticism and heading up an operation with a number of staff. However, they have only limited financial responsibilities, unlike the secretaries, who are responsible for the budget attached to the vice-regal offices. The judicial administrators who serve the Courts Administration Service federally and the provincial court systems are another close cousin of the secretaries, in that they serve a federally appointed officeholder with tenure and are responsible for the use of provincial resources to ensure the courts perform an essential function.

As issues related to the prerogative powers continue to be of interest to members of the political executive, not to mention members of the public, there is a risk that a vice-regal office that resists or questions the validity of direction offered by a head of government will once again be targeted. Canadian history is littered with instances where the political executive has taken out its frustration with the Crown's representative on the vice-regal office. The most famous examples of this have been the closing of Government Houses in Alberta, Saskatchewan, Ontario, Quebec, and New Brunswick. These occurrences would be less likely if the vice-regal offices, especially in the provinces, had greater autonomy. Rideau Hall has the benefit of being national in scope and constantly on the radar of the media. Any direct attack upon the office of the governor general—or the secretary—would probably be widely reported.

The Buckingham Palace model of complete independence from the political executive is unquestionably the gold standard in terms of ensuring the autonomy of the Crown; however, stencilling that model onto vice-regal offices is not realistic. No vice-regal office can ever attain the stature, prestige, or institutional memory embodied in the Queen and her household. Certainly the Australian federal model, whereby the office of the governor general is constituted via statute as an independent entity with authority over its budget, personnel, and human resources functions—yet accountable to the legislature—is the most realistic for ensuring vice-regal autonomy from the potential machinations of the political executive.

The final word on the importance of the independence of the vice-regal secretaries, and by extension the offices they serve, belongs to King George VI's biographer, who, in writing about the King's requirement for a secretary, reflected that "his complete independence of view must inspire confidence."[54]

Notes

1. Sir Shuldham Redfern, Memo no. 15, p. 11, quoted in David E. Smith, *The Invisible Crown* (Toronto: University of Toronto Press, 1995), 127.
2. Entry for Jean Ralluau in *Dictionary of Canadian Biography*, vol. 1, 1000 to 1700 (Toronto: University of Toronto Press, 1966), 564-65.
3. The position is not unique to Canada, and while it finds its roots in the United Kingdom, it also lives on in a number of jurisdictions, notably certain American states, India, and all of the Queen's realms large and small.
4. Vernon Bogdanor, *The Monarchy and the Constitution* (Oxford: Oxford University Press, 1998), 197.
5. Ibid., 201.
6. Ibid., 202.
7. Following a decision taken at the 1926 Imperial Conference, governors general ceased representing the British government in addition to the Sovereign. With this change and the subsequent adoption of the Statute of Westminster, governors general no longer channelled communications through the Dominions Office or any department of the British government and have since worked directly with officials at Buckingham Palace.
8. Peter Boyce, *The Queen's Other Realms* (Sydney: Federation Press, 2008), 38.
9. Ibid., 231.
10. Howard Graham, *Citizen and Soldier: The Memoirs of Lieutenant General Howard Graham* (Toronto: McClelland & Stewart, 1987), 252.
11. Sir David Smith, *Head of State: The Governor General, the Monarchy, the Republic and the Dismissal* (Sydney: Macleay Press, 2005), 41-42.
12. Ibid., 41.
13 *Office of the Governor of Queensland, Annual Report, 2011–2012* (Brisbane: State of Queensland, 2012), 6.
14. *Dictionary of Canadian Biography*, vol. 1, entry for Jean-Baptiste Patoulet, 534. Patoulet, secretary to Jean Talon (1665–1672), intendant of New France, had the task of drafting dispatches to the minister of marine.
15. John E. Hodgetts, *Pioneer Public Service: An Administrative History of the United Canadas, 1841–1867* (Toronto: University of Toronto Press, 1955), 35.
16. *London Gazette*, January 7, 1792, 5.

17. Dennis Godly, secretary to Lord Monck, was known by the derisory moniker "almighty Godly." W. L. Morton, *The Critical Years* (Toronto: McClelland & Stewart, 1964), 99.
18. Stanley to Bagot, July 11, 1842, RG 7 G.1, vol. 102, 138-39, Library and Archives Canada.
19. Ibid.
20. Elgin to Grey, June 28, 1847, in *The Elgin Grey Papers*, vol. 1 (Ottawa: King's Printer, 1937), 51.
21. Sydenham to Russell, July 1841, RG 7 G 12, vol. 58, 118, Library and Archives Canada.
22. Bagot to Stanley, May 28, 1842, MG 24A13, vol. 4, 229, Library and Archives Canada.
23. The Board of Trade was a committee of the British Privy Council that had responsibility for matters relating to trade and commerce throughout the British Empire.
24. Following his service in Canada, he would go on to become governor of Bahamas and later the Windward Islands.
25. This was Elgin's experience while serving as governor of Jamaica, where the secretary was a personal appointment that expired upon the departure or expiry of the governor. See Hodgetts, *Pioneer Public Service*, 79.
26. There were periods in Canada's pre-Confederation history when the commander-in-chief of British North America concurrently served as governor.
27. Christopher P. McCreery, "Myth and Misunderstanding: The Origins and Meaning of the Letters Patent Constituting the Office of the Governor General, 1947," in *The Evolving Canadian Crown*, ed. Jennifer Smith and D. Michael Jackson (Montreal: McGill-Queen's University Press, 2011), 32-54.
28. *Government House – Confidential*, better known as *The Green Book*, was largely written by Sir Alan Lascelles with the cooperation of the Department of the Secretary of State and the Office of the Prime Minister. Totalling 210 pages, only 250 copies of the small and confidential reference guide were printed for use by senior government officials and administrative staff at Rideau Hall. The work continued to be used as a resource into the 1980s.
29. Sir Alan Lascelles, *Green Book*, 17.
30. Ibid., 18-19.
31. Sir Shuldham Redfern, Memo no. 15, p. 11, quoted in Smith, *The Invisible Crown*, 127.
32. Ibid.
33. Lascelles's diary entry, November 6, 1945, in Duff Hart-Davis, ed., *King's Counsellor: Abdication and War: The Diaries of Sir Alan Lascelles* (London: Weidenfield and Nicholson, 2006), 365.
34. Periera retired as assistant secretary in 1946.
35. Cabinet Conclusions, March 31, 1952, RG 2, Library and Archives Canada. Also see Order-in-Council 1952-1937 noting the appointment of J. F. Delaute as secretary (administrative).
36. Cabinet Conclusions, March 31, 1952, RG 2, Library and Archives Canada. Today the appointment of the secretary is a governor-in-council appointment legally made under section 130 of the Public Service Employment Act, on the recommendation of the prime minister, who by convention acts on the advice of the governor general in relation to this appointment.

37. Boyce, *The Queen's Other Realms*, 38.
38. Robert Speaight, *Vanier: Soldier, Diplomat and Governor General* (Toronto: Collins, 1970), 376.
39. Cabinet Conclusions, October 16, 1959, RG 2, Library and Archives Canada.
40. David Twiston-Davies, *Canada from Afar: The Daily Telegraph Book of Canadian Obituaries* (Toronto: Dundurn Press, 1996), 246.
41. Boyce, *The Queen's Other Realms*, 38.
42. Prior to her appointment as secretary, Judith LaRocque was a ministerial staffer, having served as chief of staff to Ramon Hnatyshyn and later Lowell Murray.
43. See commission constituting Stephen Wallace, to do in His Excellency's name all acts on his part necessary to be done during His Excellency's pleasure, Senate of Canada, *Hansard*, December 15, 2011. The authority of the secretary to the governor general as deputy of the governor general to grant royal assent was first exercised on March 15, 2011, when Wallace granted assent to An Act to Provide for the Resumption of Air Service Operations.
44. The Royal Assent Act, 2002 allows for assent to be granted via written declaration, as opposed to the previous format whereby it could only be signified "in Parliament assembled." Assent granted by written declaration must be done in the presence of more than one member of each House of Parliament. There is a further requirement that assent be granted in Parliament assembled at least twice a calendar year.
45. Senate of Canada, *Hansard*, October 20, 2000.
46. Senator Hugh Segal, "Royal Assent: A Time for Clarity," in *The Evolving Canadian Crown*, 217.
47. House of Commons, Evidence Given before the Standing Committee on Government Operations and Estimates, October 6, 2003.
48. Adrienne Clarkson, *Heart Matters* (Toronto: Viking, 2006), 197.
49. Adrienne Clarkson, interview by Don Newman, *Politics with Don Newman*, CBC, September 19, 2003.
50. Boyce, *The Queen's Other Realms*, 112.
51. Perry S. Millar and Carl Baar, *Judicial Administration in Canada* (Montreal: McGill-Queen's University Press, 1981), 113.
52. Smith, *The Invisible Crown*, 167.
53. In New Brunswick, the secretary is styled "principal secretary," although the designations "official secretary" and "private secretary" have also been used at various times. In Prince Edward Island, the senior administrative officer is called executive assistant.
54. John Wheeler-Bennett, *King George VI: His Life and Reign* (London: Macmillan, 1958), 820.

14

CROWN PREROGATIVE DECISIONS TO DEPLOY THE CANADIAN FORCES INTERNATIONALLY: A FITTING MECHANISM FOR A LIBERAL DEMOCRACY

ALEXANDER BOLT[1]

En vertu de la loi canadienne, c'est le gouvernement qui prend la décision de déployer les forces armées du pays à l'étranger en exerçant la prérogative royale. Ce qui a été critiqué au motif d'une atteinte aux libertés qui compromettrait le principe démocratique. Selon un volet ciblé de cette critique, la prérogative de la Couronne ne constitue pas l'autorité légale en matière de déploiement des Forces canadiennes (FC) ; le reste de la critique soutenant que cette autorité devrait résider ailleurs. D'après l'élément central de l'ensemble de la critique, toute décision de déploiement devrait ainsi relever du Parlement, son volet ciblé en faisant une exigence.

Or l'auteur souligne qu'en vertu de la loi actuelle, la prérogative de la Couronne constitue de fait l'autorité responsable du déploiement des FC à l'étranger, et qu'il est à la fois contrefactuel et irresponsable de prétendre le contraire. Il ajoute qu'une fois compris dans le contexte du gouvernement responsable, le mécanisme décisionnel de cette prérogative convient tout à fait à une démocratie libérale. Il termine en contestant l'argument selon lequel la décision devrait revenir au Parlement, estimant que ce changement n'offrirait aucun supplément démocratique et qu'il pourrait, suivant le mécanisme retenu, affaiblir l'orientation donnée aux FC ou se révéler opérationnellement impraticable.

INTRODUCTION

Whether it be battlegroups to Afghanistan or Bosnia and Herzegovina, task forces to Libya, smaller supporting units to Israel or the Democratic Republic of the Congo, or the Disaster Assistance Response Team to Sri Lanka, the Canadian Forces (CF) deploy abroad on operations. In addition to requiring an international law basis,[2] such deployments must be authorized under Canada's domestic law. In all cases, such authorization flows from the executive under authority sourced in the Crown prerogative. While the executive may choose to engage with Parliament regarding a deployment decision, it is not required by law (or convention) to do so.

At first blush, this seems an ill fit with Canada's system of liberal democracy. Decisions as important as projecting Canadian power abroad and deploying our men and women in uniform, the argument goes, should be reserved for Parliament. Executive decision-making under the Crown prerogative is illiberal in that it violates the democratic principle, and the law should be changed.

At the extreme end of this argument lies the position that Crown prerogative-sourced deployment decisions are so manifestly illiberal that they are unlawful, and that, in fact, the lawful authority to deploy the Canadian Forces does rest with Parliament. This position is counterfactual and ultimately irresponsible: the Crown prerogative is the legal authority for CF deployments, and Parliament has not seized this power through the passage of legislation (even if it can be considered to have the power to do so).

More interesting is the question of whether Parliament *should* be engaged in deployment decisions at law (which would require a legal change from the status quo), a question I would answer in the negative. Too important a debate to reduce to platitudes, it is unhelpful to malign the prerogative and associate the negative viewpoint with apology for unfettered executive action. While Parliament is not engaged directly in deployment decisions, such decisions are made within the sophisticated and enlightened responsible government system, and members of Parliament, the press, and the electorate are more implicated than might first appear. Implicated, that is, if they choose to be; even as the current system is not a bad one because it is not used to its potential, "enhancing" it to allow for more parliamentary involvement does not guarantee more thoughtful (or democratic) decision-making. Looked at from the other direction, there is no democratic surplus to be obtained through legally enhancing Parliament's role. In addition, legal parliamentary engagement in deployment decisions presents important problems that must be weighed in the balance. In the final analysis, our existing system in which CF deployment decisions are based in Crown prerogative authority is a fitting one in a liberal democracy.

The Crown Prerogative Authority to Deploy the Canadian Forces

According to Professor Peter Hogg, the Crown, or royal, prerogative consists of "the powers and privileges accorded by the common law to the Crown."[3] An important source of authority, it is properly used in relation to a wide range of subject matters, from the issuance of passports, through the administration and disposal of public lands, to the conduct of foreign affairs.[4] There can be no doubt that authority to deploy the Canadian Forces flows from a Crown prerogative power of long duration.[5]

The Crown prerogative to deploy the Canadian Forces is not, in fact, exercised by the Queen as titular head of the Crown in Canada, nor, in the main, by her representative the governor general. Rather, through law and convention the power falls to the political executive and in practice is exercised by cabinet or its parts (by the prime minister, who defines the consensus of cabinet; by cabinet committees; or by individual ministers).[6] Parliament plays no direct legal role in the exercise of the Crown prerogative to deploy the Canadian Forces.[7]

The Critical View

Importantly, in the context of challenges to the use of the Crown prerogative in Canada today, critics often draw upon an outmoded definition put forward by Professor Dicey (1835–1922). Writing at a time much different from our own, Professor Dicey, who popularized the idea of the "rule of law," described the Crown prerogative as "the residue of discretionary or arbitrary authority, which at any given time is left in the hands of the Crown."[8] Aside from being too narrow, in that it does not address Crown privileges,[9] this definition comes laden with value judgements: the Crown prerogative is a "residue" (bringing to mind the idea that it is a source of law that is small, possibly insignificant, and a remainder following a process), it is "left in the hands of the Crown" (suggesting that failure to seize it might be classed as an oversight), and it is authority that is exercised in a way that is "discretionary" (suggesting secretiveness) or even "arbitrary" (implying that Crown prerogative decisions are random, capricious, or whimsical). This definition lends itself to circular arguments; those who use it in a criticism of the Crown prerogative are already half-way there.

The Crown prerogative is the frequent subject of presumptive attack. It is old, but not properly described as anachronistic[10] or as something like "the clanking of mediaeval chains of the ghosts of the past."[11] Just as one cannot make the argument that the Crown prerogative is a good idea just because it has a long history, neither is it presumptively a bad one for the same reason. Nor is it helpful to baldly announce that the Crown prerogative is "not compatible with 21st century democracy,"[12] or to suggest it is so obviously out of step with present-day foundational legal principles—like the rule of law—that it is manifestly unlawful.[13] Related, in that it stresses the supposed "otherworldliness" of the Crown prerogative, is the position that it is something like "a mysterious esoteric science which can only be understood by initiates."[14] The Crown prerogative does not have a public relations team; how well known or understood it is speaks more to the degree of academic and public interest than to its fittingness as a proper source of legal authority.

At source, these arguments concern the idea that the use of the Crown prerogative to authorize military deployment is illiberal in that it is undemocratic. It would be better, the positive side of this argument goes, if certain decisions were made with greater adherence to the spirit of representative democracy: at law, Parliament should control deployment decisions.

The Crown Prerogative: The Domestic Legal Authority for CF Deployment Decisions

Criticism of the Crown prerogative authority to deploy the Canadian Forces can be taken to the extreme of denying its existence. The only real argument that can be made in support is that this historical power has been displaced by statute.[15] While, as a general rule, legislation can seize ground formerly occupied by the prerogative, Philippe Lagassé has recently made a persuasive case that this would not be the case for certain Crown powers in respect of the Canadian Forces: this class of powers—which includes the power to deploy the Canadian Forces—is sourced not in the Crown prerogative but in the Constitution.[16] If this position is correct, then the argument that authority for CF deployments is sourced in statute law is unavailable,[17] since a statute purporting to seize this power from the Crown and move its legal basis to legislative control would not be sufficient and instead a constitutional amendment would be required.[18]

Whatever one may make of Professor Lagassé's argument, the fact remains that even if Parliament could seize from the Crown the authority to deploy, it has not done so.[19] A form of the opposing argument with superficial appeal is that the National Defence Act[20] (NDA) works to limit or displace the associated Crown prerogative power, particularly in sections 4 and 31. However, the "management and direction" of the Canadian Forces, confirmed for the minister of national defence in NDA section 4, does not supplant the prerogative authority to deploy the Canadian Forces.[21] For its part, the NDA section 31 authority granted to the governor-in-council to place elements of the Canadian Forces on "active service"[22] is not linked directly with deployment, but instead brings a number of administrative consequences.[23] One need not be on active service to be deployed, and one can be on active service without being deployed. In fact, right now all regular members of the Canadian Forces—the vast majority of whom are not deployed at any given time—are on active service in Canada and abroad as a class.[24]

In point of fact, the executive does act on the basis of Crown prerogative authority to make deployment decisions.[25] No Canadian court has found that the historic Crown prerogative power to deploy the Canadian Forces has been displaced by the NDA or any other statute; instead, court pronouncements have reaffirmed it. In one 2002 case concerning a claim flowing from Canadian bombing in Kosovo, the source of the authority to participate in the NATO-led campaign was not an issue, with the defendant conceding it was "founded in the Crown's prerogative."[26] In 2003, the Federal Court heard two cases challenging executive discretion to enter the war in Iraq. Aside from making the point that the matters were premature, since the government had not made such a decision, the court twice affirmed that the Crown prerogative would be the relevant source of authority.[27]

Consistent with the state of affairs that sees CF deployments decided upon under Crown prerogative authority with no formal role for Parliament, there have been several attempts at change. The 1994 Special Joint Committee on Canada's Defence Policy, the 1997 Somalia Commission of Inquiry, and an April 2000 report of the Standing Committee on Foreign Affairs each called for enhanced parliamentary oversight of defence matters; however, their recommendations were not implemented. At least two private member's bills (introduced in 1994 and 1998) unsuccessfully sought an amendment to the NDA to provide for a vote in the House of Commons before the Canadian Forces were deployed overseas.[28]

One other point needs to be made: neither the placement (or maintenance) of the Canadian Forces on active service nor a "take note" debate in the House of Commons is a requirement for a CF deployment by convention.[29] Practice cannot be equated with convention. Governments have the right to use whatever mechanism they choose for the purpose of consulting Parliament on deployment decisions,[30] and they have not used one consistently. While there have been many deployments over a long time period,[31] in broad brushstrokes the practice from 1950 to 1992 saw governments use a placement or maintenance on "active service" as a procedure to have the lower House consider some of the deployments.[32] Since then, in some (but not all) cases, governments have moved toward the use of take-note debates, with or without a vote for missions, including those in the former Yugoslavia,[33] peacekeeping in Ethiopia and Eritrea,[34] and the mission in Afghanistan.[35] Some missions were not subject to consultation,[36] and on several occasions different governments have announced that Parliament need not be consulted on a deployment decision.[37] Take-note debates not only concern government decisions to deploy CF elements, but can also relate to decisions *not* to do so: the government decision not to support the US-led operation in Iraq was the subject of take-note debates on October 1-2, 2002. Hence, neither active service designations nor take-note debates can be characterized as mechanisms designed to cede executive authority: active service designations merely engage additional administrative and disciplinary elements and are not directly connected with deployment, and take-note debates consider a separate government decision.[38]

There is no authority for the position that the CF deployment authority rests with Parliament.[39] It must be concluded that those who hold this position are not making a factual argument but rather a normative one. It is to this more interesting matter—whether the authority to deploy the Canadian Forces *should* be based in the Crown prerogative—that this chapter now turns.

The Democratic Legitimacy of Basing Deployment Decisions in the Crown Prerogative

The history of the Crown prerogative shows that it has developed in a sophisticated and careful way and in line with liberalism and modern representational democracy.[40] It survived the Glorious Revolution and modern developments in democracy, not because reformers forgot about it or the Crown was so strong it could beat back challenges, but because it is useful and helpful. Far from being a tool of autocratic power, it is for the benefit of the people.[41]

The democratic legitimacy of the executive's CF deployment decisions can be understood only in light of the wider governing context. Perhaps especially as Canadian politics are intertwined with those of the United States in news reporting and political analysis, it is easy to lose sight of Canada's system of responsible government. For Hogg, Monahan, and Wright, "the conventions of responsible government have subjected the prerogative powers to democratic control."[42] In fact, recalling the important distinctions between the Canadian and US political systems is a useful method for identifying aspects of the Canadian system that help democratize executive decision-making.

Canada's cabinets are almost always made up of ministers drawn from the elected, lower, house of Parliament: each cabinet minister is both a member of government and a member of Parliament. Two follow-on facts bear stressing.

First, and contrary to the US system where senior officers of the executive branch are appointed from a variety of positions and oftentimes from outside of elected politics, in almost all cases Canadian cabinet members must be elected: those who exercise the Crown prerogative have been chosen by the electorate. While it is true to say that it is only a segment of the electorate that is responsible for returning each cabinet member, the fact remains that cabinet members owe their positions to Canadian people, without whom an appointment to the cabinet would be impossible.

Second, cabinet ministers sit in the lower House and are subjected to questioning from other Commons members, including an "institutionalized opposition bent on demonstrating the inappropriateness and inefficiencies of government policy."[43] Unlike the US system, where cabinet members play no role in Congress, Canadian cabinet ministers are routinely questioned in the House about executive decisions, including those arising from the exercise of the Crown prerogative to deploy the Canadian Forces. Members of the government face questions posed orally during question period and in writing on the order paper, as well as in special debates and in parliamentary committees struck to examine issues including deployments (and other issues touching on the Canadian Forces).[44] These questions are not exclusively of the "soft ball" type addressable with non-answers. For example, on May 15, 2006, Dawn Black, MP for New Westminster-Coquitlam, put Question 33 on the order paper. The "question" consisted of 29 detailed and sophisticated sub-questions (marked (a) – (cc)), on issues surrounding the deployment in Afghanistan and in particular the treatment of detainees.[45]

Under the convention of individual ministerial responsibility, if the minister of national defence cannot explain or fix a problem identified within the portfolio (including problems related to deployments), then he or she will be pressured to resign. The prime minister may be compelled to remove an incompetent or controversial minister as well. A minister can also be moved in a cabinet shuffle.[46] In addition, government answers, as well as news reporting and academic analysis, can influence voters selecting members of Parliament in follow-on elections and through this mechanism deciding which political party will be asked by the governor general to form the government. While deployment decisions are not the only issue considered by voters, the nature of these decisions speaks to the complexity of politics more than to possible undemocratic elements in our system.

Not insignificantly, the cabinet must answer in caucus for its decisions. In line with the convention of party loyalty these caucus meetings are held in camera, but they can present a check on cabinet action.[47]

Intimately connected with this institutionalized holding of the government to account for its decisions through questioning and debate, a government in the Canadian system endures only as long as it holds the confidence of the House of Commons. While US presidents, vice-presidents, and cabinet members can be removed from office, this requires impeachment by a majority in the House of Representatives, followed by trial in the Senate with conviction established by a two-thirds majority. The mechanism is used only for allegations of illegal acts. In Canada, governments can fall because of differences of opinion, and the comparable process is a much easier one requiring a simple majority vote in the House of Commons on a vote of confidence (which can be in respect of a vote on routine business).

In addition to its role in questioning the government, the House of Commons has a number of functions in matters of defence.[48] Most significantly, Parliament is concerned with the business of supply, a matter of no small importance in the context of CF deployment decisions that place a great strain on the country's coffers.[49]

Whether Parliament, its members, and the press use the system to its potential, however, is another matter: while related, capacity and performance are different things. It has been suggested that the Canadian public and its elected representatives have displayed a limited interest in defence matters for decades, but that this may have changed given the country's military experience in Afghanistan.[50] One hopes this is a correct assessment; certainly the question in 2013 of a CF deployment in Mali generated a great deal of media and parliamentary interest.[51] Either way, there is no guarantee that giving the system the potential for greater democratic involvement (if, or however, that may be done) will actually spur parliamentarians into greater engagement. Critics of Crown prerogative-based deployment decisions as undemocratic might find their ire more profitably directed at the way in which the mechanism is applied rather than the mechanism itself.[52]

No Democratic Surplus from Parliamentary Engagement in Deployments

Considered in the abstract, there is a superficial allure to parliamentary involvement in deployment decisions. In theory, important decisions would be made by a wider body of officials than those who sit in cabinet, allowing a greater number of viewpoints to be expressed and providing constituents a more direct route to influence. Perhaps all of this would lead to increased "democratic legitimacy."[53] But would parliamentary engagement in CF deployment decisions deliver a democratic surplus? Even isolated from the problems associated with mechanisms for parliamentary engagement in CF deployment decisions discussed below, I suggest the answer is no.

The first order of business is to define the legal[54] mechanism for parliamentary engagement in CF deployment decisions. Canada's Parliament is bicameral, consisting of the House of Commons and the Senate (and the Crown). At the outset, it can be said that having Canada's unelected Senate involved in CF deployment decisions—an option advocated by some, including, perhaps understandably, the Standing Senate Committee on Foreign Affairs[55]—will not deliver any democratic surplus. It is only through the involvement of the House of Commons that such a surplus could arise. Any mechanism for engaging the House of Commons would be based on legislation, and there are two broad options. The first option would see legislation from Parliament that granted CF deployment decision-making power to some component of the executive. Democratization under this option would consist only in the fact that Parliament had substituted a legislative authority for the historical Crown prerogative power to deploy the Canadian Forces. The second option, which presumably would deliver a greater democratic effect, would be legislation requiring that the House of Commons be engaged in CF deployment decisions. This mechanism would be a two-stage democratization of deployment decision-making: the placement of deployment authority on a legislative footing, and the requirement for the exercise of this authority to be accomplished with involvement of the elected lower House.

There is precedent for the first option, and it is by far the most likely one. The National Defence Act now provides an executive decision-making process for certain domestic CF deployments: section 273.6(1) provides that the governor-in-council or the minister of national defence (MND) may authorize the Canadian Forces "to perform any duty involving public service," and section 273.6(2) legislates a mechanism and requirements for the governor-in-council or the MND to "issue directions authorizing the Canadian Forces to provide assistance in respect of any law enforcement matter."[56] The executive retains the authority, and this authority is statutorily unfettered: notably, by virtue of 273.6(4), it is the governor-in-council, and not Parliament or the House of Commons, that can issue directions in respect of the MND's related domestic deployment authorities. Gains in line with democratic principles on this option would be minimal. In effect, this option would result in a legislation of the status quo. The only addition to the democratic ledger would be a theoretical one: for those who oppose the very idea of Crown privilege and power not rooted in parliamentary grant, this option would have the welcome effect of supplanting another Crown prerogative subject area.

While it might seem that option two—the entrenchment in legislation of a House of Commons role in deployment decision-making—has great potential for democratic surplus, other factors must be kept in mind.

In a majority government environment with the existing convention of party loyalty, the democratic gain from a Commons vote on an executive decision is effectively zero (unless the government chose to hold free votes for military deployments, which would be unlikely given the stakes involved and the possibility that such votes might be matters of confidence). But even outside of majority governments (or within them if MPs are permitted to vote on their conscience), one must ask whether deployment decisions would be different. History has shown strong support across party lines for a given military operation.[57] The opposition has not voted against government decisions to deploy.[58] It has been suggested that debates do not typically deal with broader "geopolitical reasons or interests" relating to the deployment, but instead with the narrow idea of the CF's ability to perform.[59]

At least some advocates for change to deployment decision mechanisms are pessimistic about the gains from parliamentary engagement. One Australian paper argued that US congressional engagement has been "a limited deterrent to wars of aggression" and that we should be careful not to place too much stock in such mechanisms. It concluded that a requirement for parliamentary approval (in both houses) might not be enough on its own.[60]

In all likelihood, Commons votes on CF deployment decisions would be cast as confidence votes, causing opposition parties to colour decision-making with the very important question of whether saying "no" to the deployment is worth the price of voting out the government and causing a general election. In addition, this complex calculus—which could oftentimes value elections tactics over the merits of the CF deployment decision itself—could take place in an environment of national security threat that would be exacerbated were Parliament to be dissolved.[61]

Related to this is a point concerning the relationship between democracy and government accountability. With executive decision-making based in the Crown prerogative, the government is responsible for decisions.[62] If, ultimately, it is accountability we are after with our focus on democracy—suggested by the use of the term "democratic accountability" in the Crown prerogative criticism context[63]—then we have to ask whether there are gains with a parliamentary approval mechanism. In his important study on defence accountability structures, Professor Lagassé argues there may not be. Were opposition MPs to vote with the government on a CF deployment, accountability would be decreased since it would be shared between the government and opposition. To the extent of its acceptance of government policies, the opposition would be blunted in the performance of its role as institutionalized government critic.[64] The situation is worse with a minority government, since the opposition in that case must vote with the government or cause it to fall.[65] Quite apart from the problems associated with parliamentary engagement in CF deployment decisions (a matter discussed below), such engagement would not result in democratic surplus.

Problems with Parliamentary Engagement in Deployment Decisions

Leaving aside the fact that existing decision-making mechanisms are legitimate ones and that parliamentary engagement options will not deliver a democratic surplus, there are problems associated with these options.

The first parliamentary engagement option—the simple placement of executive decision-making on a statutory footing—presents problems associated with legislative translation: in order for it to cover the myriad conceivable (and inconceivable) circumstances that might require a CF deployment, the statutory grant of authority would have to be very broad. Professor Irvin Studin has identified precisely the same problem with the wording of the Emergencies Act related to "war emergencies," which he describes as "laconic."[66] There would be no real statutory guidance given to the executive in its decision-making beyond a bald grant of authority. Almost certainly, the executive could satisfy the legal requirements of the statute with minimal analysis of, and statements on, the prevailing situation.

By contrast, the existing procedure under the Crown prerogative captures the executive's decision in a record. Such record could be a very detailed record of a decision following a memorandum to cabinet, or it could be a letter of authorization containing the mission strategic objectives. What is important is that, even at their least detailed, these recorded authorizations restrain CF activity in terms of numbers, dates, geographic scope, and mission objectives. Follow-on military orders flow directly, and mission creep is avoided. This practice of structured and constraining executive direction has developed in the Crown prerogative authorization context. It is unlikely a similar requirement would, or could,[67] be made a statutory imperative.

An interesting example of "authority interplay" that raises comparable issues is that between the Crown prerogative-sourced Canadian Forces Armed Assistance Directives (CFAAD)[68] and NDA section 273.6(2). Both sources of authority relate to CF assistance to law enforcement and would apply in overlapping circumstances. The Crown prerogative-based CFAAD, however, is more detailed and constraining. The 273.6(2) regime is set out in one sentence divided into a chapeau and two requirements; the CFAAD, by contrast, consists of nine paragraphs and contains a regime for pre-positioning, decision-making on force composition, command and control, and, ultimately, meeting RCMP requests for armed assistance to deal with the situation. In short, the legislative-footing option would replace the existing practice of detailed, constraining, executive direction under Crown prerogative authority with a regime of executive direction referencing wide, general grants of statutory authority.

The second option—that of having a Commons vote on deployments—raises important questions as to practical workability. Consider the following cases.

On September 11, 2001, the United States was attacked. The next day the North Atlantic Council—the principal political decision-making body within NATO, on which Canada is a member and which operates by consensus—issued a statement that if determined to be an attack against the United States, it was against them all.[69] As such, it is arguable that as of September 12, 2001, Canada was committed to assist NATO in its eventual exercise of collective self-defence in Afghanistan, at least at the political level. In the event, on October 7, 2001, Prime Minister Chrétien announced a sizable CF military engagement in Afghanistan.[70]

On December 26, 2004, an undersea earthquake occurred in the Indian Ocean, generating tsunamis that hit several countries in Southeast Asia causing a humanitarian disaster. On January 2, 2005—one week after the event and on the margins of the holiday period—Prime Minister Paul Martin announced that Canada would send the CF Disaster Assistance Response Team (DART) to Sri Lanka.[71]

In both of these cases, the Canadian executive worked at breakneck speed, engaging with allies, coming to legal and political grips with difficult situations, assessing response options, and preparing for military intervention. Aside from the pace of this work, it demanded the analysis of an ever-changing and growing body of intelligence. There are serious questions about whether the House of Commons could have debated and decided on these CF deployments in any meaningful way (let alone any way that would enhance democratic legitimacy). MPs would have had to take on the unforecasted and complex analysis required in addition to their normal and considerable workloads and programmed holiday breaks. It has been noted that, unlike with much public policy, when it comes to CF deployments Canada oftentimes does not set the agenda; instead, the executive finds itself reacting to the decisions of others, including allies, NATO, and the UN, making parliamentary input difficult or, perhaps, "impossible."[72]

Importantly, the analysis required would concern not just the immediate issue of the deployment, its requirements and costs and what military assets are best suited and can be spared, but also the myriad other factors that must be considered in coming to a deployment decision, including bilateral and multilateral relations, treaty obligations, and often complex questions of international law. There is a strong argument to be made that the executive is best placed to perform the required analysis—which concerns not an isolated issue but a range of factors—and that parliamentary structures are not competent to do so.[73]

Delays in CF deployments can lead to national security risks, loss of available military tactics, corresponding risk to CF members and, in the case of humanitarian deployments (such as that to Sri Lanka), an increase in suffering. Any advantages of surprise will be compromised for deployments involving the possible or probable use of force against adversaries.[74] This is not to say that speed should be obtained at the expense of analysis, but, as in so many things, it is a matter of balance. Regardless of what mechanism is put in place, there will be concerns that decision-makers are rushing to decisions. The important point is that burdening the CF deployment mechanism with additional procedure will necessarily lead to delays that are, arguably, unnecessary and unacceptable.

CF deployment decisions oftentimes involve information that must remain secret, either because it is provided by allies with caveats to this effect or because it is collected in a way necessitating limited distribution. Indeed, it is not only intelligence that has security concerns; in many cases the fact of negotiations with allies on possible deployments and the contents of these negotiations must be kept secret. While secrecy issues can be mitigated in a variety of ways, they will always remain and will need to be dealt with, leading in the worst cases to lengthy delays or a stalled deployment analysis. Even where a standing house committee is "security cleared" to the appropriate level,[75] deployment debates would either consider incomplete information in public or the complete picture in camera. Neither of these solutions is perfect if the aim is to democratize deployment decisions.

In addition, debates on CF deployments are in many cases best conducted in secret. Recalling the rationale for conducting cabinet committee and caucus meetings in camera, such debates are best in an environment that encourages the free flow of ideas and arguments without concern for public perception. With public debates, this element is lost, and in fact the public arena may present incentives to weaken debate. One does not need to look too far into the realm of the possible to imagine Commons debates on important CF deployment decisions deteriorating into cheap political point-scoring exercises narrowly focused on "sound bite" issues at the expense of the broad-based, difficult, and sophisticated analysis required.

Conclusion

It is too easy, and ultimately unhelpful, to write off the Crown prerogative as "pre-democratic."[76] This historic source of executive power is the basis for CF deployment authorizations, and I have suggested here that the supposed problem of the democratic deficit may be more apparent than real. Seemingly straightforward proposals for change are not; maybe the "parliamentary engagement Emperor" has no clothes. We should continue the important debate on the availability of democracy gains through the use of other mechanisms, but there is much to suggest that the current system is a fitting one for our liberal democracy and that obvious solutions wither in the light of analysis.

A form of this debate took place in the United Kingdom following that country's intervention in Iraq (which proved to be deeply unpopular). In 2004, a House of Commons committee published a report colourfully titled "Taming the Prerogative," arguing for a statutory provision requiring parliamentary approval for a decision to enter into an armed conflict. Three years later, following consideration of a House of Lords committee report and government comments, the Commons committee published a follow-up report, entitled "Constitutional Renewal," drawing back from its original hard line and falling in with the Lords committee's conclusions to have a convention rather than a law. The UK story continues: in early 2011 the coalition government announced it would proceed with a legislation approach, but it is proving very difficult to come up with suitable language. The government was still without a law in 2013.[77]

Perhaps it is correct to say that even if Parliament (as well as courts) could curtail the Crown prerogative, they have chosen not to do so;[78] and perhaps this reflects considered wisdom. The law is not the answer for every grievance. It may be that enhanced effectiveness using existing structures is a better approach than criticism of those structures. Politics must be allowed to take up its rightful place.

Notes

1. The views expressed in this chapter are the author's alone. They do not necessarily reflect, nor should they be taken to reflect, the views of the Government of Canada, the Department of National Defence, the Canadian Forces, or the Office of the Judge Advocate General.
2. Article 2(4) of the Charter of the United Nations prohibits the "threat or use of force," and possible legal exceptions include operations under UN Security Council resolution, consent of the host state, or in lawful exercise of self-defence.
3. Peter W. Hogg, *Constitutional Law of Canada,* looseleaf ed. (Scarborough, ON: Thomson Carswell, 1997), 1.9.
4. See, for example, Paul Lordon, *Crown Law* (Toronto: Butterworths, 1991), 75-105. The Crown prerogative power to deploy the Canadian Forces is a federal power.
5. Craig Forcese, *National Security Law* (Toronto: Irwin Law, 2008), 153; see also Lordon, *Crown Law,* 81; the seminal case of *Chandler* v. *D.P.P.,* [1962] 3 All E.R., 146; and O. H. Phillips and Paul Jackson, *O. Hood Phillips' Constitutional and Administrative Law,* 7th ed. (London: Sweet and Maxwell, 1987), 345.
6. For a more detailed discussion of the relevant law and convention, see Alexander W. Bolt, "The Crown Prerogative as Applied to Military Operations" (Office of the Judge Advocate General, Ottawa, 2008); and Philippe Lagassé, "Parliamentary and Judicial Ambivalence toward Executive Prerogative Powers in Canada," *Canadian Public Administration* 55, no. 2 (2012): 12.
7. Michael Dewing and Corinne McDonald, "International Deployment of Canadian Forces: Parliament's Role" (Library of Parliament, 2006), 1.
8. A. V. Dicey, *Introduction to the Study of the Law of the Constitution,* 10th ed. (London: Macmillan,1959), 424.
9. Hogg, *Constitutional Law,* 1.9, note 76.
10. See, for example, UK, House of Commons, SN/IA/4335, "Parliamentary Approval for Deployment of the Armed Forces: An Introduction to the Issues" (2007) and the discussion of Lord Holme's remarks, 16.
11. The quotation is from Lord Roskill in *Council of Civil Service Unions* v. *Minister for the Civil Service,* [1984] 3 All E.R. 935 (H.L.), 955, cited in M. Elliott and Amanda Perreau-Saussine, "Pyrrhic Public Law: Bancoult and the Sources, Status and Content of Common Law Limitations on Prerogative Power," *Public Law* 697 (2009): 710. Borrowed from another case where it was applied in a different context, Lord Roskill used the quotation in reference to arguments on the judicial reviewability of Crown prerogative decisions.
12. See discussion of criticisms by the group Charter 88 in UK, House of Commons, SN/IA/4335, 11.
13. See, for example, the dissenting opinion of DeP. Wright J. in *Aleksic* v. *Canada (Attorney General)* (2002), 215 D.L.R. (4th) 720 (Ont. Div. Ct.), 724.

14. This phrase comes from a discussion on the common law more broadly, and its idea is rejected, the court instead referring to a system "founded on broad principles of common sense applicable to the every day conditions of civilised life" (*R. v. Grills* (1910), 11 C.L.R. 400, 412). The connection to the Crown prerogative is made in H. V. Evatt, *The Royal Prerogative* (Sydney: Law Book Co., 1987), 16. See also SN/IA/4335, 3, describing the Crown prerogative as "difficult to explain and define."
15. This is the argument made by DeP. Wright J. in *Aleksic*, 724.
16. Philippe Lagassé, "The Crown's Powers of Command-in-Chief: Interpreting Section 15 of Canada's Constitution Act, 1867," *Review of Constitutional Studies* 15, no. 3 (2013).
17. Similarly, the US War Powers Resolution—which purports to require congressional approval of certain troop deployments—has been considered unconstitutional by successive administrations.
18. More broadly, any associated remedy would be extremely difficult to put into place, bringing into question whether the problem is worth the remedy.
19. See, e.g., Forcese, *National Security Law*, 154.
20. R.S.C. 1985, c. N-5.
21. See, e.g., Lordon, *Crown Law*, 82, who, even as he describes this section as granting "control" and "disposition" of the Canadian Forces to the minister of national defence, affirms the Crown prerogative right to "station" the Canadian Forces.
22. Article 31(1) of the NDA provides that the governor-in-council may place the Canadian Forces or part of it on "active service" in certain circumstances, including "in consequence of any action undertaken by Canada under the North Atlantic Treaty."
23. See NDA ss. 30(1) and 77, 88, and 97.
24. P.C. 1989-583 (April 6, 1989). This continues a situation in place since P.C. 1950-4365 of September 9, 1950, at the time of participation in the Korea action. While the order-in-council reads "for the purpose of fulfilling Canada's obligations under the North Atlantic Treaty," this is not operative text, as it is not possible to be on active service for one purpose but not another: see NDA s. 31(2) deeming all CF members on active service to be such "for all purposes."
25. For a discussion of who within the executive makes deployment decisions and through what mechanism, see Bolt, "The Crown Prerogative."
26. *Aleksic*, 729.
27. *Blanco* v. *Canada* (2003), 231 F.T.R., 7; *Turp* v. *Chrétien* (2003), 111 C.R.R. (2d) 184 (F.C.), 188 (citing *Blanco*).
28. Bill C-295 was introduced December 7, 1994, and M-380 on June 10, 1998. For a wider discussion on these attempts at change, see Dewing and McDonald, "International Deployment," 6-7.
29. Forcese, *National Security Law*, 155. Irvin Studin, "The Strategic Constitution in Action: Canada's Afghan War as a Case Study," *German Law Journal* 13, no. 5 (2012), 419, considers the argument (see 429n30, 441n54), but seems to reject it (429n30). Cf., e.g., James W. J. Bowden, "The Demise of Responsible Government and the Crown Prerogative on Defence," *Parliamentum* (blog), February 26, 2012, http://parliamentum.org/2012/02/26/crown-prerogative-on-defence/.
30. Studin, "Strategic Constitution," 441-42.

31. For a more detailed discussion on parliamentary consultation mechanisms over time, see Dewing and McDonald, "International Deployment," appendices 1 and 2.
32. Beginning with order-in-council P.C. 1950-4365 (Korea) and ending with P.C. 1992-2519 of December 7, 1992 (Somalia), and including, for example, P.C. 1964-389 (Cyprus) and P.C. 1990-1995 (Iraq).
33. For example, on January 25, 1994, March 29 and December 4, 1995, October 7, 1998, and April 12, 1999.
34. On October 17, 2000.
35. For example, on September 21 and October 15, 2001, January 28, 2002, and November 15, 2005.
36. For example, in East Timor, Macedonia, and Haiti.
37. Most recently, Prime Minister Harper announced that Parliament need not be consulted on the government's extension of the Afghan mission: "Afghan Training Mission Doesn't Need Vote: PM," *CBC News*, November 12, 2010.
38. The contentious take-note debate on May 17, 2006, considered a two-year extension of Canadian engagement in Afghanistan. The related motion, which passed with 149 yeas to 145 nays, was framed in terms of lower house "support" of the government's decision.
39. The blending of the descriptive and the normative can be more subtle. Perhaps a commentator will say that the Crown prerogative can be used only in respect of some CF deployments, in some circumstances, or that assertions of Crown prerogative powers are inappropriate unless the courts have made express acknowledgements of those precise powers.
40. See Bolt, "The Crown Prerogative as Applied to Military Operations"; Lagassé, "Parliamentary and Judicial Ambivalence."
41. Philippe Lagassé, "Accountability for National Defence," Institute for Research on Public Policy, Study 4 (2010), 7.
42. Peter W. Hogg, Patrick J. Monahan, and Wade K. Wright, *Liability of the Crown*, 4th ed. (Toronto: Carswell, 2011), 25.
43. M. M. Atkinson and David C. Docherty, "Parliament and Political Success in Canada," in *Canadian Politics in the 21st Century*, 5th ed., ed. Michael S. Wittington and Glen Williams (Scarborough: Nelson, 2000), 5.
44. Today we have the Commons Standing Committee on National Defence and the Senate Committee on Foreign Affairs and International Trade.
45. Question 33 was made an order for return, and the answer was tabled September 18, 2006; a revised answer was tabled on March 19, 2007 (Canada, Sessional Paper No. 8555-391-33-01).
46. Recent movements from the position of minister of national defence include Art Eggleton (2002) and Gordon O'Connor (moved in a cabinet shuffle 2007).
47. One historic example is the dropping of gun control laws in the face of backbencher revolt: Atkinson and Docherty, "Parliament and Political Success in Canada," 21.
48. Lagassé lists eight parliamentary functions related to defence ("Accountability for National Defence," 11). Of course there are other players in deployment decisions; for example, Studin refers to "the federalism dynamic" (431).
49. According to the government, the incremental cost of the 2001–11 portion of the Afghanistan mission was estimated at $11.3 billion (http://www.afghanistan.gc.ca/canada-afghanistan/news-nouvelles/2010/2010_07_09.

aspx?view=d). The significant costs of the mission in Libya were also the subject of media controversy: see, for example, "Libya Mission's Final Costs Reach $347M," *CBC News*, May 11, 2012. The final decision on the Lockheed Martin F-35 will have implications for future CF deployments.

50. Lagassé, "Accountability for National Defence," 3, 5.
51. Editorial, "Parliament Must Debate Any Military Mission in Mali," *Toronto Star*, January 1, 2013; Campbell Clark and Geoffrey York, "Harper Rules Out 'Direct' Canadian Military Mission in Mali," *Globe and Mail*, January 8, 2013, http://www.theglobeandmail.com/news/politics/harper-rules-out-direct-canadian-military-mission-in-mali/article7044771; Laura Payton, "Harper Wants 'Broad Consensus' before Extending Mali Help," *CBC News*, January 23, 2013; J. L. Granatstein, "Why the Pacifist Left Is Marginalized on Mali," Arguments, *Ottawa Citizen*, February 6, 2013. Granatstein bemoaned the "tiresome refrain" of certain Mali commentators viewed as conducting weak and partisan analysis of a difficult problem. All of this debate can only be a good thing.
52. For example, Lagassé argues that parliamentarians must work to ensure greater adherence to responsible government principles rather than have principles weakened by change ("Accountability for National Defence," 6). See also M. Bright, "Does Parliamentary Oversight of Canadian Peacekeeping Work?" *Vanguard* 4, no. 4 (1999): 7. Bright argues that oversight flows from greater information to Parliament rather than "micro-management of Cabinet."
53. Canada, Standing Senate Committee on Foreign Affairs (SSCFA), *The New NATO and the Evolution of Peacekeeping: Implications for Canada* (April 2000), 76.
54. Note that UK studies have recommended a non-legal convention (formalized in a resolution) as a fix for a perceived democratic deficit in the use of the Crown prerogative for military deployments. See, for example, Joint Committee on the Draft Constitutional Renewal Bill, *Draft Constitutional Renewal Bill, Volume 1: Report* (London: Stationery Office, 2008); UK, House of Commons, SN/IA/4335, 18-19. As non-legal, this option is not weighed here.
55. SSCFA, *The New NATO*, 76-77.
56. There is a carve-out. Pursuant to section 273.6(3), the legislated mechanism does not apply to "assistance that is of a minor nature."
57. Dewing and Corinne McDonald, "International Deployment," 5.
58. Ibid., 6.
59. Ibid., 5. This might be considered another forum for legitimate Commons discussions on ways and means.
60. Alison Broinowski, ed., *Why Did We Go to War in Iraq? A Call for an Australian Inquiry* (Carton, Victoria: Iraq War Inquiry Group, 2012), 59.
61. Lagassé, "Accountability for National Defence," 18.
62. *Canada v. Khadr*, [2010] SCC 3, paras. 37 and 39.
63. See, e.g., UK, House of Commons, SN/IA/4335, 10.
64. Lagassé, "Accountability for National Defence," 9. "Every time an opposition party votes with the government, a measure of accountability is lost" (12). Lagassé applies this analysis to the Afghanistan mission (13, 16).
65. Ibid., 15.

66. Studin suggests the Emergencies Act is "most laconic" in its treatment of war emergencies, since "it is near impossible for legislation to restrict or condition the entirety executive behaviour in the context of the most serious national emergencies or situations" ("Stategic Constitution," 430n33; see also 438n52).
67. It would appear such a legislated requirement would be unique in Canadian statute law. In its formulation it would face the same challenges as the underlying grant of authority: how to empower the Crown to act in the myriad possible scenarios that might be faced.
68. Order-in-Council P.C. 1993-64, March 30, 1993.
69. NATO, "Statement by the North Atlantic Council," Press Release 124, September 12, 2001.
70. Canadian Chargé d'affaires a.i. of the Permanent Mission to the President of the Security Council, letter, October 24, 2001.
71. CBC News, "Disaster Relief: Canada's Rapid Response Team," January 13, 2010, http://www.cbc.ca/news/canada/story/2010/01/13/f-disasters-military-dart.html.
72. Dewing and McDonald, "International Deployment," 4. One option would be retrospective approval, but problems with this approach include the exposure to criminal liability for good faith actions, and the matter of executive deployment authorizations that have been actioned but not subsequently confirmed (see, e.g., UK, House of Commons, SN/IA/4335, 26; Joint Committee, *Draft Constitutional Renewal Bill*, 92).
73. Lagassé, "Accountability for National Defence," 7. For Supreme Court of Canada acknowledgment of the complex decisions made by the executive and the related "limitations of the Court's institutional competence," see *Canada v. Khadr*, [2010] SCC 3, paras. 37, 39, and 47.
74. UK, House of Commons, SN/IA/4335, 24.
75. An option discussed by Iraq War Inquiry Group, "Why Did We Go to War in Iraq?" 61.
76. See the SN/IA/4335 discussion of Lord Holme's remarks, 16.
77. Foreign Secretary Hague's promise was made on March 21, 2011, during debates on the Libya mission. See, e.g., "War Footing Commons Veto 'Dangerous' as Doubt Cast over Plans," *Telegraph*, January 4, 2013, http://www.telegraph.co.uk/news/uknews/defence/9779726/War-footing-Commons-veto-dangerous-as-doubt-cast-over-plans.html; Andrew Sparrow, "PMQs and Release of the Coalition's Pledge Audit: Politics Live Blog," *Guardian*, January 9, 2013.
78. Lagassé, "Parliamentary and Judicial Ambivalence," 157.

Part 4

First Nations and the Crown

15

"Recollecting Sovereignty": First Nations–Crown Alliance and the Legacy of the War of 1812

Stephanie Danyluk

L'histoire de la participation des Premières Nations à la guerre de 1812 remet en question l'assertion de souveraineté prééminente de la Couronne canadienne et met en évidence la pérennité de leurs droits à l'autodétermination et à la souveraineté partagée avec le Canada. Ce chapitre analyse les diverses expressions de la souveraineté autochtone à travers les récits historiques de convergence et d'échanges politiques entres les Premières Nations de l'Ouest et la Couronne dans le cadre de la guerre de 1812.

Étant donné la façon dont les Premières Nations de l'ouest envisageaient la souveraineté avant cette guerre, on ne peut considérer ces alliances comme une affirmation de souveraineté de la Couronne à l'encontre des peuples autochtones. Inscrivant ce dossier historique dans le contexte des récits oraux des Premières Nations, l'auteure soutient que la mémoire historique de la guerre de 1812 continue d'exprimer d'importantes dimensions politiques de l'alliance entre la Couronne et les Premières Nations et qu'elle justifie la revendication de souveraineté partagée. Ce qui constitue un préalable à la création d'un troisième ordre de gouvernement découlant de ce partage de souveraineté. Les références à un conflit vieux de deux siècles s'appliquent ainsi aux enjeux actuels de droits, de titres et de gouvernance, de sorte qu'un troisième ordre gouvernement autochtone viendrait reconnaître l'importance des liens historiques entre la Couronne et les Premières Nations tout en réaffirmant que celles-ci ont délégué – et non cédé – leur autorité à la Couronne.

> "Canada's Aboriginal peoples were in every sense key to the victory that firmly established Canada as a distinct country in North America. Now, of course, much has changed in 200 years. The war, contrary to a lot of expectations of the time, ushered in a long peace between Canada and the United States. The Americans are now our great friends and allies. Canada

> is a peaceful and prosperous federation stretching from coast to coast to coast. Yet one of the constants over the decades has been the loyal service of Canada of its Aboriginal peoples during times of great need."
>
> —Prime Minister Stephen Harper[1]

The bicentennial of the War of 1812 provided the Canadian government with a welcome opportunity to recognize the role of First Nations in the founding of Canada. A War of 1812 National Recognition Ceremony acknowledging descendants of the Crown's Aboriginal allies was held in Ottawa on October 25, 2012, at which time these allies were awarded medals and banners created by the Canadian Heraldic Authority. Although Prime Minister Harper recognized the fidelity of First Nations peoples in their relationship with the Crown and their contribution to Canada, his words overlooked instances in Canada's past where this loyalty was not reciprocated and First Nations sovereignty was undermined. Conversely, while First Nations' memories of the War of 1812 highlight their alliance with the Crown, they do so in a way that reinforces their autonomy, asserting that they were not subordinates in this relationship. First Nations exercised their right to self-determination on a nation-to-nation level as equal partners in the alliances formed during this war. Indeed, the history of First Nations' participation in the War of 1812 challenges the Canadian Crown's claim to pre-eminent sovereignty and demonstrates First Nations' lasting right to self-determination and shared sovereignty with Canada.

Oral histories of Crown promises made to Western Nations allies in the War of 1812 reveal that these commitments constituted a treaty relationship. To fully understand the lasting significance of these promises for First Nations today, it is necessary to examine both their historical context and the manner in which they are understood by Indigenous peoples as a commitment to protect their sovereignty. At the time of the War of 1812, the nations residing throughout the Great Lakes and upper Mississippi included the Dakota, Fox, Kickapoo, Menominee, Ojibwa, Ottawa, Potawatomi, Sauk, and Winnebago, who were collectively referred to by the British as the "Western Indian Nations." According to the testimony of the Western Nations, alliances formed with the Crown were constituted by shared promises that allowed each nation to retain sovereignty and provided for the protection of their autonomy and territory. In other words, these First Nations were self-governing nations entering into a nation-to-nation agreement.

This historical context buttresses claims to autonomy on the part of these nations today and supports the idea of shared sovereignty through the establishment of a First Nations third order of government. When First Nations recall the War of 1812, they see more than just a historical event. Rather, they link this event to a history of promises made by the Crown to protect their sovereignty. In this chapter, I argue that promises made during the War of 1812 were an extension of a long-standing treaty relationship between the Crown and First Nations, whereby the former recognized the autonomy, sovereignty, and territory of Western Nations.[2] This chapter shows how First Nations came to this interpretation of the promises made during the war and highlights how the Crown's promises constituted a treaty from a First Nations' perspective. I examine how sovereignty was understood by Western Nations prior to the War of 1812, illustrate some of the complexities of the alliances, and conclude with a study of the continuing legacy of the Crown's promises. This alliance sets a precedent for establishing a third order of government flowing from the shared sovereignty between First Nations and the Crown.

First Nations, the Crown, and Shared Sovereignty

Shared sovereignty is a concept that First Nations have historically accepted and applied. Indigenous inhabitants of North America have long had systems of government that allowed them to maintain autonomous territory and governance, while partaking in close partnerships and common causes. For example, by the mid-eighteenth century, the Sauk and Fox lived in small separate groups, but would come together seasonally at large villages such as Saukenuk along the Rock River.[3] The Winnebago were divided into clans which lived together in towns or villages that were governed by two civil leaders. These leaders came together to form a larger council.[4] The Pottawatomi also had leaders within each village who would come together to consult with one another at various times. The Dakota Nation was made up of four separate groups. Each group acted autonomously and had its own civil and military leaders, who usually gathered for a general council each spring.[5] The larger governing structure of the Dakota Nation was called the Oceti Sakowin, or the Seven Council Fires, and included the Lakota and Nakota Nations. Trade relationships existed among the Oceti Sakowin Nations, and these groups would come together each summer for this purpose.[6] These nations had a polity of their own and their own approach to establishing alliances. In particular, treaties and ceremonies between Indigenous nations strengthened these relationships, be it for building political liaisons, conducting trade, or providing military support. For example, an alliance between Sauk and Fox occurred in the mid-1730s, merging these groups as one, although both groups maintained separate leadership.[7] In addition, the Pottawatomi had a confederacy with the Ojibwa and Ottawa.[8] Thus, each nation acted as an autonomous political entity, but this autonomy was complemented by confederacies and flexible systems of governance.

Similarly, Indigenous inhabitants of North America did not see their relationship with the Crown as one of subordination. When First Nations partnered or allied themselves with the Crown, they regarded themselves as independent nations, maintaining their right to self-determination. First Nations that entered into agreements with the Crown would not have seen these arrangements as reducing their autonomy or sovereignty.

Specific cultural protocol was important in the establishment of alliances. Nations employed wampum and the calumet to signal the gravity and importance of councils, negotiations, and agreements. Wampum belts were used as a reminder of a treaty or an agreement, and the calumet was smoked with due ceremony to seal alliances and signify agreements. Gift-giving was also significant, and it was expected that there would be periodic exchanges of food and goods over the duration of an alliance. As alliances between the Western Nations and the British Crown were cemented through the eighteenth century, large gatherings and ceremonies involving cultural protocol became customary.

Yet ceremonies and protocol of this kind may have held a different significance for First Nations participants than for the representatives of the Crown. For instance, the records of councils held by Sir William Johnson with groups of Western Nations throughout the 1760s document the extensive use of protocols and ceremonies incorporating both the calumet and the wampum, such as at the Council at Niagara in 1764 to ratify the Royal Proclamation.[9] John Borrows points out that "First Nations had a perspective of the document that contradicts claims to British sovereignty found in the Proclamation."[10] Whereas the British viewed the Proclamation as a unilateral declaration and First Nations as passive receivers, First Nations saw the Proclamation as a recognition of their autonomy that they actively ratified.[11] As Burrows explains, "They expected the Crown to protect their interests, and not allow them to be interfered with, especially with regard to their land use and means of livelihood."[12] Hence, not only do earlier ceremonies and agreements with the Crown help explain the actions of these Western Nations as allies of the British in the War of 1812, they also shed light on how the Crown–First Nations alliances of this war would have been interpreted differently by the parties involved.

The War of 1812 and Crown–First Nations Relations

Although the War of 1812 is often dismissed as a relatively minor conflict, it has remained an important part of the history of participating First Nations. Many factors are cited as causes of the war: trade restrictions on American goods, the impressment of Americans into the British Navy, and generally poor relations between the two nations. Described by a Virginia Republican as a "land grab," the war began in June 1812. With the British engaged in a long and costly conflict with Napoleon, the Americans found this to be an opportune moment to strike. What the Americans thought would last only six weeks continued for two-and-a-half years. Perhaps the most significant factor cited for First Nations participation was British support for Indigenous peoples against American expansion. The expansion of American settlement had ushered in an era of harsh and often brutal takeovers of First Nations lands. Acting on behalf of their autonomous nations, First Nations leaders were seeking to protect their own social, political, and cultural systems as much as they looked to aid their British allies. Indigenous leaders sought the establishment of an independent First Nations homeland, and alliances with the British were formed with this in mind. Clearly, the Indigenous peoples had at least as much at stake in the rising conflict with the Americans as the British.

During the War of 1812, the British understood that attracting First Nations' support depended on their Indigenous allies believing that their sovereignty and territory were protected.[13] Given the importance of having the assistance of First Nations, the British were prepared to convey the sense that this was the Crown's intent. The Western Nations were valuable military allies in the War of 1812 and, according to General Proctor, "the most powerful and the most warlike of the Indians."[14] The participation of the Western Nations in the War of 1812 is remarkable for the sheer number of warriors. Of the 10,000 documented First Nations participants, at least 8,710 were "Western Indians" who were located in the territories of Michigan, Illinois, and Indiana and considered to be under the jurisdiction of the American government at the start of the war.[15] While British correspondence makes it clear that, to some officials, engaging First Nations warriors was more about the exploitation of their force than it was about protecting Indigenous territories, the large-scale participation of the Western Nations in the War of 1812 was driven by the interest of these nations to protect their sovereignty and territories.[16]

First Nations participants did not cede military or political power to British officials, but delegated this authority. Their actions make it clear that these warriors were directed by both British commanders and their own First Nations leaders as was deemed fit. Reactions to growing conflict with the Americans provide evidence of the belief on the part of the Western Nations that they were acting autonomously. At a council of Shawnees, Kickapoo, and Winnebago approximately two weeks prior to the beginning of the war, one chief was quoted as declaring, "If we hear of any of our people having been killed, we will immediately send to all the nations on or toward the Mississippi, and all this island will Rise as one man."[17] The initial battle, which took place at Fort Michilimackinac, is indicative of the type of support that was provided by these First Nation allies. Well over 300 First Nations people participated in this battle, with the entire force totalling approximately 550 men. The Americans capitulated to the British force almost immediately, and the British secured the fort without a drop of blood spilt. This victory was significant, as news of the British success attracted many First Nations initially hesitant to ally with the British. But perhaps equally significant is the report to Sir George Prevost that the First Nations forces were commanded by the chiefs of their individual tribes: the continued control of these leaders over their forces is indicative of maintenance of their political autonomy.[18]

The Dakota, Fox, Kickapoo, Menominee, Ojibwa, Ottawa, Potawatomi, Sauk, and Winnebago remained loyal to the British during the war, fighting at Fort Michilimackinac, Detroit, Sandusky, Prairie du Chien, and other battles that took place either near or within their territory. In the effort to preserve autonomy, the Western Indian allies maintained strong control over their territories throughout the war. Indeed, there are many instances where these First Nations allies acted independently to protect their families and territories. The battle at Rock River on July 21, 1814, provides one example. The Indigenous inhabitants of Rock River, including many women, aided in the attack against American invaders, jumping on board their ships and beating back the Americans with hoes and setting fire to their decks.[19] The defence of Prairie du Chien provides another example of autonomous action. Following defeat of the Americans at Prairie du Chien in June 1814, Dakota Chief Little Crow told British officials at Mackinac, "I have sent the Americans from La Prairie du Chien, and then I came here to drive them away."[20] At this time, British Colonel William McKay reported that the Winnebago "behaved in a most villainous manner," plundering the village and killing some of the inhabitants.[21] They were reprimanded by Colonel McKay, who recounted that these Winnebago "audaciously" replied that "they are under no obligations to us but they have themselves preserved the Country."[22] Their actions were likely in retaliation for the murder of seven members of the Winnebago Nation by the Americans at Prairie du Chien.[23] However indignant the British commanders were at this expression of self-rule, the words and actions of these Western Nations participants suggest that they were acting independently in the protection of their jurisdiction and believed that this was their right as partners in this alliance.

First Nations–Crown relationships at the time of the War of 1812 illustrate that the authority of the Crown was accepted with the consent of the First Nations allies. These nations delegated military authority to British officials in order to protect their values and livelihood. They did not surrender their territory, sovereignty, or their right to self-determination through their participation in this alliance. Indeed, the protection of their sovereignty was asserted in promises made by the Crown. For First Nations, what this promised protection meant was the continuation of their ability to act autonomously as self-governing nations. These promises were often delivered at large councils, accompanied by presentations of flags, medals, and wampum.[24] There is documentation of numerous promises that include the protection and maintenance of the territory, rights, and privileges of these nations. A speech prepared by Major-General Francis De Rottenburg and delivered by Robert Dickson at a council at Michilimackinac in January 1813 is representative of these types of promises. Dickson was instructed to address the nations employing "a few strings of wampum."[25] At this council he declared, "The object of the war is to secure to the Indian Nations the boundaries of their Territories."[26] He then distributed medals and flags and continued,

> My Children, that you may bear in mind the Alliance now renewed between you and my White Children, I give you a flag and a medal to be preserved in your Nation forever: by looking at this flag you will remember it came from your English Father, and when any of my Chiefs shall see it, they shall take you by the hand and do you all the good they can.[27]

Here, Dickson appeals to these groups as autonomous nations, pledging the protection of the Crown. Dickson's words alone may not seem enough to signify a treaty, but accompanied as they were by established treaty protocols, including gifts and wampum, these promises mirror those made at the Niagara council.[28] These agreements were less about authority and control than they were about the merging of political power and will. James Sákéj Youngblood Henderson refers to treaties of this kind as "prerogative treaties," in that they "recognized and empowered dual legal systems and mutual rights of self-determination" and "created a bilateral sovereignty of a kinship state in a shared territory."[29] Speeches such as Dickson's held much significance for First Nations, in their view asserting their sovereignty and highlighting the political dimensions of First Nations–Crown alliance as a nation-to-nation agreement.

In the minds of the First Nations people, these were solemn treaty promises. With the signing of the Treaty of Ghent, however, the Crown's promises were left unfulfilled. The territory of the Western Nations was handed over to the Americans, effectively leaving the rights and privileges of these nations unprotected. British commander Lieutenant-Colonel McDouall was one of the most vocal opponents of the abandonment of the Western Nations allies. Vehemently opposed to the British surrender of Prairie du Chien to the Americans, he expressed his view to Sir George Murray that the Americans were in violation of article 9 of the Treaty of Ghent and asserted that this territory had always belonged to members of the Western Nations:

> My perplexity is as great as ever, as to the order, sent me through Lt. Col. Harvey, to give up Fort McKay & the Prairie des Chiens, to the Americans, as the ninth article of the Treaty affords the most clear and circumstantial evidence, that the great extent of Country from the Mississippi, so shamefully seized upon, by the Americans in June last, & from which they were

> expelled in the ensuing month, reverts again to the Indians, as it is expressly stipulated that they are restored to all the possessions, rights, & privileges, which they enjoyed in 1811.[30]

He went on to state, "Instead of the flattering promises, which I was so lately instructed to make to them, being realized, the Whole Country is given up. A breach of faith, is with them an utter abomination, & never forgotten."[31] Lieutenant-Colonel McDouall's words indicate the blatant disregard of promises to protect the sovereignty, territory, rights, and privileges of these allies. Whereas Western First Nations had allied with the Crown in good faith, this failure set off a course of events that fatally limited the sovereignty of the Western Nations.

Western Nations and the Crown following the War

First Nations leaders made efforts to retain their alliance with the Crown in spite of these broken promises. Following the communication of the contents of the Treaty of Ghent to the leaders of the First Nations allies, responses from these leaders affirm that—at least from their perspective—this was a treaty relationship through which their autonomy was protected.[32] At a council held at Drummond Island on June 29, 1816, Colonel William McKay informed the Dakota and others that their territory was officially under the jurisdiction of the Americans. Afterwards, Wabasha proclaimed,

> But these steps must not be adopted before we hear from our Great English Father at Quebec. Though there is a Barrier unexpectedly placed between you and us, yet we stretch our arms over all obstructions and reach our English Father's hand which we hold with a strong grasp, and never will let go as long as we live.[33]

Here, Wabasha speaks a discourse of allegiance without disempowerment. His representation of the Dakota extending their hands and rejecting obstacles in the maintenance of this relationship highlights the Dakota's belief in their ability to choose to remain a part of this alliance in spite of the consequences of the signing of the Treaty of Ghent. In the eyes of First Nations, their relationship with the Crown did not dissolve with the end of the war; they continued to recognize the commitments and obligations that accompanied this alliance.

The conclusion of the War of 1812 was followed by a time of dispossession and subjugation for many of the allies of the Western Nations, in spite of the efforts of British commanders and First Nations alike. While some of these groups became fragmented and separated—either through land surrenders or policies of removal on the part of the American government—many continued to uphold their connections to the British Crown.[34] Although the Western Nations were now under the jurisdiction of the American government, Crown officials continued to receive them into Canada, offering protection to those who desired to settle across the border. Throughout the 1830s and 1840s, some 5,000 to 9,000 First Nations people moved from American to Canadian territory, although they may not have settled permanently.[35] But while these nations were received in Canada, they were not given a land base or privileges in line with those Indigenous groups who occupied traditional territory in Canada. If, according to the promises made by the Crown through Robert Dickson and others, the object of the war had been to secure to the Indian Nations the boundaries of their territories, the representatives of the Crown had certainly failed.

Indeed, the failure on behalf of the Crown to sufficiently uphold its promises was acknowledged by its own representatives. In 1836, the lieutenant governor of Upper Canada, Sir Francis Bond Head, wrote to British colonial secretary Lord Glenelg regarding the imperative of maintaining promises made during the War of 1812. He explained, "It must be recollected that in our Wars with the Americans, we gladly availed ourselves of the services of the Indians, whom invariably we promised we never would desert." Head went on to say,

> These rude ceremonies had probably little effect upon our officers, but they sunk [sic] deep in the minds of the Indians.... On our part, little or nothing documentary exists—the promises which were made, whatever they might have been, were almost invariably verbal, those who expressed them are now mouldering in their graves. However, the regular delivery of the presents proves and corroborates the testimony of the Wampums, and by whatever sophistry we might deceive ourselves, we could never succeed in explaining to the Indians of the United States, that their Great Father was justified in deserting them.[36]

The solemnity of the promises as they are described by Head supports the continued insistence on the part of Western Nations that these oaths and ceremonies constituted a treaty relationship and suggests that the Crown—either through willfulness or forgetfulness—has broken its promises.

Whereas there were some efforts by the Crown to maintain the commitment to the Western Nations throughout the first half of the nineteenth century, by the mid-nineteenth century, this had changed. As military and trade partners, the Western First Nations were no longer valuable to the Crown. Additionally, in the eyes of the newly formed Canadian government, increased settlement of Canadian territories prompted the need to control the movement of First Nations. These changes had severe consequences for many of the Western First Nations as governments began to exercise sovereignty over these people and their territories. Indeed, by 1862, many of the Dakota in Minnesota had grown weary of the American failure to provide annuity payments promised in exchange for their land surrender. On the brink of starvation, they rebelled against the encroaching settlers in a conflict often referred to as the Minnesota Uprising. At this time, a group of approximately 1,000 Dakota fled northward, many rejecting participation in the rebellion. They arrived near Fort Garry, presenting the King George III medals received in the War of 1812, and requested land based on Crown promises.[37] They established informal settlements in Manitoba and Saskatchewan over the next decade.

The Dakota in Western Canada continued to draw from these promises to justify a claim to autonomy. In the early 1870s, when Treaties One and Two were being negotiated, the lieutenant governor of Manitoba and the North West Territories met with Dakota leaders, who requested adherence to treaty. In December 1871, Lieutenant Governor Archibald reported,

> When I asked their business with me, they declared that they and their forefathers had always been faithful to the Crown. They showed four or five medals of the time of George III, which had been presented by British officers in the time of that sovereign, and which had been transmitted from father to son, in the families of chiefs, and held as a sacred treasure from that day to this.
>
> They said that the Officers from whom their ancestors had received these medals, had assured them that the bearers of the medals, wherever they should be, would receive for themselves and their families, whenever they asked for it, the protection of the Sovereign and the flag.
>
> They then placed on the ground a British flag and piled the medals on it, and went on to say that they came to ask for that protection and for a piece of land to live on and cultivate. They were willing to take it anywhere the Queen chose to give it, but they wished to settle and to till the soil for a livelihood.[38]

The Dakota based their claim to land in the prairies on promises from the War of 1812, as they had done on their arrival near Fort Garry in 1862. Historically, the territory of the Dakota extended into the newly formed Canadian nation. Yet the Crown excluded them from treaty negotiations. As foretold by Lieutenant Governor Head, the War of 1812 promises were forgotten. It was made clear that the reserve lands eventually offered to the Dakota—a land base drastically smaller than that of the treaty nations—were not a right, but were given because "it would be good policy or consented with humanity."[39] In spite of the long history of alliance with the British and promises made to the Dakota, Canadian officials took the stance that the Dakota were American Indians.

Treaties and Shared Sovereignty Today

Although the circumstances of the relationship between the Crown and First Nations have changed over time, what remains is the insistence of First Nations that the relationship is built on a foundation of treaty promises. Memories of these promises stand as an assertion that the alliance with the British Crown was a long-standing, government-to-government relationship. For the Dakota, their involvement provides both the context and the justification for rights and privileges overlooked by the Crown and the Canadian government. Contemporary oral histories of the War of 1812 maintain the historic focus on alliances. Testimonies persist in maintaining claims to rights and title by the Dakota in Canada. Recollecting stories told to him by his grandfather, Henry Two-Bears, Robert Goodvoice explained,

> The Dakotas, they have these medals. And these medals were made in England. And a man came from England, across the sea they said, across the big waters and brought them, brought the medals and the councillors badges and these pledges and give it to the Dakotas. They were not made in Canada, the medal was made in England. So this is the only proof that they have that they are the people that fought side by side with Robert Dickson and his army.... And this Robert Dickson was right there and he was the one that told them, he is the one that asked them to help them to fight and he is the one that asked them to quit fighting and he is the one that told them to stay over there and he is the one that told them—any time they want—to cross the border back to the north, back into Canada.[40]

Not only are the promises of Dickson central to Goodvoice's testimony, but the King George III medals, as they did for the Dakota chiefs who asserted their right to land in 1871, continue to represent their right to reside in Canada. Other oral testimonies assert that the promises made during the War of 1812 were part of a treaty relationship with the Crown. In 1970 Elder Sam Buffalo explained, "The Dakota who are now residing in Canada won this right in the Seven Fire treaty with the British government in 1812. And this is why there was no hesitation for some of the Dakota people to enter into Canada."[41] These oral histories challenge the position of the colonial and Canadian governments that the Dakota were American refugees; they also assert that the promises of the Crown are central to current issues of rights, title, and governance. Placing the promises made during the War of 1812 into their broader historical context reveals that—to the Western Nations at least—these promises were part of a historic treaty relationship with the Crown.

The self-determination evident through the history of the War of 1812 signifies that Western Nations like the Dakota have had a history of functioning as autonomous nations. To cite one example, Dakota communities such as the Whitecap Dakota First Nation are taking advantage of the bicentennial of the War of 1812 as a strategic method to realize their sovereignty. The chief of Whitecap Dakota First Nation, Darcy Bear, stated, "The betrayal of the British links to the larger story of the betrayal of all the First Nations allies with the signing of the Treaty of Ghent, but the Dakota story is different. We have a proud past."[42] Focusing on the alliance with the Crown, Bear described the Dakota as nation builders: "We want to be part of the fabric of the nation on the basis of the contribution of our ancestors."[43] He went on to explain that Dakota involvement in the War of 1812 demonstrates their ability to "rebuild strong relationships, so that our relationship [with Canada] moves forward in a good way—the ways our ancestors would have done it—sitting down in good faith and correcting this historical wrong."[44]

Establishing a third order of government centred on First Nations sovereignty and self-determination offers one means of addressing these historical wrongs. The 1996 Royal Commission on Aboriginal Peoples (RCAP) proposed the establishment of "three orders of government with distinct but overlapping spheres of authority."[45] This proposal has been echoed by Greg Poelzer and Ken Coates, who point to self-government as a method of instituting a First Nations third order of government.[46] Poelzer and Coates explain that this is not an entirely new concept, as shared sovereignty is founded on historical principles and approaches to First Nations–Crown relations: "A third order of government, sharing sovereignty with federal and provincial governments, is consistent with the historical and institutional foundations of Canada."[47] As expressed in the RCAP final report, "Over time and by a variety of methods, Aboriginal peoples became part of the emerging federation of Canada while retaining their rights to their laws, lands, political structures and internal autonomy as a matter of Canadian common law."[48] The authority of the Crown was delegated, not ceded, by First Nations through the treaty process.[49] In other words, alliances or treaty processes affirmed—rather than subordinated—First Nations sovereignty. These sovereignties merely coalesced at times to work in partnership.

The history of Western Nations in the War of 1812 provides a precedent for the establishment of a First Nations third order of government; in this historical context, Bear indicates the desire to establish a new approach to enacting sovereignty. His statement supports the observation of Poelzer and Coates that building a third order of government "means building a relationship that involves Aboriginal people reconciling their political aspirations with both federal and provincial governments."[50] The Whitecap Dakota First Nation's efforts to secure its political autonomy are demonstrated through joint government initiatives such as the First Nations Lands Management Act, self-governance, the Whitecap education co-governance model, and the pursuit of reconciliation with

Canada. Through these intergovernmental arrangements, they have identified methods to secure their sovereignty in cooperation with both provincial and federal governments. Similarly, the 1996 RCAP report describes "shared sovereignty" as "a hallmark of the Canadian federation and a central feature of the three-cornered relations that link Aboriginal governments, provincial governments and the federal government."[51] The future of First Nations governance almost certainly lies in such a model, which provides all three orders of government with distinct but overlapping spheres of authority.

Memories of the War of 1812 continue to support claims to Aboriginal rights and title. Not all of the Western Nations held or hold the same opinions on this alliance, but for some, these oral histories have taken on new meaning. These references are not simply an attempt to profit from the past. References to a conflict two centuries ago apply to current issues of rights, title, and governance. A First Nations third order of government would both recognize the significance of the historical relationship between First Nations and the Crown and reaffirm that the authority of the Crown was delegated, not ceded, by First Nations. Changes to the political landscape over the past two centuries mean that First Nations are no longer able to enact sovereignty in same way as they did at the time of the War of 1812. However, these nations still look to regain the sovereignty that they have lost and are seeking new methods to reclaim this autonomy. The perspective of First Nations aligns with that expressed in Prime Minister Harper's address at the War of 1812 National Recognition Ceremony. Weaving these allied nations into the narrative of Canadian history, the War of 1812 continues to be remembered as a moment when these First Nations were autonomous and allows us to look forward to a time when they may one day share sovereignty with the Crown.

Notes

1. Prime Minister Stephen Harper, presentation at the War of 1812 National Recognition Ceremony (Rideau Hall, Ottawa, October 25, 2012), http://www.pm.gc.ca/eng/media.asp?category=2&id=5127.
2. John Borrows, "Wampum at Niagara: The Royal Proclamation, Canadian Legal History and Self-Government," in *Aboriginal Treaty Rights in Canada*, ed. Michael Asch (Vancouver: University of British Columbia Press, 1998), 155-72.
3. Emma H. Blair, ed., *The Indian Tribes of the Upper Mississippi Valley and Region of the Great Lakes: As Described by Nicolas Perrot, French Commandant in the Northwest* (Lincoln: University of Nebraska Press, 1996), 355.
4. Ibid., 302.
5. Paul L. Stevens, "Wabasha Visits Governor Carleton, 1776: New Light on a Legendary Episode of Dakota-British Diplomacy on the Great Lakes Frontier," *Michigan Historical Review* 16, no. 1 (1990): 21-48.

6. David McCrady, *Living with Strangers: The Nineteenth-Century Sioux and the Canadian-American Borderlands* (Toronto: University of Toronto Press, 2006), 3.
7. Garrick A. Bailey and William C. Sturtevant, eds., *Handbook of North American Indians,* vol. 2 (Washington, DC: Smithsonian Institution, 2008), 636.
8. Blair, *The Indian Tribes,* 302.
9. "Niagara and Detroit Proceedings, July-September 1761," in *The Papers of Sir William Johnson,* vol. 3, ed. James Sullivan (Albany: University of the State of New York, 1921), 454.
10. Borrows, "Wampum at Niagara," 156-60.
11. Ibid., 155.
12. Ibid., 168.
13. Ibid., 168.
14. Michigan Pioneer and Historical Society, *Michigan Historical Collections,* vol. 15 (Lansing: Darius D. Thorpe, State Printers and Binder, 1889), 220.
15. Robert S. Allen, *His Majesty's Indian Allies: British Indian Policy in the Defence of Canada, 1774–1815* (Toronto: Dundurn, 1996), 219-20.
16. Ibid.
17. Michigan Pioneer and Historical Society, *Michigan Historical Collections,* 90.
18. Ibid., 112, 140.
19. T. G. Anderson, Captain Commanding, Fort McKay, Prairie du Chien, to Lt. Colonel McDouall, Commanding Michilimackinac, September 14, 1814, RG 8 C Series, vol. 1709, reel C-3840, 117-23, Library and Archives Canada.
20. Colonial Office 42, vol. 157, folio 12, as an enclosure in Sir George Prevost to Lord Bathurst, July 18, 1814.
21. Michigan Pioneer and Historical Society, *Michigan Historical Collections,* 622-25.
22. Ibid., 626.
23. Ibid., 610.
24. Speech delivered by Lt. Colonel McDouall to the Indian Chiefs and Warriors at Michilimackinac, June 5, 1814 [Doc. 112] RG 8 C Series, vol. 1219, reel C-3526, 238-41, Library and Archives Canada.
25. [Noah Freer], Military Secretary, Quebec, to Sir John Johnson, Superintendent General and Inspector General of the Indian Department, January 14, 1813, RG 8 C Series, vol. 257, 17-20, Library and Archives Canada.
26. "Speech of Robert Dickson Esquire to Indian Tribes, 18 January 1813," prepared by Major General Francis De Rottenburg, endorsed by John Johnson, Montreal, January 18, 1813, McCord Museum of Canadian History, M640, as cited in Allen, *His Majesty's Indian Allies,* Appendix C, 223-24.
27. Ibid.
28. Borrows, "Wampum at Niagara," 164.
29. James [Sákéj] Youngblood Henderson, "Empowering Treaty Federalism," *Saskatchewan Law Review* 58 (1994): 248-52.
30. Michigan Pioneer and Historical Society, *Michigan Historical Collections,* vol. 14, 136.
31. Ibid.
32. Ibid., 479-86.
33. Ibid., 480-81.

34. James A. Clifton, "A Place of Refuge for All Time: Migration of the American Potawatomi into Upper Canada, 1830 to 1850," Canadian Ethnology Service Paper No. 26 (National Museums of Canada, Ottawa, 1975), 25-28.
35. Ibid., 65.
36. Sir F. B. Head to Lord Glenelg, November 20, 1836, quoted in Robert Surtees, *Treaty Research Report: The Manitoulin Treaties* (Ottawa: Treaties and Historical Research Centre, 1986), 11.
37. Allen, *His Majesty's Indian Allies*, 197; McCrady, *Living with Strangers*, 18.
38. Adams G. Archibald to Joseph Howe, Secretary of State for the Provinces, December 27, 1871, RG 10 Series A, vol. 363, reel C-9596, Library and Archives Canada.
39. McCrady, *Living with Strangers*, xvi.
40. Robert Goodvoice, excerpt from transcript, June 15–October 15, 1977, R-1334, Saskatchewan Archives.
41. Samuel Buffalo, excerpt from transcript, September 8, 1977, R-1345, Saskatchewan Archives.
42. Darcy Bear, interview, April 4, 2012, Whitecap Dakota First Nation.
43. Ibid.
44. Ibid.
45. Royal Commission on Indigenous Peoples (RCAP), *Royal Commission Report on Aboriginal Peoples*, vol. 2, *Restructuring the Relationship* (Ottawa: Royal Commission on Indigenous Peoples, 1996), 215.
46. Greg Poelzer and Ken Coates, "Aboriginal Peoples and the Crown in Canada: Completing the Canadian Experiment," in *Continuity and Change in Canadian Politics: Essays in Honour of David E. Smith*, ed. Hans J. Michelmann and Cristine de Clercy (Toronto: University of Toronto Press, 2006), 164.
47. Ibid., 149.
48. RCAP, *Restructuring the Relationship*, 193-94.
49. Henderson, "Empowering Treaty Federalism."
50. Poelzer and Coates, "Aboriginal Peoples and the Crown," 164.
51. RCAP, *Restructuring the Relationship*, 240-41.

16

The Aboriginal Peoples and the Crown

J. R. (Jim) Miller

Historiquement, les liens entre la Couronne et les Premières Nations du Canada reposaient sur une forme de parenté établie et périodiquement renouvelée par des cérémonies autochtones regroupant alors Amérindiens et immigrés, l'usage d'une parenté assignée pour réunir ces deux populations représentant l'adoption par les nouveaux arrivants d'une pratique autochtone. Cette relation fondée sur une forme de parenté sous-tend aux XVIIe et XVIIIe siècles des liens commerciaux et militaires, avant de s'appuyer au XIXe siècle sur les traités territoriaux conclus en maintes parties du pays. Hélas, après que la population non autochtone se fut imposée en force et en nombre, la Couronne canadienne a perdu de vue toute dimension de parenté. Dès lors et pendant plus d'un siècle, le Canada a vu les peuples autochtones comme des populations administrées plutôt que des collectivités auxquelles il était rattaché. Aussi faut-il raviver aujourd'hui cette forme de parenté fondée sur le respect mutuel pour rétablir les relations plus saines et plus fructueuses du passé.

Two historical vignettes from the age of Queen Victoria reveal the essential elements that make up the relationship between Canada's Crown and Indigenous peoples. In the autumn of 1862, a large number of Dakota made their way north from Minnesota to Red River, the British territory across the "Medicine Line," as First Nations people called the international border. They were seeking sanctuary in British territory from the US military. There, they told Hudson's Bay Company officials, effectively representatives of the Crown, that they were allies of the British monarch, and that George III had made them promises when they allied themselves with Britain in the War of 1812.[1] This was hardly a new argument by the Dakota. When they had met with Saulteaux leaders in Red River in 1860, they showed them their George III medals, emblems of their alliance with the Crown.[2] In other words, to both Indigenous and immigrant leaders in Manitoba, the Dakota made the case that they had a claim to reside in British territory because of their alliance with the Crown. Later, in 1881, a close relative of Queen Victoria received similar evidence of First Nations' ties to the Crown during his tour of the West. Governor General Lorne was the son-in-law of Queen Victoria, having married Princess Louise. On Lorne's extensive trip, he encountered leaders who reminded him of their ties to the Queen. When he parleyed with the Dakota in Manitoba, they made a point of wearing their George III medals for the occasion.[3] At Fort Qu'Appelle, Lorne encountered Chief Kahkishiway, one of the original negotiators of Treaty 4 in 1874. Kahkishiway greeted Lorne with the words, "I am glad to see you my Brother-in-Law."[4]

How do we explain these encounters? Why would Dakota make a major point of having medals that were given to them by George III in recognition of their taking up arms with the British? And why would Kahkishiway, a Plains chief, regard the Queen's son-in-law as his brother-in-law? The answers reveal the nature of the links between First Nations and the Crown. First Nations regard themselves not as subjects, but as allies of the monarch, either as a result of having been in alliance with Britain or as a consequence of having made treaty with the Queen of Britain. But their alliance is not just a practical matter of mutual aid for mutual benefit. It is embedded in a kinship relation between them that led Kahkishiway to regard and address the governor general as his brother-in-law. Kinship and alliance are the heart of the ties to the Crown. Understanding these ties allows us to appreciate where we as a country have gone wrong in the past and, perhaps, to discern how we might improve relations in the future.

Those ties historically have had a highly personal quality to them. That characteristic came out in the terms that northeastern woodlands First Nations, the first Indigenous people to meet Europeans in present-day Canada, had for the representatives of the Crown from the earliest days. To Native people in early Quebec, the French governor was known and addressed as Onontio, meaning mountain. Why? Because the first governor of New France was Charles Montmagny, whose surname connoted mountain. And every governor of the French colony after Montmagny was also Onontio in the minds and speech of First Nations diplomats. In British settlements to the south a similar pattern prevailed from the seventeenth century onward. The governor of New York, for example, was known as Corlaer for the simple reason that the first European to enter into a treaty with the Iroquois was Arent von Curler, a Dutchman who concluded an agreement with them on behalf of New Holland. And so, thereafter, every British governor was addressed as "Corlaer," a version of von Curler, at least down until George Washington became the first president of the United States. Washington was known in the Iroquois language as Town Destroyer because of his role in an expedition that invaded and laid waste to Iroquoia in 1775.[5] And so successive presidents have been known to the Iroquois by that negative term. The significance of these linguistic curiosities is that, while Indigenous relations with Europeans were cemented in kin-like structures, those with the king's local representative had a highly personal quality—Onontio or Corlaer—as well.

The arrangements that established these distinctive ties were present in Native-European interactions from the earliest days of contact. Europeans came to the eastern shores of the future Canada from the seventeenth century onward to trade and, because of rivalries with other strangers, in search of alliances with First Nations that would strengthen them against those rivals. From the First Nations' standpoint, there was no distinction between trading with people and aiding them in their struggles. The two functions were but two sides of the same coin, and that coin was kinship. That linkage was illustrated as early as 1603 in an encounter between Samuel de Champlain and the Montagnais chief Anadabijou. The chief, who was engaged in hostilities with the Iroquois, was most welcoming, listening to Champlain's offer of friendship and then saying to his followers "that in truth they ought to be very glad to have His Majesty for their great friend." The tie between alliance and trade in the mind of First Nations was revealed the next morning when Anadabijou told his people they were going to "break camp and go to Tadoussac, where their good friends were," to trade.[6]

As revealing as this evidence of the tie between commerce and diplomacy were the steps the Montagnais chief had taken before declaring he and his people should be glad to have the King of France as their friend. Anadabijou had given the French party a warm welcome, feasted them in his lodge, and, after the Europeans had made their proposal, responded systematically. He "began to smoke tobacco, and to pass on his pipe" to the French leaders as well as "certain other Sagamores who were near him. After smoking for some time, he began to address the whole gathering, speaking with gravity, pausing sometimes a little, and then resuming his speech ..." Then he pronounced that they should be glad to have a relationship with the French King.[7] What Champlain and the other visitors had experienced in Anadabijou's lodge was the Indigenous protocol—formal welcome, speech-making, and smoking the pipe—by which First Nations brought strangers into their circle of kinship. The Aboriginal ceremonies were essential to ensure that unknown strangers were not a threat to the Native peoples. Making and keeping them kin was the method used to ensure continuing friendship between disparate peoples.

The use of Indigenous protocols to make kin was widespread in relations between First Nations and Europeans, and these ceremonies were also used through intermediaries to make kin of European monarchs. Once the Hudson's Bay Company initiated trade at the mouths of rivers flowing into Hudson Bay in the early 1670s, it too found its personnel drawn into the world of Indigenous kinship and ceremony. Indeed, the governors of the company were soon instructing post commanders to conduct ceremonies in accordance with the practice of the local people, including the use of the pipe. For their part, First Nations who travelled to the HBC posts participated in such ceremonials first to establish a relationship through fictive kinship and thereafter to renew it. Their insistence on these procedures is revealed most clearly in how the trading captains of the visiting parties conducted themselves at the conclusion of exchange. First Nations who were satisfied with how they had been treated would leave their pipe at the post for the next visit; those who were dissatisfied would take their pipe away with them, signifying that the relationship was ended. As an observer noted, "Each leader leaves his grand calumet at the fort he trades at unless he is affronted, and not designed to return next summer, which is sometimes the case."[8]

For obvious reasons, prominent in the exchanges that went on in commercial, diplomatic, and treaty relationships was the language of kinship and family. It was usually the case that both sides, European and Indigenous, referred to the European leaders as "our Father" or "our Great Father" or, later, "our Great White Mother," Victoria. They also used terms like "Brother" or, as seen earlier, "Brother-in-Law" to capture the kin-like relationship that the use of Aboriginal protocol had created and renewed regularly. But of course both sides used the language of family in the way they understood it from their own cultural background. So, for example, when Europeans used terms like the British "Father" and his North American "Children," it was often with a connotation of subordination of the children to the parent. Such implications were to be expected of people from a society in which children were "to be seen and not heard" and in which offspring were expected to be obedient and dependent. But that was not the case with the familial language that First Nations used, for the simple reason that childhood in their societies was radically different from the subordination that prevailed among Europeans. In North American culture, childhood was a time of great freedom during which children had a right to expect protection and assistance from adults. The social dynamics were strikingly different and so, accordingly, were the meanings that the two parties attached to their shared rhetoric of kinship and family.[9] The fact that the same words meant different things to Native and newcomer would in time cause difficulties between the parties.

The process by which the particular ties between the Crown and Indigenous peoples emerged out of the general relationships created for the pursuit of trade and alliance was one that unfolded over the two centuries prior to the advent of Victoria's reign in 1837. While trade and diplomacy continued to dominate relations between Indigenous and immigrant in northeastern North America through the seventeenth and well into the eighteenth centuries, after 1700 the alliance function bulked ever larger because of new preoccupations among the Europeans. From 1700 until approximately 1760, France and Britain were engaged in a worldwide struggle for supremacy, a contest that had its North American aspect. In the forests of the new continent, interchanges between First Nations and

Europeans were increasingly dominated by diplomacy as both Britain and France earnestly sought Indigenous allies to assist them in their rivalry. For the First Nations, for example the Iroquois, whether they allied themselves and fought with a foreign power was determined by their own interests. And although the use of Aboriginal protocol such as welcomes, feasts, and smoking the pipe remained prominent in the exchanges, increasingly trade was a support for diplomacy so far as the Europeans were concerned. Even in regions in which the prime furs had been overhunted, France in particular maintained trading posts as a means to preserve the kin-based alliances that were essential to ensure diplomatic and military support. As Anadabijou's behaviour had demonstrated over a century earlier, commerce and alliance were two facets of the kinship tie.

This phase of interactions came to a dramatic conclusion in the 1750s and 1760s in a way that altered the relationship between North American peoples and the British Crown. The British, of course, prevailed in the Seven Years' War, the climactic showdown with France, and soon found themselves faced with the challenge of integrating some strange new colonies, such as Quebec, into their imperial system. In the autumn of 1763, King George III issued a Royal Proclamation that revolutionized his and the British government's relations with the First Nations of the eastern half of North America. Most of the Royal Proclamation of 1763 dealt with new arrangements such as those for government and justice in the former French colonies Britain had acquired, but a crucial half-dozen paragraphs at the end of the document focused directly on the Crown's future relations with First Nations.

To discourage reckless expansion into Indian Country by land-hungry settlers in the Thirteen Colonies, the Proclamation effectively closed off the interior, recognizing the region beyond the Appalachian Mountain range as Indian territory. Settlement there was prohibited, and trade in the region was to be regulated by the governor of the respective colonies east of the mountainous watershed. This policy was intended to prevent collisions between American expansionists and restive former allies of the French who were worried about their lands. To that end, the Proclamation recognized lands beyond the western boundaries of the colonies as "lands reserved to them ... as their Hunting Grounds" and referred to Indians "with whom We are connected and who live under Our Protection." Equally important, King George's Proclamation said that if a First Nation community wished to dispose of some of its territory, the land "shall be purchased only for Us, in Our Name, at some public Meeting or Assembly of the said Indians to be held for that Purpose by the Governor or Commander in Chief of Our Colonies respectively within which they shall lie."[10] Dealing for land was to be the exclusive prerogative of the Crown and its representatives, and such dealings were to take place openly so that the First Nations people involved would know what was transpiring.

It would be difficult to exaggerate the importance of the Royal Proclamation of 1763 for Indigenous peoples' relations with the Crown or for Native-newcomer relations more generally. It provided Crown recognition of some form of First Nations' possessory right to their territories, and it promised that the Crown would have a direct role in the observance and protection of those rights. More immediately significant was the fact that the formula the Proclamation outlined—obtained by the Crown at a public meeting organized by the monarch's direct representative in the colonies—became the protocol for making a new form of treaty, the agreements by which First Nations conveyed or agreed to share the use of their lands with European newcomers. In other words, it was the foundation of the territorial treaty system. More generally in the longer term, the Proclamation became the symbol of the protective role that the Crown played in relation to First Nations. For example, to early twentieth-century First Nations in British Columbia struggling to get provincial authorities even to recognize that Aboriginal title existed in the Pacific province, the Proclamation stood, in the words of political scientist Paul Tennant, as "the critically important statement of political justice pertaining to those goals. Britain, the source of the proclamation and in the early period still having colonial authority over Canada, came to be seen as the only possible source of remedy to the injustice being perpetrated in British Columbia."[11]

Indeed, the Crown in Britain became a beacon of hope and help for First Nations aggrieved with the colonial, or later provincial and national, governments they faced. London and the King became the place of pilgrimage of leaders, such as the Mohawk Joseph Brant, who sought guarantees of assistance from Britain. Brant sought Crown help as a condition of his people's support of Great Britain in the American Revolutionary War. More generally, a pattern of travelling to London to petition the Crown for assistance developed in eastern British North America and spread all the way to the Pacific Ocean. For example, an Anicinabe woman, Nahnebahwequa, with the help of Quaker supporters, travelled to London in 1860 and obtained an audience with Queen Victoria in search of help in securing lands that she had lost to colonial officials because, they said, she had married a non-Indian. Neither Brant nor Nahnebahwequa succeeded in their mission, but the Crown nonetheless became the place that First Nations—British Columbian groups seeking recognition of their Aboriginal title in the early decades of the twentieth century or Mohawk sovereignists trying to secure Crown recognition of their status as allies rather than subjects of the Crown in the 1920s—repaired frequently. This practice culminated in the unsuccessful lobbying in London by First Nations to prevent patriation of the constitution without their agreement in the early 1980s.[12]

Usually First Nations, and occasionally Métis, were more successful dealing with the Crown's representatives in treaty negotiations back in

North America. The formula for making territorial treaties that the Royal Proclamation had spelled out was followed, with greater or lesser fidelity, in the making of three series of treaties in the future Ontario between the 1780s and the 1860s. The precise terms of these Upper Canadian treaties matter less for our purposes here than the protocol and symbolism that accompanied them. The familiar practices of formal greetings, gifts, feasting, and the rhetoric of family were features of these talks, especially in the first half-century after treaty-making began in the future Ontario. At Port Hope in 1811, for example, a Crown representative addressed the First Nation:

> Children – I am happy to see you, and I return thanks to the Great Spirit, that has been pleased to enable us to meet at this place in good health. Children – I am sent by Your Father the Governor to make an agreement with you for the purchase of a small piece of land, the plan of which I now lay before you.... Children – As your women and children must be hungry, I have brought some of Your Great Father's Bread and milk, and some ammunition for your young men, which I will give you before we hear this.[13]

Or the parleys in 1818 at the Credit River west of Toronto, at which William Claus, "having saluted the Chief and Indians in the usual manner, addressed them as follows. My children, I am come here by the desire of your Great Father, to speak to you on the subject of the remainder of your Country." And the session concluded with Claus distributing "the Presents which your Great Father annually sends out for the comfort of his Indian children."[14] There was a good deal of presumption in the Crown representative's use of the term "children" to address the Mississauga leaders.

By Confederation, then, the practice of incorporating the image of the Crown in all negotiations between the settler government and First Nations had become well established. Although the traditions of using Indigenous protocol to make and renew kinship as an aid to treaty-making were beginning to weaken, they still had some force. The way in which Canadian First Nations viewed the Crown as kin and ally was made explicit in an address of the Six Nations to the heir to the throne, the Prince of Wales, during his visit to British North America in 1860:

> Brother, – We, the Chiefs, Sachems and Warriors of the Six Nations in Canada are glad of the opportunity to welcome to our native land, the Son of our Gracious Sovereign Queen Victoria, and to manifest our continued loyalty and devotion to the person and Crown of your Royal Mother. We return thanks to the Great Spirit that he has put it in to your Royal highness's mind to come to this country, and that He has preserved your Royal Highness safe, that we may meet together this day. He has ordained Princes and Rulers to govern his people; and it is His will that our beloved Queen, Your Royal Mother, is so preeminent in power and virtue.

> Brother, – Although we have been separated from our Sovereign by the "Great Water," yet have we ever kept the chain of friendship bright, and it gives us joy to meet with the Heir Apparent to the Throne, that we may renew and strengthen that chain, which has existed between the Crown of England and the Six Nations for more than two hundred years. Our confidence in our Sovereign is as lasting as the stars in Heaven. We rejoice at the presence among us to fill the place of your Royal Mother, and her illustrious predecessor, whom we also love.[15]

The address by the Six Nations nicely captured the key concepts in the relationship of the Crown and First Nations. Kinship, specifically the equal familial relationship implied in the term "Brother," was evoked by the way its several sections saluted the Prince as "Brother." As well, alliance was highlighted by references to "the chain of friendship," the Covenant Chain of alliance and mutual support between the Iroquois and the Crown that had developed in the late seventeenth and eighteenth centuries.

If the use of Aboriginal protocol had begun to wane in the mid-century Upper Canadian treaties, it would soon be reinvigorated and restored to its central place as a result of treaty negotiations that took place in the former Hudson's Bay Company lands, Rupert's Land, in the 1870s. The First Nations of the western woodlands and plains had formed their understanding of and approach to Europeans in the fur trade, a system of exchange in which the kinship tie was a central component. They would carry those attitudes into discussions about forging a new relationship with representatives of the Crown. So far as their new negotiating partners were concerned, at a time when relations between western plains nations and the American government erupted into widespread, destructive warfare, the fledgling government of Canada was aware that negotiating with the Indigenous populations was the only way it could make effective the theoretical title it had gained from the Hudson's Bay Company by the transfer Rupert's Land in 1869–70. Had Canada's political leaders ever thought otherwise, their clumsy conduct in Red River in 1869 incited a Métis resistance and disabused them of any naïve notions about western Native people. Some government leaders realized that they possessed an advantage over their American neighbours in the fact that they were subjects of the British Queen. They could play on the contrast between the warring Americans, led by their "long knives," or sabre-wielding cavalry, and the more pacific tradition of relations between Britain and her Canadian colonies and First Nations. This strategy was all the more likely to be successful after the North West Mounted Police, with their red serge uniforms, were created and made their way west in 1874. The Great White Queen Mother, Victoria, was a superior draw to the Town Destroyer in Washington.

Both Crown representatives and First Nations leaders who favoured making treaty employed the image of the Crown, along with the rhetoric of family and usually Indigenous protocol, to advance their arguments during the negotiations between 1871 and 1877. With the exception of negotiations preceding Treaty 4, at which tensions ran high because one of the First Nations groups harboured lingering resentment over the transfer of Rupert's Land, the smoking of the pipe and sometimes other protocol figured prominently in the proceedings. Both sides were always cognizant, too, of the place of Queen Victoria in their discussions. The Crown representative who negotiated four of the seven agreements, Alexander Morris, in 1873 lobbied the prime minister to establish a force equipped with red serge because "50 men in red coats are better than 100 in other colours," and he happily included mounted police escorts in his treaty parties to remind First Nations of the tie to the Crown once the police were in the region.[16] In negotiations, he emphasized that he and his fellow commissioners came on behalf of the Crown. "I wish you to understand we do not come here as traders, but as representing the Crown, and to do what is just and right," he informed the restive Saulteaux at the talks for Treaty 3 in 1873.[17] And at Fort Qu'Appelle in 1874, Morris brought the monarch directly into the talks: "What I have to talk about concerns you, your children and their children, who are yet unborn, and you must think well over it, as the Queen has thought well over it. What I want, is for you to take the Queen's hand, through mine, and shake hands with her for ever..."[18] For government representatives to use such rhetoric might not have been surprising, but it is important to note that the tactics resonated with chiefs whose actions suggested they subscribed to similar beliefs.

A powerful example of the way in which pro-treaty chiefs included Queen Victoria in their rationale for making an agreement comes from a private caucus of leaders at Fort Carlton in August 1876, on the eve of Treaty 6 negotiations. At this gathering, two senior Cree chiefs, Mistawasis and Ahtahkakoop, who favoured entering treaty, worked to persuade the doubters and opponents within their ranks of the benefits of treaty. First, Mistawasis addressed the skeptics, asking, "Have you anything better [than treaty] to offer our people?" To him it appeared "that the Great White Queen Mother has offered us a way of life when the buffalo are no more. Gone they will be before many snows have come to cover our heads or graves if such should be." He contended that the Queen would put an end to the selling of alcohol that was often devastating to Plains peoples and would "stop the senseless wars among our people, against the Blackfoot, Peigans, and Bloods." Mistawasis's colleague, Ahtahkakoop, continued the case for treaty. He argued that resisting the oncoming tide of settlement was futile, as the experience of southern nations fighting "the Long Knives" showed. He urged the assembled leaders to choose "the right path now while we yet have a choice," go where "the Queen Mother has offered us a new way," and take up agriculture. He ended his oration with the words, "I will accept the Queen's hand for my people." Mistawasis added, "I for one will take the hand that is offered."[19]

At the face-to-face negotiations, numerous chiefs alluded to the centrality of Queen Victoria to treaty-making. During talks at Fort Ellice, shortly after Treaty 4 was concluded at Fort Qu'Appelle, Long Claws responded to Commissioner Alexander Morris after another of the official's references to Victoria—"the Queen is willing to help her children"—by saying, "My father—I shake hands with you, I shake hands with the Queen."[20] During the negotiation of Treaty 7 at Blackfoot Crossing in 1877, the venerable Chief Crowfoot alluded to Victoria's red-coated warriors: "If the Police had not come to the country where would we all be now? Bad men and whiskey were killing us so fast that very few, indeed, of us would have been left to-day. The Police have protected us as the feathers of the bird protect it from the frosts of winter.... I am satisfied. I will sign the treaty."[21] A few years earlier, at Fort Qu'Appelle, another chief had needed more assurance about the protective powers of the Queen that would flow from treaty. Kamooses had asked, "Is it true you are bringing the Queen's kindness? Is it true you are bringing the Queen's messenger's kindness? Is it true you are going to give my child what he may use? Is it true you are going to give the different bands the Queen's kindness? Is it true that you bring the Queen's hand? Is it true you are bringing the Queen's power?" And Morris had responded, "Yes, to those who are here and those who are absent, such as she has given us." Kamooses persisted, "Is it true that my child will not be troubled for what you are bringing him?" Morris replied, "The Queen's power will be around him."[22] As these exchanges revealed, like Mistawasis and Ahtahkakoop, many Plains chiefs who chose to enter treaty saw becoming kin with Queen Victoria through protocols and the treaty agreement as a way to access the Crown's power to protect and assist them in challenging times, all the more so when compared to what their cousins south of the Medicine Line were experiencing with the "long knives" who represented Washington.

The western treaties of the 1870s embodied the Crown rhetorically, practically, and legally. To state the most obvious point, the written versions of the treaties that the Government of Canada produced specified that the pacts were between Victoria and her red children. Treaty 2, the Manitoba Post Treaty, was typical of them all. It was headed "Articles of a Treaty made and concluded this twenty-first day of August, in the year of our Lord one thousand eight hundred and seventy-one between Her most Gracious Majesty the Queen of Great Britain and Ireland ..." and the Saulteaux. The first paragraph of the government text mentioned "her Most Gracious Majesty" four more times, culminating in the statement that the treaty was provided so that the First Nations "may know and be assured of what allowance they are to count upon and receive from Her Majesty's bounty and benevolence."[23] The problem, as it turned out though, was that the western nations who made treaty between 1871 and 1877 could not "count upon" and did not "receive" expeditiously the aid they had been promised when the plains economy collapsed with the disappearance of the bison in 1879. The federal government's response was legalistic, niggardly, and dilatory, much to the cost of hard-pressed Plains peoples. By the early 1880s, observers were reporting that extreme hardship and even starvation were noticeable in parts of the prairies.

These disappointing developments were the backdrop to the governor general's tour of the West in the summer of 1881. The numbered treaties were hardly concluded when First Nations began to express their frustration over the way they were being dishonoured. At the payment of annuities at Fort Qu'Appelle in 1878, for example, Kahkishiway said, "Our Great Mother told us to try hard and sustain her. We have done so. Now we ask for our Great Mother to be charitable."[24] Louis O'Soup, like Kahkishiway a party to the agreement in 1874, was blunter. He wanted "all he had said [to be] put on paper and given to our Great Mother, and if what they wanted was not granted the paymaster need not come back next year."[25] Chiefs adopted more diplomatic language in appealing to and remonstrating with Lord Lorne three years later, but there was no mistaking their frustration. Kanasis said, "We want a Reformation of the Treaty" and explained, "We can't make our living by what was given to us by The Treaty." And Louis O'Soup explained the significance of his earlier threat not to accept further annuities if treaty implementation did not improve.

> I think we don't understand each other thoroughly. I wish to make it plain when they say let us break the Treaty. The first person Governor Morris came here and made this Treaty. You will receive help for 20 years and again he promised the Indian should never starve. Now they have told you a little of their starvation. Of course when a person breaks their promises that person is first to break the treaty.... Why they ask to break the Treaty is because since treaty was made they have found they have not enough to keep them alive.[26]

Implicit in the comments and actions of the frustrated chiefs was their understanding of the treaties they had made such a short time ago. Through treaty-making ceremonies, including rhetoric, they had enlarged the circle of kinship and drawn the Queen and her Canadian subjects and government within it. It was the relationship that the treaties created that mattered to them, not the precise words of the government's version of it, just as it was all the speeches that the Queen's commissioners had made to them that counted. They found that their generosity in extending kinship and sharing their territory was not reciprocated, and they threatened to regard the treaties as terminated. Just as a disgruntled fur-trade captain would retrieve his pipe from the trading post if dissatisfied, they would signal the relationship was ended by refusing annuities in future. And, they emphasized, they regarded the government, not themselves, as having broken the treaty.

In the spring of 1876 the Canadian Parliament passed an Indian Act that sought to regulate all aspects of First Nations' lives. The statute, largely a consolidation of existing legislation that affected First Nations, had been under development since 1871. At that time, complaints from First Nations individuals and organizations had spurred the Macdonald government to begin a process of review and revision that extended well into the administration of Alexander Mackenzie.[27] For governments of both parties, the motivation underlying the 1876 measure appears to have been to tidy up legislation dealing with First Nations. The Indian Act enshrined in law the widely held view that First Nations were, and should be treated as, legal minors under the trusteeship of the federal government.

Unfortunately, however, once the treaties were concluded, the government began to relate to First Nations as administered peoples according to the terms of the Indian Act, rather than as kin-like partners on the basis of the treaty relationship. From the 1880s until the late twentieth century, Canada dealt with First Nations as though they were the dependent children that the Indian Act said they were. It ignored its commitments about respecting First Nations' ways, including mobility and gathering rights, and imposed limits to their movements and harvesting. Canada reneged on its promises in the first six numbered treaties of the 1870s to supply "schools on reserves" by relying increasingly on custodial residential schools that were usually located well away from the students' home communities. The Dominion forgot its oral promises not to interfere with First Nations' practices by aggressively promoting the Christian religion and, until 1951, outlawing First Nations observances such as the Potlatch of the North West Coast and the summer dances of the prairies. Similarly, Canadian policy sought to alter First Nations' ways of governing themselves and using land in favour of Euro-Canadian practices such as elective institutions and individual property ownership on reserves. And when First Nations resisted this barrage of coercive measures—as they did repeatedly in every part of country—the Canadian government responded with great coercion. For example, the introduction of Family Allowances in the 1940s became a means of compelling attendance at unpopular schools by threatening to withhold the monthly payments.[28] In the latter decades of the twentieth century, Canada relied less than it had earlier on coercion in applying its policies, but its underlying assumption that it knew better than First Nations people what is good for them has never disappeared.

The sorry truth of relations between First Nations and the Crown ever since passage of the Indian Act has been that this radical shift in the approach to relations on the federal government's part has perverted and poisoned relations between the federal government and First Nations. Unlike First Nations, who continued to think in terms of kinship that included the Crown, sharing, and reciprocal approaches, the Canadian government has treated First Nations as legal dependants, the status that the Indian Act assigned them in 1876. As Louis O'Soup said to Victoria's son-in-law in 1881, "we don't understand each other thoroughly." Different culturally-based uses of the rhetoric of family reflected that incomprehension. For centuries relations between Indigenous peoples and the Crown had been characterized by kinship and alliance, made and renewed by Aboriginal protocols. That relationship worked well; Native and newcomer related in a harmonious and mutually beneficial way. But in the late nineteenth century, the government of Sir John A. Macdonald unilaterally shifted its understanding and practice of maintaining the relationship to one marked by domination and authoritarianism. Although the record is not clear, it appears that the federal government made that shift either not realizing the impact it would have on western First Nations who had recently concluded treaties or under the assumption that the decline of the western economy, especially the bison, weakened First Nations there so much that they were no longer a military threat. Whatever the Macdonald government's motivation, relating to First Nations in an authoritarian, trustee-ward manner was not in accord with the earliest Canadian historical tradition, and it was not the basis on which treaties, including the late-nineteenth-century pacts, had been negotiated. Those agreements sought to make us kin, not superior and subordinate. That fatal step in 1876 blighted government–First Nations relations by the 1880s and has soured the relationship ever since.

If Canada wants to recapture that healthier relationship, it needs to restore relations to their historic character. That pressing need was implicit in the grassroots movements that erupted in protest against the Harper government's legislation affecting First Nations generally, and its budget omnibus bills in particular, during the winter of 2012–13. The Idle No More movement, which began in Saskatoon on November 11, 2012, and Chief Theresa Spence of Attawapiskat in the Treaty 9 region of northern Ontario, who began a highly publicized partial fast in early December, both made the historic importance of the Crown's links to First Nations explicit. At the centre of Idle No More—and the justification for its demand that the omnibus bills be repealed—was the movement's insistence on the primacy of the treaty relationship in government–First Nations relations. Similarly, the notion of kinship through the Crown with the Queen's non-Native subjects was embodied in rhetoric that Idle No More used. For example, during a demonstration on Parliament Hill on January 28, 2013, a group of First Nations women, garbed in the colourful and melodious dresses of jingle dancers, carried a sign that read "Remember Canada: You are a treaty partner."[29] For her part, in her unsuccessful demand that both the governor general and the prime minister meet with her and First Nations leaders to resolve outstanding issues, Chief Spence highlighted treaties and the Crown–First Nations relationship. The campaign by Chief Spence failed to bring about the change she sought, and the long-term impact of Idle No More cannot yet be assessed, but their fundamental message is clear. If and when the Crown again becomes the Great Mother or Father to whose government Native people can look for fraternal, reciprocal treatment, this country will have found a solution to what we non-Natives mistakenly call "the Indian problem."

Acknowledgements

I would like to thank the Social Sciences and Humanities Research Council of Canada, whose Standard Research and Gold Medal Prize Grants supported the research on which this chapter is based, and my colleagues Lesley Biggs and Bill Waiser for reading and commenting on an earlier draft.

Notes

1. Peter Douglas Elias, *The Dakota of the Canadian Northwest: Lessons for Survival* (Winnipeg: University of Manitoba Press, 1988), 17.
2. Sarah Carter, "'Your Great Mother across the Salt Sea': Prairie First Nations, the British Monarchy and the Vice-Regal Connection to 1900," *Manitoba History* 48 (Autumn/Winter 2004–2005): 36.
3. *The Globe* (Toronto), September 13, 1881, cited in Carter, "Your Great Mother," 36.
4. Notes of Lord Lorne's interviews with chiefs, 1881, RG 10 Records of the Department of Indian Affairs, vol. 3768, file 33,642, Library and Archives Canada.
5. Barbara Graymont, *The Iroquois in the American Revolution* (Syracuse: Syracuse University Press, 1972), 221.
6. H. P. Biggar, ed., *The Works of Samuel de Champlain*, 6 vols. (Toronto: Champlain Society, 1922–26), 1:98-101.
7. Ibid., 1:104.
8. Quoted in J. R. Miller, *Compact, Contract, Covenant: Aboriginal Treaty-Making in Canada* (Toronto: University of Toronto Press, 2009), 20. For HBC trade protocol in general, see 14-21.
9. On the rhetoric of family and kin-making, see Harold Cardinal and Walter Hildebrandt, eds., *Treaty Elders of Saskatchewan: Our Dream Is That Our Peoples Will One Day Be Clearly Recognized as Nations* (Calgary: University of Calgary Press, 2000), 18-19, 33-34, and 41-42; John L. Tobias, "The Origins of the Treaty Rights Movement in Saskatchewan," in *1885 and After: Native Society in Transition*, ed. F. Laurie Barron and James B. Waldram (Regina: Canadian Plains Research Center, University of Regina, 1986), 248-49.
10. Royal Proclamation of 1763, Charles S. Brigham, *British Royal Proclamations Relating to America. Transactions and Collections of the American Antiquarian Society* (Worcester, MA, 1911), 215-17.

11. Paul Tennant, *Aboriginal Peoples and Politics: The Indian Land Question in British Columbia, 1849–1989* (Vancouver: University of British Columbia Press, 1990), 71.
12. J. R. Miller, "Petitioning the Great White Mother: First Nations' Organizations and Lobbying in London," in *Reflections on Native-Newcomer Relations: Selected Essays* (Toronto: University of Toronto Press, 2004), 217-41.
13. Minutes of a meeting with the Mississauga Indians of the River Moira, Smith's Creek, July 24, 1811, CO 42, 351, Colonial Office Correspondence, Upper Canada, 1811, Despatches, reel B295, 138-39, Library and Archives Canada.
14. Record of a Council at River Credit, October 27, 28, and 29, 1818, Claus Family Fonds, vol. 11,109-12, reel G-1480, Library and Archives Canada.
15. Presentation reproduced in the exhibition "Victorian Ideals, Victorian Values: Oronhyatekha, M.D.," Royal Ontario Museum, May 29, 2002. The exhibition was created by the Woodland Cultural Centre, Brantford, in collaboration with the Royal Ontario Museum.
16. A. Morris to J. A. Macdonald, January 16, 1873, MG 26A Sir John A. Macdonald Papers, vol. 252, 113998-4003, Library and Archives Canada.
17. Alexander Morris, *The Treaties of Canada with the Indians* (Saskatoon: Fifth House, 1991; 1st ed. Toronto: Belfords, Clarke, and Co., 1880), 67. Citations are from the 1991 edition.
18. Morris, *Treaties*, 90.
19. The caucus, from which these statements are taken, was attended by the Métis interpreter whom Mistawasis and Ahtahkakoop had hired, Peter Erasmus. Erasmus recorded the speeches in his memoir, *Buffalo Days and Nights*, ed. Irene Spry (Calgary: Fifth House, 1990), 246-50.
20. Morris, *Treaties*, 124.
21. Ibid., 272.
22. Ibid., 117-18.
23. Treaty 2, ibid., 316-17.
24. James Trow, *Manitoba and North West Territories: Letters by James Trow* (Ottawa: Department of Agriculture, 1878), 53.
25. Ibid. Trow, an MP and chair of the Commons Immigration and Colonization Committee, was an observer at the annuity payments. For the significance of refusing annuity payments, see Miller, *Compact, Contract, Covenant*, 302; and *New York Times* online, June 27, 1973, accessed August 27, 2007, for a news item on a band in the Great Slave Lake area of the Northwest Territories that refused its annuities as a protest against maladministration by the federal government.
26. Notes of Lord Lorne's interviews with chiefs, 1881. These comments were made at the Fort Qu'Appelle gathering.
27. John Leslie and Ron Maguire, *The Historical Development of the Indian Act*, 2nd ed. (Ottawa: Treaties and Historical Research Centre, Department of Indian and Northern Affairs, 1979), 59-69.
28. J. R. Miller, *Skyscrapers Hide the Heavens: A History of Indian-White Relations in Canada*, 3rd ed. (Toronto: University of Toronto Press, 2000), chap. 11, "The Policy of the Bible and the Plough," 254-82.
29. *Globe and Mail*, January 29, 2013, A1.

Conclusion: The Contentious Canadian Crown

Philippe Lagassé

Ce dernier chapitre porte sur les débats et conflits suscités par la complexité de la Couronne. S'appuyant sur les textes de cet ouvrage et d'autres études sur la monarchie constitutionnelle du Canada, l'auteur y analyse trois conceptions concurrentes de la Couronne : héréditaire, collective et constitutionnelle. La première est centrée sur les aspects familiaux et britanniques de la Couronne, la deuxième lui prête un rôle dans le développement d'une communauté politique et de la nation canadienne, la troisième y voit une source d'autorité souveraine au Canada. Les désaccords au sujet de la Couronne surgiraient ainsi lorsque les tenants de ces différentes conceptions s'opposent sur leur importance relative s'agissant d'établir la pertinence de la Couronne et le sens à lui donner. L'auteur met aussi en évidence les failles de chacune des conceptions et conclut en proposant des moyens d'enrichir le débat sur la Couronne au Canada.

"The crown," the British constitutional historian Frederic Maitland argued, "is a convenient cover for ignorance."[1] Referring at once to the monarch, the state, and the executive, Maitland believed that the concept meant so many things that it actually meant nothing. For Maitland and his contemporary disciples, "the crown does nothing but lies in the Tower of London to be gazed at by sight-seers." The present volume casts doubt on this dismissive analysis, as do the many important studies of the Crown that have appeared since Maitland's history of the British Constitution was first published in 1908. Far from being a mere ornament, the Crown was and remains a critical element in the Westminster tradition. Nonetheless, we must admit that Maitland's comment touches a nerve: there is some truth to what he observed. Maitland was correct that the Crown can act as a cover, but he was wrong that it covers ignorance. Rather, it covers complexity. The Crown is not simple; it is inherently obscure. This does not imply that the Crown is immaterial—quite the opposite. Yet it is also true that the Crown's complexity is a source of confusion and contention.

When people discuss the Crown but understand it differently, disagreement is inevitable. Debates about the Crown that surrounded the Idle No More movement in 2012 and the royal succession bill in early 2013 offer two examples of such disagreements. Writings on the Crown in Canada reveal that such disagreements are common. The nature of the Crown is contentious owing to its complexity.

In this concluding chapter, I will present three prevalent conceptions of the Crown in Canada: the hereditary Crown, the communal Crown, and the constitutional Crown. Although these understandings are by no means exhaustive, they remain the most pertinent in discussions of Canada's constitutional monarchy today. The first focuses on the familial and British aspects of the Crown. The second stresses the Crown's role in building a sense of political community and Canadian nationhood. The third is concerned with the Crown as the source of sovereign authority in Canada. I outline these conceptions with reference to the contributions included in this volume, to other scholarly analyses, and to opinion pieces about the monarchy that have been published in recent years. My aim is to identify fault lines that divide Canadians when they talk and think about the Crown. Further, I examine disagreements that exist among those who share the same basic definition of the Crown. In so doing, my second aim is to highlight the debates within the debate. The chapter concludes with a brief reflection on how we might improve discussions of the Crown in Canada, in spite of its inescapable complexity.

The Hereditary Crown

Heredity is necessarily associated with the Crown. The fact that the throne is occupied by successive members of one house, the Windsors, is a testament to this facet of the monarchy. This is the familial nature of the Crown. Canada's kings and queens are not elected, nor must they be vetted as part of a formal process of appointment. Canadian sovereigns are anointed based on their bloodline and order of birth. While republics can have political dynasties, they are not a fundamental component of that type of political order. This is clearly not the case in Canada's constitutional monarchy. The Canadian Crown is linked with a particular family, and the Windsors are the most recognizable representatives of the institution, notwithstanding their lack of residence in Canada.

Notable commentators laud the familial character of the Crown. Columnist Andrew Coyne notes that the monarchy's strength lies in its heredity.[2] The Royal Family, he writes, is a symbol of "the collective inheritance that is the sum of many generations' work.... Monarchy is the symbolic representation of that idea, the passing of the generations in the house of Windsor mirroring the passing of the generations at large, back and back into antiquity."[3] John Fraser, Master of Massey College, captures a similar sentiment in his book, *The Secret of the Crown: Canada's Affair with Royalty*.[4] For Mr. Fraser, the Crown's place in Canada is inexorably tied to the affection that Canadians feel for the Royal Family. In her chapter in this book, Carolyn Harris reminds us that this is not merely a reflection of the attachment to the current Queen or admiration for the Duke and Duchess of Cambridge. Canadians, Dr. Harris demonstrates, were equally attached to Lord Lorne and Princess Louise during their first years at Rideau Hall. From the perspective of these observers, the Royal Family provides an important connection between Canadians and the Crown.

The familial aspect of the Crown, however, is an attractive target for critics. They argue that Canada's hereditary monarchy is a shameful symbol of aristocratic privilege, discrimination, and undemocratic pretences. Columnist Janice Kennedy asks, "In civilizations that long ago accepted equality as a social cornerstone, what possible justification could there be for even the notion of monarchy? For the idea of elevating fellow humans to the very top of the heap for no reason other than birth?"[5] Jonathan Kay, the comment page editor for the *National Post*, shares Ms. Kennedy's aversion. In his estimation, the reverence of family and blood is "just a sentimental way of taking the side of feudalism lite."[6] Historian Michael Bliss, meanwhile, scorns Canadians for their acceptance of the Windsors and the exclusionary rules that govern which members of their family ascend to the throne: "Our head of state will be the person who by accident of birth, not for any other reason, happens to be King or Queen of Great Britain. That person must also be a member of the Church of England. No Catholics, atheists, Confucians, Muslims, Jews, or Canadians need apply."[7]

Family, a notion that most Canadians surely associate with the Crown, fuels a heated debate about the monarchy in Canada. This hereditary component of the Crown is a powerful means of creating personal affection for the institution among Canadians, while at the same time it may be employed to argue that the monarchy is antiquated and elitist.

Professor Bliss's comments about the Royal Family point to the other hereditary aspect of the Crown; namely, the monarchy is part of Canada's British inheritance. Regardless of how Canadian the Crown has become over the past century, there is no denying that the institution came to Canada from the United Kingdom. Quebec was of course ruled by French monarchs when the province was the colony of New France, as Senator Serge Joyal reminds us in his chapter. In that sense, Canada's status as a monarchy predates the arrival of the British Crown on the territories that would eventually make up Canada. But the form and substance of the contemporary Canadian Crown are derived from the United Kingdom, not the *Ancien Régime*.

The residual Britishness of the Crown is evidenced in a number of ways. Powers and privileges that the Crown possesses in Canada can be properly understood only with reference to the historic authorities and rights of its British counterpart.[8] The Canadian Sovereign also shares the official names and designations of the British Sovereign. The present queen is Queen Elizabeth the Second in Canada, although Canada did not exist at the time of Queen Elizabeth I, because the Canadian Crown is an outgrowth of the British Crown, not a Canadian invention. Furthermore, the Britishness of the Crown has been acknowledged, and to some extent celebrated, by the Conservative government of Prime Minister Stephen Harper. During the press conference in January 2013 announcing the tabling of Bill C-53, An Act to Assent to Alternations in the Law Touching on the Succession to the Throne, heritage minister James Moore reminded Canadians that they share a monarch with Great Britain and that the two states, along with fourteen other Commonwealth realms, share a common Crown.[9] While this argument may rile those who uphold the legal distinctiveness of the Canadian Crown, there is no denying that the Canadian and British Crowns are under a personal union. Indeed, as Ian Holloway argues in his chapter, absent an amendment to Canada's Constitution, the Canadian and British monarch must be the same person.

Critics of the Crown have been as eager as supporters to stress that the institution was inherited from Great Britain and that the monarchy retains a latent Britishness. They have posited that Canada will only be truly independent once the individual who personifies the Canadian state is not simultaneously the monarch of the United Kingdom. A severing of this personal union is upheld as the final, still unachieved, step toward Canadian independence and national maturity. In the words of Roland Paris, "Why does Canada have a foreign head of state?... Shouldn't the next step be to 'Canadianize' the office of head of state?"[10] Some critics believe that any reference to royalty, monarchy, or the Crown is a reminder of Canada's former status as a British colony. Hence, historian J. L. Granatstein opposed the revival of royal designations for the Canadian air force and navy because, in his mind, they represent a homage to Canada's colonial past rather than a recognition of the military's relationship with the Canadian Crown.[11] A portion of the Canadian public, it appears, is not unsympathetic to this view. A recent Harris/Decima poll suggests that approximately 40 percent of Canadians see the monarchy a relic of Canada's colonial past.[12]

The Britishness of the Canadian Crown is a sensitive topic, even among monarchists. While certain supporters of Canada's monarchy see no reason why the Crown's inherited ties to the British throne should make the institution any less Canadian,[13] other monarchists prefer to distance Canada's Crown from its British counterpart.[14] The latter believe that for many Canadians, the traditional Britishness of Canada's monarchy is an argument for its abolishment. Canada's republicans are determined to remind the public of the Crown's British heredity for the same reason.[15]

The Communal Crown

Canadians are surrounded by the Crown, whether they realize it or not. The designation "royal" is attached to countless organizations, from the Royal Ontario Museum to the Royal Society of Canada to the Royal Canadian Mounted Police. Streets in most cities are named after monarchs and vice-regal officers. Crowns adorn highways, military units, and crests across the country. The Queen's name and image are everywhere, from arenas to schools to the national currency. In each of these manifestations, the Crown is meant to serve as a unifying element within the Canadian community. Indeed, whenever the Crown is discussed as a symbol or a dignified institution in the Bagehotian sense, it is the communal nature of the Crown that is evoked.

In *The Evolving Canadian Crown*, Paul Benoit describes this communal aspect of the Crown as "state ceremonial," the constitutional monarch's "liturgical authority."[16] The liturgical Crown reflects the values of the Canadian polity. When the Crown manifests itself in this way, Dr. Benoit argues, the purpose is to engage Canadians in a form of secular worship. Along similar lines, in *The Crown in Canada*, Frank MacKinnon argues that as the non-partisan but authoritative representatives of the Canadian state, the Sovereign and her vice-regal officers attend to civil society, bringing Canadians together in recognizing notable events and praiseworthy citizens.[17] Ultimately, this communal dimension serves to produce an emotional bond among Canadians of different regions, religions, ethnicities, and political affiliations. Through symbol and ceremony, the Crown helps to build Canada as a nation. Seen from this perspective, the Crown reflects Canada unto itself.

Most Canadians who encounter the Crown will do so within this communal rubric. Every year, the governor general and lieutenant governors take part in numerous celebrations and events across the country. While politicians will participate in occasions that emphasize the activities of government or their party, the vice-regal officers recognize causes and achievements of importance to Canadians as a whole. In fact, as Christopher McCreery's chapter on the lieutenant governors shows, this function has contributed to the Crown's growing presence in the provinces. Although this division of labour between politicians and vice-regal officers is often blurred, the principle remains: while parliamentarians will cater to civil society to build electoral support, the Crown can be deployed to lift certain occasions and endeavours above the partisan fray for the benefit of all Canadians.

The communal aspect of the Crown also frames most of the Queen's and Royal Family's activities in Canada. While the Sovereign will occasionally come to Canada to perform a constitutional duty, such as the signing of the Constitution Act, 1982, visits from the Queen and members of the Royal Family are largely focused on community-building and "state ceremonial." The presence of the Queen and members of her family at Canada Day celebrations, for example, serves not only to fill a Canadian appetite to meet the Royal Family, but more fundamentally to establish a bond between citizens and those who personify the Crown. Similarly, having the Sovereign and other royals attend local events contributes to the Canadianization of the Crown, making it an institution that Canadians can identify as their own. *Ottawa Citizen* columnist Dan Gardner has remarked that the Queen's attendance at hockey games cements the affection that Canadians feel for the Crown as a unifying symbol of their nation.[18]

The Crown's role in the honours system and in granting Canadians access to heraldry can be properly understood only with reference to this communal component of Canadian constitutional monarchy. Canada's honours such as the Order of Canada recognize the achievements and societal contributions of praiseworthy Canadians. These honours are specifically bestowed by the governor general to avoid any sense of partisan reward. Although many former politicians belong to the Order of Canada, they owe the honour to the Crown, not a political party or fellow partisan. The Canadian Heraldic Authority is housed at Rideau Hall, under the direction of the governor general, for similar reasons. Although the Authority's "principal objective is to ensure that all Canadians who wish to use heraldry will have access to it,"[19] the office also guarantees that these symbols are provided for the community as a whole, and not for the interests of a particular party. Christopher McCreery's many writings about Canadian honours and symbols of authority emphasize the Crown's role in building this sense of community.[20] It is significant that all provinces except Quebec have placed the Crown and the lieutenant governor at the core of their honours system.

Richard Berthelsen's contribution to this volume further highlights how innovations in the presentation of the speech from the throne emphasize the communal role of the Crown. While most speeches from the throne are increasingly partisan, certain jurisdictions, notably Quebec, have moved toward a less overtly political throne speech. Mr. Berthelsen sees this trend as a positive development, one that lifts the Crown above partisan politics and stresses the institution's function as a unifying element within a political community.

In the Westminster tradition, the Crown serves as the concept of the state.[21] Recognizing the Crown as the state in Canada sheds light on the other functions that the monarchy fulfils in the Canadian political community. For instance, it explains why oaths are sworn to the Sovereign. The desired effect of these oaths is to establish a sense of obligation, duty, and belonging to Canada through a pledge to the Sovereign as the embodiment of the Canadian state. Hence, new Canadian citizens do not swear an oath to the government or Parliament; instead, they swear an oath to the Queen. Civil servants take an oath to the Queen as well, a reminder that their ultimate loyalty is to the state, not to the government of the day or even Parliament. Parliamentarians, too, swear an oath to the Queen, reminding them that they are not only accountable to the electorate but must be loyal to the state as well.[22]

Canada's military personnel have a unique relationship with the Queen, based on the Crown as the locus of supreme military command authority. The Canadian Armed Forces (CAF) are servants of the Crown, not Parliament or the people. As with the civil service, their underlying loyalty is to the Crown as the state. However, the Sovereign also stands at the top of Canada's military command structure. All orders and directives to the armed forces formally flow from the Crown's command authority. Furthermore, the Sovereign and the governor general, as commander-in-chief of Canada, have a fiduciary responsibility toward those who take up arms in defence of the realm. Thus, the Crown serves a critical unifying function within the Canadian military community, acting as the paramount source of command authority, the focus of the armed forces' loyalty and service, and the guardian of the CAF's honour and welfare. It is for these reasons that showing respect and reverence for the Queen is a duty for those who wear a Canadian military uniform.[23]

The relationship between First Nations and the monarchy involves notions of community and the Crown as state as well. As J. R. Miller explains in his chapter, the Crown–First Nations relationship is based on ties of kinship and alliance among Indigenous communities, the Sovereign, and the monarch's representatives. Rather than being engaged in a strictly legal arrangement, the Crown–First Nations relationship is steeped in a sense of common cause and mutual obligation and respect, at least in principle. As Stephanie Danyluk's chapter further highlights, the Western Nations who allied themselves with the Crown during the War of 1812 did so as sovereign nations. Recognizing that the Crown and First Nations still exist under a form of shared sovereignty, Ms. Danyluk argues, would help ease tensions between Canadian governments and Indigenous peoples.

Disagreements surrounding the governor general's role in the 2012–2013 Idle No More movement reflected a similar divergence of views. Whereas commentators assumed that First Nations protestors wanted Governor General David Johnston to meet with cabinet ministers and chiefs as a representative of Her Majesty's government, it is far more likely that they saw the governor general as a representative of the Crown and the Canadian state. As Tom Flanagan noted at the time, the presence of the governor general as a personal manifestation of the state would have reinforced the argument that Crown–First Nations relations should be understood as a nation-to-nation interaction based on principles of shared sovereignty, and not one of hierarchy with a subnational group petitioning the federal government.[24] Having the governor general attend as a personification of the state would have reinforced the notion that the Crown and chiefs encounter one another as the heads of equally sovereign peoples.

Further, Senator Serge Joyal recalls in his chapter that the communal Crown was a respected institution in Quebec society from as early as the conquest of 1759 to the Quiet Revolution. French-Canadian civic and religious leaders recognized the efforts that the Crown made in preserving language rights and the Roman Catholic Church in Quebec following the capitulation of New France. They appreciated the benefits of British parliamentarism and the extension of traditional English liberties to the Canadas. While this positive inclination toward the Crown has since dissipated in Quebec, the senator's contribution captures a time when Quebecers accepted the Crown as an integral part of their political community.

Of course, the communal Crown is not without its critics. Skeptics wonder if Canadians still feel any real connection to the Crown. While the Royal Family may be admired, critics argue that royalty no longer commands any liturgical authority or ceremonial reverence. As non-residents, moreover, members of the Royal Family cannot serve as effective symbols of the Canadian polity or state. Janice Kennedy captures this sentiment: "The time has come to stop salivating after a family of upper-class Brits.... It's time to stop festooning their symbols with maple leaves and pretending they belong to us."[25] And while Canada's governors general and lieutenant governors might be suitable understudies, they lack the tenure and personal presence of the monarch.[26] Furthermore, being appointed on the recommendation of governments, they might be said to lack the apolitical aura that the Sovereign enjoys. If these objections were valid, they would raise doubts about the ability of vice-regal officers to serve as effective representatives of the Crown in its communal capacity. It must be noted, however, that this is a rather muted critique. As John D. Whyte's chapter in this volume suggests, the vice-regal officers have performed their communal functions with a good deal of success, enough to lead republicans to argue that the monarchy is superfluous insofar as the governors have effectively displaced the Sovereign in this respect.

The Conservative government's emphasis on the monarchy might also raise concerns that the Crown has been politicized. Specifically, in making the restoration of the monarchy in the Canadian political community such a central part of their government's legacy, it is possible that the institution will be associated with one political party.[27] The Crown's capability to act as an apolitical, non-partisan symbol of Canada could wane as a result. Not accidentally, this trepidation exists because previous Liberal and Progressive Conservative governments sought to minimize the role of the Crown as a Canadian symbol. If the Conservatives' revival of the monarchy appears out of place to some, it owes much to the subtle marginalization of the Crown as a Canadian emblem from the mid-1960s to the 2000s.[28] Nonetheless, the effort to reduce the importance of the

Crown during these decades allows critics to argue that the Conservatives' embrace of the Crown is at odds with the political neutrality of the institution. The counter-argument is that if Canada's monarchial tradition is to be revived, as it was previously diminished, this must be led by the elected government of the day.

A lack of knowledge about the Crown's role as the concept of the state has presented challenges for the institution's communal functions as well. The fact that the Crown serves as the state is rarely acknowledged, even within the legal establishment or in debates where this reality is consequential. The widespread ignorance about this facet of the Crown contributes to the confusion over why oaths are sworn to the Sovereign, whether the monarch is Canadian, the granting of royal monickers, and the Queen's role as the embodiment of the Canadian polity. Canadians are so unaware that the Crown is the state that the ceremonies and rites that depend on this notion may be at risk of losing their meaning and resonance. Indeed, John Whyte argues that in today's Canada the very legitimacy of the authority that is said to flow from the Crown has been supplanted by the de facto reality of popular sovereignty and republican values. If this reading were correct, the liturgical authority of the Crown would be reduced to a novelty—if it survived at all.

It is not difficult to find evidence supporting Professor Whyte's contention. The need to swear oaths to the Queen is regularly challenged or treated as entirely pro forma.[29] Use of the term "public service" in lieu of the more constitutionally-accurate "civil service" is indicative of a greater comfort with republic notions of government.[30] High-ranking military officers have stated that the armed forces serve Parliament.[31] In her commentary on Senator Joyal's chapter, Linda Cardinal suggests that the ambivalence Quebecers currently feel toward the Crown may be part of a deeper legacy of modernity and republicanism that predates the Quiet Revolution. Prominent Liberal and New Democratic politicians have voiced support for abolishing the monarchy on the grounds (stated by John Whyte) that it no longer accords with Canada's political values or effectively represents the Canadian polity.[32] For those who are opposed to the monarchy, these ways of thinking demonstrate that Canada would be well on the road to republicanism if it were not for a complicated constitutional amending formula.

And yet there are reasons to think that the power of the communal Crown is far from extinguished. If many Canadians are unfamiliar with the Crown as the non-partisan fount of authority and as the concept of the state, it may be because they were not reminded of these facets of the monarchy for many decades. As Peter H. Russell notes in his chapter, Canadians remain uneducated about the Crown. If more Canadians were aware of the communal functions that the institution serves, it is possible that the public's respect and support for the Crown would grow. With the Harper government making a concerted effort to remind Canadians that they live in a constitutional monarchy, it is not unlikely that the Crown's place within Canada's political community will garner greater recognition. Indeed, it is important to recall that many established symbols of Canada, such as the national flag, the Charter of Rights and Freedoms, and bilingualism and multiculturalism, did not gain spontaneous acceptance. They became cemented within Canada's national identity only after several years and, in some cases, decades. The Crown, which has been part of Canada since well before Confederation, has long been integral to the Canadian national story and has strong roots. This history will facilitate efforts to revive a sense of national attachment to the Crown. At this juncture, it is impossible to tell whether these factors will be sufficient to counteract other forces that distance Canadians from the monarchy. Yet it is premature to assume that Canadians will inevitably be divorced from an institution that has been an ever-present part of their country.

The Constitutional Crown

The Crown is the keystone of the Canadian Constitution. As the source of sovereign authority, it is vital for the operation of Canada's legislatures, executives, and judiciaries. Yet the Crown's place in the Constitution is usually overlooked in favour of higher-profile institutions such as the House of Commons, cabinet, and Supreme Court. As David E. Smith argued in his seminal book on Canada's constitutional monarchy, the Crown is invisible, despite being the first principle of Canadian government.[33] This is the hallmark of the constitutional Crown: critical but clandestine. The hiddenness of the constitutional Crown does not make it incomprehensible, however. Provided one is willing, in Lord Atkin's and Lord Roskill's terms, to study the contemporary relevance of "the clanking mediaeval chains of the ghosts of the past,"[34] it is possible to draw the constitutional Crown out of the shadows.

The Queen is one part of the federal Parliament alongside the House of Commons and the Senate. Together they form the legislative power known as the Crown-in-Parliament. The clearest manifestation of the Crown-in-Parliament is the granting of royal assent to bills that have passed the House of Commons and Senate. No bill becomes a law until royal assent is given. Although royal assent is now seen as a formality, it signifies that the Crown's authority is required to give effect to legislation. The speech from the throne is another representation of the Crown-in-Parliament. With these speeches, the Crown can outline the legislative goals that the government has set out for a parliamentary session. As per section 54 of the Constitution Act, 1867, any parliamentary vote, resolution, address, or bill that involves the expenditure of money must obtain a royal recommendation before it is adopted or passed. Submitted by cabinet ministers, royal recommendations ensure that the House of Commons and Senate cannot use their legislative authority to impose policy and spending choices on the executive. Since ministers are held to account for government policy and public expenditures, their control of royal recommendations guarantees that they are only responsible for policies and expenditures that they have endorsed. Accordingly, this aspect of the Crown-in-Parliament serves to reinforce the principles of responsible government. Legislation that touches upon the Crown's powers or privileges, furthermore, must obtain the consent of the Crown.[35] In principle, this allows the Crown to express concern regarding bills that undermine the independence and constitutional functions of the Sovereign or the governor general, and permits cabinet to protect the Crown's prerogative powers from ill-advised statutory infringements.

Whereas the operations of the Crown-in-Parliament are largely uncontroversial, the Crown's powers *over* Parliament have been the subject of significant contention. Scholars disagree about when the governor general or a lieutenant governor can refuse to act on the advice of a first minister to prorogue or dissolve the legislature. Views on this question can be divided into two camps. The first sees the Sovereign's representatives as active parliamentary referees, arbitrating between political parties who are vying to form a government. In this view, which is well represented by Peter Russell's chapter in this book, the vice-regal officers are expected to play a robust role in defending parliamentary democracy and ensuring that the Crown's powers are not abused for partisan gain. In practice, this means that the governors can refuse to prorogue or dissolve the legislature if they believe that a first minister is seeking to avoid votes of non-confidence, gain undue political advantage over the opposition, or inhibit legislative scrutiny of the executive.

The alternative view holds that the vice-regal officers are better understood as constitutional fire-extinguishers,[36] implying that they should only refuse the advice of a first minister to prorogue or dissolve the legislature in the most exceptional of circumstances.[37] Thus, a governor would exercise discretion only in times of emergency or when a first minister was undoubtedly attempting to undermine the legislature and the democratic process. For the supporters of this view, the foundation of responsible government is that the Crown acts on the advice of those holding the confidence of the lower house; unless this confidence is formally withdrawn, it is not for the Sovereign's representative to refuse the advice of the first minister. Robert E. Hawkins defends this view in his contribution to this book, noting that the governors will only act when there can be no question that they *must* act. James W. J. Bowden and Nicholas A. MacDonald have argued for this perspective as well,[38] and their chapter demonstrates that this is the position articulated in the 1968 *Manual of Official Procedure of the Government of Canada*.

Crown powers are a pivotal component of the executive's strength in Canada. Prerogative powers related to appointments, mercy, international affairs, secrecy of information, and the machinery of government provide prime ministers and cabinet with a significant source of authority over the affairs of government and matters of state. As David E. Smith argues in his chapter, prerogative power has been vital to the centralization of authority in the office of the prime minister and in the development of the administrative state. For Dr. Smith, the importance of these powers belies the notion that the Crown is merely a dignified institution; in reality, monarchical authority remains a salient and efficient part of the executive. In making this argument, Dr. Smith states that the executive's powers and authority are not wholly determined by the legislature in Canada. Prerogatives that canonical legal scholars were quick to dismiss in the nineteenth and early twentieth centuries have proved resilient to parliamentary displacement. Despite all that has been written about the need to curtail the dominance of the executive, legislatures have been hesitant to supplant the Crown's remaining prerogatives, and the courts have been remarkably deferential toward governmental decisions and actions that flow from prerogative authority.[39]

Alexander Bolt's chapter examines one of the Crown's most significant prerogative powers: the authority to deploy the armed forces. Lieutenant-Colonel Bolt demonstrates that, contrary to an increasingly popular view, this power does not belong with the House of Commons. It continues to flow from the Crown and is exercised at the discretion of ministers. Arguably, having the House of Commons approve exercises of Crown prerogatives would dilute the executive's responsibility and limit the ability of opposition parties to hold the government to account. This may be one reason why governments are seeking legislative sanction of decisions that flow from prerogative authority. Having the House of Commons vote its approval of controversial government decisions launders exercises of the prerogative, giving them a democratic sheen that complicates later efforts to hold the executive to account.

An appreciation of the Crown's role in the Constitution clarifies relations between Parliament and the executive. Canada's Constitution Act, 1867 vests executive authority in the Queen. This means that governing is done in the Crown's name and that all the powers of the executive flow either from the Crown's prerogatives or from authorities granted to the Crown by statute. Although is it commonly held that the legislature and executive are fused in the Westminster tradition, the Crown's status as the executive power shows that this is not accurate. As noted by James Bowden and Nicholas MacDonald in their chapter, when cabinet ministers govern, they exercise the authority of the Crown as the executive, not the powers of Parliament or even the Crown-in-Parliament. The Crown as the executive power is constitutionally distinct from the Crown's role in the legislature. Similarly, although cabinet members are drawn from Parliament, this does not mean that Parliament governs. Ministers of the Crown are members of Parliament by convention, but the powers and authorities that an individual wields as a Crown minister are not those of the individual as an MP. These are two separate and distinct positions—one in the executive, the other in the legislature—that are held by the same individual. Owing to the principles and practices of Westminster-style parliamentary democracy and responsible government, this means that cabinet links, but does not fuse, the executive and legislature.[40]

The Canadian executive itself can be subdivided according to how its members relate to the Crown as the executive power. The Sovereign and vice-regal governors make up the formal executive. The secretaries to the Sovereign and governors, whose roles and functions are outlined in Christopher McCreery's second chapter, belong to the formal executive as well. Ministers of the Crown belong to the political executive. They are responsible for the affairs of government and are accountable to the legislature. Although their power and authority flow from the Crown, their right to govern stems from the fact that they must command the confidence of the elected house of the legislature. Civil servants, the armed forces, and the police comprise what can be called the permanent executive. While they follow the directives of ministers and are accountable to them, their service is to the Crown, which ensures that they remain in place, operating the machinery of government and fulfilling their duties to the state as different cabinets come and go. The independence that officials, military officers, and the police enjoy vis-à-vis the government of the day ultimately resides in their service to the Crown.

Judicial independence is vital to Canadian constitutionalism and the rule of law. Yet this does not mean that judges and the courts are detached from the Crown. On the contrary, the authority that courts wield descends to them from the Crown as the fount of justice. Indeed, though the judiciary ensures the rule of law, justice is administered in the name of the Sovereign. Judges, moreover, are appointed by the Crown acting on the advice of cabinets. Equally significant, the Crown acts as the prosecutor in criminal cases, and the prerogative power of prosecution is exercised by the Crown's attorneys general. As the Supreme Court of Canada has found, prosecutorial discretion "finds its source in the Attorney General's role as the official legal advisor to the Crown."[41] And because it flows from the Crown's prerogative, prosecutorial discretion is insulated from interference by the courts.[42]

No discussion of the judiciary's interaction with the Crown should ignore how the courts have employed the monarchy to shape Canadian federalism. In a sequence of nineteenth- and twentieth-century decisions, the judiciary found that the federal and provincial Crowns were co-equal sources of sovereign authority, with the result that Ottawa could not claim to be the pre-eminent level of government in Canada.[43] Instead, the Canadian federation was understood, in David E. Smith's words, to be a "compound monarchy," with two separate orders of government.[44] This meant, among other things, that the federal government could not give effect to treaties that fell under the provinces' legislative competencies. Since the passage of the Constitution Act, 1982, furthermore, the unanimous consent of the federal Parliament and provincial legislatures has been required to change the offices of the Sovereign, governor general, and lieutenant governors. In effect, each of the provinces has been given the power to veto amendments aiming to remove the Crown from the Canadian Constitution.

The Crown is the source and foundation of Canada as a sovereign state; this is arguably the monarchy's most significant constitutional function. When the Dominion of Canada was confederated in 1867, the new country was a self-governing British colony under the sovereign powers and authority of the Crown of Great Britain and Ireland. At the Imperial Conference of 1926, it was agreed that the self-governing colonies would have control of their own affairs. The legal instrument that formalized this arrangement was the 1931 Statute of Westminster. Although not explicitly stated in the document nor fully appreciated at the time, the Statute of Westminster allowed for a gradual division of the Crown. Indeed, the divisibility of the Crown was necessary to ensure that the self-governing colonies could act as fully independent states. In the lead-up to the patriation of the Canadian Constitution, British law lords recognized that the Canadian Crown was distinct from the British Crown, and this division of the Crowns made Canada separate and independent from the United Kingdom.[45] The passage of the Canada Act, 1982, which ended the British Parliament's power to legislate for Canada, merely affirmed the sovereign independence that the development of the Canadian Crown had brought into force after 1931.

In spite of the Crown's centrality in the Constitution, it remains shrouded in mystery, and those committed to understanding the institution's various constitutional permutations are few in number, mostly confined to academia and the bureaucracy. But this does not diminish the reality that the Canadian Constitution cannot be properly understood without reference to the Crown. If recent trends are any indication, moreover, interest in the Crown in growing among scholars and those advocating for constitutional reform. While the constitutional Crown is unlikely to attract as much attention as its hereditary and communal components, it will remain central to debates about the institution's future.

Debating the Crown

Few aspects of Canada's constitutional monarchy are simple or self-evident. The Crown as a concept and an institution has evolved for over a thousand years. It has also taken on a particular style and importance in the Canadian context, owing to its ties with First Nations, role in federalism, and entrenchment in the written Constitution. The Crown cannot be reduced to the Sovereign, a symbol, or a source of authority—yet it is each of these things. Canada's constitutional monarchy is about the Royal Family, the country's past as part of the British Empire, a sense of community and nationhood, and the fundamental idea and legal foundation that underpins power in the state. Nor is this list exhaustive. Though not discussed here, the Canadian Crown has international and philosophical components as well. Complexity characterizes the Crown.

Improving debate about the Crown in Canada involves acknowledging this complexity. This holds as much for supporters of the Crown as it does for critics. Scholars who focus on the constitutional importance of the Crown would do well to acknowledge and understand the affection shown the Royal Family. In many ways, these are vastly different topics, but they are both vital parts of the Crown. Similarly, though many monarchists insist that the Crown is Canadian, avoiding the institution's inherent Britishness appears disingenuous. Moreover, however attractive it is for critics to frame the monarchy debate around the privileges or nationality of the Royal Family, this strategy is doomed to fail when confronted with the Crown's role in the constitutional and the political community. Indeed, the lack of interest that many republican critics have toward the communal and constitutional Crown helps explain the movement's difficulty in mobilizing Canadians. Railing against royalty will only go so far when Canada's constitutional structure is at stake.

In response to Maitland, then, we should say that the Crown is not a cover for ignorance, but rather that refusing to acknowledge the complexity of the Crown encourages ignorance. It stands to reason that debates and discussions about Canada's constitutional monarchy are better served when the Crown's complexity is acknowledged and embraced.

Notes

1. Frederic W. Maitland, *The Constitutional History of England* (1908; repr., Union, NJ: Lawbook Exchange, 2001), 418.
2. Andrew Coyne, "The Queen, and a Nationalism Built on Love," *Postmedia News*, June 4, 2012.
3. Andrew Coyne, "We're All in the Royal Family," *Macleans.ca*, July 8, 2011.
4. John Fraser, *The Secret of the Crown: Canada's Affair with Royalty* (Toronto: House of Anansi Press, 2012).
5. Janice Kennedy, "Don't Reform Monarchy, Abolish It," *Winnipeg Free Press*, December 1, 2011.
6. Jonathan Kay, "Behind the Pageant and Princesses, It's Just Feudalism Lite," *National Post*, June 6, 2012.
7. Michael Bliss, "It's Time to Retire the Royals," *National Post*, January 21, 2011.
8. Canadian legal studies examining the Crown in depth rely on British precedents, concepts, and cases. See, for instance, Paul Lordon, *Crown Law* (Toronto: Butterworths, 1991).

9. Canadian Heritage, "Backgrounder: Introduction of Line of Succession Legislation," January 31, 2013.
10. Roland Paris, "No Republicanism, Please – We're Canadian," *OpenCanada.org*, July 1, 2011.
11. Prithi Yelaja, "Royal Military Renaming Slammed as Colonial Throwback," *CBC.ca*, August 17, 2011.
12. Harris/Decima, "Desire to Maintain Monarchy Has Grown Significantly in English Canada," press release, May 24, 2012.
13. Michael Valpy, "The Monarchy: Offshore, But Built In," *Globe and Mail*, August 23, 2012.
14. Philippe Lagassé, "The Queen Is the Canadian Crown," *Ottawa Citizen*, January 9, 2012.
15. On Britishness and Canadian identity, see C. P. Champion, *The Strange Demise of British Canada: The Liberals and Canadian Nationalism, 1964–1968* (Montreal and Kingston: McGill-Queen's University Press, 2010), chap. 1.
16. Paul Benoit, "State Ceremonial: The Constitutional Monarch's Liturgical Authority," in *The Evolving Canadian Crown*, ed. Jennifer Smith and D. Michael Jackson (Montreal and Kingston: McGill-Queen's University Press, 2012).
17. Frank MacKinnon, *The Crown in Canada* (Calgary: Glenbow-Alberta Institute / McClelland & Stewart West, 1976), chap. 2.
18. Dan Gardner, "Truly, the Queen of Canada," *Ottawa Citizen*, August 29, 2012.
19. "Canadian Heraldic Authority," www.gg.ca, accessed April 20, 2013.
20. Christopher McCreery, *The Order of Canada: Its Origins, History, and Development* (Toronto: University of Toronto Press, 2005); *The Canadian Honours System* (Toronto: Dundurn, 2005); *On Her Majesty's Service: Royal Honours and Recognition in Canada* (Toronto: Dundurn, 2008).
21. Martin Loughlin, "The State, the Crown, and the Law," in *The Nature of the Crown: A Legal and Political Analysis*, ed. Maurice Sunkin and Sebastian Payne (Oxford: Oxford University Press, 1999).
22. MacKinnon, *The Crown in Canada*, 21-22.
23. For the legal foundations of the relationship between the Crown and armed forces, see the Federal Court case of *Chainnigh v. Attorney General of Canada*, 2008 FC 69.
24. Tom Flanagan, "Native Talks with the Crown Challenge Canada's Very Existence," *Globe and Mail*, January 25, 2013.
25. Janice Kennedy, "The Queen Is Not Canadian," *Ottawa Citizen*, January 13, 2012.
26. See David E. Smith, *The Republican Option in Canada, Past and Present* (Toronto: University of Toronto Press, 1999).
27. Chantal Hébert, "Can Federal Liberals Make the Old New Again?," *Toronto Star*, October 10, 2012.
28. Dan Gardner, "The Republican in Rideau Hall," *Ottawa Citizen*, February 11, 2009.
29. Tobi Cohen, "NDP's Pat Martin Wants to Drop Queen from Citizenship Oath," *Postmedia News*, April 18, 2013.
30. Robert Watt, "The Crown and Its Employees," in *The Nature of the Crown: A Legal and Political Analysis*, ed. Maurice Sunkin and Sebastian Payne (Oxford: Oxford University Press, 1999).

31. In his last speech as chief of the Defence staff, General Rick Hillier noted that "we are servants of Parliament." See "Harper Hints New Chief of Defence Will Be on Shorter Leash," *Ottawa Citizen,* July 3, 2008.
32. Jane Taber, "Liberals Vote to Keep Monarchy, Legalize Pot at Convention," *Globe and Mail,* January 15, 2012; Jane Taber, "Put Monarchy to a Vote, NDP Leadership Hopeful Says," *Globe and Mail,* November 30, 2011.
33. David E. Smith, *The Invisible Crown: The First Principle of Canadian Government* (Toronto: University of Toronto Press, 1995).
34. Lord Roskill paraphrased this line from Lord Atkin. See *United Australia v. Barclays Bank,* [1941] A.C. 1, 29 (H.L.) and *Council of Civil Service Unions v. Minister for the Civil Service* [1985] A.C. 374.
35. Alistair Fraser, W. F. Dawson, and John A. Holtby, *Beauchesne's Rules & Forms of the House of Commons of Canada* (Toronto: Carswell, 1989), 213.
36. Frank MacKinnon, *The Crown in Canada,* chap. 7.
37. Robert MacGregor Dawson, *The Government of Canada,* 5th ed. (Toronto: University of Toronto Press, 1970), 161.
38. Nicholas A. MacDonald and James W. J. Bowden, "No Discretion: On Prorogation and the Governor General," *Canadian Parliamentary Review* 34, no. 1 (2011).
39. Philippe Lagassé, "Parliamentary and Judicial Ambivalence toward Executive Prerogative Power in Canada," *Canadian Public Administration* 55, no. 2 (2012): 157-80.
40. Dennis Baker, *Not Quite Supreme: The Courts and Coordinate Constitutional Interpretation* (Montreal and Kingston: McGill-Queen's University Press, 2010), chapters 3 and 4.
41. *Krieger v. Law Society of Alberta,* [2002] 3 S.C.R 372, 2002 SCC 65, para. 25.
42. Ibid.
43. D. Michael Jackson, *The Crown and Canadian Federalism* (Toronto: Dundurn, 2013).
44. Smith, *The Invisible Crown,* 12.
45. *The Queen v. the Secretary of State for Foreign and Commonwealth Affairs* [1981] 4 C.N.L.R.

General Bibliography on the Crown in Canada

D. Michael Jackson

Books

Ajzenstat, Janet. *The Canadian Founding: John Locke and Parliament*. Montreal and Kingston: McGill-Queen's University Press, 2007.

—. *The Once and Future Canadian Democracy: An Essay in Political Thought*. Montreal and Kingston: McGill-Queen's University Press, 2003.

Ajzenstat, Janet, Paul Romney, Ian Gentles, and William Gairdner, eds. *Canada's Founding Debates*. Toronto: University of Toronto Press, 2003.

Ajzenstat, Janet, and Peter J. Smith, eds. *Canada's Origins: Liberal, Tory, or Republican?* Ottawa: Carleton University Press, 1997.

Allen, Robert S. *His Majesty's Indian Allies: British Indian Policy in the Defence of Canada, 1774–1815.* Toronto: Dundurn, 1996.

Anson, Sir William R. *The Law and Custom of the Constitution*. Vol. 2, *The Crown*. Oxford: Clarendon Press, 1908.

Aucoin, Peter, Mark D. Jarvis, and Lori Turnbull. *Democratizing the Constitution: Reforming Responsible Government*. Toronto: Emond Montgomery Publications, 2011.

Bagehot, Walter. *The English Constitution*. London: Oxford University Press, 1961.

Baker, Dennis. *Not Quite Supreme: The Courts and Coordinate Constitutional Interpretation*. Montreal and Kingston: McGill-Queen's University Press, 2010.

Barnett, Anthony, ed. *Power and the Throne: The Monarchy Debate*. London: Vintage, 1994.

Bastien, Frédéric. *La Bataille de Londres: Dessous, secrets et coulisses du rapatriement constitutionnel*. Montreal: Boréal, 2013.

Batt, Elizabeth. *Monck, Governor General, 1861–1868: A Biography*. Toronto: McClelland & Stewart, 1976.

Bedell Smith, Sally. *Elizabeth II: The Life of a Modern Monarch*. New York: Random House, 2012.

Berger, Carl. *The Sense of Power: Studies in the Ideas of Canadian Imperialism*. Toronto: University of Toronto Press, 1970.

Bissell, Claude. *The Imperial Canadian: Vincent Massey in Office*. Toronto: University of Toronto Press, 1986.

Black, Charles E. Drummond. *The Marquess of Dufferin and Ava... Diplomatist, Viceroy, Statesman*. London: Hutchinson, 1903.

Black, Edwin. *Divided Loyalties: Canadian Concepts of Federalism*. Montreal: McGill-Queen's University Press, 1971.

Blatherwick, John. *Canadian Orders, Decorations and Medals.* 5th ed. Toronto: Unitrade Press, 2003.

Bogdanor, Vernon. *The Monarchy and the Constitution*. Oxford: Oxford University Press, 1995.

Bousfield, Arthur, and Garry Toffoli. *Fifty Years the Queen: A Tribute to Elizabeth II on Her Golden Jubilee*. Toronto: Dundurn, 2002.

—. *Home to Canada: Royal Tours 1786–2010*. Toronto: Dundurn, 2010.

—. *The Queen Mother and Her Century: An Illustrated Biography of Queen Elizabeth the Queen Mother on Her 100th Birthday*. Toronto: Dundurn, 2000.

—. *Royal Observations: Canadians and Royalty*. Toronto: Dundurn, 1991.

—. *The Royal Tour of 1939: Royal Spring and the Queen Mother in Canada*. Toronto: Dundurn, 1989.

Boyce, Peter. *The Queen's Other Realms: The Crown and Its Legacy in Australia, Canada and New Zealand*. Sydney: Federation Press, 2008.

Bradford, Sarah. *Elizabeth: A Biography of Her Majesty The Queen*. Toronto: Key Porter Books, 1996.

Brun, Henri, Guy Tremblay, and Eugénie Brouillet. *Droit constitutionnel*. 5e édition. Cowansville: Éditions Yvon Blais, 2008.

Buchan, John. *Canadian Occasions*. Toronto: Musson, 1941.

Buchan, William. *John Buchan: A Memoir*. Toronto: Griffin House, 1982.

Buckner, Phillip, ed. *Canada and the End of Empire*. Vancouver: University of British Columbia Press, 2005.

Buckner, Phillip, and R. D. Francis, eds. *Canada and the British World*. Vancouver: University of British Columbia Press, 2006.

Butler, David, and D. A. Low, eds. *Sovereigns and Surrogates: Constitutional Heads of State in the Commonwealth*. London: Macmillan, 1991.

Canada. Privy Council Office. *Manual of Official Procedure of the Government of Canada.* Prepared by Henry F. Davis and André Millar. Ottawa: Government of Canada, 1968.

The Canadian Press. *Canada's Queen. Elizabeth II: A Celebration of Her Majesty's Friendship with the People of Canada*. Toronto: John Wiley & Sons, 2008.

Cardinal, Linda, and David Heaton, eds. *Shaping Nations: Constitutionalism and Society in Australia and Canada*. Ottawa: University of Ottawa Press, 2002.

Champion, C. P. *The Strange Demise of British Canada: The Liberals and Canadian Nationalism, 1964–1968*. Montreal and Kingston: McGill-Queen's University Press, 2010.

Cheffins, Ronald, and Ronald Tucker. *The Constitutional Process in Canada.* 2nd ed. Toronto: McGraw-Hill Ryerson, 1976.

Chevrier, Marc. *La République au Québec, une idée suspecte*. Montreal: Boréal, 2012.

Chitty, Joseph. *A Treatise on the Law of the Prerogatives of the Crown.* London: Butterworths, 1820. Reprinted by Lawbook Exchange, 2010.

Clarkson, Adrienne. *Heart Matters: A Memoir.* Toronto: Viking Canada, 2006.

Coady, Mary Frances. *Georges and Pauline Vanier: Portrait of a Couple*. Montreal and Kingston: McGill-Queen's University Press, 2011.

Coates, Colin M., ed. *Imperial Canada, 1867–1917*. Edinburgh: Centre of Canadian Studies, 1997.

—. *Majesty in Canada: Essays on the Role of Royalty*. Toronto: Dundurn, 2006.

Cotton, Peter Neive. *Vice-Regal Mansions of British Columbia*. Vancouver: Elgin Publications, 1981.

Couture, Claude, et Paulin Mulatris. *La nation et son double. Essais sur les discours postcoloniaux au Canada*. Québec : Les Presses de l'Université Laval, 2012.

Cowan, John. *Canada's Governors General, Lord Monck to General Vanier*. Toronto: York Publishing, 1965.

Cox, Noel. *A Constitutional History of the New Zealand Monarchy: The Evolution of the New Zealand Monarchy and the Recognition of an Autochthonous Polity*. Saarbrücken: VDM Verlag Dr. Müller, 2008.

Creighton, Donald. *The Road to Confederation: The Emergence of Canada, 1863–1867*. Toronto: Macmillan, 1964.

Dawson, R. McGregor. *Constitutional Issues in Canada, 1900–1931*. London: Oxford University Press, 1933.

—. *The Government of Canada*. 5th ed. Revised by Norman Ward. Toronto: University of Toronto Press, 1970.

—. *The Principles of Official Independence: With Particular Reference to the Political History of Canada*. London: P. S. King & Son, 1922.

Dempsey, L. James. *Warriors of the King: Prairie Indians in World War I*. Regina: Canadian Plains Research Center, University of Regina, 1999.

Dicey, A. V. *Law of the Constitution*. 10th ed. Introduction by E. C. S. Wade. London: Macmillan, 1962.

Diefenbaker, John G. *Those Things We Treasure*. Toronto: Macmillan, 1972.

Dimbleby, Jonathan. *The Prince of Wales: A Biography*. New York: William Morrow and Company, 1994.

Evatt, H. V. *The Royal Prerogative*. Sydney: Law Book Company, 1987.

Evatt and Forsey on the Reserve Power. A complete and unabridged reprint of H.V. Evatt, *The King and His Dominion Governors* (2nd ed., 1967) and Eugene A. Forsey, *The Royal Power of Dissolution in the British Commonwealth* (reprint, 1968), together with a new introduction by Eugene Forsey. Sydney: Legal Books, 1990.

Farthing, John. *Freedom Wears a Crown*. Toronto: Kingswood House, 1957.

Forcese, Craig, and Aaron Freeman. *The Laws of Government: The Legal Foundations of Canadian Democracy*. Toronto: Irwin Law, 2005.

Forsey, Eugene A. *Freedom and Order: Collected Essays*. Toronto: McClelland & Stewart, 1974.

—. *A Life on the Fringe: The Memoirs of Eugene Forsey*. Toronto: Oxford University Press, 1990.

—. *The Royal Power of Dissolution of Parliament in the British Commonwealth*. Toronto: Oxford University Press, 1943. Reprinted with corrections as an Oxford in Canada paperback, 1968.

Forsey, Helen. *Eugene Forsey: Canada's Maverick Sage*. Toronto: Dundurn, 2012.

Fraser, Andrew. *The Spirit of the Laws: Republicanism and the Unfinished Project of Modernity*. Toronto: University of Toronto Press, 1990.

Fraser, John. *Eminent Canadians: Candid Tales of Then and Now*. Toronto: McClelland & Stewart, 2000.

—. *The Secret of the Crown: Canada's Affair with Royalty*. Toronto: House of Anansi Press, 2012.

Galbraith, J. William. *John Buchan: Model Governor General*. Toronto: Dundurn, 2013.

The Governors General of Canada from Viscount Monck to David Johnston. Ottawa: New Federation House, 2013.

Grant, George. *Lament for a Nation: The Defeat of Canadian Nationalism*. Third reprint. Toronto: McClelland & Stewart, 1970.

Gwyn, Sandra. *The Private Capital: Ambition and Love in the Age of Macdonald and Laurier*. Toronto: McClelland & Stewart, 1984.

Hall, Trevor. *Royal Canada: A History of Royal Visits to Canada since 1786*. Godalming, Surrey, UK: Archive Publishing, 1989.

Happy & Glorious. A Celebration of the Life of HM Queen Elizabeth II. London: Cassell Illustrated, 2006.

Hardman, Robert. *A Year with the Queen*. New York: Simon & Schuster, 2007.

—. *Her Majesty: Queen Elizabeth II and Her Court*. New York: Pegasus Books, 2012.

Hart-Davis, Duff, ed. *King's Counsellor. Abdication and War: The Diaries of Sir Alan Lascelles*. London: Phoenix, 2007.

Heard, Andrew. *Canadian Constitutional Conventions: The Marriage of Law and Politics*. Toronto: Oxford University Press, 1991.

Hnatyshyn, Gerda, and Paulette Lachapelle-Bélisle. *Rideau Hall: Canada's Living Heritage*. Ottawa: Friends of Rideau Hall, 1994.

Hogg, Peter. *Constitutional Law of Canada*. 5th ed. Toronto: Carswell, 2007.

Hogg, Peter, Patrick J. Monahan, and Wade K. Wright. *Liability of the Crown*. 4th ed. Toronto: Carswell, 2011.

Hryniuk, Margaret, and Garth Pugh. *"A Tower of Attraction": An Illustrated History of Government House, Regina, Saskatchewan*. Regina: Government House Historical Society / Canadian Plains Research Center, University of Regina, 1991.

Hubbard, Robert H. *Ample Mansions: The Viceregal Residences of the Canadian Provinces*. Ottawa: University of Ottawa Press, 1989.

—. *Rideau Hall: An Illustrated History of Government House, Ottawa*. Montreal and Kingston: McGill-Queen's University Press, 1977.

Hubbard, Ruth, and Gilles Paquet, eds. *The Case for Decentralized Federalism*. Ottawa: University of Ottawa Press, 2010.

Jackson, D. Michael. *The Crown and Canadian Federalism*. Toronto: Dundurn, 2013.

—, ed. *Honouring Commonwealth Citizens: Proceedings of the First Conference on Commonwealth Honours and Awards, Regina, 2006*. Toronto: Ontario Ministry of Citizenship and Immigration, 2007.

Jennings, Sir Ivor. *Constitutional Laws of the Commonwealth*. Oxford: Clarendon Press, 1952.

—. *The Law and the Constitution*. 5th ed. London: University of London Press, 1959.

Joyal, Serge. *Le Mythe de Napoléon au Canada français*. Montreal: Del Busso, 2013.

—, ed. *Protecting Canadian Democracy: The Senate You Never Knew*. Montreal and Kingston: McGill-Queen's University Press, for Canadian Centre for Management Development / Centre canadien de gestion, 2003, 2005.

Joyal, Serge, and Paul-André Linteau, eds. *France-Canada-Québec : 400 ans de relations d'exception*. Montreal : Presses de l'Université de Montréal, 2008.

Keith, Arthur Berriedale. *The Constitutional Law of the British Dominions*. London: Macmillan, 1933.

—. *The King and the Imperial Crown: The Powers and Duties of His Majesty*. London: Longmans, Green, 1936.

Kennedy, William Keith. *Lord Elgin*. London: Oxford University Press, 1926.

—. *The Sovereignty of the British Dominions*. London: Macmillan, 1929.

Lacey, Robert. *Majesty: Elizabeth II and the House of Windsor*. New York: Harcourt Brace Jovanovich, 1977.

—. *Royal: Her Majesty Queen Elizabeth II*. London: Little, Brown, 2002.

Latham, R. T. E. *The Law and the Commonwealth*. Oxford: Oxford University Press, 1949.

Léger, Jules. *Jules Léger: gouverneur-général du Canada, 1974–1979: Textes et réflexions sur le Canada / Jules Léger: Governor General of Canada, 1974–1979: A Selection of His Writings on Canada*. Montreal: Éditions de l'Hexagone, 1989.

Leigh, Wendy. *Edward Windsor: Royal Enigma. The True Story of the Seventh in Line to the British Throne*. New York: Simon & Schuster, 1999.

Lemieux, Frédéric, Christian Blais, and Pierre Hamelin. *L'histoire du Québec à travers ses lieutenants-gouverneurs*. Quebec: Les Publications du Québec, 2005.

Lennox, Doug. *Now You Know Royalty*. Toronto: Dundurn, 2009.

Lipset, Seymour Martin. *Continental Divide: The Values and Institutions of the United States and Canada*. New York: Routledge, 1990.

Lordon, Paul. *Crown Law*. Toronto: Butterworths, 1991.

Loughlin, Martin. *Foundations of Public Law*. Oxford: Oxford University Press, 2010.

—. *The Idea of Public Law*. Oxford: Oxford University Press, 2003.

Low, Anthony. *Constitutional Heads and Political Crises*. London: Macmillan, 1988.

Lownie, Andrew. *John Buchan: The Presbyterian Cavalier*. Toronto: McArthur & Company, 2004.

MacDonnell, Tom. *Daylight upon Magic: The Royal Tour of Canada – 1939*. Toronto: Macmillan, 1989.

MacKinnon, Frank. *The Crown in Canada*. Calgary: Glenbow Alberta Institute / McClelland & Stewart West, 1976.

MacMillan, Margaret, Marjorie Harris, and Anne L. Desjardins. *Canada's House: Rideau Hall and the Invention of a Canadian Home*. Toronto: Alfred A. Knopf Canada, 2004.

MacNutt, W. Stewart. *Days of Lorne: Impressions of a Governor General*. Fredericton: Brunswick Press, 1955.

Mallory, J. R. *The Structure of Government*. Rev. ed. Toronto: Gage, 1984.

Marshall, Geoffrey. *Constitutional Conventions: The Rules and Forms of Political Accountability*. Oxford: Oxford University Press, 1984.

Martin, Stanley. *The Order of Merit: One Hundred Years of Matchless Honour*. London: I. B. Tauris, 2007.

Massey, Vincent. *On Being Canadian*. Toronto: Dent, 1948.

—. *Speaking of Canada: Addresses by the Right Hon. Vincent Massey, C.H., Governor General of Canada, 1952–1959*. Toronto: Macmillan, 1959.

—. *What's Past Is Prologue: The Memoirs of Vincent Massey*. Toronto: Macmillan, 1963.

McCreery, Christopher. *The Canadian Forces' Decoration / La Décoration des Forces canadiennes*. Ottawa: Department of National Defence / Ministère de la Défense nationale, 2010.

—. *The Canadian Honours System*. Toronto: Dundurn, 2005.

—. *On Her Majesty's Service: Royal Honours and Recognition in Canada*. Toronto: Dundurn, 2008.

—. *The Order of Canada: Its Origins, History and Development*. Toronto: University of Toronto Press, 2005.

—. *The Order of Military Merit / L'Ordre du mérite militaire*. Ottawa: Department of National Defence / Ministère de la Défense nationale, 2012.

McKenna, Mark. *The Captive Republic: A History of Republicanism in Australia 1788–1996*. Melbourne: Cambridge University Press, 1996.

McWhinney, Edward. *The Governor General and the Prime Ministers: The Making and Unmaking of Governments*. Vancouver: Ronsdale Press, 2005.

Messamore, Barbara J. *Canada's Governors General, 1847–1878: Biography and Constitutional Evolution*. Toronto: University of Toronto Press, 2006.

Michelmann, Hans J., and Cristine de Clercy, eds. *Continuity and Change in Canadian Politics: Essays in Honour of David E. Smith*. Toronto: University of Toronto Press, 2006.

Miller, Carman. *The Canadian Career of the Fourth Earl of Minto: The Education of a Viceroy*. Waterloo: Wilfrid Laurier University Press, 1980.

Miller, J. R. *Compact, Contract, Covenant: Aboriginal Treaty-Making in Canada*. Toronto: University of Toronto Press, 2009.

Monahan, Patrick J., and Byron Shaw. *Constitutional Law*. 4th ed. Toronto: Irwin Law, 2013.

Monet, Jacques. *The Canadian Crown*. Toronto: Clarke Irwin, 1979.

—. *The Last Cannon Shot: A Study of French-Canadian Nationalism, 1837–1850*. Toronto: University of Toronto Press, 1969.

—. *La Monarchie au Canada*. Ottawa : Le Cercle du livre de France, 1979.

Morton, W. L. *The Canadian Identity*. Madison: University of Wisconsin Press; Toronto: University of Toronto Press, 1965.

—. *The Kingdom of Canada: A General History from Earliest Times*. Toronto: McClelland & Stewart, 1963.

Mowatt, Claire. *Pomp and Circumstances*. Toronto: McClelland & Stewart, 1992.

Munro, Kenneth. *The Maple Crown in Alberta: The Office of Lieutenant-Governor, 1905–2005*. Victoria: Trafford Publishing, 2005.

Noonan, James. *Canada's Governors General at Play: Culture and Rideau Hall from Monck to Grey, with an Afterword on Their Successors, Connaught to LeBlanc*. Ottawa: Borealis, 2002.

Noonan, Peter W. *The Crown and Constitutional Law in Canada*. Calgary: Sripnoon, 1998.

Nuendorff, Gwen. *Studies in the Evolution of Dominion Status. The Governor Generalship of Canada and the Development of Canadian Nationalism*. London: George Allen & Unwin, 1942.

Oliver, Peter. *The Constitution of Independence: The Development of Constitutional Theory in Australia, Canada, and New Zealand*. Oxford: Oxford University Press, 2005.

Olmsted, Richard A., ed. *Decisions of the Judicial Committee of the Privy Council relating to the British North America Act, 1867, and the Canadian Constitution, 1867–1954*. 3 vols. Ottawa: Queen's Printer, 1954.

Patmore, Glenn A. *Choosing the Republic*. Sydney: University of New South Wales, 2009.

Pike, Corinna A.W., and Christopher McCreery. *Canadian Symbols of Authority: Maces, Chains and Rods of Office*. Toronto: Dundurn, 2011.

Pimlott, Ben. *The Queen: A Biography of Elizabeth II*. London: HarperCollins, 1996.

Radforth, Ian. *Royal Spectacle: The 1860 Visit of the Prince of Wales to Canada*. Toronto: University of Toronto Press, 2004.

Romney, Paul. *Getting It Wrong: How Canadians Forgot Their Past and Imperilled Confederation*. Toronto: University of Toronto Press, 1999.

Russell, Peter H. *Constitutional Odyssey: Can Canadians Be a Sovereign People?* 3rd ed. Toronto: University of Toronto Press, 2004.

—. *Two Cheers for Minority Government: The Evolution of Canadian Parliamentary Democracy.* Toronto: Emond Montgomery Publications, 2008.

Russell, Peter H., and Cheryl Milne. *Adjusting to a New Era of Parliamentary Government: Report of a Workshop on Constitutional Conventions*. Toronto: David Asper Centre for Constitutional Rights, 2011.

Russell, Peter H., and Lorne Sossin, eds. *Parliamentary Democracy in Crisis.* Toronto: University of Toronto Press, 2009.

Saywell, John T. *The Lawmakers: Judicial Power and the Shaping of Canadian Federalism*. Toronto: University of Toronto Press, for Osgoode Hall Law Society, 2002.

—. *The Office of Lieutenant Governor: A Study in Canadian Government and Politics.* Toronto: University of Toronto Press, 1957; Rev. ed., Toronto: Copp Clark Pitman, 1986.

Segal, Hugh. *The Right Balance: Canada's Conservative Tradition.* Vancouver: Douglas & McIntyre, 2011.

Senior, Hereward, and Elinor Kyte Senior. *In Defence of Monarchy.* Toronto: Fealty Enterprises, 2009.

Seward, Ingrid. *Prince Edward: A Biography*. London: Century, 1995.

Shea, Kevin, and John Jason Wilson. *Lord Stanley: The Man behind the Cup*. Bolton, ON: Fenn Publishing, 2006.

Smith, David E. *Across the Aisle: Opposition in Canadian Politics.* Toronto: University of Toronto Press, 2013.

—. *The Canadian Senate in Bicameral Perspective*. Toronto: University of Toronto Press, 2003.

—. *Federalism and the Constitution of Canada*. Toronto: University of Toronto Press, 2010.

—. *The Invisible Crown: The First Principle of Canadian Government.* Toronto: University of Toronto Press, 1995. Reprinted with a new preface, University of Toronto Press, 2013.

—. *The People's House of Commons: Theories of Democracy in Contention.* Toronto: University of Toronto Press, 2007.

—. *The Republican Option in Canada, Past and Present*. Toronto: University of Toronto Press, 1999.

Smith, Goldwin. *Canada and the Canadian Question*. Toronto: Hunter Rose, 1891; new ed., edited by Carl Berger, University of Toronto Press, 1971.

Smith, Janet Adam. *John Buchan: A Biography*. Toronto: Little, Brown, 1965.

—. *John Buchan and His World.* London: Thames and Hudson, 1979.

Smith, Jennifer, and D. Michael Jackson, eds. *The Evolving Canadian Crown*. Montreal and Kingston: Institute of Intergovernmental Relations, School of Policy Studies, Queen's University, McGill-Queen's University Press, 2012.

Smith, Sir David. *Head of State: The Governor-General, the Monarchy, the Republic and the Dismissal*. Sydney: Macleay Press, 2005.

Speaight, Robert. *Vanier, Soldier, Diplomat and Governor General: A Biography*. Toronto: Collins, 1970.

Stamp, Robert M. *Kings, Queens and Canadians: A Celebration of Canada's Infatuation with the British Royal Family*. Toronto: Fitzhenry & Whiteside, 1987.

—. *Royal Rebels: Princess Louise & the Marquis of Lorne*. Toronto: Dundurn, 1988.

Stursburg, Peter. *Roland Michener: The Last Viceroy*. Toronto: McGraw-Hill Ryerson, 1989.

Sunkin, Maurice, and Sebastian Payne. *The Nature of the Crown: A Legal and Political Analysis*. New York: Oxford University Press, 1999.

Swan, Conrad. *Canada: Symbols of Sovereignty*. Toronto: University of Toronto Press, 1977.
—. *A King from Canada*. Stanhope, Durham, UK: The Memoir Club, 2005.
Tidridge, Nathan. *Canada's Constitutional Monarchy*. Toronto: Dundurn, 2011.
—. *Prince Edward, Duke of Kent: Father of the Canadian Crown*. Toronto: Dundurn, 2013.
Tizard, Catherine. *The Role of the Governor-General of New Zealand*. Wellington: Government House, 1977.
Trudel, Marcel. *Mythes et réalités dans l'histoire du Québec*. Vol. 1. Montreal: Éditions Hurtubise HMH, Cahiers du Québec, collection Histoire, 2001.
Twomey, Anne. *The Chameleon Crown: The Queen and Her Australian Governors*. Sydney: Federation Press, 2006.
Vance, Jonathan F. *A History of Canadian Culture*. Toronto: Oxford University Press, 2009.
—. *Maple Leaf Empire: Canada, Britain, and Two World Wars*. Toronto: Oxford University Press, 2012.
Vanier, Michel, and George Cowley, eds. *Only to Serve: Selections of Addresses by Governor General Georges P. Vanier*. Toronto: University of Toronto Press, 1970.
Vipond, Robert C. *Canadian Federalism and the Failure of the Constitution*. Albany: State University of New York Press, 1991.
Ward, Norman. *Dawson's Government of Canada*. Toronto: University of Toronto Press, 1987.
Weston, Hilary M. *No Ordinary Time: My Years as Ontario's Lieutenant-Governor*. Toronto: Whitfield Editions, 2007.
Wheare, Sir Kenneth. *The Constitutional Structure of the Commonwealth*. Oxford: Clarendon Press, 1960.
—. *The Statute of Westminster and Dominion Status*. 5th ed. London: Oxford University Press, 1953.
Williams, Jeffery. *Byng of Vimy: General and Governor General*. Toronto: University of Toronto Press, 1992.
Willis-O'Connor, H. *Inside Government House*. Toronto: Ryerson Press, 1954.
Winterton, George. *Monarchy to Republic*. Melbourne: Oxford University Press, 1986.
—. *Parliament, the Executive and the Governor-General*. Melbourne: Melbourne University Press, 1983.
Woods, Shirley E. *Her Excellency Jeanne Sauvé*. Toronto: Macmillan, 1986.

Educational Booklets

Aird, John Black. *Loyalty in a Changing World: The Contemporary Function of the Office of Lieutenant Governor of Ontario*. Toronto: Office of the Premier, 1985.
Canadian Honours and Awards Bestowed upon Members of the Canadian Forces / Distinctions honorifiques conférées aux membres des Forces canadiennes. Ottawa: Canadian Forces / Les Forces canadiennes, 2012 (annually).
Découvrir le Canada. Les droits et responsabilités liés à la citoyenneté. Guide d'étude. Ottawa: Ministre des Approvisionnements et Services Canada, 2011.
Discover Canada. The Rights and Responsibilities of Citizenship. Study Guide. Ottawa: Minister of Public Works and Government Services Canada, 2011.
Forsey, Eugene A. *Les Canadiens et leur système de gouvernement*. Septième édition. Ottawa: Ministre des Approvisionnements et Services Canada, 2010.

—. *How Canadians Govern Themselves*. 7th ed. Ottawa: Minister of Supply and Services Canada, 2010.

Jackson, D. Michael. *The Canadian Monarchy in Saskatchewan.* 2nd ed. Regina: Government of Saskatchewan, 1990.

—. *Images of a Province: Symbols of Saskatchewan / Images d'une province: les symboles de la Saskatchewan*. Regina: Government of Saskatchewan, 2002.

—. *Royal Saskatchewan: The Crown in a Canadian Province*. Regina: Government of Saskatchewan, 2007.

—. *La Saskatchewan royale: la Couronne dans une province canadienne.* Regina: Gouvernement de la Saskatchewan, 2007.

MacLeod, Kevin S. *La Couronne canadienne: La monarchie constitutionnelle au Canada*. Ottawa : Ministère du Patrimoine canadien, 2008. Nouvelle édition, 2012.

—. *A Crown of Maples: Constitutional Monarchy in Canada*. Ottawa: Department of Canadian Heritage, 2008. New edition, 2012.

Pomp & Circumstance: An Historical Celebration of Queen's Park. Toronto: Legislative Assembly of Ontario, 1984.

Silver Jubilee: Royal Visit to Canada, Six Days in the Life of the Queen. Ottawa: Deneau & Greenberg, 1977.

Stanley, George F. G. *The Role of the Lieutenant Governor / Le role du lieutenant-gouverneur.* Fredericton: Legislative Assembly of New Brunswick / Assemblée législative du Nouveau-Brunswick, 1992.

Symbols of Canada / Les symboles du Canada. Ottawa: Department of Canadian Heritage / Ministère du Patrimoine canadien, 2010.

Chapters in Books

Arnot, David. "We Are All Treaty People." In *Saskatchewan Politics: Crowding the Centre,* edited by Howard A. Leeson. Regina: Canadian Plains Research Center, University of Regina, 2009.

Bercuson, David J., and Barry Cooper. "From Constitutional Monarchy to Quasi Republic: The Evolution of Liberal Democracy in Canada." In *Canadian Constitutionalism, 1791–1991*, edited by Janet Ajzenstat. Ottawa: Canadian Study of Parliament Group, n.d. [1992].

Burke, Fred. "The Office of Lieutenant Governor." In *Provincial Government and Politics*, edited by Ronald C. Rowat. Ottawa: Carleton University, 1973.

Chevrier, Marc. "L'idée républicaine au Québec et au Canada français – les avatars d'une tradition cachée." In *L'idée républicaine dans le monde, XVIIIe / XXIe siècles.* Vol. 2. Edited by Paul Baquiast and Emmanuel Dupuy. Paris : L'Harmattan, 2007.

Galbraith, J. William. "John Buchan in Canada: Writing a New Chapter in Canada's Constitutional History." In *John Buchan and the Idea of Modernity*, edited by Kate Macdonald and Nathan Waddell. London: Pickering & Chatto, 2013.

Haverstock, Lynda M. "Bestowing Honours: The Other Side." In *Honouring Commonwealth Citizens: Proceedings of the First Conference on Commonwealth Honours and Awards, Regina, 2006,* edited by D. Michael Jackson. Toronto: Ontario Ministry of Citizenship and Immigration, 2007.

Hubbard, R. H. "Viceregal Influences on Canadian Society." In *The Shield of Achilles: Aspects of Canada in the Victorian Age,* edited by W. L. Morton. Toronto: McClelland & Stewart,1968.

Jackson, D. Michael. "The Crown in Saskatchewan: An Institution Renewed." In *Saskatchewan Politics: Crowding the Centre,* edited by Howard A. Leeson. Regina: Canadian Plains Research Center, University of Regina, 2009.

—. "Political Paradox: The Lieutenant Governor in Saskatchewan." In *Saskatchewan Politics: Into the Twenty-First Century,* edited by Howard A. Leeson. Regina: Canadian Plains Research Center, University of Regina, 2001.

Miller, J. R. "Petitioning the Great White Mother: First Nations' Organizations and Lobbying in London." In *Reflections on Native-Newcomer Relations: Selected Essays*. Toronto: University of Toronto Press, 2004.

Monet, Jacques. "La Couronne." In *Le Système parlementaire canadien,* edited by Manon Tremblay and Marcel Tremblay. Quebec : Les Presses de l'Université Laval, 1995.

—. "The Personal and Living Bond." In *The Shield of Achilles: Aspects of Canada in the Victorian Age,* edited by W. L. Morton. Toronto: McClelland & Stewart, 1968.

Morton, W. L. "Lord Monck, His Friends, and the Nationalizing of the British Empire." In *Character and Circumstance,* edited by John S. Moir. Toronto: Macmillan, 1970.

Murray, Lowell. "Which Criticisms Are Founded?" In *Protecting Canadian Democracy: The Senate You Never Knew,* edited by Serge Joyal. Montreal and Kingston: McGill-Queen's University Press, 2003, 2005.

Poelzer, Greg, and Ken Coates. "Aboriginal Peoples and the Crown in Canada: Completing the Canadian Experiment." In *Continuity and Change in Canadian Politics: Essays in Honour of David E. Smith,* edited by Hans J. Michelmann and Cristine de Clercy. Toronto: University of Toronto Press, 2006.

Rasmussen, Merrilee D. "Legislatures in Saskatchewan: A Battle for Sovereignty?" In *Saskatchewan Politics: Crowding the Centre,* edited by Howard A. Leeson. Regina: Canadian Plains Research Center, University of Regina, 2009.

Saywell, John T. "The Lieutenant-Governors." In *The Provincial Political System, Comparative Essays,* edited by David Bellamy, Jon Pammett, and David Rowat. Toronto: Methuen, 1976.

Smith, David E. "Saskatchewan and Canadian Federalism." In *Saskatchewan Politics: Into the Twenty-First Century,* edited by Howard A. Leeson. Regina: Canadian Plains Research Center, University of Regina, 2001.

Williams, John. "'The Blizzard and Oz': Canadian Influences on the Australian Constitution, Then and Now." In *Shaping Nations: Constitutionalism and Society in Australia and Canada,* edited by Linda Cardinal and David Heaton. Ottawa: University of Ottawa Press, 2002.

Articles

Aucoin, Peter, and Lori Turnbull. "Electoral Reform, Minority Government, and the Democratic Deficit: Removing the Virtual Right of First Ministers to Demand Dissolution." *Canadian Parliamentary Review* 27, no. 2 (2004).

Baker, Dennis. "'The Real Protection of the People': The Royal Recommendation and Responsible Government." *Journal of Parliamentary and Political Law* 4 (2010).

Banks, Margaret. "If the Queen Were to Abdicate: Procedure under Canada's Constitution." *Alberta Law Review* 28 (1990).

Benoit, Paul. "A Job for Mrs. Clarkson." *Policy Options* 20, no. 9 (1999).

—. "Parliament and Democracy in the 21st Century: The Crown and the Constitution." *Canadian Parliamentary Review* 25, no. 2 (2002).

—. "The Queen's Prerogatives." *The Literary Review of Canada* 5, no. 7 (1996).

—. "Remembering the Monarch." *Canadian Journal of Political Science* 15, no. 3 (1982).

Benoit, Paul, and Garry Toffoli. "More Is Needed to Change the Rules of Succession for Canada." *Canadian Parliamentary Review* 36, no. 2 (2013).

Boily, Frédéric. "La « crise de la prorogation » vue du Québec." *Constitutional Forum constitutionnel* 18, no. 1 (2009).

Bolt, Alexander. "The Crown Prerogative as Applied to Military Operations." Office of the Judge Advocate General, Strategic Legal Paper Series, Issue 2 (2008).

Bowden, James W. J., and Nicholas A. MacDonald. "Writing the Unwritten: The Officialization of Constitutional Conventions in Canada, the United Kingdom, New Zealand, and Australia." *Journal of Parliamentary and Political Law* 6, no. 1 (2012).

Boyce, Peter. "Review of *Head of State*." *Australian Journal of Public Administration* 6, no. 2 (2006).

Cairns, James. "Bringing Parliament to the People: A Meditated-Politics Approach to the Speech from the Throne." Paper prepared for Canadian Political Science Association meetings, University of Saskatchewan, May–June 2007.

Carter, Sarah. "'Your Great Mother across the Salt Sea': Prairie First Nations, the British Monarchy and the Vice-Regal Connection to 1900." *Manitoba History* 48 (2004–2005).

Cheffins, Ronald I. "The Royal Prerogative and the Office of Lieutenant Governor." *Canadian Parliamentary Review* 23, no. 1 (2000).

Chevrier, Marc. "La République néo-française." *Bulletin d'histoire politique* 17, no. 3 (2009).

Cox, Noel. "The Theory of Sovereignty and the Importance of the Crown in the Realms of the Queen." *Oxford University Commonwealth Law Journal* 2 (2002).

Craven, Greg. "The Developing Role of the Governor-General: The Goldenness of Silence." *Federal Law Review* 32, no. 2 (2004).

Davison, Charles B. "Prorogation: A Powerful Tool Forged by History." *Law Now* 34, no. 2 (2009).

Desserud, Donald Anton. "The Governor General, the Prime Minister and the Request to Prorogue." *Canadian Political Science Review* 3, no. 3 (2009).

Forsey, Eugene A. "The Crown and the Constitution." *Dalhousie Review* (Spring 1953).

—. "The Role of the Crown in Canada since Confederation." *The Parliamentarian* 60, no. 1 (1979).

Freeman, Damien. "The Queen and Her Dominion Successors: The Law of Succession to the Throne in Australia and the Commonwealth of Nations." *Constitutional Law and Policy Review* 4, no. 28 (2001).

Gagnon-Guimond, Renée. "Leurs Majestés au Québec : la visite royale de 1939." *La Revue d'histoire du Québec* 5, no. 4 (1990).

Galbraith, J. William. "Fiftieth Anniversary of the 1939 Royal Visit." *Canadian Parliamentary Review* 12, no. 3 (1989).

Guly, Christopher. "The Perils of Prorogation." *The Lawyer's Weekly* 29, no. 6 (2010).

Hawkins, Robert E. "'The Monarch Is Dead; Long Live the Monarch': Canada's Assent to Amending the Rules of Succession." *Journal of Parliamentary and Political Law* 7, no. 3 (2013).

Heard, Andrew. "The Governor General's Decision to Prorogue Parliament: A Chronology and Assessment." *Constitutional Forum constitutionnel* 18, no. 1 (2009).

Heintzman, Ralph. "The Meaning of Monarchy." *Journal of Canadian Studies / Revue d'études canadiennes* 12, no. 2 (1977).

Henderson, James (Sákéj) Youngblood. "The Perspectives of Aboriginal Peoples of Canada on the Monarchy: Reflections on the Occasion of the Queen's Golden Jubilee." *Constitutional Forum constitutionnel* 13 (2003).

Hicks, Bruce. "British and Canadian Experience with the Royal Prerogative." *Canadian Parliamentary Review* 33, no. 2 (2010).

—. "The Crown's 'Democratic' Reserve Powers." *Journal of Canadian Studies / Revue d'études canadiennes* 44, no. 2 (2010).

—. "Guiding the Governor General's Prerogatives: Constitutional Convention versus an Apolitical Decision Rule." *Constitutional Forum constitutionnel* 18, no. 2 (2009).

—. "Lies My Fathers of Confederation Told Me: Are the Governor General's Reserve Powers a Safeguard of Democracy?" *Inroads* 25 (2009).

Hogg, Peter. "The 2008 Constitutional Crisis: Prorogation and the Power of the Governor General." *National Journal of Constitutional Law* 27 (2010).

Hurley, James Ross. "The Royal Prerogative and the Office of Lieutenant Governor: A Comment." *Canadian Parliamentary Review* 23, no. 2 (2000).

Jackson, D. Michael. "The Development of Saskatchewan Honours." Research paper for the Senior Management Development Program, Saskatchewan Public Service Commission, 1990.

—. "How the Monarchy Protects Canadian Values." *Canadian Speeches: Issues of the Day* 9, no. 2 (1995).

Kirk-Greene, and H. M. Anthony. "The Governors-General of Canada, 1867–1952: A Collective Profile." *Journal of Canadian Studies / Revue d'études canadiennes* 12, no. 4 (1977).

Kong, Hoi. "Towards a Civic Republican Theory of Canadian Constitutional Law." *Review of Constitutional Studies* 15 (2011).

Lagassé, Philippe. "Accountability for National Defence: Ministerial Responsibility, Military Command and Parliamentary Oversight." *IRPP Study*, no. 4 (2010).

—. "The Crown's Powers of Command-in-Chief: Interpreting Section 15 of Canada's Constitution Act, 1867." *Review of Constitutional Studies* 18, no. 2 (2013).

—. "Parliamentary and Judicial Ambivalence toward Executive Prerogative Powers in Canada." *Canadian Public Administration / Administration publique du Canada* 55, no. 2 (2012).

Lovewell, Mark. "The Inconvenient Crown." *Literary Review of Canada* 20, no. 5 (2012).

MacDonald, Nicholas A., and James W. J. Bowden. "The Manual of Official Procedure of the Government of Canada: An Exposé." *Constitutional Forum constitutionnel* 20, no. 1 (2011).

—. "No Discretion: On Prorogation and the Governor General." *Canadian Parliamentary Review* 34, no. 1 (2011).

Mallory, J. R. "The Appointment of the Governor General: Responsible Government, Autonomy and the Royal Prerogative." *Canadian Journal of Economics and Political Science* 26, no. 1 (1960).

—. "The Lieutenant Governor's Discretionary Powers." *Canadian Journal of Economics and Political Science* 27 (1961).

Malloy, Jonathan. "The Executive and Parliament in Canada." *Journal of Legislative Studies* 10, no. 2/3 (2004).

McWhinney, Edward. "The Constitutional and Political Aspects of the Office of the Governor General." *Canadian Parliamentary Review* 32, no. 2 (2009).

—. "Constitutional Guidelines for a Governor General in Minority Government Situations." *Canadian Parliamentary Review* 29, no. 3 (2006).

—. "Fixed Election Dates and the Governor General's Power to Grant Dissolution." *Canadian Parliamentary Review* 31, no. 1 (2008).

—. "'The Line Over Which He Must Not Pass': Defining the Office of Governor General, 1878." *Canadian Historical Review* 86, no. 3 (2005).

—. "'On a Razor Edge': The Canadian Governors-General, 1888–1911." *British Journal of Canadian Studies* 13, no. 2 (1998).

Messamore, Barbara J. "Conventions of the Role of the Governor General: Some Illustrative Historical Episodes." *Journal of Parliamentary and Political Law* 4 (2010).

Milliken, Peter. "Appropriation Acts and Governor General's Warrants." *Canadian Parliamentary Review* 13, no. 2 (1990).

Monet, Jacques. "La Couronne du Canada." *Journal of Canadian Studies / Revue d'études canadiennes* 11, no. 4 (1976).

Moore, Christopher. "Maple Leaf Crown." *Canada's History* [formerly *The Beaver*], (June–July 2012).

Morrison, Katherine L. "The Only Canadians: Canada's French and the British Connection." *International Journal of Canadian Studies / Revue internationale d'études canadiennes* 37 (2008).

Munro, Kenneth. "Canada as Reflected in Her Participation in the Coronation of Monarchs in the Twentieth Century." *Journal of Historical Sociology* 14, no.1 (2001).

—. "The Turmoil Surrounding the Prorogation of Canada's 40th Parliament and the Crown." *Constitutional Forum constitutionnel* 18, no. 1 (2009).

Neary, Peter. "Confidence: How Much Is Enough?" *Constitutional Forum constitutionnel* 18, no. 1 (2009).

—. "The Morning after a General Election: The Vice-Regal Perspective." *Canadian Parliamentary Review* 35, no. 3 (2012).

Neitsch, Alfred Thomas. "A Tradition of Vigilance: The Role of Lieutenant Governor in Alberta." *Canadian Parliamentary Review* 30, no. 4 (2007).

Nicholson, Rob. "Changing the Line of Succession to the Crown." *Canadian Parliamentary Review* 36, no. 2 (2013).

O'Connell, D. P. "Canada, Australia, Constitutional Reform and the Crown." *The Parliamentarian* 60, no. 1 (1979).

O'Donnell, Dan. "Lord Lisgar: From Governor of New South Wales to Governor-General of Canada." *Journal of the Royal Australian Historical Society* 76 (1991).

Patmore, Glenn A. "Choosing the Republic: The Legal and Constitutional Steps in Canada." *Queen's Law Journal* 32, no. 2 (2006).

Patmore, Glenn A., and John D. Whyte. "Imagining Constitutional Crises: Power and (Mis)behaviour in Republican Australia." *Federal Law Review* 25 (1997).

Poole, Thomas. "Judicial Review at the Margins: Law, Power, and Prerogative." *University of Toronto Law Journal* 60, no. 1 (2010).

Roberts, Edward. "Ensuring Constitutional Wisdom during Unconventional Times." *Canadian Parliamentary Review* 32, no. 1 (2009).

Russell, Peter H. "Discretion and the Reserve Powers of the Crown." *Canadian Parliamentary Review* 34, no. 2 (2011).

—. "Principles, Rules and Practices of Parliamentary Government: Time for a Written Constitution." *Journal of Parliamentary and Political Law* 6, no. 2 (2012).

Sharp, Mitchell. "Depoliticizing the Speech from the Throne." *Parliamentary Government* 8, no. 4 (1989).

Smith, David E. "Bagehot, the Crown and Canadian Constitutionalism." *Canadian Journal of Political Science* 28, no. 4 (1995).

—. "Empire, Crown and Canadian Federalism." *Canadian Journal of Political Science* 24, no. 3 (1991).

—. "Queen Elizabeth II and Canada: Fifty Years On." *The Beaver* (February–March 2002).

—. "Republican Tendencies." *Policy Options / Options politiques* 20, no. 4 (1999).

—. "Republics, Monarchies and Old Dominions." *Canadian Parliamentary Review* 20, no. 4 (1997–1998).

—. "Re: The Royal Prerogative and the Office of Governor General." *Canadian Parliamentary Review* 23, no. 3 (2000).

Sossin, Lorne. "The Rule of Law and the Justiciability of Prerogative Powers: A Comment on Black v. Chrétien." *McGill Law Journal* 47 (2002).

Stacey, C. P. "Lord Monck and the Canadian Nation." *Dalhousie Review* 14 (1934).

Stilborn, Jack. "The Role of the Governor General: Time to Revisit the Visits." *Policy Options* 30, no. 7 (2009).

Studin, Irvin. "Constitution and Strategy: Understanding Canadian Power in the World." *National Journal of Constitutional Law* 28, no. 1 (2010).

Thompson, Robert W. "Canada, Secularity and a Constitutional Monarchy." *National Journal of Constitutional Law* 18 (2005/2006).

Tremblay, Guy. "Limiting the Government's Power to Prorogue Parliament." *Canadian Parliamentary Review* 33, no. 2 (2010).

Twomey, Anne. "Changing the Rules of Succession to the Throne." *Public Law* (April 2011).

—. "The Governor-General's Role in the Formation of Government in a Hung Parliament." *Public Law Review* 22, no. 1 (2011).

—. "The Royal Succession and the De-patriation of the Canadian Constitution." *Constitutional Critique* (blog), February 4, 2013. http://blogs.usyd.edu.au/cru/2013/02/the_royal_succession_and_the_d.html.

Whitelaw, William Menzies. "Lord Monck and the Canadian Constitution." *Canadian Historical Review* 21 (1940).

—. "Responsible Government and the Irresponsible Governor." *Canadian Historical Review* 13 (1932).

Whyte, John D. "The Australian Republican Movement and Its Implications for Canada." *Constitutional Forum constitutionnel* 4, no. 3 (1993).

Theses

Boisvert, Étienne. "La monarchie britannique, une institution populaire: Dieu et mon droit… et l'opinion publique?" MA thesis, Université de Sherbrooke, 2012.

Henry, Wade A. "Royal Representation, Ceremony, and Cultural Identity in the Building of the Canadian Nation, 1860–1911." PhD diss., University of British Columbia, 2001.

Palmer, Sean. "The Ramifications of Sharing a Head of State: A Study in the Implications of a Structure." PhD diss., Auckland University of Technology, 2010.

Rasmussen, Merrilee D. "The Decline of Parliamentary Democracy in Saskatchewan." MA thesis, University of Regina, 1994.

Wilcox, Victoria M. "Prime Minister and Governor-General: Mackenzie King and Lord Tweedsmuir, 1935–1940." MA thesis, Queen's University, 1976.

Court Rulings

D. Michael Jackson and Philippe Lagassé*

Major court decisions related to the Crown in Canada

***Church v. Blake* (1875) 1 Q.L.R. 177**

Justice Taschereau ruled in Quebec Superior Court that the prerogative of escheats (the right of the government to receive estates of the intestate) did not belong to the provincial Crown: "…ces droits appartiennent au souverain. Or, sous notre constitution, la souveraintè est à Ottawa. Il n'y a que là que Sa Majesté soit directement représentée." However, this ruling was overturned by the Quebec Court of Queen's Bench in 1876, holding that escheats fell within provincial jurisdiction.

***Lenoir v. Ritchie* (1879) 3 S.C.R. 575**

Hearing an appeal on precedence of provincially-appointed Queen's Counsel, the Supreme Court of Canada declared that Nova Scotia legislation providing for the appointment of Queen's Counsel was ultra vires "because the lieutenant-governor had no right to exercise, nor the legislature to confer, this prerogative power." The provinces were thus "royally demoted."[1] (But see *Liquidators of the Maritime Bank v. The Receiver General of New Brunswick, infra.*)

***Mercer v. Attorney General for Ontario* (1881) 5 S.C.R. 538**

With Justice Taschereau appointed to the Supreme Court of Canada in 1875, the composition of the Court had changed. In this case, involving an intestate estate, a majority of the Court held that while escheats were a part of the royal prerogative, the provincial government, through the office of the lieutenant governor, could have no claim on them.

*The editors acknowledge the assistance of John D. Whyte in preparing this summary.

---

[1] Robert C. Vipond, *Liberty and Community: Canadian Federalism and the Failure of the Constitution* (Albany: State University of New York Press, 1991), 66, 68.

***Russell v. The Queen* (New Brunswick) (1882) UKPC 33**

William Russell appealed his conviction under the Canada Temperance Act. The Judicial Committee of the Privy Council upheld the federal statute on the ground of Parliament's residual jurisdiction to legislate for "peace, order and good government" when the subject of legislation did not clearly fall within provincial heads of power, even if it might bear on provincial jurisdictions. (In later cases, some judges sought to limit the significance of *Russell* and the scope of residual federal jurisdiction through claiming that the federal temperance legislation was held to be valid only because it was enacted in the context of a national emergency relating to alcohol usage.)

***Hodge v. The Queen* (Canada) (1883) UKPC 59**

Archibald Hodge challenged his conviction under an Ontario liquor statute. The Judicial Committee of the Privy Council upheld Ontario's right to administer its own liquor licensing system as a matter of property and civil rights in the province. The implication of this decision was that there can be concurrent federal and provincial legislation when a regulatory subject matter has two primary aspects. Equally significant was the decision that the provincial legislature was not a mere delegated authority but held direct legislative powers under the 1867 Constitution. The Judicial Committee identified provincial legislatures as co-sovereign legislative bodies and affirmed the constitutional doctrine of coordinate federalism.

***The Queen v. Bank of Nova Scotia* (1885) 11 S.C.R. 1**

In *The Queen v. Bank of Nova Scotia*, the Supreme Court of Canada determined that in bankruptcies the Crown had preference over other creditors as a matter of Crown prerogative, but this entitlement inhered only in the federal, not the provincial, Crown.

***Liquidators of the Maritime Bank v. The Receiver General of New Brunswick* [1892] A.C. 437**

Liquidators revisited the question of the Crown's precedence over other creditors. Lord Watson, for the Judicial Committee of the Privy Council, dismissed the argument that Confederation had severed the connection between the Crown and the provinces. He ruled that the provincial Crown retained precedence over other creditors on the basis of its loan being "a Crown debt," since "a Lieutenant-Governor, when appointed, is as much a representative of Her Majesty for all purposes of provincial government as the Governor General himself is for all purposes of Dominion government." He stated that "the object of the [British North America] Act was neither to weld the provinces into one, nor to subordinate provincial governments to a central authority, but to create a federal government in which they should all be represented, entrusted with the exclusive administration of affairs in which they had a common interest, each province *retaining* its independence and autonomy."

***Attorney-General for Canada v. Attorney-General for Ontario* [1898] A.C. 247**

Lord Watson, for the Judicial Committee of the Privy Council, confirmed that the prerogatives of the provincial Crown included the right to appoint Queen's Counsel, as had been asserted by Ontario and Nova Scotia since *Lenoir v. Ritchie*.

***Bonanza Creek Gold Mining Co. v. The King* (1916) 1 A.C. 566**

In *Bonanza Creek*, Viscount Haldane ruled for the Judicial Committee of the Privy Council that an Ontario company incorporated under letters patent issued by the lieutenant governor had the status and capacity of a natural person and could, therefore, take out mining leases in the Yukon.

***Re Initiative and Referendum Act* [1919] A.C. 935, 49 D.L.R. 18 (P.C.)**

The Manitoba act in question provided for legislation to be adopted and put into effect by popular referendum, as well as through the regular legislative process. It was held by the Judicial Committee of the Privy Council to be unconstitutional because it interfered with the lieutenant governor's constitutional role in granting royal assent and therefore amended the provincial vice-regal office enshrined in section 92(1) of the British North America Act. Lord Haldane referred to the position of the lieutenant governor "as directly representing the Sovereign in the province."

***A.G. v. De Keyser's Royal Hotel Ltd.* (1920) A.C. 508 (H.L.)**

De Keyser is a British case, still routinely cited by Canadian courts in cases involving prerogative powers, which held that governments must act with statutory authority when a statute and prerogative occupy the same legal ground. The case reaffirmed the supremacy of Parliament and statute over the Crown and its prerogatives in the United Kingdom.

***Toronto Electric Commissioners v. Snider* [1925] UKPC 2**

In *Snider*, the Judicial Committee of the Privy Council held federal industrial relations legislation to be ultra vires because the legislation interfered with provincial jurisdiction over "property and civil rights in the province," which includes the regulation of contracts of employment. The Committee found there to be no emergency with respect to industrial relations that would warrant federal interference with a matter under provincial jurisdiction. In his opinion for the Committee, Lord Haldane said that the provinces were "in a sense like independent kingdoms with very little Dominion control over them" and "should be autonomous places as if they were autonomous kingdoms."

***Reference re a Resolution to Amend the Constitution* [1981] 1 S.C.R. 753**

In the *Patriation Reference*, the Supreme Court of Canada noted that the constitutional order is expressed through both constitutional laws and constitutional conventions. Conventions are governmental practices that are repeated over time in like circumstances and that reflect norms necessary to the sensible operation of the relationship between the constitutional elements of the state. Conventions can be more significant to constitutional integrity than some constitutional laws, but they are not enforced by the courts. In this reference case, the Supreme Court of Canada identified conventions relating to constitutional amendment without issuing any orders directing compliance.

***The Queen v. The Secretary of State for Foreign and Commonwealth Affairs* [1981] 4 C.N.L.R.**

In an appeal from the denial of an application made by three First Nations organizations, Lord Denning of the English Court of Appeal stated that "it was recognized that, as a result of constitutional practice, the Crown was no longer indivisible. [...] As a result, the obligations of the Crown under the Royal Proclamation [of 1763] and the Indian treaties became the obligations of the Crown in respect of Canada." Lord Justice May added, "In matters of law and government the Queen of the United Kingdom is entirely independent and distinct from the Queen of Canada."

***Guerin v. The Queen* [1984] 2 S.C.R. 335**

The Supreme Court of Canada held that the federal Crown holds a fiduciary duty to First Nations' interests that goes beyond legal technicalities and contractual language and rules. This duty rests on the Royal Proclamation of 1763 and that document's creation of a duty on the Crown to conduct dealings with First Nations to prevent exploitation and pursue the best interests of "Indians." The court stated that Aboriginal oral tradition carried great weight in interpreting this duty.

***Operation Dismantle v. The Queen* [1985] 1 S.C.R. 441**

In *Dismantle*, the Supreme Court of Canada considered whether the Canadian government's decision to allow American cruise missile testing in Canada violated the "right to life, liberty, and security of the person" in section 7 of the Charter of Rights and Freedoms. Although the Court found that there was no rights violation in this case, the justices held that Crown prerogatives on which diplomatic relations with foreign nations are based were susceptible to judicial review (and judicial remedy) if the exercise of this prerogative power, or any other act of the executive founded on Crown prerogative, violated constitutional law.

Alberta Government Telephones v. Canada **[1989] 2 S.C.R. 225**
As part of its ruling on whether Alberta Government Telephones, as an agent of the provincial Crown, was immune from federal regulatory jurisdiction over interconnecting works, the Supreme Court noted that the federal legislation did not purport to bind the provincial Crown. The Court endorsed the requirement that an intention to bind the Crown in right of Canada, or of a province, must be clearly expressed in the legislation.

M. v. Home Office **[1994] 1 A.C. 377**
M. v. Home Office is a British case that affirmed that the Crown's immunity from injunctions does not extend to ministers or other Crown servants acting in their official capacity. Lord Templeman noted that "judges cannot enforce the law against the Crown as Monarch because the Crown as Monarch can do no wrong, but judges enforce the law against the Crown as executive and against the individuals who from time to time represent the Crown."

Roach v. Canada **(Minister of State for Multiculturalism and Citizenship) (C.A.) [1994] 2 F.C. 406**
The federal Court of Appeal considered whether requiring candidates for citizenship to swear an oath to the Queen violated candidates' Charter rights to espouse republicanism. The appeal was dismissed on the basis that, as long as Canada is a constitutional monarchy with the Sovereign as its head of state, requiring the swearing of an oath to the Queen accords with the Constitution's fundamental structure and confirms candidates' acceptance of (although not necessarily agreement with) that basic structure.

Delgamuukw v. British Columbia **[1997] 3 S.C.R. 1010**
In *Delgamuukw* the Supreme Court of Canada gave clearer scope to claims for Aboriginal title and Aboriginal rights. These two claims are distinct but related. Aboriginal title arises at the time Crown sovereignty is asserted over land and becomes a legal burden on the Crown's title. Aboriginal occupation is enough to establish title, and proof of specific continued uses of territory is not required. Aboriginal rights may be infringed by governments but only when there is a compelling reason to do so and the infringement is consistent with the fiduciary relationship between the Crown and Aboriginal peoples. This case both recognized a robust idea of Aboriginal title and confirmed the consultation and compensatory elements of meeting the fiduciary duty of the Crown.

Reference re Remuneration of Judges **[1997] 3 S.C.R. 3**
The Supreme Court of Canada identified constitutional principles derived from the Constitution's preamble and from purposes implied by other

constitutional provisions. These principles related to the independence of judges and served as the basis for the Court's requirements with respect to relations between provincial governments and provincial courts.

***Reference re Secession of Quebec* [1998] 2 S.C.R. 217**

In the *Secession Reference,* the Supreme Court of Canada identified principles on the basis of the written constitutional text. "These principles inform and sustain the constitutional text; they are vital unstated assumptions upon which it is based."[2] From these principles, the Court articulated the constitutional requirements that relate to an initiative taken by a province to secede from Canada.

***R. v. Marshall (No. 1)* [1999] 3 S.C.R. 456**

The Supreme Court of Canada made clear that "the Honour of the Crown is always at stake in its dealings with Aboriginal people [...] Interpretations of treaties and statutory provisions which have an impact upon treaty or Aboriginal rights must be approached in a manner which maintains the integrity of the Crown." This principle was applied in the interpretation of a 1760 treaty, thereby protecting a Mi'kmaq right to harvest eels.

***Campbell v. British Columbia* (2000) B.C.S.C. 1123**

The Supreme Court of British Columbia upheld the recognition in the Nisga'a treaty of Aboriginal rights, including the right of self-government. That treaty recognized Nisga'a jurisdiction to make laws. The court held that provincial legislation implementing this recognition did not violate constitutional provisions relating to the head of state or the legislative powers of the federal and provincial governments. Constitutional recognition of Aboriginal rights includes the capacity to exercise governmental powers outside structures of government expressly set out in the Constitution Act, 1867.

***Black v. Chrétien (Prime Minister)* [2001] 54 O.R. (3d) 215, 199 D.L.R. (4th) 228 (C.A.)**

The Ontario Court of Appeal ruled that the prime minister's exercise of the prerogative power with respect to relations between states to deny a Canadian citizen—Conrad Black—a British peerage was not subject to judicial review. Executive prerogatives exercised by prime ministers should be approached with a degree of deference by the courts, especially when their use does not violate the Constitution.

---

[2] Brian Slattery, "Why the Governor General Matters," in *Parliamentary Democracy in Crisis,* ed. Peter H. Russell and Lorne Sossin (Toronto: University of Toronto Press, 2009), 83.

***Ross River Dena Council Band v. Canada* SCC 54 [2002] 2 S.C.R. 816**
In *Ross River*, the Supreme Court of Canada found that the prerogative power to create First Nations reserves had been displaced by the Indian Act by necessary implication. The case helped refine the conditions for determining whether a prerogative power has been displaced by necessary implication of legislative provisions.

***O'Donohue v. Canada, 2003* CanLII 41404 (ON SC)**
In *O'Donohue*, the Ontario Superior Court considered whether the provisions of the Act of Settlement, 1701 relating to monarchical succession violate the protection of equality in section 15(1) of the Canadian Charter of Rights and Freedoms. The court held that a principle of symmetry and union exists with respect to the Canadian monarch, so that the Canadian monarch is identified as the same person as the United Kingdom monarch. This principle is an element of Canadian constitutional law and, therefore, should not be interrupted by the operation of the Charter of Rights.

***Haida Nation v. British Columbia (Minister of Forests),* [2004] 3 S.C.R. 511, 2044 SCC 73**
In *Haida*, the Supreme Court of Canada found that the honour of the Crown toward First Nations must be "understood generously" and that it imposes a duty on governments to "consult with Aboriginal peoples and accommodate their interests" when undertaking actions that might affect Aboriginal right or title. However, the Court specified that "the Crown is not under a duty to reach an agreement; rather, the commitment is to a meaningful process of consultation in good faith." The scope and duties surrounding the honour of the Crown toward First Nations have been further specified by the Supreme Court in the cases of *Mikisew Cree First Nation v. Canada (Minister of Canadian Heritage)* (2005) 3 S.C.R. 388 and *Manitoba Métis Federation Inc. v. Canada (Attorney General)* 2013 SCC 14.

***Chainnigh v. Attorney General of Canada,* 2008 FC 69**
Chainnigh addressed the obligation of military officers to honour and swear allegiance to the Queen in Canada. In dismissing the application for judicial review of this obligation, the Federal Court of Canada outlined the nature of the relationship between the Sovereign and armed forces, and found that oaths to the Queen flow from her position within the military command structure as the fount of military command authority. The oath of allegiance to the commander is a suitable military condition.

***Conacher v. Canada (Prime Minister)* 2009 FC 920 [2010] 3 F.C.R. 411**
In *Conacher* the Federal Court examined whether an amendment to the Canada Elections Act (setting fixed election dates) established a convention or other restraint that would unconstitutionally limit the prime minister's discretion with respect to advising the governor general to dissolve

Parliament. The Federal Court found that the legislation did not impair the prime minister's discretion to advise that Parliament be dissolved.

***Canada (Prime Minister) v. Khadr*, 2010 SCC 3, [2010] 1 S.C.R. 44**
In *Khadr*, the Supreme Court of Canada ruled unanimously that, although the federal government had been a party to a violation of the appellant's Charter right to being treated according to fair procedures while being held in a foreign jail, the specific remedy sought against the government could not be ordered since that remedy would entail interference with the government's prerogative powers with respect to the conduct of relations between states. The Court found that this prerogative power had not been supplanted by legislation governing the Department of Foreign Affairs and International Trade and, therefore, that actions taken or not taken with other states are not amenable to the normal judicial supervision of the exercise of statutory powers. The principle of subjecting exercises of prerogative powers to constitutional standards is affirmed in this case, but judicial remedies must operate within the constraint that the exercise of prerogative powers cannot be judicially prescribed.

***McAteer et al. v. Attorney General of Canada*, 2013 ONSC 5895**
In *McAteer*, the Ontario Superior Court of Justice was asked to consider whether swearing an oath to the Queen of Canada in order to obtain Canadian citizenship violated the applicants' rights under the Charter of Rights and Freedoms. In this ruling, Morgan J. found that the citizenship oath constituted a type of compelled expression, but that it was justified under section 1 of the Charter. As part of his ruling, Morgan J. made several significant observations about the Sovereign's role in Canada. He noted that the "Crown sits at the sovereign apex of the legal and political system" and that in swearing an oath to the Queen, new citizens were expressing their loyalty toward "the institution of the state that she represents." More precisely, he argued that "the oath to the Queen is in fact an oath to a domestic institution that represents egalitarian governance and the rule of law."

Queen's Policy Studies
Recent Publications

The Queen's Policy Studies Series is dedicated to the exploration of major public policy issues that confront governments and society in Canada and other nations.

Manuscript submission. We are pleased to consider new book proposals and manuscripts. Preliminary inquiries are welcome. A subvention is normally required for the publication of an academic book. Please direct questions or proposals to the Publications Unit by email at spspress@queensu.ca, or visit our website at: www.queensu.ca/sps/books, or contact us by phone at (613) 533-2192.

Our books are available from good bookstores everywhere, including the Queen's University bookstore (http://www.campusbookstore.com/). McGill-Queen's University Press is the exclusive world representative and distributor of books in the series. A full catalogue and ordering information may be found on their web site (**http://mqup.mcgill.ca/**).

For more information about new and backlist titles from Queen's Policy Studies, visit http://www.queensu.ca/sps/books.

School of Policy Studies

Building More Effective Labour-Management Relationships, Richard P. Chaykowski and Robert S. Hickey (eds.) 2013. ISBN 978-1-55339-306-1

Navigationg on the Titanic: Economic Growth, Energy, and the Failure of Governance, Bryne Purchase 2013. ISBN 978-1-55339-330-6

Measuring the Value of a Postsecondary Education, Ken Norrie and Mary Catharine Lennon (eds.) 2013. ISBN 978-1-55339-325-2

Immigration, Integration, and Inclusion in Ontario Cities, Caroline Andrew, John Biles, Meyer Burstein, Victoria M. Esses, and Erin Tolley (eds.) 2012. ISBN 978-1-55339-292-7

Diverse Nations, Diverse Responses: Approaches to Social Cohesion in Immigrant Societies, Paul Spoonley and Erin Tolley (eds.) 2012. ISBN 978-1-55339-309-2

Making EI Work: Research from the Mowat Centre Employment Insurance Task Force, Keith Banting and Jon Medow (eds.) 2012. ISBN 978-1-55339-323-8

Managing Immigration and Diversity in Canada: A Transatlantic Dialogue in the New Age of Migration, Dan Rodríguez-García (ed.) 2012. ISBN 978-1-55339-289-7

International Perspectives: Integration and Inclusion, James Frideres and John Biles (eds.) 2012. ISBN 978-1-55339-317-7

Dynamic Negotiations: Teacher Labour Relations in Canadian Elementary and Secondary Education, Sara Slinn and Arthur Sweetman (eds.) 2012. ISBN 978-1-55339-304-7

Where to from Here? Keeping Medicare Sustainable, Stephen Duckett 2012. ISBN 978-1-55339-318-4

International Migration in Uncertain Times, John Nieuwenhuysen, Howard Duncan, and Stine Neerup (eds.) 2012. ISBN 978-1-55339-308-5

Life After Forty: Official Languages Policy in Canada/Après quarante ans, les politiques de langue officielle au Canada, Jack Jedwab and Rodrigue Landry (eds.) 2011. ISBN 978-1-55339-279-8

From Innovation to Transformation: Moving up the Curve in Ontario Healthcare, Hon. Elinor Caplan, Dr. Tom Bigda-Peyton, Maia MacNiven, and Sandy Sheahan 2011. ISBN 978-1-55339-315-3

Academic Reform: Policy Options for Improving the Quality and Cost-Effectiveness of Undergraduate Education in Ontario, Ian D. Clark, David Trick, and Richard Van Loon 2011. ISBN 978-1-55339-310-8

Integration and Inclusion of Newcomers and Minorities across Canada, John Biles, Meyer Burstein, James Frideres, Erin Tolley, and Robert Vineberg (eds.) 2011. ISBN 978-1-55339-290-3

A New Synthesis of Public Administration: Serving in the 21st Century, Jocelyne Bourgon, 2011. ISBN 978-1-55339-312-2 (paper) 978-1-55339-313-9 (cloth)

Recreating Canada: Essays in Honour of Paul Weiler, Randall Morck (ed.), 2011. ISBN 978-1-55339-273-6

Data Data Everywhere: Access and Accountability? Colleen M. Flood (ed.), 2011. ISBN 978-1-55339-236-1

Making the Case: Using Case Studies for Teaching and Knowledge Management in Public Administration, Andrew Graham, 2011. ISBN 978-1-55339-302-3

Centre for International and Defence Policy

Afghanistan in the Balance: Counterinsurgency, Comprehensive Approach, and Political Order, Hans-Georg Ehrhart, Sven Bernhard Gareis, and Charles Pentland (eds.), 2012. ISBN 978-1-55339-353-5

Security Operations in the 21st Century: Canadian Perspectives on the Comprehensive Approach, Michael Rostek and Peter Gizewski (eds.), 2011. ISBN 978-1-55339-351-1

Institute of Intergovernmental Relations

Paradigm Freeze: Why It Is So Hard to Reform Health-Care Policy in Canada, Harvey Lazar, John N. Lavis, Pierre-Gerlier Forest, and John Church (eds.), 2013. ISBN 978-1-55339-324-5

Canada: The State of the Federation 2010, Matthew Medelsohn, Joshua Hjartarson, and James Pearce (eds.), 2013. ISBN 978-1-55339-200-2

The Democratic Dilemma: Reforming Canada's Supreme Court, Nadia Verrelli (ed.), 2013. ISBN 978-1-55339-203-3

The Evolving Canadian Crown, Jennifer Smith and D. Michael Jackson (eds.), 2011. ISBN 978-1-55339-202-6

The Federal Idea: Essays in Honour of Ronald L. Watts, Thomas J. Courchene, John R. Allan, Christian Leuprecht, and Nadia Verrelli (eds.), 2011. ISBN 978-1-55339-198-2 (paper) 978-1-55339-199-9 (cloth)

The Democratic Dilemma: Reforming the Canadian Senate, Jennifer Smith (ed.), 2009. ISBN 978-1-55339-190-6